The Old Testament 12 Step Workbook

A 90 Day Program of Bible-Based Addiction Recovery

By Boruch Binyamin

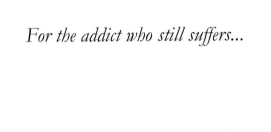

For the addict who still suffers...

Welcome

Mᴜ NAME IS BORUCH, AND I AM AN ALCOHOLIC.

Twenty-two years ago, I walked into an AA meeting and spoke those words out loud for the first time. It was also the first time I had been honest with myself about what was going on in my life for many years. With God's help, I have remained sober in AA since then. I wrote this workbook to help my brothers and sisters in the rooms achieve recovery using inspiration taken from the Bible. It is based on my understanding of Biblical texts as a Jew, but I believe that anyone who has a spiritual appreciation for the divinity of the Holy Scriptures can find this a valuable resource for recovery. The spiritual principles I discuss should be relevant to anyone in recovery who is interested in spiritual growth and conscious contact with a Higher Power. However, the ideas in this book should not be interpreted as the exclusive or authoritative Jewish view on the Bible as it relates to recovery. Such a work would be far beyond my level of knowledge.

There is no correct way to use this workbook. I encourage you to, as they say in the rooms, "Take what you like and leave the rest." However, there is a suggested process contained within its pages: Over a period of one 90 days, read the Old Testament verse for each day. For each day, there is a set of questions and a space for personal journaling based on the 12 steps of Alcoholics Anonymous. To get the most out of this workbook, consider setting aside some time to think about the reading, answer the questions, and do some journaling.

A few quick notes on the material: The Biblical verses cited in the book are translated from the original Hebrew, so they may read differently from traditional texts you may have seen before. Also, in certain places, I have incorporated insights from the ancient Rabbis who interpreted the Old Testament. I refer to them as "The Commentators."

May God grant you the greatest of blessings and success on your personal journey to serenity and recovery from addiction.

Boruch

Contents

The 12 Steps of Alcoholics Anonymous

1. We admitted we were powerless over alcohol - that our lives had become unmanageable.
2. Came to believe that a Power greater than ourselves could restore us to sanity.
3. Made a decision to turn our will and our lives over to the care of God as we understood Him.
4. Made a searching and fearless moral inventory of ourselves.
5. Admitted to God, to ourselves and to another human being the exact nature of our wrongs.
6. Were entirely ready to have God remove all these defects of character.
7. Humbly asked Him to remove our shortcomings.
8. Made a list of all persons we had harmed, and became willing to make amends to them all.
9. Made direct amends to such people wherever possible, except when to do so would injure them or others.
10. Continued to take personal inventory and when we were wrong promptly admitted it.
11. Sought through prayer and meditation to improve our conscious contact with God as we understood Him, praying only for knowledge of His will for us and the power to carry that out.
12. Having had a spiritual awakening as the result of these steps, we tried to carry this message to alcoholics and to practice these principles in all our affairs.

Genesis Workbook

Genesis 1:1 – "In the beginning of God's creating the Heavens and the earth..."

God created the world and everything in it. If we ever needed a quick wakeup call about who we are, where we and all that we value comes from, we need to read no further than this opening line of The Torah. Everything is in His hands. Your life, your success or failure – in life and recovery, is in God's hands. The one that is powerful enough to create the world can be the Higher Power that can give you the strength to deliver you from addiction. Everything that you have, all your possessions, all your money, comes from God. In recovery, it helps to remember this fact. If you think, "I made this money myself. I did it myself. I relied on myself," – that is self-seeking, and self-involvement that can interfere with recovery. If you trust in God to give you the income and possessions you need, that you can handle, and no more, then you can begin to be satisfied with what you have. You will start to worry less about financial insecurity, a big driver of addiction and relapse.

Questions to Ponder	
What does it mean to you, in recovery, that God created the entire universe?	
If you accept this as the truth, does it affect your view of the world and other people?	
For today: Can you think of your money and possessions not as yours, but as something God has given to you?	

Step 1: We admitted we were powerless over alcohol - that our lives had become unmanageable.

Journaling Exercise: Describe how your powerlessness over alcohol affected your ability to experience and participate in the universe that God created.

Day 2

Genesis 1:5 – "God called to the light: "Day," and to the darkness He called: "Night." And there was evening and there was morning, one day."

God separates light from darkness. When we are in the grip of our addictions, our lives are permanently dark. We live in an eternal night of the soul as we desperately grasp for our next hit of whatever it is that we think will fix us. God created light – He has the power to bring us into the light of recovery. He turns the long night of addiction and the struggle of recovery to the light of sobriety and good recovery. God also created time. By separating night and day, He gave us the days of our lives and the days of our recovery. As we say in the program, it's a day at a time. God gives us that day at a time.

Questions to Ponder	
Has the process of recovery changed your sense of time? How so?	
Do you think God can take you from personal "darkness" to "light"? If so, how?	
For today: Has a belief in a higher power has lit up your life today? If so, how?	

Step 1: We admitted we were powerless over alcohol - that our lives had become unmanageable.

Journaling Exercise: Did the power of alcohol and drugs "darken" your life, concealing the good things in your life and enabling you to hide the bad things? How does it feel now that God's light is shining on your powerlessness over alcohol and drugs?

Day 3

Genesis 2:15 – "God took the man and placed him in the Garden of Eden, to work it and to guard it."

What work was Adam supposed to do in the Garden of Eden? After all, everything grew on its own. God wanted Adam to observe God's commandments and grow in spiritual awareness. That was Adam's "work."

As recovering addicts, this is our work as well. Our job in recovery is to work on ourselves. If we work on ourselves, devoting ourselves to follow the commandments and learning, dedicating ourselves to increasing our spiritual selves, we are doing the important task that has been assigned to us in recovery. Like Adam, we have a clear mission. Sometimes, though, in the fog of our illness, we cannot see how simple the assignment is. Our homework in recovery, therefore, is to think about the simplicity, but enormity of this work. We can do it, though. By telling us about Adam's work in the Garden of Eden, God is showing us how to do our work in recovery.

Questions to Ponder	
What do you think God's mission is for you in life?	
Do you think the fog of addiction interfered with your sense of purpose in life? If so, how?	
For today: What will you do today to get in touch with God's mission for you in life?	

Step 2: Came to believe that a Power greater than ourselves could restore us to sanity.

Journaling Exercise: In what ways can you relate – or not relate - to Adam's mission of believing in a higher power greater than yourself?

Genesis 3:9 – "God called out to the man and said to him, 'Where are you?'"

After Adam and Eve had eaten the forbidden fruit of the Tree of Knowledge, they hid from God. Or, in reality, they tried to hide. God then asks, 'Where are you?' as if He didn't already know.

As recovering addicts, we can learn two important concepts from this verse. On one level, we should understand that God sees all of our deeds, even if we are trying to hide from Him. We may be able to fool others, or even ourselves, if we are faking our way through recovery, but God knows what is going on. We cannot hide. If we are ready to do the work, we should understand that this is an opportunity and a blessing, not a punishment. Being unable to hide from God also means that God is with us always. We are never alone, and that could be a comforting thought to those of us who struggle with isolation in recovery. In addition, this verse introduces the idea of God giving us the chance to repent. God knows where Adam and Eve are. He is asking because he wants to give them the chance to admit what they did and repent. God has mercy on us so much of the time, even when we don't deserve it. God gives us the chance to repent, make amends, and say we are sorry. If we are working well in recovery, we will perceive when this opportunity is being extended to us and act on it.

Questions to Ponder	
Have you ever tried to fool others into believing you were someone other than what you really were at the time? If so, how?	
Do you now feel an awareness that God is watching, giving you a chance to admit to yourself that you are powerless over your addiction? If so, how?	
For today: What would you like God to see you do today?	

16

Step 2: Came to believe that a Power greater than ourselves could restore us to sanity.

Journaling Exercise: What would you say to God if He asked you, "Where are you?" today?

Genesis 6:16 – "A window shall you make for the Ark, and to a cubit finish it from above."

Why does God tell Noah to make the window "from above," that is, a skylight? Some Commentators even say that the window was actually a special gem that allowed light to enter, but made it impossible to see out of. The Sages teach that Noah was enough of a righteous man to be saved from the flood, but not righteous enough to be worthy of witnessing the destruction of the world.

In the program, we need to be careful not to let ourselves be exposed to too much that is traumatic. While we can't avoid life's daily stresses, we should be very circumspect about going out of our way to witness and deal with troubling circumstances. Observing and talking about stressful events can damage our sobriety.

Questions to Ponder	
Have you ever had the experience of witnessing something that you wished you had not? Did it affect your serenity?	
Do you feel a need to see everything and everyone all the time? If so, is this good or bad for you?	
For today: What will you do to deal with life's stresses in a healthy way?	

Step 3: Made a decision to turn our will and our lives over to the care of God as we understood Him.

Journaling Exercise: In what ways can you relate, or not relate, to Noah turning his life over to the care of God in the Ark – with a window that let in light but shielded him from seeing images that would traumatize him?

Genesis 8:1 – "God remembered Noah and all the beasts and all the animals that were with him in the Ark."

The Sages teach that the Ark was too small to hold all of the animals. There was no way that the animals, Noah and his family, and all the food they needed would have fit in the Ark, even if it had been a hundred times larger than it was. How did everything fit in? The Sages teach that God made a miracle, so as the animals entered the Ark, the interior of the boat got larger and larger, so all of God's creatures could be safe inside.

In recovery, we sometimes feel that we are not up to the great task of sobriety. Temptation is everywhere, and we alone are too weak to resist. This line of The Torah tells us that we are not alone, that if we take the first step, then God can help us the rest of the way, "opening us up" on the inside to the message of recovery the way He opened up the Ark.

Questions to Ponder	
Have you ever experienced the feeling that God is doing for you what you could not do for yourself?	
Have you ever had the feeling that God has enabled the impossible to happen in order for you to live and get into recovery?	
For today: How is God "expanding the ark," so to speak, to help you in recovery?	

Step 3: Made a decision to turn our will and our lives over to the care of God as we understood Him.

Journaling Exercise: Are there aspects of your life and recovery that you think are "too big" for God to handle? Can you imagine that God, like His miracle of the Ark, will always be "big enough" to enable you to turn your life and will over to God?

Genesis 13:7 – "And there was quarrelling between the herdsmen of Abram's livestock and the herdsmen of Lot's livestock..."

Lot became rich from Pharaoh's gifts for the sole reason that he was Abraham's nephew. However, instead of being grateful and deferential to his uncle, who had enabled him to amass a large amount of unearned wealth, Lot instead grows resentful of Abraham's "encroachment" onto his pasture lands. This behavior should look very familiar to anyone who has either suffered from addiction or been close to a person struggling with addiction. Despite great gifts and success, the addict is miserable, fractious, and greedy. More, more, more – the addict wants more of whatever it is he craves, and no amount of it will ever do. It can get to the point where the addict will turn on those who feed him. Like Lot, the addict gets into a fight with the one who made his whole life possible. As recovering addicts, we need to search ourselves and be honest with ourselves when we act in this way. A good goal for recovery is to root out and eliminate this kind of self-centered behavior.

Questions to Ponder	
Do you think you have ever taken what God has given you for granted?	
Have you ever resented what God has given you as unfair?	
For today: Can you try to be conscious of resentments you may have about not being given enough in life?	

Step 4: Made a searching and fearless moral inventory of ourselves.

Journaling Exercise: In your fourth step work, can you identify moments in your life when you were acting like Lot and his herdsmen – always wanting more, more, more despite the consequences or how it looked to others?

Genesis 17:2 – "[God said to Abraham] I will set my covenant between Me and you, and I will increase you most exceedingly."

Alcoholics Anonymous, and all of the related recovery programs, originated with one famous phone call in the 1930s, when Bill W called "Dr. Bob" and asked if he could talk in order to avoid an overpowering urge to get drunk. Dr. Bob agreed to the meeting, and the two men stayed sober together. And, 70 years later, there are millions of sober people all over the world … just because Dr. Bob took the call and agreed to talk to Bill W. When God said to Abraham, "I will increase you most exceedingly," we can understand that to mean, on one level at least, that Abraham has many descendants in the covenant. Those who make the covenant of Abraham and follow God are the "increase" of Abraham. He was just one man, but he has millions of descendants. In recovery, too, when we work with others and extend ourselves to help other addicts stay in recovery, we are increasing the group of people that started with Bill W and Dr. Bob. Each positive step we take in helping others in recovery leads to more growth in recovery, and ultimately, more support for ourselves when we need it.

Questions to Ponder	
How do you think you have influenced your "descendants" – e.g. family and friends?	
Have you been helped by another sober person in your recovery? If so, how?	
For today: Can you help another recovering addict stay clean and sober?	

Step 4: Made a searching and fearless moral inventory of ourselves.

Journaling Exercise: As you look at your life from the perspective of the fourth step, can you see moments where you may have made a promise and then broken it? Do you think recovery can prepare you to enter into covenants with God and other people? If not, why?

Day 9

Genesis 19:17 – "Flee for your life! Do not look behind you nor stop anywhere in the plain; flee to the mountain lest you be swept away."

When Lot, accompanied by his wife and daughters, were fleeing from the destruction of Sodom, they were given this famous piece of advice, which Lot's wife did not obey. Lot's wife turned around to look, and she was turned into a pillar of salt. We might wonder, what's so bad about looking back? The answer can teach us about recovery: When we get the chance to live a sober life, it is nothing less than a miracle where we "flee for our lives" from destruction and insanity. If we are wise, we will never look back, much less go back, to the old way we were. Of course, it is tempting ... many of us have felt the strong, seductive pull of addiction calling as we struggle through recovery. Yet, even to look back is dangerous, as the verse shows. Looking back is the first step to going back.

Questions to Ponder	
Do you think you were ever given a chance, by God, to escape nearly certain death?	
Are you tempted to "look back" fondly at your time of using?	
For today: Can you avoid the temptation to look back at your addict experience?	

Step 5: Admitted to God, to ourselves and to another human being the exact nature of our wrongs.

Journaling Exercise: Is it possible to do the fifth step, admitting to God, yourself and others, the exact nature of your wrongs while avoiding gazing back affectionately at your history of drinking and using – like Lot's wife?

Genesis 24:19 – "When she [Rebecca] finished giving him [Eliezer] the drink, she said, 'I will draw water even for your camels until they have finished drinking.'"

It is with this remarkable act of kindness that Rebecca proves herself to be worthy to marry Isaac. The incident is striking, and it connects with issues of recovery. On one level, the pure effort involved is amazing, and that can tell us a lot about Rebecca. Without being asked, she waters 10 camels – a big job for a little girl. Plus, she does so happily while the camels' owners and his companions, all of whom are able-bodied men, sit and watch. Most of us, if we were in that situation, would probably say, "Why don't you get your own water?" But not Rebecca. She has great values and character. In recovery, we can find inspiration in this story. We should be willing to make the effort, even when it doesn't appear to be a reasonable use of our time. There is usually a God-given reason that we are being asked to do something in recovery, and if we question it too much, we may miss the opportunity to help someone, as well as ourselves.

Questions to Ponder	
Has anyone ever made a big effort to help you, perhaps without even being asked? How do you feel about that?	
Have you been asked to do something in recovery that you didn't undertand? Did you do it? How did you feel about it?	
For today: How can you make an effort for your own recovery and others'?	

Step 5: Admitted to God, to ourselves and to another human being the exact nature of our wrongs.

Journaling Exercise: The fifth step takes courage and commitment. In the process, can see yourself (or not see yourself) acting like Rebecca, who was willing to make an effort to do the right thing without perhaps understanding the immediate payoff?

Genesis 25:20 – "Isaac was forty years old when he took Rebecca, daughter of Bethuel the Aramean from Paddan-Aram, sister of Laban, the Aramean, as a wife for himself."

Why does The Torah repeat itself here, telling us again that Rebecca was the sister of Laban, and that Laban was an Aramean? We already know this, so The Torah is emphasizing the facts to make a point. Rebecca was one of the most righteous people who ever lived. Yet, she came from a family of idolaters and swindlers. The contrast is profound. Not only did she grow up to be different from her family, she grew up to be the opposite kind of character by many orders of magnitude. As recovering addicts, we can find inspiration in the story of Rebecca. Many of us come from less-than-perfect family backgrounds, and we may find, as we do our steps, that our families of origin played a role in shaping our addictive selves. Yet, we are God's children, too, and like Rebecca, we can develop a healthy distance from whatever bad influences were present in our upbringings.

Questions to Ponder	
How has your family of origin affected your addiction and recovery?	
Do you feel that you were influenced negatively by your family of origin? If so, how can you take positive steps to get away from that influence?	
For today: Think about how you are also God's child. Does this belief change your view of your family of origin?	

Step 6: Were entirely ready to have God remove all these defects of character.

Journaling Exercise: Rebecca grew up among people with immense defects of character, yet she became one of the most righteous people who ever lived. In your personal story, can you identify (or not identify) with her challenge of removing defects of character she might have inherited from her family of origin? Can you connect this to the sixth step?

Genesis 25:21 – "Isaac entreated God opposite his wife, because she was barren. God allowed Himself to be entreated by him, and his wife Rebecca conceived."

The Sages note that Isaac was 60 years old when Rebecca gave birth. Since he got married at 40, we can deduce that Rebecca was barren for 20 years. We should have a lot of compassion for Rebecca. She was told she was going to be the mother of a great nation, and nothing happened for 20 years, despite her fervent prayers. It is a testament to her supremely high level of righteousness and spiritual development that Rebecca never despaired of fulfilling her purpose in life. We can derive inspiration in recovery from this fact alone. However, in addition, we can also learn a valuable recovery lesson from Rebecca and Isaac's devotion to prayer to accomplish a goal that was set out for them. They never stopped praying, for 20 long years, to get the child they knew prophetically was meant for them. They never wavered. There is a great concept here for recovery: namely, that prayers are never wasted, and that the answer to our prayers may not come instantly. In recovery, we pray for many things, including serenity and sobriety. The answer may not be immediately recognizable, but we should never abandon our prayers.

Questions to Ponder	
Have you ever prayed for something but found that your prayers were not answered (Yet)?	
Do you feel that you have a destiny in life, like Rebecca and Isaac?	
For today: What will you pray for in recovery?	

Step 6: Were entirely ready to have God remove all these defects of character.

Journaling Exercise: The sixth step may take time. In what ways can you connect becoming entirely ready to have God remove defects of character with Isaac and Rebecca's great patience in waiting for God to grant them their wish of having a child?

Genesis 27:22 – "So Jacob drew close to Isaac his father, who felt him and said, 'The voice is Jacob's voice but the hands are Esau's hands.'"

In this famous verse, Isaac is tricked into giving the blessing, bestowing the leadership of the Jewish people forever, to Jacob, not Esau. And, this verse gives us a great tool to use in recovery. The contrast between the "voice of Jacob" and the "hands of Esau" provides us with a helpful image to gauge our own behavior. The voice refers to what we say, while the hands are where we take action. This verse should force us to ask ourselves if we are acting in the same way that we speak. Do we say with our voices that we are going to do commandments and help others in the program, but then, with our hands, do nothing? Or, do we take positive actions with our hands despite what we do or don't say? In recovery, we should try to act as we say we act, rather than speaking with the good voice of Jacob, while we do evil with the hands of Esau.

Questions to Ponder	
Have you ever talked the talk in the "voice of Jacob" but done things that were not so good, with the "hands of Esau"?	
Are you following God's will for yourself or simply paying lip service to the concept?	
For today: Can you bring together your hands and voice – acting in a way that matches the things you say about yourself?	

Step 7: Humbly asked Him to remove our shortcomings.

Journaling Exercise: The word "humbly" is key to understanding the seventh step. You have to be humble to ask God to remove your shortcomings. Reflect on your process of trying to become humble, perhaps thinking about times when you "speak with the voice of Jacob" but take actions "with the hands of Esau."

Day 14

Genesis 28:12 – "And he dreamt, and behold! A ladder was set earthward and its top reached heavenward; and behold! Angels of God were ascending and descending on it."

In this famous scene, we see "Jacob's Ladder" full of ascending and descending angels. For recovery, this moment is a plum of wisdom on numerous fronts. Let's touch on two issues. Like all of us, Jacob had angels that helped him accomplish his great purposes in his life. Yet, unlike you and I, he was privileged to actually see them. If we could know about the angels that God dispatches to help us and protect us in our daily lives, we might be more appreciative of the life we have been given. Additionally, the image of going up and down the ladder is a great metaphor for the way we work, or don't work, our programs. Every day, we are either moving toward recovery, or away from it. This is a choice we must make. If we choose to ignore recovery, we inevitably go down the ladder and our program suffers, perhaps even to the point of relapse. Ignoring our program is equivalent to choosing to turn away from it. No action equals negative action. Conversely, if we choose to do the work, and improve our programs, we ascend the ladder and grow in recovery and spirituality.

Questions to Ponder	
Can you relate to the idea of going up and down a ladder, from recovery to addiction and back?	
If you've been "down the ladder," how have you gotten yourself back up?	
For today: How will you seek conscious contact with your Higher Power to advance up the "ladder" of spiritual growth in recovery?	

Step 8: Made a list of all persons we had harmed, and became willing to make amends to them all.

Journaling Exercise: The eighth step can be stressful, as we think about people we have harmed. As you think about specific people, can you imagine that you're either going up or down the "ladder" of spiritual growth suggested by Jacob's dream?

Genesis 32:25 – "Jacob was left alone and a man wrestled with him until the break of dawn."

The "man" was actually an angel of Esau, and Jacob's victory over him portends that Jacob will prevail over Esau in the long term. As addicts, we should be able to relate to the idea of struggling all night with a powerful adversary that fights us without any clear cause. Yet, we can prevail, if we have faith in God. Jacob is injured in the struggle, but he survives. So too have we been injured in our lengthy struggles with addiction, but we can go on and live full lives. The struggle between Jacob and the angel can inspire us to believe that things will be okay for us if we pray and also do our footwork. The promise is fulfilled when we see that Esau embraces Jacob instead of killing him (Genesis 33:4). For recovery purposes, we can view this event as a great example of "letting go" of a life-long resentment. Though of course the story is more complicated than that, we should still be impressed with Esau's ability to embrace the brother he had sworn to kill for so many years. In our own lives and recovery processes, we might also benefit from this idea – releasing ourselves from the bondage of resentments and embracing our brothers. It can only improve our serenity if we do it with sincerity and God's help.

Questions to Ponder	
Have you ever had the experience of struggling or fighting with someone and not understanding what it was even about?	
Do you think that someone you fought with in addiction was actually trying to help you, but you couldn't see it?	
For today: Can we embrace someone we once resented or even hated?	

Step 9: Made direct amends to such people wherever possible, except when to do so would injure them or others.

Journaling Exercise: Wrestling with your past, as Jacob wrestled with the angel, is part of the ninth step. As you work the ninth step, can you relate to the idea of wrestling with a mysterious, powerful enemy for no identifiable reason?

Genesis 37:20 – "Come now therefore, and let us slay him, and cast him into one of the pits…"

It is far too superficial an analysis to say that Joseph's brothers wanted to kill him merely because of spite. After all, we are talking about Jacob's sons, who were some of the most righteous men who ever lived. Yet, in this verse, they do something that seems to be completely wrong. How can this be? One interpretation is that the brothers were acting in accordance to what they considered to be a solemn duty to protect the nation of Israel from the leadership of Joseph, whom they considered unfit to lead. Taking responsibility for the future of the Jewish people, they took action. Because they felt they were doing the right thing, the brothers feel no remorse, and are even able to deceive their father for many years, despite his immense grief, about the true whereabouts of Joseph. The lesson in this story for those of us in recovery is to be circumspect about situations where we are completely certain that we are taking the correct action, if that action might hurt someone. Or, worse, if we are convinced that we are doing God's will, we owe it to everyone, including ourselves, to give the idea a thorough review before taking action. Only God knows what God's will really is. We can't know, so we should be very careful about being so sure of ourselves in these kinds of situations.

Questions to Ponder	
Have you ever felt that you knew exactly the right thing to do about a situation, but in retrospect it was wrong?	
Did you ever decline to take advantage of the wisdom of an elder person who could have helped you make a better life decision?	
For today: Are you willing to ask God for guidance on important life decisions?	

Step 10: Continued to take personal inventory and when we were wrong promptly admitted it.

Journaling Exercise: In this verse, Jacob's brothers make a mistake and then cover it up for more than 20 years. They did not promptly admit that they were wrong. Does this resonate with your past life experience?

Day 17

Genesis 41:2 – 41:4 - "And, behold, there came up out of the river seven cows, well-favored and fat-fleshed; and they fed in the reed grass. And, behold, seven other cows came up after them out of the river, ill favored and lean-fleshed; and stood by the other cows upon the brink of the river. And the ill-favored and lean-fleshed cows did eat up the seven well-favored and fat cows."

Pharaoh dreams of fat cows coming out of the river, which are later eaten by emaciated cows. The dream portends seven years of plenty, followed by seven years of famine. This famous image can serve as a helpful guide to sobriety on many levels. As we have probably experienced in our own lives, a period of acting out in our addiction can easily rob us of whatever "abundance" we have built up in previous years. Addictions, like the lean cows, can consume money, family, relationships and accomplishments with awesome ease. We would all do well to be vigilant about warding off the addictive attacks that lay in wait for us. On another level, the approach that Joseph recommends to Pharaoh, that the Egyptians store grain in anticipation of the famine, is a good metaphor for working a program. As we advance in sobriety, we need to create our own "storehouses" of program tools, relationships, and behavior to help us when the inevitable "lean years" of addiction stalk us. If you have any amount of sober time, you can probably relate to the feeling of being under attack from your addictive impulses. The more time you have, and the better you have worked your program, the more ability you will have to weather the attack, as the Egyptians did the famine.

Questions to Ponder	
Have you experienced today's version of "fat" and "lean" years? How did they affect your addiction and recovery?	
Has addiction ever robbed you of abundance (material, spiritual, emotional)?	
For today: Can you prepare yourself for the "lean" times that are inevitably heading your way at some point?	

42

Step 11: Sought through prayer and meditation to improve our conscious contact with God as we understood Him, praying only for knowledge of His will for us and the power to carry that out.

Journaling Exercise: Have prayer and meditation improved your conscious contact with God to the point where you can foresee how your life may have "lean" and "fat" times – and enable you to prepare yourself? In this context, "lean" and "fat" might mean wealth, happiness, serenity and so forth.

Genesis 48:5 – "And now thy two sons, who were born unto thee in the land of Egypt before I came unto thee into Egypt, are mine; Ephraim and Manasseh, even as Reuben and Simeon, shall be mine."

Thus does Jacob make Joseph's sons, Ephraim and Manasseh into his "own" and creates for them a full inheritance as tribe leaders of Israel. Ephraim and Manasseh each have their own tribes, equal in stature to those of their uncles – Simeon, Reuben, and so on. But, Joseph has no tribe of his own. Why is there no tribe of Joseph? At first glance, this seems unfair. Joseph was designated as the leader, he saved everyone's life, he served and sacrificed mightily for the good of all Israel. Yet, he gets no tribe of his own. Of course, that isn't necessarily true. Joseph gets two tribes, not one. They just don't bear his name. From the perspective of recovery, we can see the "tribes" of Joseph in two distinct ways, each of which can help us understand our journey in recovery. At one level, Joseph might react with resentment at his father's decree. "Why can't I have my own tribe?" he might complain. That is how all of us have acted at some point in our addiction and recovery. Righteous anger at being left out of something. Yet, Joseph does not complain, because he understood that not only was he getting a double portion, he was also realizing the vision of Israel's future through his children. As a mature person, he takes pride in the success of his children, and even though he doesn't get the "credit" in name recognition, he is still happy for them. His behavior should be an inspiration to us.

Questions to Ponder	
Have you ever resented not getting something you thought was owed to you?	
Are you able to appreciate that someone you love has gotten something special instead of resenting it?	
For today: If you have a resentment, can you look at it carefully and see if there is something in it to actually be thankful for?	

Step 12: Having had a spiritual awakening as the result of these steps, we tried to carry this message to alcoholics and to practice these principles in all our affairs.

Journaling Exercise: Practicing these principles sometimes means working through resentments about what you "deserved but didn't get." Have you experienced this sort of resentment in recovery? Have you been able to "practice these principles" and achieve serenity despite the resentment?

Exodus Workbook

Exodus 1:1 – "Now these are the names of the sons of Israel, who came into Egypt with Jacob; every man came with his household."

The book of Exodus begins with a list of the names of the sons of Jacob who went down to Egypt. In fact, the Hebrew name for the book of Exodus is "Shemos," which means "Names." At this time the exile of Egypt is underway, and the Israelites will have to endure centuries of slavery before being freed by Moses. From the perspective of an addict or co-addict, we might be able to identify with the Israelites at this stage of their existence. Suddenly, a once prosperous group of people is relegated to slavery. As addiction progresses, we too see this type of transformation. Slowly, sometimes quickly, we are rendered into slaves of the addiction. In recovery, we try to release ourselves from the enslavement of addiction. This opening verse of Exodus, therefore, might give us some hope in the process. The Children of Israel have names, even as they are forced into bondage. Each of us also has a name, an identity as a sober person, a child of God, who longs to be free. In meetings we say, "Hi, my name is … I'm an alcoholic." This is not an accident. The program wants us to remember our name, remember who we are, who we were, and who we might be. With a name, we are less enslaved by our addictions.

Questions to Ponder	
Were you called by a different name (i.e. a "street name") when you were drinking or using? What name do you go by now? Is it different? Does it make you feel differently about yourself?	
Can you relate to the idea expressed in the verse regarding a free person sent into slavery? Did drinking or using create a form of slavery for you?	
For Today: This verse refers to the names of a family. Think about how drinking or using affect your relationship with your family. Did they have a different name for you when you were drinking or using?	

Step 1: We admitted we were powerless over alcohol - that our lives had become unmanageable.

Journaling Exercise: Losing control over your identity, expressed in your name, can be a strong indication of powerlessness over alcohol or drugs. As one sober friend explains, "My name changed from 'Jeff' to 'dog,' 'crackhead' and 'hey you.'" Can you relate?

Day 20

Exodus 1:8 – "Now there arose a new king over Egypt, who knew not Joseph."

The new Pharaoh did not know Joseph, nor did he understand how Joseph had saved the kingdom from famine. The assumption we make is that if he had known about Joseph, he would not have enslaved the Israelites out of fear of their potential disloyalty. To him, the Israelites were merely a threatening group of foreigners, not the descendants of a great man who had, if nothing else, greatly enriched the house of Pharaoh. In recovery, we can probably identify with both Pharaoh and the Israelites in this part of the story. When we are drinking and using, we often conveniently "forget" those people who have contributed to our success and well-being and associate instead with new, downward companions. We may even lash out and try to destroy friends and family who care about us because they are interfering with our addictive drives. On the flip side, our behavior may cause those who cared about us in the past to "forget" about us. Like the Israelites in the story, we may get burned by people we thought were our friends, though perhaps it is due to our own actions. Finally, this verse should remind us that it is dangerous for us to place too much importance on the goodwill of other people to assure our recovery. Only God has the ultimate power to help us in recovery. If we place our faith in God and pray for recovery, then it will not matter if the people in our lives forget who we are.

Questions to Ponder	
Did you ever "forget" someone from your life who didn't approve of your drinking or using?	
Did you find a new group of "friends" to hang around with when you were drinking or using? Were they good for you or appreciate who you were?	
For Today: Think about times when you might have lashed out in anger at someone who loved you and was trying to help you overcome your addiction?	

Step 1: We admitted we were powerless over alcohol - that our lives had become unmanageable.

Journaling Exercise: Think about how unmanageable our lives become when we "forget" the people who truly love us. What can that tell us about the power of addiction and our powerlessness over it?

Exodus 2:3 – "And when she could not longer hide him, she took for him an ark of bulrushes, and daubed it with slime and with pitch; and she put the child therein, and laid it in the reeds by the river's brink."

The Sages teach, "Many designs are in a man's heart, but the counsel of God – only it will prevail." The story of Moses is nothing less than a sequence of miracles, all of which run counter to the cruel decree of Pharaoh that all Jewish boys be killed. Pharaoh had heard from his astrologers that the future savior of the Jewish people was to be born within the next period of time. Thus, he told his soldiers to find and kill all Jewish boys. Despite this ruling, and the subsequent slaughter, Moses not only survived, but was raised right under the nose of the ruling dynasty that he would one day destroy. Many designs were in Pharaoh's heart, but only God will prevail.

As we struggle with recovery, we should remember that the designs in our heart, both good and bad, will only be realized as God sees fit. When we start to think that we are running the show, and that our will, not God's, is what counts, we are heading for trouble.

Questions to Ponder	
Have you ever had a "design in your heart" that God's will prevented from happening?	
Do you feel God's will for you in your life? If so, what are you experiencing?	
For Today: Are you struggling with trying to "run the show" on your own? How is it going for you?	

Step 2 - Came to believe that a Power greater than ourselves could restore us to sanity.

Journaling Exercise: God gives us opportunities to come to Him and be protected by God on our journey to recovery. If you have felt God offering you an opportunity to come to Him, to come to believe that a Power greater than yourself could restore you to sanity, describe the feeling and the overall experience that led up to it.

Exodus 2:12 – "And he looked this way and that way, and when he saw that there was no man, he smote the Egyptian, and hid him in the sand."

There are two well-known interpretations of this verse. Moses looked around and there was no one present, so he smote the Egyptian. That is, he felt that he would not be observed so he went ahead with his attack thinking he was alone. Alternatively, the phrasing in Hebrew that says Moses saw, "lo ish," or "no man" around, indicates that he was not alone, but that there were no "men" around him. By "no man," the Commentators indicate that Moses was not surrounded by women and children, but rather he was surrounded by many people, including men, but that nobody was acting "like a man." Nobody was doing the right thing, and lashing out against cruelty and injustice. Moses decided to be a man, to act like a man, and take action. Everyone else was too afraid of the Egyptians, too absorbed in the slave mentality, to do anything. Have you ever been in this situation? You know the right thing to do, but you are too afraid to act? Perhaps when we confront problems in our recovery, or the bad behavior of addicts in our lives, we might want to take the path blazed by Moses in this story: do the right thing. Don't be cowed by the power of others. Only God has the power in life. Be a man (or woman) and get yourself into the right action.

Questions to Ponder	
Did you struggle with "doing the right thing" when you were drinking and using? How so?	
In what ways can you relate, or not relate, to being afraid of other people whom you think have power over you?	
For Today: Are you finding it easier or harder to "do the right thing" for yourself or others?	

Step 2 - Came to believe that a Power greater than ourselves could restore us to sanity.

Journaling Exercise: In what ways do you think Moses was inspired by a belief in a Power greater than himself to "do the right thing" and slay the Egyptian taskmaster?

Exodus 4:10 – 4:11 – "And Moses said unto the Lord: 'Oh Lord, I am not a man of words, neither heretofore, nor since Thou hast spoken unto Thy servant; for I am slow of speech, and of a slow tongue.' And the Lord said unto him: 'Who hath made man's mouth? Or who maketh a man dumb, or deaf, or seeing, or blind? Is it not I, the Lord?"

Being a man of great humility, Moses did not at first want to accept the immense assignment that God had bestowed upon him. He says, "I am not a man of words," a phrase that has been interpreted to mean either that he stuttered, was not a good public speaker, or did not, in fact speak the language itself very well. God's response is very instructive for our recovery. God says, essentially, that whatever Moses' perceived speech flaws may be, they matter not. God says, "Who hath made man's mouth?" God is in control. God made the mouth, the words, the ears of the listeners, and on and on. What God wants is what is going to happen. Moses will be a channel of God's will, his own self doubts notwithstanding. What an inspiration! We can learn from this story that we can do anything, even those things we consider impossible for us, if it is in keeping with God's will for us.

Questions to Ponder	
Is there something you want to do in your life that you have thought was impossible? Has getting into recovery changed your perspective?	
Do you feel as if you are in control of everything in your life? Where does that leave God?	
For Today: Think about your most serious defects of character. Do you think God can help you overcome them, as He did with Moses and his problems with speech?	

Step 3- Made a decision to turn our will and our lives over to the care of God as we understood Him.

Journaling Exercise: In this verse, Moses is basically giving God an excuse for why he cannot carry out the commandment to speak to Pharaoh, demanding the he free the Israelite slaves. Can you relate to this sort of fear of taking on a big, difficult task?

Exodus 7:13 – "And Pharaoh's heart was hardened, and he hearkened not unto them; as the Lord had spoken."

Pharaoh acts like an alcoholic. No matter how bad things get, he doesn't listen. Like an alcoholic who will not admit that he has a problem, even after the kind of unceasing series of disasters that only an alcoholic can experience, Pharaoh will not change his mind. His heart is hardened. Of course, God hardens Pharaoh's heart too, but it was a pretty hard heart to begin with.

This verse can open our eyes to the ways that addiction destroys our lives through the power of denial. How many wrecked cars, arrests, divorces, arguments, job losses, and so on, will it take before our hearts become less hardened to the reality of our addiction? Like Pharaoh, we have all white knuckled our way through crisis after crisis, blaming others for our problems and refusing to acknowledge the truth – that we are the ones at fault. This verse tells us to wake up and soften our hearts, to hear the truth at long last.

Questions to Ponder	
Have you ever ignored a problem that was caused by your drinking or using? What were the consequences?	
Looking back at your time of drinking and using, can you see situations that, in retrospect, were warning signs that you chose to ignore or rationalize?	
For Today: Is addiction "hardening your heart," so to speak, hardening yourself to want to return to drinking and using regardless of the consequences to yourself and others?	

Step 3- Made a decision to turn our will and our lives over to the care of God as we understood Him.

Journaling Exercise: Making a decision to turn our wills over to the care of God requires that we soften our hearts. Can you think of ways that your heart may have been too "hardened" before you were ready to do the third step?

Exodus 13:17 – "And it came to pass, when Pharaoh had let the people go, that God led them not by the way of the land of the Philistines, although that was near; for God said: 'Lest peradventure the people repent when they see war, and they return to Egypt.'"

God understood that the Israelites, so recently freed from slavery, might not be able to handle an abrupt confrontation with the Philistines that could result from taking a direct route from Egypt to the Land of Israel. This part of the Exodus story is rich with symbolism for our daily lives and struggle with recovery and addiction. We can learn from this verse that sometimes, it is wise to take an indirect approach to our worst problems, take baby steps and build our strength. If we take the plunge prematurely, we may suffer a backlash and find ourselves in worse trouble than before we started. For example, let's say you drank over resentment that you felt you were owed a raise at work. Then, newly sober, you decide to barge into your boss's office and demand a raise – that would not be good sober behavior. The result, in fact, might be a reaction that could lead you right back to the bottle. Instead, a wise approach might be to carefully plan a request for a raise, working with a sponsor to understand the most effective way to approach the situation. Or, perhaps even more importantly, learn to trust God to guide you on the right path to confronting the problem. This is the lesson of Exodus 13:17.

Questions to Ponder	
Whom should you trust in figuring out how to deal with important issues in sobriety: yourself, an experienced elder or God?	
When you look at a major decision in sobriety, can you see a quick, easy path that might be dangerous, versus a longer, more deliberate and healthy path to figuring out the right thing to do?	
For Today: Is God holding you back from the abrupt, fast and toxic approach to solving a problem in sobriety?	

Step 4 - Made a searching and fearless moral inventory of ourselves.

Journaling Exercise: As you work on your fourth step, can you think of situations where you took a fast, easy, but perhaps toxic approach to solving a personal problem? What were the consequences?

Exodus 14:11 – "And they said unto Moses: 'Because there were no graves in Egypt, hast thou taken us away to die in the Wilderness? Wherefore hast thou dealt thus with us, to bring us forth out of Egypt?'"

Here we see fear turning into anger, a classic challenge for the recovering addict. With the Egyptian army closing in, the trapped Israelites lash out at Moses, the one who has saved them from slavery. I think we've all been here. After the enslavement of addiction, you're on your way in recovery. But of course, it's not easy. You feel trapped, fearful, miserable. What do you do? Your fear emerges as anger at the very people who are trying to help you. And, what's driving it? A lack of faith. It's hard to imagine how the Israelites, who have just witnessed miracle after miracle from God (He liberated them and came close to destroying the most powerful king on Earth), are ready to deny their faith the minute that fear overtakes them. Yet, that is the addict's way, and it's the job of a recovering addict to seek the strength and faith in a higher power to overcome that fear. The waters will part if we can transform that fear into a stronger faith.

Questions to Ponder	
Have you ever experienced fear turning into anger?	
In what ways has fear gotten in the way of your seeing the blessings you have in your life?	
For Today: Do you feel at all trapped, with no way out? What is happening? Is the situation as bad as you thought?	

Step 4 - Made a searching and fearless moral inventory of ourselves.

Journaling Exercise: As you work your fourth step, can you spot events and experiences where fear was making you angry – like the Israelites in this verse?

Exodus 19:5 – "And now, if you hearken well to My voice and observe My covenant you shall be to Me the most beloved treasure of all peoples, for Mine is the entire world."

It may be hard for an addict to appreciate that he or she will be one of the treasured peoples of God. We get so run down, so caught up in our disease and self-loathing, that we can forget that we are people of God. And, while it may seem impossible to get to the place of being one of the treasured people, you are already there. The human soul is innately perfect, from God's perspective. Its potential needs to be cultivated, though, through focus on conscious contact with God, doing the right thing and being of service to others. All you have to do is listen to the word of God – however you receive that word, e.g. through the Bible, prayer, meditation and so forth. However, the challenging part of the work involves acting sober and engaging in sober behavior.

Questions to Ponder	
Do you feel as if you are treasured by God? If so, how? If not, what do you think is blocking the feeling?	
Are you able to perceive the word of God? If so, how? If not, what do you think is blocking you?	
For Today: What do you think God will do for you today versus the work you must do for yourself?	

Step 5 - Admitted to God, to ourselves and to another human being the exact nature of our wrongs.

Journaling Exercise: By admitting to God to ourselves and to another human being the exact nature of our wrongs, in what ways can we avoid polluting ourselves – God's treasure – our bodies and souls?

Exodus 19:17 – "Moses brought the people forth from the camp toward God."

The Commentators interpret the phrase "toward God" as meaning that God was waiting for the Israelites, waiting for them to come to Him. He contrasts this behavior with that of a regular monarch (or any political leader, realistically), who waits for the people to assemble before arriving on the scene. Can you imagine a presidential candidate standing on stage, waiting for the crowd to show up? Never. But, here's God, the King of the Universe, waiting for us. There's a very powerful idea in this for recovery. God is waiting for us. All we have to do is approach. In the depths of addiction, we may consider ourselves beyond hope, beyond care, but nothing could be further from the truth. Each of us, no matter how degraded we become, has a standing appointment to see the most powerful force in the universe one on one, whenever we want. All we have to do is be willing to take the steps toward God to make it happen.

Questions to Ponder	
Does knowing that God waits for you, for whenever you're ready, change your view of God, or of yourself?	
Can you learn anything about the nature of ego and vanity by contrasting God's readiness to wait for you with a worldly leader's unwillingness to wait for anyone?	
For Today: In what ways do you feel worthy/not worthy of having a "standing appointment" with the King of the Universe?	

Step 5 - Admitted to God, to ourselves and to another human being the exact nature of our wrongs.

Journaling Exercise: Just as God was waiting in the Wilderness for the Israelites, God waits for you to admit to Him, yourself and another human being the exact nature of your wrongs. Does this truth make you want to hurry to do your fifth step, or delay? Why?

Exodus 20:1 – 20:2 – "God spoke all of these statements [The Ten Commandments] saying: I am God, your God, Who has taken you out of the land of Egypt, from the house of slavery."

Many have commented that the first commandment isn't really a commandment, at least at first glance. The announcement that "I am God, your God…" doesn't seem to be commanding us to do anything, or not do anything. Yet it is, in many ways. One way to interpret the first commandment is to understand it as an instruction to be aware of God. You could think of it as saying, in effect, "Understand that I am God" or "Believe that God is in your life, in the world." Being commanded to believe in God's presence is a necessary step for recovery. The second step in the 12 steps of AA is, "Came to believe that a Power greater than ourselves could restore us to sanity." Coming to believe in God is a gentler form of being commanded to believe in God. In some recovery cases, it might be better to think that you're being commanded. It will help you crash through barriers of belief that will impede your recovery. Then, we have the powerful idea that God has taken us out of the house of slavery. Addiction is a form of slavery. God can take us out from our personal Egypt, the place where we serve the drugs and alcohol, no matter how destructive they are for our lives.

Questions to Ponder	
Do you struggle with a belief in a higher power? If so, what is motivating that struggle?	
Can you relate/not relate to the idea of a "personal Egypt" – addiction's "enslavement" of us?	
For Today: How do you feel about being commanded to believe that there is a Higher Power in your life?	

Step 6 - Were entirely ready to have God remove all these defects of character.

Journaling Exercise: In order to do the sixth step, you have to have a belief in a Higher Power. Does the first commandment help you feel entirely ready to have God remove all of your defects of character? If so, how? If not, why not?

Exodus 20:3 – "You shall not recognize the Gods of others."

This commandment, one of The Ten Commandments, is an exhortation not to worship idols. You may think, wow, that's not so hard. I don't bow down to statues of other Gods. I'm off the hook, right? Well, technically maybe so, but perhaps not. Idolatry comes in many different forms. The Jewish people were released from their craving for idolatry – it used to be a serious hunger for every Jew, believe it or not, to worship idols – but God lifted that desire. Today, we are not drawn so much to idolatrous religions. Yet, we often worship, in effect, money, status, other people, fame, and so forth. Again, you're thinking, I'm not doing that. But, take a careful look at your life. What's driving your day-to-day activities? Where is your motivation coming from? Is it to serve God and be aware of God in your life, or is it to make enough money to impress your friends? Serving our secular idols is spiritually harmful in and of itself, but it is also a big factor in addiction. In the rooms, we hear story after story about people who tried to fill up their empty lives with possessions and meaningless achievements. The lack of fulfillment inherent in this kind of activity created a void that addiction could fill with all of its toxins. The goal is to understand when you are giving your power away to an idol, religious or secular.

Questions to Ponder	
Can relate/not relate to the idea that we may have tried to fill up our lives with material possessions or non-spiritual experiences?	
When you were drinking or using, do you think you elevated your drug of choice to the status of being an idol – an inanimate being that had power over you? Did you "serve" that idol?	
For Today: How are you balancing the drive to achieve and earn money in day to day life with the equally (or more) important drive to achieve serenity and conscious contact with a Higher Power?	

Step 6 - Were entirely ready to have God remove all these defects of character.

Journaling Exercise: Being ready to have God remove all of your defects of character means being ready to accept God as the central Higher Power in your life – replacing any fake gods or "idols" that we tend to worship today, e.g. money, power, success, prestige. As you work on your sixth step, how can you think about moving God to the center of your consciousness and moving everything else, the "idols" so to speak, off to the side or out of the way completely?

Exodus 21:24 – "...an eye for an eye, a tooth for a tooth, a hand for a hand, a foot for a foot..."

This is one of the most famous, and most famously misunderstood, phrases in the entire Bible. Understanding the difference between what "an eye for an eye" really means, as opposed to what a lot of people think it means, can teach us a lot about sobriety and recovery. A lot of people think "an eye for an eye" is about revenge. If someone pokes you in the eye, poke them in the eye, and so forth. Get even! But, curiously, it is not about that at all. "An eye for an eye" is a formula for civil damages, meaning if someone harms you to the tune of $20, they owe you $20. It's a profound difference, when viewed from the perspective of recovery. For many of us, addictive behavior is fueled by feelings of revenge and resentment, the wanting to gauge out the eyes of someone who hurt us. True recovery and sobriety occurs, however, when you are ready to pay damages yourself, to make amends to people you have harmed. If you took $20, pay back $20. Do it. You'll feel a lot better about yourself and you will be building your sobriety. That's the true meaning of "an eye for an eye."

Questions to Ponder	
When you were drinking and using, did you experience a desire to take revenge on people you thought had wronged you? Did you act on those feelings? How did it go?	
Are you wanting to take revenge on people now that you are in recovery? If so, what's driving the feeling? Do you think it's good for your recovery?	
For Today: Are you feeling that you owe someone "an eye for their eye" so to speak, but the actual amends might be a lot simpler and clearer than that?	

Step 7 - Humbly asked Him to remove our shortcomings.

Journaling Exercise: In what ways does humbly asking God to remove our shortcomings require us to be clear about our defects and not exaggerate them? In this context, an eye for an eye means that we should ask God to remove our actual shortcoming, in equal proportion to their reality, not the reality that our fear, shame and resentment may make them out to be.

Day 32

Exodus 22:20 – "You shall not taunt or oppress a stranger, for you were strangers in the land of Egypt."

This verse stresses the need for Jews to be kind to strangers, to be hospitable and charitable with others – all in the context of having once been strangers themselves in Egypt, and never to forget that experience. So it is in the program, where we are encouraged to be kind to newcomers and those in early sobriety (or newly back from relapses.) Newcomers are fragile and need our most generous nature. This should probably seem pretty obvious, but there's more to it than meets the eye. The majority of us, even in our most degraded state, are probably not going out of our ways to be hateful to newcomers. Yet, we should all work on noticing when we are not giving our fullest selves to newcomers. For example, in a tight meeting with regular attendees, it's easy to fall into a club-like mentality and not be as welcoming to newcomers as we should be. On a deeper level, this verse can be viewed as a comment on the evolution of self that occurs in recovery. In many ways, the new, sober self is a "stranger" to the old, familiar addict. The sober world is an alien place. We are aliens in the sober world. We need to be kind to ourselves.

Questions to Ponder	
Can you relate/not relate to the idea of being a stranger in a strange place?	
How did you feel when you went to your first meeting? Did the people at the meeting extend themselves to you and make you feel welcome?	
For Today: How are you feeling about the suggestion that you be kind to newcomers?	

Step 8 - Made a list of all persons we had harmed, and became willing to make amends to them all.

Journaling Exercise: In what ways might you feel like a stranger as you make a list of persons you have harmed? i.e. in some ways you're a new person who is going to make amends for things you might not have considered wrong before.

Exodus 25:31 – "You shall make a Menorah of pure gold, hammered out shall the Menorah be made..."

As we noted in yesterday's piece, Moses was supposed to hammer the golden Menorah out of a single piece of gold. According to experienced goldsmiths, this is virtually impossible to do. So, how did Moses, who had no goldsmith skills at all, actually make the Menorah? The Commentary tells us that God told Moses to throw a lump of gold into a fire. God would take over at that point and let the fire miraculously shape the Menorah. This image is rich with meaning for addiction recovery. We, too, are like lumps of gold. If we are willing to be thrown into the "fire" of recovery, trusting God, we too can be shaped into something beautiful and spiritual. It takes trust and courage. Similarly, there are going to be moments in recovery when we simply won't believe the value in the advice we are being given. A direction from a sponsor might sound as plausible as, "Throw the gold into the fire. A Menorah will come out." But, it will, if we trust God and listen to those with more experience than us.

Questions to Ponder	
Can you relate/not relate to the idea of being an unformed piece of gold? Is there a better you hiding inside that needs to be shaped by spiritual practice?	
Can you relate/not relate to the notion of being improved by being "thrown in the fire" so to speak?	
For Today: Does something seem impossible to accomplish? Do you think it might be possible if you, like Moses, take a leap of faith and do what God wants to do?	

Step 9 - Made direct amends to such people wherever possible, except when to do so would injure them or others.

Journaling Exercise: Making direct amends may seem as difficult as taking a lump of gold and hammering it into a perfect Menorah. In what ways can you use the symbolism of this verse to help you prepare for the seemingly impossible task of making direct amends?

Day 34

Exodus 30:17 – "God spoke to Moses, saying: 'You shall make a copper Laver and its base of copper, for washing; place it between the Tent of Meeting and the Altar, and put water there. From it, Aaron and his sons shall wash their hands together with their feet.'"

This rather simple instruction, that Moses should make a copper vessel for water used for washing, can give us some important insights into recovery. Technically, the Priests needed to wash both their hands and feet before they entered the Tabernacle to perform the sacrificial services. In spiritual terms, the washing refers to a cleansing of impurity from the hands and feet that is required for service to God. There are many modern-day references to this in religious observance: washing of hands before eating, praying, and so forth. We can take this idea of washing into recovery as well. When we work on sobriety, we need to wash off the toxic spiritual matter that is contaminating our souls. Addiction is a filthy business, in spiritual terms, if not in physical reality. We need to wash off the poison of addiction and toxic people if we want to engage in serious recovery. And, like the Priests, we need to wash both our hands and our feet, in symbolic terms. The hands represent our actions. We need to cleanse ourselves of the spiritual impurity resulting from what we have done. The feet represent where we've been. We need to clean off the effects of being in places where we should not have gone.

Questions to Ponder	
Does the symbolism of the verse resonate with you: washing the hands referring to cleansing your deeds and washing the feet referring to where you are and where you are heading?	
How do you handle toxic people and situations now that you are in recovery? Do you have way to "wash off" their effects on you?	
For Today: Are there any toxic influences you want to "wash away," so to speak, as way to get ready to seek conscious contact with God?	

Step 10 - Continued to take personal inventory and when we were wrong promptly admitted it.

Journaling Exercise: Thinking about the verse's description of the Laver, the washing vessel, in what ways can you relate the concept of cleansing yourself of spiritual toxins with the tenth step's suggestion of continuing to take personal inventory?

Day 35

Exodus 32:17 – "Joshua heard the sound of the people in its shouting, and he said to Moses, 'The sound of battle is in the camp.'"

Moses did not know that the Israelites had made a golden calf when he descended with the stone tablets containing The Ten Commandments. But, he heard the noise made by the wild dancing and celebration going on in front of the idol. To Joshua, his helper, it was the "sound of battle." What was it: celebration or battle? It was both, really. The blurring of the boundary between celebration and strife can easily define what was going on in the Israelite camp. Yes, the Israelites were celebrating their new "god," but they were also – at least some of them – struggling with the dissonance that the golden calf represented. They knew better. They had sworn to follow the one True God quite recently. They knew what they were doing was wrong, but many could not stop themselves. So it is with addiction. In a relapse, most of us know we are doing the wrong thing, but we can't stop. It's a battle, a battle we must fight over and over, in many cases. As was the case with the Israelites, it is faith in the one True God that will help us win the battle and stay sober.

Questions to Ponder	
Have you ever felt like a celebration was actually a battle (i.e. you were "enjoying yourself" so much you felt as if you were in a fight?)	
Does recovery remind you of a struggle between a false god and a true Higher Power?	
For Today: Are you struggling with the temptation to drink and use? If so, can you relate to the feelings of the Israelites in this verse, who were tempted into idolatry to relieve their fears?	

Step 11 - Sought through prayer and meditation to improve our conscious contact with God as we understood Him, praying only for knowledge of His will for us and the power to carry that out.

Journaling Exercise: Have ever been tempted into relapse or "worshipping a false god," as per the verse? In what ways can the eleventh step help you regain conscious contact with God?

Exodus 38:8 – "He made the laver of copper and its base of copper."

The laver was an elaborate washing basin made of copper. It allowed the Priests to wash the hands and feet at the same time in preparation for doing the services in the Tabernacle. The Commentators tell us that the copper used to fashion the laver came from the polished copper mirrors that the women had used in Egypt. This idea can inspire us in recovery on two separate levels. The Israelite women used their mirrors to beautify themselves and make themselves attractive to their husbands. That they would part with these mirrors for the sake of building the Tabernacle is itself a striking fact. Sacrifice of personal pleasure for the sake of holiness is a major message in recovery. Recovery can lead to pleasure and joy, but it can often involve sacrificing fun, irrelevant activities that distract us from our primary purpose. The mirrors also have a powerful backstory. During the period of enslavement, many men did not want to father children who would grow up in slavery. The women knew better. They knew that the future generation would be free, so they used the mirrors to beautify themselves, to encourage their husbands to be intimate with them and ensure a Jewish future. We should keep in mind these mirrors, and the brave women who used them, as we struggle in the depths of addiction and recovery. There will be a better future if we do the work.

Questions to Ponder	
When you were drinking or using, did you think much about your future? Did you feel you had a future?	
Has recovery made you think about sacrificing some personal pleasure for the sake of getting better (at least temporarily?).	
For Today: Is addiction affecting your ability to be intimate with other people?	

Step 12 - Having had a spiritual awakening as the result of these steps, we tried to carry this message to alcoholics and to practice these principles in all our affairs.

Journaling Exercise: When you think about carrying the message to alcoholics, in what ways could you talk about the possibility of a different future for people who are still drinking or using?

Leviticus Workbook

Leviticus 1:1 – "He called to Moses and God spoke to him from the Tent of Meeting..."

According to The Commentators, God called to Moses in a loud voice, but only Moses could hear it. This makes sense, of course, because Moses was a great prophet and was able to speak directly with God. There is a lesson here for recovery. God may be speaking to us, but we need to learn to listen for God's voice. If we tune in, the voice of God might be loud and clear, but if we are not paying attention, we hear nothing. The idea of a loud voice that you can't hear, however, is also a terrific metaphor for the warnings we ignore as we plunge into addiction. The danger signs are screaming at us, sometimes literally, but we choose to be deaf to them. The addiction is too alluring. We need to quiet ourselves down on the inside if we want to hear the voice of God in our lives. For some of us, this might actually mean talking a little more softly. The rooms are full of people who are in love with their own loud voices. Recovery happens when we learn to enjoy a little silence and hear what others have to say, especially the One who speaks the truth.

Questions to Ponder	
Have you ever had trouble detecting the "voice of God" in your life? (Most likely not literally the voice of God, but God's message to you?"	
Can you relate/not relate to the idea that perhaps your own voice is so loud at times that it blots out God's voice in your life?	
For Today: Can you make time to be in a quiet place to help you focus on your recovery?	

Step 1: We admitted we were powerless over alcohol - that our lives had become unmanageable.

Journaling Exercise: When you took the first step, was it in response to a message you received in your life? Was that message possibly from God, though perhaps delivered by a person? (e.g. a judge, a family member, a doctor?)

Leviticus 5:5 – "When one shall become guilty regarding one of these matters, he shall confess what he sinned."

The Torah lists a number of sins that a person should confess, and for which he should bring a guilt offering to the Priest. These include refusing to bear witness to a financial transaction, and thus causing someone to suffer a monetary loss, as well as touching spiritually contaminated objects. In recovery, we have the equivalent. Not being straight with people in financial dealings is one of the classic signs that an addiction is getting out of control. The loss of the moral compass, the dishonesty – these are the defects of character that lead to worse addiction problems and lapses in recovery. Similarly, downward companionship, hanging around with toxic, dangerous people, is a major threat to recovery. But, like the sins described in The Torah, they should be confessed. Call them out. Telling a sponsor that you spent time with your old drug dealer is a great way to break the spell and get yourself on the right track, even if your addict self is pulling you in the wrong direction.

Questions to Ponder	
Have you ever done something that resulted in another person losing money (or something valuable like time or a relationship)?	
In recovery, are you still drawn to toxic, dangerous people? What are you doing about it?	
For Today: Do you need to call out a behavior that you haven't discussed with anyone before – to make it have less power over you?	

Step 2 - Came to believe that a Power greater than ourselves could restore us to sanity.

Journaling Exercise: In what ways can the experience of wronging another person or spending time with a toxic, dangerous person lead you to see that only a Higher Power can restore you to sanity?

Leviticus 6:6 – "A permanent fire shall remain aflame on the Altar; it shall not be extinguished."

The fire on the Altar symbolizes the eternal devotion of the Israelites to God. It never goes out. Alternatively, it should never be let to go out. Like any fire, it needs to be tended and fueled to keep burning. Without attention, it will quickly die out. Recovery is much the same. We need to be constant in our tending of our inner "fire" of recovery. We should commit to keeping it burning at all times, never extinguishing it. We need to be passionate about recovery – on fire – so to speak. This may not be as hard as it sounds. Once burning, a fire is relatively easy to maintain. If we can create a good recovery program for ourselves, it will not be a superhuman effort to keep it going. If we do let the fire go out, then the work of setting a new one will be challenging. Starting a fire from nothing is a lot harder than keeping a good fire going. This is true for real fires and symbolic spiritual/recovery fires. We need to be constant and vigilant in our efforts to maintain our focus – our "fire" – in recovery.

Questions to Ponder	
Can you envision your recovery as a permanent fire, like the one that "shall remain aflame on the Altar"?	
What might threaten to extinguish the "permanent fire" of your recovery? What can you do to prevent that from happening?	
For Today: What can you do today to "tend to the fire" of your recovery – to keep it going over the long term?	

Step 3- Made a decision to turn our will and our lives over to the care of God as we understood Him.

Journaling Exercise: If you turn your life and will over to the care of God, will that help you establish a "permanent fire" of strong spiritual growth in recovery?

Leviticus 11: 3 – "Everything among the animals that has a split hoof, which is completely separated into double hooves, and that brings up its cud – that one you may eat."

This verse describes one of the basic laws of kosher food, which is that only cud-chewing animals with split hooves may be eaten. Cows are okay. Horses are not. There are many dietary laws in Judaism and few make any real sense. Why is a split hoof okay, but a single hoof is off limits? It seems arbitrary. At some level, it's worth going through the spiritual exercise of just accepting that this is God's will for Jewish people. One interpretation that resonates with recovery is to reflect on what it means to touch the ground. While the idea of having one's "feet on the ground" is generally considered to be positive, there are aspects of being attached to the ground that may not be so healthy. The ground – dirt – can be seen as origin of our animalistic tendencies. Our most base appetites, our worst ethical behavior, are of course "natural." All's fair in nature, where you prey on the weak, eat everyone else's food and so forth. That's the way of the animal kingdom, but not what God has in mind for human beings. One of The Bible's main messages is that we have to rise above our animal instincts and learn to act like human beings. So, eating animals that don't touch the ground with a single foot, but which have a split, should remind us to be wary of our connections to pure nature.

Questions to Ponder	
When you were active in your addiction, did you do things that were "perfectly natural" but which, in retrospect were wrong or unhealthy for you?	
Can you relate/not relate to the idea that there may be differences between your human self and your lower, animal self? What are the differences?	
For Today: Think about how recovery has helped you rise above animalistic tendencies.	

Step 4 - Made a searching and fearless moral inventory of ourselves.

Journaling Exercise: As you work your fourth step, can you spot incidents where your behavior was driven by animalistic instincts, which you perhaps rationalized at the time as being "only natural…"

Day 41

Leviticus 11:9 – "This may you eat from everything that is in the water: everything that has fins and scales in the water, in the seas, and in the streams, those you may eat."

This section of The Torah lists many types of animals that Jews may or may not eat. It's the foundation of kosher dietary laws. Putting aside the technicalities of kosher laws, which are quite complex, there is a simple spiritual concept embodied in all the regulations about what kinds of foods are acceptable from God's perspective. One interpretation is that God wants us to be careful about what we consume. Being disciplined about what we eat is an important aspect of a general spiritual discipline. Eating is so basic, so routine, that we can do without thinking. This is true of so many other areas of life. We can go on autopilot and plow through our day without being aware of what's going on, who we are, or how we affect others. This is not good for sobriety. Similarly, we should be conscious of what we are taking into ourselves, in a broader sense than diet. What ideas are we consuming, what attitude and opinions? We should be vigilant about what we take in, because what we take in will ultimately come back out. If we surround ourselves with toxic, negative people, we risk becoming toxic and negative ourselves. At the very least, that toxicity will affect us. The kosher dietary laws are designed to remind us, by making us watch what we eat, to be careful about what else we consume.

Questions to Ponder	
Have you ever gone "on autopilot" with routine but important activities like being with family or friends? What was the result?	
In what ways can you connect the idea of watching what you eat with the broader idea of being careful about the kinds of ideas and opinions you absorb?	
For Today: Think about people in your life, perhaps identifying toxic individuals who should be avoided in the future.	

Step 4 - Made a searching and fearless moral inventory of ourselves.

Journaling Exercise: As you work your fourth step, can you see experiences where you "digested" toxic beliefs and thinking from others, perhaps without realizing it?

Leviticus 13:45 – "And the person with tzaraas in whom there is the affliction – his garments shall be rent, the hair of his head shall be unshorn, and he shall cloak himself up to his lips he is to call out 'Contaminated, contaminated.' He shall dwell in isolation, outside the camp."

This is quite an image. The afflicted person needs to tear his clothes, not cut his hair, and walk about calling, "Contaminated, contaminated," so that people will be aware that he has the disease. This verse has several interesting contradictions. For one thing, if tzaraas is not a communicable disease, why does the sufferer need to warn people that he is approaching? One thought is that the spiritual contamination that is afflicting him may affect them. Being around spiritually diseased people can have a negative impact on our own sobriety and peace of mind. Another view is that a person with tzaraas is telling people how much pain he is in so that others will pray for him. A third, fascinating interpretation, from Rabbi Hirsch, is that the person with tzaraas is actually saying "you are all contaminated." Being contaminated, he assumes that everyone else is as well. This might sound familiar for those of us in recovery. When we are acting out, we sometimes assume that everyone else in the world is as ill as we are. It's a psychological phenomenon called projection. Finally, is the sufferer in isolation, outside the camp or in the camp warning people that he is contaminated? It's both. He or she is isolated, even while among others. Self-destructive habits of negative speech and deprecating others cuts him off from people. In this way, the sufferer is like so many addicts – alone in a crowd.

Questions to Ponder	
Do you think that a spiritually bad attitude is contagious? How so?	
Can you relate/not relate to the idea of mentally projecting your illness onto others? i.e. assuming that everyone around you thought and acted the same way you did, when they didn't?	
For Today: Think about times when your behavior cut you off from others, perhaps people you cared about, or who cared about you.	

Step 5: Admitted to God, to ourselves and to another human being the exact nature of our wrongs.

Journaling Exercise: If your fourth step includes episodes where your behavior was driven by spiritually contaminated thinking, in what ways can you work on clearing out this contamination by admitting to God, to yourself and another human being the exact nature of your wrongs?

Day 43

Leviticus 13:45 – "He shall dwell in isolation, outside the camp."

God puts the person suffering from tzaraas into isolation. He is to spend time with himself, away from others. This isolation can be seen as a rebuke for anti-social behavior. By making him be alone, God is attempting to make the sufferer of tzaraas feel the pain of isolation – the pain that he or she has caused others by gossip and slander. When we act out against others, especially through negative speech, we cause others to feel pain and isolation. God gives us tzaraas and isolates us to make us reflect on that destructive act. The challenge is to take the rebuke and use it as an opportunity to learn about ourselves. As addicts, we are usually self-serving and self-seeking, so we typically respond to rebuke with denial, rationalization and more acting out. The verse can help us think about positive, constructive ways to deal with the isolation caused by our addictive behaviors. If we are strong and do the work, we can use the pain of isolation, which is a natural part of recovery, as an opportunity to learn about ourselves.

Questions to Ponder	
Being alone can be helpful in recovery, but too much isolating can be bad. How can you figure out the right balance for yourself?	
Can you relate/not relate to the idea that being isolated from others is a proper rebuke for self-seeking behavior that caused pain to others?	
For Today: Think about how being rebuked can help us learn about ourselves and grow.	

Step 5: Admitted to God, to ourselves and to another human being the exact nature of our wrongs.

Journaling Exercise: In what ways can the process of admitting to God, yourself and another human being the exact nature of your wrongs make you feel less isolated from others?

Leviticus 14:9 – "On the seventh day he shall shave off all his hair – his head, his beard, his eyebrows, and all his hair he shall shave off."

Why would this action be necessary for cleansing oneself of the spiritual malady of tzaraas? The eyes are significant, according to the commentators, because it is the eyes that look with envy and jealousy. So many sins of speech begin with the eyes. The eyes covet. The eyes judge. The eyes envy. All of these emotions can drive people to gossip and slander. The act of removing some of the superficial beauty of the eyes is intended to remind the person with tzaraas to guard his eyes better. Our own stories probably bear this idea out. Passionate feelings of envy and resentment, which can be huge forces for negativity and addictive acting out, are often initiated by what we see. Wow, look at his fancy car! Look at my ex-wife's new boyfriend! Look at my friend's cool job! Look, look, look – then feel. And, it's not always pretty. The imperative here is to relearn how we look at things. Instead of, "Look at the fancy car. Why can't I have one?" perhaps it would be healthier to think, "Look at the fancy car. That guy has a high car payment. Maybe he hates that expensive car. I don't have to worry about an expensive car. I have the car that I need. I need to move on."

Questions to Ponder	
Can you relate/not relate to the idea that recovery can benefit from "guarding the eyes" – not looking with envy and resentment at what others have? (Or seem to have)	
Looking back on your time of addiction, can you now see that people you envied and resented perhaps didn't quite have all what you thought they did? (e.g. the guy with the big car really just had a big car payment?)	
For Today: Focus on how you can "guard your eyes" in recovery.	

Step 6 - Were entirely ready to have God remove all these defects of character.

Journaling Exercise: In what ways can becoming ready to have God remove your defects of character involve getting better at "guarding your eyes" against coveting and envying what you see in others?

Leviticus 14:33 – 14:35 – "God spoke to Moses and Aaron, saying: 'When you arrive in the land of Canaan that I give you as a possession, and I will place a tzaraas affliction upon a house in the land of your possession; the one to whom the house belongs shall come and declare to the Priest, saying: Something like an affliction has appeared to me in the house.'"

Tzaraas can also afflict your house, it turns out. Imagine what that looks like. You're sitting at home, slandering and gossiping when all of a sudden, the walls start to show strange stains and deformities. It's a fascinating image, and one that can tell us something about the way spiritual contamination spreads. Tzaraas of the body is a physical ailment that comes from the spiritual toxin of gossip and slander. If you talk down about others, you may get tzaraas of the body. But why the house? This actually makes a great deal of sense. When we spew toxic gossip and waste our spiritual selves denigrating others, we poison our homes as well. The spiritual environment, the "vibes" if you will, in the home of someone who gossips negatively will be deadly. The tzaraas of the house is actually helpful to the one who is gossiping. It's a wakeup call to change his ways. The home of an addict is the same. The self-seeking, self-destructive behavior of the addict taints his home, and almost always the lives of those who share that home. If only the walls of an addict's house would develop a mysterious rash to alert them to the harm they are causing, it would be a sign that things need to change.

Questions to Ponder	
Do you think that being negative and denigrating others can affect the tone of the home and family?	
Have you ever seen a sign that you needed to change the way you spoke and acted in your home? (Perhaps not the walls changing colors but something that clearly signaled that your behavior was toxic and destructive?)	
For Today: Focus on not talking about other people. (i.e. consider how you feel when you badmouth others? Does it make you feel better? For how long?)	

Step 6 - Were entirely ready to have God remove all these defects of character.

Journaling Exercise: Can you envision the sixth step helping you make your role in the home and family more healthy and positive? How so?

Leviticus 16:7 – 16:10 – "He [Aaron] shall take the two he-goats and stand them before God, at the entrance of the Tent of Meeting. Aaron shall place lots upon the two he-goats: one lot 'for God' and one lot 'for Azazel.' Aaron shall bring near the he-goat designated by lot for God, and make it a sin offering. And the he-goat designated by lot for Azazel shall be stood alive before God, to provide atonement through it, to send it to Azazel to the Wilderness."

These verses describe the handling of the two goat sacrifices in the Yom Kippur service. One goat is offered on the Altar. The other, "for Azazel," is sent out into the Wilderness to die. The basic idea here is that Aaron, the High Priest, is essentially transferring the sins of the Israelites onto the goats. One is offered. One is sent away. The idea of casting lots to determine the fates of two goat offerings will likely seem alien in today's world. Yet, there's an idea here that should resonate with anyone working a program. The act of sending the goat into the Wilderness reminds us of the act of "turning it over" to God. AA suggests that we should try to purge ourselves of negative, addictive-triggering feelings and thoughts by "turning them over" to God and letting God sort out what they mean. It's an odd process when you start it, but it works. God understands what to do with destructive, toxic feelings, even if we can't handle them. We should turn over our addiction-fueling feelings to God, as if we were putting them onto a goat designated "for Azazel" and sending them out into the Wilderness to die. Then, we can go back to focusing on our recovery.

Questions to Ponder	
How are you doing with the process of turning things over to a Higher Power?	
Does the image of the Priest placing the sins of the Israelites onto a goat help you visualize how you might turn your issues over to a Higher Power?	
For Today: Focus on turning over negative, toxic feelings. This may not be a consistent reflex early in recovery.	

Step 7 - Humbly asked Him to remove our shortcomings.

Journaling Exercise: The seventh step is all about turning things over to your Higher Power. As you work the seventh step, can the process of visualizing the goat of Azazel in the verse help you let God take away your defects of character?

Leviticus 19:1 – 19:2 – "And the Lord spoke to Moses, saying, speak to the entire congregation of the Children of Israel, and say to them, 'You shall be holy, for I, the Lord, your God, am holy.'"

God is speaking to us, through Moses, telling us that we are each holy. When God says, "You shall be holy," He means you – yes you. Why are we holy? As the verse says, we are holy because God is holy. God says, "You shall be holy, for I, the Lord, your God, am holy." That's pretty cool, isn't it? We can be holy because God is holy. Of course, we have to do our part. What God is trying to communicate, I think, is that each of us has the potential to be truly holy, to be spiritually complete up to whatever level we can manage. It takes focus and work to get to that level, but God has implanted within each of us a special, personal flame of holiness that we can ignite. Each of us has the potential to have a personal relationship with God. I heard a great example of this at a meeting once, where a man said, "I wanted to tell God how big my problems were. Instead, I told my problems how big my God was."

Questions to Ponder	
What does it mean to you to feel holy? E.g. to be living in a spiritually whole, sound way? Have you experienced some version of this?	
If you think your problems are big, does it help to imagine that God is bigger than your problems?	
For Today: Focus on feeling holy. If this feels difficult, what do you think is getting in your way?	

Step 7 - Humbly asked Him to remove our shortcomings.

Journaling Exercise: The seventh step can be helped along by focusing on our potential to be holy. As we think about humbly asking God to remove our shortcomings, in what ways can we be successful with the step work by paying attention to our innate holiness?

Leviticus 19:3 – "Every man shall fear his mother and his father, and you shall observe My Sabbaths. I am the Lord, your God."

The commandment to honor one's mother and father can be a perplexing challenge to addicts. Everyone's relationship with his or her parents is complicated, but for addicts, it can be toxic. In some cases, recovery will require detaching from parents who are catalysts for acting out, perhaps as a result of their own addiction issues or abuse. For most of us, though, it's a little more nuanced. One truth to comprehend, though, is that we need to make peace with our parents if we want good recovery and serenity. How can we do this? One approach is to practice forgiveness and release yourself from resentment you feel toward them. This is easier said than done, but it can be an immense relief. Conversely, you will have amends to make to them. What? You are already disagreeing, but think about it carefully. Your step work should rigorously examine ways in which you disrespected and wronged your parents. In some cases, the best approach will be to make "living amends," where you use your current relationship with your parents to be good to them, making up for past wrongs. (You can't un-wreck the car from 10 years ago anyway, so why try?) At the same time, as The Commentators point out about this verse, respect for one's parents should not override the Sabbath. A good relationship with parents requires mutual respect. If your parents cannot understand and respect your spiritual practice in recovery, you will need to set boundaries. You should not violate the Sabbath (either literally or symbolically) to please your parents.

Questions to Ponder	
How do you think your relationship with your parents affected your addiction?	
In what ways do you think your parents are influencing your recovery? (Even if they are no longer living, your parents might still be affecting your recovery.)	
For Today: Think about ways you can make amends to your parents.	

Step 8 - Made a list of all persons we had harmed, and became willing to make amends to them all.

Journaling Exercise: Should you include your parents on your eighth step amends list? Why or why not?

Leviticus 19:4 – "You shall not turn to the worthless idols, nor shall you make molten deities for yourselves. I am the Lord, your God."

What does it mean to "turn" to an idol? Technically, it means worshipping a false god instead of the one true God. The "turning" implies that the worshipper is in a state of emotional and spiritual need, so he "turns" to the idol and, in effect, turns away from God. A broader, recovery-based interpretation might be that, as addicts, our addictions often find us turning to spiritually empty solutions to make our lives better. Of course, these solutions – money, sex, power, status, fun – provide no answers, nor sustenance for us. Generally, they make things worse. If you crave money, no amount of money will make you happy. Of course, the drugs and alcohol themselves, the gambling, the sexual acting out, are all just modern incarnations of idolatrous passions. They are all-consuming and ultimately worthless. They drain us of our spiritual potential. As we get into recovery, there's a temptation to "turn ourselves" to these false gods once again. If only we were richer, we might think to ourselves, then we won't feel so empty and want to use drugs all the time. That's incorrect. You're using drugs because you're trying to fill your soul with a worthless, idolatrous material. It won't get you anywhere. This is what The Torah is trying to tell us. Do not worship idols. Instead, focus on the true God.

Questions to Ponder	
When you were active in your addiction, did you ever feel as if you were pursuing "false gods" like money, sex, power, fun and so forth?	
If the modern idols of money, sex, power, etc. tempted you, what do you think you were trying to fix about yourself by pursuing them?	
For Today: Do you feel drawn to the false gods of today, away from the true God?	

Step 8 - Made a list of all persons we had harmed, and became willing to make amends to them all.

Journaling Exercise: As you prepare your eighth step list, can you think of anyone whom you might have harmed in your pursuit of "false gods" in life? E.g. money, sex, power, fun etc.

Leviticus 19:9 – "When you reap the harvest of your land, you shall not complete your reaping to the corner of your field, and the gleanings of your harvest you shall not take."

The verse instructs farmers not to harvest their entire crop. Rather, they are to leave the corners of their fields, as well as any grain that falls on the ground during the harvest, for the poor to collect. This commandment is of course one of charity, but it's actually deeper even than that. Why not, for example, just harvest all of your crops and write a check to the poor? Wouldn't that be more efficient? Yes and no. There are two reasons for leaving your crop for gleaning. One is that it reminds the farmer that his wealth and harvest are gifts from God, gifts that God wants him to share with those who have less. Farming is very hard work, so it's totally understandable that a farmer will feel entitled to every bit of grain that he has labored to grow. God wants to interrupt that tempting thought. And, having real, poor people gathering in your remnant crop is a tangible, human reminder of how much good God has done for the farmer. In program, we should emulate this commandment and give of ourselves to our fellows – in person, one on one. We should not hog our recovery and good fortune. We should share it with the newcomers and the relapsers, people who are waiting at the corners of our fields, so to speak, desperately in need of help.

Questions to Ponder	
Have you shared your experience, strength and hope with others? How did it go? How did you feel about the experience?	
Do you feel inhibited from sharing your recovery with others? What do you think is getting in your way?	
For Today: Can you share your recovery with someone else in the program?	

Step 9 - Made direct amends to such people wherever possible, except when to do so would injure them or others.

Journaling Exercise: One challenge in the ninth step is to understand that not everyone on your list will understand or appreciate your recovery. Sharing your recovery with people on your amends list might backfire. As you think about making amends, can you think of people on your list who may not want to hear an extended description of how your recovery process works? Why do you think they may not be interested?

Leviticus 19:11 - 19:12 – "You shall not steal, you shall not deny falsely, and you shall not lie to one another. You shall not swear falsely by My Name, thereby desecrating the Name of your God – I am God."

What does it mean to "deny falsely?" It means to deny that a piece of stolen property is stolen. The person who steals is accused of stealing. He then may even falsely swear an oath to God, i.e. "I swear to God," that the property is actually his. According to The Commentators, this verse shows a progression of bad behavior that starts with theft. First, we steal. Then, we deny that the stolen property came into our possession illegally. Then, we just wind up lying to everyone about anything. It's a natural progression for an addict who digs himself deeper and deeper into a lie to appear innocent. At worst, the addict starts to believe the lie. That is truly toxic. He says, "That store I stole from was ripping me off with their high prices. I'm just taking back what's mine." This is a passage into a gateway of a completely false life dominated by lying – a journey into the toxic secrecy of addiction. Addiction thrives in the mind of a liar and the two conditions feed on each other. The liar becomes a bigger addict, and the addict becomes a bigger and better liar, all in the name of getting and using. We can only break the addictive cycle if we can find the strength to stop lying. Of course, God will help us with this challenge, if we can make ourselves swear honestly to God. If you say, "I swear to God that I will stop using" and you try your hardest to make this oath stand, you will make progress toward sobriety.

Questions to Ponder	
Did you tell lies when you were active in your addiction?	
If you were dishonest with others (and yourself) during your addiction, did the process of lying feed on itself, digging you into a deeper hole? How so?	
For Today: Is there something that God wants you to be honest about today, perhaps to yourself?	

Step 9 - Made direct amends to such people wherever possible, except when to do so would injure them or others.

Journaling Exercise: Are you making any amends for lying or "denying falsely" as per the verse? If so, what were the circumstances? How do you feel about it now? How will you make amends?

Leviticus 25:1 – 25:4 – "God spoke to Moses on Mount Sinai, saying: Speak to the Children and Israel and say to them: When you come into the land that I give you, the land shall observe a Sabbath rest for God. For six years you may sow your field and for six years you may prune your vineyard; and you may gather in its crop. But the seventh year shall be a complete rest for the land, a Sabbath for God; your field you shall not sow and your vineyard you shall not prune."

This is the law of the "Sabbatical" (Shemitah) year, the biblical practice of letting the land lay fallow every seventh year. Shemitah gives us a great way to think about the responsibility we need to take for ourselves, along with the faith that we need to have in God to provide for us. Yes, God provides for us, but we must do our part. On the seventh year, God will take care of us. The land must rest. We can be free from the hard work of farming so we can concentrate on our relationship with God. In modern life, the Shemitah concept can help us remember not to get overly caught up in physical wealth and possessions. If you're working seven days a week, you're not having faith in God to provide for you. You're thinking that you alone are responsible for your wealth, and chances are, you aren't satisfied with what you got. Guess what. You never will be. This feeling of never being satisfied can be a big driver of addictive acting out. You get so tired and stressed by it all that a drink or a drug seems like a great way to tune out. It's only when you release yourself from this treadmill and accept that God is taking care of you – provided you do your part – then you will begin to be happy with what you've been given.

Questions to Ponder	
What are you responsible for in your life? What things can you trust God to do for you?	
Have you ever over-worked while worrying excessively about providing for yourself (and perhaps your family)? Did that feeling affect your addiction?	
For Today: Are you feeling stress about whether or not you will be able to provide for yourself in recovery?	

Step 10 - Continued to take personal inventory and when we were wrong promptly admitted it.

Journaling Exercise: As you continue to take personal inventory in the tenth step, can you identity situations where you were feeling as if you alone had to do it all – that God would not help you manage your life and recovery?

Leviticus 26:3 – 26:4 – "If you will follow My decrees and observe My commandments and perform them; then I will provide rains in their time, and the land will give its produce and the tree of the field will give its fruit."

If you follow God's law, God will reward you. That's the idea behind this verse. In this case, specifically, God it telling the Israelites that if they follow His law when they live in the Promised Land, they will reap a bountiful harvest. In our own lives, we should find that we are rewarded spiritually and materially by following God's laws. It may not always seem that way, of course, but God is not a push-button satisfaction machine. God rewards us with the experiences that we need to have. Ultimately, though, it's true. It's a simple program: Don't drink. Work the steps. You will be okay. It's virtually guaranteed. Part of the challenge is accepting the reward that God has given us for our devotion. It may not be what we expect, but it will be good for us. Sometimes God surprises us with rewards that we did not realize we needed.

Questions to Ponder	
By following the program (God's law for addicts), are you experiencing your own "bountiful harvest" of good things in life?	
Does it ever seem that, even though you are trying to follow God's will, things aren't working out for you? How do you feel about it? What might you do differently to make the situation better?	
For Today: What do you think God's will is for you today? Do you think God might reward you for following His will for you today?	

Step 11 - Sought through prayer and meditation to improve our conscious contact with God as we understood Him, praying only for knowledge of His will for us and the power to carry that out.

Journaling Exercise: How do you interpret the phrase, "improve our conscious contact with God"? The step implies that we can do better today at achieving conscious contact than we did yesterday. In what ways can you realize this improvement for yourself?

Leviticus 26:19 – "I will break the pride of your might; I will make your Heaven like iron and your land like copper."

God continues the warning of what will happen to the Israelites if they ignore God's laws in the land that He is giving them. God will "break the pride of your might." In recovery, there's a concept known as "self-will run riot." If we believe that our own strength and abilities are enough to save us from drugs and alcohol, let alone all of life's difficulties, we are heading for disaster. God's will is what matters. It can be tricky to make this work, of course. We need to believe in ourselves to be successful in recovery. Yet, we have to temper that belief in ourselves with a faith in God. Trying to go it alone, fueled only by ego and self-will, we will likely find our lives to "be like copper," yielding nothing.

Questions to Ponder	
Have you experienced "self will run riot"? e.g. situations where your belief in your self, or your need to serve your needs overrides healthy behavior… where your troubles are truly of your own making? (See p. 62 of The Big Book)	
How do you balance a healthy belief in the self with the dangers of excessive self-seeking?	
For Today: What is your self-will? (We all have it… it's normal…) But, is it aligned with, or opposed to God's will for you today?	

Step 12 - Having had a spiritual awakening as the result of these steps, we tried to carry this message to alcoholics and to practice these principles in all our affairs.

Journaling Exercise: In what ways does practicing the principles of the 12 steps in all of your affairs require you to remain aware of your self-will and its role in how you live your life?

Numbers Workbook

Numbers 1:1 – "God Spoke to Moses in the Wilderness of Sinai..."

The Book of "Numbers" is so named because of the census that occurs in it. However, in Hebrew the book is called "Bamidbar," which means "in the Wilderness." The book is set in the Wilderness of Sinai, where the Israelites received The Torah and wandered for 40 years before entering the Promised Land. It's an interesting contrast: Numbers, implying plenty, and wilderness, which contains nothing. In some ways, the Wilderness of Sinai was both. It was an empty place, a desert. Yet, it was also filled to the brim with holy people and spiritual life. As addicts, we have all probably felt at some time as if we were in "a wilderness" of the soul, a place of great emptiness and meaninglessness. The insight that can help us at these moments is that the void of the wilderness exists to be filled. You can fill it with your personal spiritual growth or you can languish in its arid futility. God is in the wilderness, though, if you're seeking Him. That's the message in this first line of the book. God spoke to Moses in the Wilderness. He can speak to you, too.

Questions to Ponder	
Can you relate to the idea that addiction is like a wilderness?	
If addiction is empty like a wilderness, can you also see it as a space to be filled with new ideas, new spirituality, a new you?	
For Today: Do you feel as if you are going into a personal wilderness today or out of one?	

Step 1: We admitted we were powerless over alcohol - that our lives had become unmanageable.

Journaling Exercise: In what ways can you connect admitting that you are powerless over alcohol to the idea of being in a personal wilderness?

Numbers 1:5 – "These are the names of the men who shall stand with you: For Reuben, Elizur son of Shedeur."

The Bible proceeds to list the names of each tribal leader, before detailing the headcount of each tribe. Why does The Bible tell us their names? One interpretation is that it underscores the importance of the individual in the group. There was a big group, the Israelites, divided into tribes. Within each tribe were individuals. Naming individuals emphasizes the personal responsibility that each person had to take. By counting those individuals, God is reminding them that they have a personal obligation to follow His law. God is also saying, "You count." We have names, too. Names count. They confer unique individuality on each of us. We introduce ourselves at meetings by name. We are anonymous, but not unidentified. God counts us by name, too, in His own way. We should never forget that. No matter how bad we feel, how low we have fallen, we still have a name. We are still God's children. We count.

Questions to Ponder	
Does the phrase "I count" seem different to you in recovery than it might have during your time of drinking or using drugs?	
Do you consider yourself to be one of God's children? If so, what does it mean to you to be one of God's children? If not, why not?	
For Today: What obligations do you have today to follow God's laws? What will you do today to make yourself count as one of God's children?	

Step 2 - Came to believe that a Power greater than ourselves could restore us to sanity.

Journaling Exercise: In what ways might a Power greater than yourself make you feel as if you count, as if you have a name – that you are one of God's children?

NOTE: This segment refers to the "Sotah," a married woman suspected of adultery by secluding herself with another man. The material may seem strange to some modern readers. It's worth noting, though, that The Torah also forbids a married man from secluding himself with a woman. Whatever punishment a woman might receive for this behavior will also be carried out against the man. I am including verses about the Sotah because they show how it is possible to turn to God to gain understanding and solutions for seemingly insoluble problems.

Numbers 5:11 – 5:13 – "God spoke to Moses, saying, 'Speak to the Children of Israel and say to them: Any man whose wife shall go astray and commit treachery against him; and a man could have lain with her carnally, but it was hidden from the eyes of her husband, and she became secluded and could have been defiled – but there was no witness against her – and she had not been forced...'"

This verse describes the process which the Priest performs when a married woman is accused of possible adultery because she secluded herself with another man, a charge she denies. The Priest performs a ritual to determine if the woman is telling the truth. For our purposes, what caught my eye here was the phrase "hidden from the eyes of her husband." What behaviors do we hide from others? What secrets are we carrying around, allowing to poison our thinking and actions? There's a great saying in recovery, which is, "You're only as sick as your secrets." Though this is a bit simplistic, it's also quite true in its essence. Secrecy is the breeding ground of addictive acting out and relapses. The healthy thing to do is bring those secrets out into the light of day. You don't have to publicize them. Telling your sponsor is a good step to take. But, by admitting your secrets, you reduce their power over you.

Questions to Ponder	
Do you have secrets that you feel are affecting your serenity and recovery? If so, what do you think you should do about them?	
If there are experiences you have had, which you conceal from others (or even yourself, sometimes), how do you think they are affecting your state of mind?	
For Today: How can you focus on acting in ways that will never have to be kept secret later?	

Step 3- Made a decision to turn our will and our lives over to the care of God as we understood Him.

Journaling Exercise: In what ways does turning your will and life over to the care of God require you to stop concealing your behavior from God and other people?

Day 58

Numbers 9:15 – "On the day the Tabernacle was set up, the cloud covered the Tabernacle that was a tent for the Testimony, and in the evening there would be upon the Tabernacle like a fiery appearance until morning."

The Bible describes how God's presence was made physical through a "Cloud of Glory" that covered the Tabernacle during the day and transformed into a "Pillar of Fire" by night. It must have been quite a sight! This is one of the many miracles that God did for the Israelites when they were wandering in the Wilderness. God gave the Israelites a constant reminder that He was there, present among them. How comforting, and perhaps frightening at times, that must have been. Today, we have no such physical reminder of God's presence. It's easy to think that God is absent, or impossible to find. Yet, God is still present. God has just chosen not to make His presence known in such a clear and obvious way. Our challenge in recovery is to recognize that God is around us at all times, as if we ourselves were surrounded in a cloud of glory by day and had our paths illuminated by Godly fire at night.

Questions to Ponder	
Do you feel that God is around you at all times? If so, what makes you feel that way? If not, why not?	
Do you feel comforted by the idea that God is around you at all times? Or, perhaps, does it make you nervous, like God sees everything that you're doing?	
For Today: Can you try to spot God's hidden presence in your life?	

Step 4 - Made a searching and fearless moral inventory of ourselves.

Journaling Exercise: In what ways can you think of the fourth step as a list of things that God has seen, but you wish He hadn't?

Day 59

Numbers 11:4 – 11:6 – "The rabble that was among them cultivated a craving, and the Children of Israel also wept once more, and said, 'Who will feed us meat? We remember the fish we ate in Egypt free of charge; the cucumbers, melons, leeks, onions, and garlic. But now, our life is parched, there is nothing; we have nothing to anticipate but the manna.'"

Here we have the Israelites, who have been freed from centuries of crushing, soul-destroying slavery by miraculous acts of God, who have been given The Torah, the greatest spiritual revelation in human history, who have been kept alive by a miraculous food that falls from the sky, and what is their problem? They miss the free cucumbers they used to get when they were slaves. That's right: cucumbers and leeks. They're complaining to Moses about that. Sound familiar? It should. We all do this, unfortunately, especially when we're struggling with addiction recovery. Chances are, if you had a serious addiction problem, you're lucky to be alive. If you're sober, it's because God wanted to give you another chance at life. Yet, the addict's nature is to be dissatisfied. Nothing is good enough. Life is terrible. Acting out and using drugs appears to be a solution, or at least an anesthetic to make it all go away, at least for a while. If only we could see what is really going on in those moments. Like the Israelites, we have been delivered from the slavery of addiction. Yet, we also complain about our state of affairs. If we could think clearly, we would be in gratitude. That's the choice we need to make.

Questions to Ponder	
What are you complaining about in recovery? Whatever it is, is it really so bad?	
If there are things that don't feel right about recovery, how does your life compare now to the time when you were drinking or using?	
For Today: Can you focus on gratitude and turn over feelings of resentment about issues that are truly minor?	

Step 5: Admitted to God, to ourselves and to another human being the exact nature of our wrongs.

Journaling Exercise: Take a few experiences described on your fourth step and try to put them into perspective by comparing them to minor problems that are troubling you now, e.g. "I am upset that I missed breakfast but I need to admit to God that I once injured another person in a drunk driving incident." What can the contrasts tell you about life before and after getting sober?

Numbers 13:1 – 13:2 – "God spoke to Moses, saying, 'Send forth men, if you please, and let them spy out the land of Canaan that I give to the Children of Israel.'"

Thus begins one of the great tragedies of The Torah: The incident of the spies. Moses sends 12 accomplished men, leaders, to reconnoiter the land that God has promised them. Ten of the 12 return overcome with fear and warn the Israelites that the conquest would be impossible. Panic and rebellion ensued. The people wanted to return to Egypt. God reacted to this display of faithlessness by condemning that generation of Israelites, the slave generation, to wander for 40 years and die in the Wilderness. The key to understanding this tragedy is the phrase "if you please." God is giving Moses the option of sending the spies, and Moses decides to do it. Moses understands that the people are fearful about conquering the land, but he thinks that if 12 men they trust can scout it out, their confidence in the venture will increase. He's completely wrong. Fear takes over, and the people decide they would rather return to brutal, soul-crushing slavery rather than attempt to receive a gift they have been promised by God. Does that make any sense? No, but that's what fear does to us. The whole episode is doubly tragic because it was unnecessary. God has already told the Israelites that He will assure them the conquest of the land. That should be good enough, but it's not. As we struggle with recovery, we need to remember that God will help us be sober if we trust Him. If we decide to figure it out all on our own, we are subject to the power of our fears, a situation that can lead to personal disaster.

Questions to Ponder	
Have you ever let fear take over in your life, driving you to mistaken decisions?	
Can you relate to the fear the Israelites felt, even though they had been told that God would ensure their successful conquest of the Promised Land?	
For Today: Are you feeling fear about something that you know God can help you handle if you let Him?	

Step 6 - Were entirely ready to have God remove all these defects of character.

Journaling Exercise: For some, the sixth step seems like it doesn't involve much work. You just have to be entirely ready. Yet, being ready to have God remove all your defects of character often involves conquering your personal fear that you will be unable to change. As you do the sixth step, try to identify fears that may be getting in the way of being entirely ready to have God remove all your defects of character.

Day 61

Numbers 13:33 – "There we saw the Nephilim, the sons of the giant from among the Nephilim; we were like grasshoppers in our eyes, and so we were in their eyes."

Here, the spies are elaborating on their frightening experience with "giant" people in the Land of Israel. They saw the giants and felt as if they themselves were as small as grasshoppers. What's interesting is how they repeat the phrase, first saying, "We were like grasshoppers in our eyes," and then stating that the giants also saw them that way. This is a great example of a self-fulfilling prophecy of failure that we see so often in recovery. In the fourth step, we work at this, trying to figure out our role in problems we have had. Someone told me I was stupid, we report. What is our role in that experience? We believed them. We enabled the insult to find a nice fat target. The spies felt that they were small and powerless, so it's no surprise that they imagined the giants saw them that way as well. However, they really didn't know what the giants thought. The Rabbi of Kotsk remarked that one of the spies' mistakes here was to get overly concerned with what others were thinking. That is also a big factor in recovery. The spies were supposed to be thinking about their mission. Whatever anyone else thought should have been irrelevant. We can take cue from the Rabbi of Kotsk and focus on our own recovery and not let how we imagine others to be thinking take us off our paths.

Questions to Ponder	
What's your mission in recovery? Are you paying too much attention to others' opinions of what you're trying to accomplish?	
If you feel fear or personal degradation, is it possible that you are playing a role in allowing yourself to feel that way – by believing the opinions of others even if you don't admit it out loud.	
For Today: How can you tune out the opinions of others (or what we imagine to be their opinions)?	

Step 6 - Were entirely ready to have God remove all these defects of character.

Journaling Exercise: The sixth step is one you have to do by yourself. It's all about you and being entirely ready – an essentially internal process. In what ways might the views of other people in your life be interfering with your sixth step?

Numbers 16:1 – 16:3 – "Korach son of Izhar son of Kohath son of Levi separated himself, with Dathan and Abiram sons of Eliab, and On son of Peleth, the offspring of Reuben. They stood before Moses with two hundred and fifty men from the Children of Israel, leaders of the assembly, those summoned for meeting, men of renown. They gathered together against Moses and against Aaron and said to them, 'It is too much for you!'"

The story of Korach is one of rebellion. Korach, a prince of Israel, along with 250 followers, challenges the leadership of Moses and Aaron. Korach is, of course, misguided, but he seems to have plenty of people who want to help him topple Moses and Aaron from their heavenly-appointed roles. The Torah specifically calls out his three main co-conspirators, who are from the tribe of Reuben. The tribe of Reuben camped next to the tribe of Levi, which was Korach's group. The proximity allowed the Reubenites to become influenced by Korach's unwise rebellion. The Commentators[1] point to the problems that can arise when otherwise good people associate with those who are evil. Recovery presents similar challenges. Part of getting sober is learning to stay away from toxic, triggering people and situations. Downward companionship and associating with active addicts is a path to disaster. We need to learn how to stay away from people who can hurt our recovery, even if it's painful at first to make the change.

Questions to Ponder	
Are you close to a toxic person in your life in recovery? What is the relationship?	
Are you tempted toward downward companionship in recovery?	
For Today: How can you distance yourself from toxic people?	

---

[1] Mishnah Negaim (12:6) — "Woe to the evildoer and woe to his neighbor."

Step 7 - Humbly asked Him to remove our shortcomings.

Journaling Exercise: How can a relationship with a toxic person or a desire to seek downward companionship get in the way of humbly asking Him to remove your shortcoming?

Numbers 16:8 – 16:10 – "Moses said to Korach, 'Hear now, O offspring of Levi: Is it not enough for you that the God of Israel has segregated you from the assembly of Israel to draw you near to Himself, to perform the service of the Tabernacle of God, and to stand before the assembly to minister to them? And He drew you near, and all your brethren, the offspring of Levi, with you – yet you seek priesthood, as well!'"

Korach was from a branch of the Levite tribe that was not eligible to become High Priests. What Moses is saying here, in effect, is that Korach should be grateful to God for being selected for his specific holy role as a Levite and not covet the role of High Priest. Korach is acting like an ungrateful alcoholic. He's been granted a position of great holy responsibility, far closer to the center of spiritual life than the average Israelite. Yet, his envy for his other cousin, Aaron, is too much for him. It drives him to an act of rebellion that is so intense that it destroys him and threatens the belief system of millions of others. Dissatisfaction with what one has is a sign of the spiritual illness of addiction. If you aren't satisfied with what you have, you will never be satisfied with anything more that you get. You will always want more and you will always be angry and resentful about others who have things that you want. It's an endless trap, one that can ruin people. You can be sober and want to have more in life, but there's a spiritual balance to be struck: It's best to appreciate what you have and understand that you can work for more, but be willing to accept what God gives you.

Questions to Ponder	
Has envy of what other people possess ever driven you further into addictive behavior?	
Have you ever wanted more of something but then not been satisfied when you got it?	
For Today: Can you focus on being happy with what you have, perhaps trying to envision a healthy way to have more of something without falling prey to resentment and impatience?	

Step 7 - Humbly asked Him to remove our shortcomings.

Journaling Exercise: Humbly asking God to remove your shortcomings may involve being happy with the way you are today. How can the seventh step help you focus on what is okay with you today?

Numbers 16:4 – "Moses heard [Korach's accusation] and fell on his face."

Moses listened to Korach's outrageous accusation. Then, instead of responding to Korach, he "falls on his face" – meaning he went right into an intense state of prayer. Moses wanted God's help in understanding what was going on and how he should react to Korach. It's a remarkable display of faith, self-control, humility and spiritual health. Moses is a great role model for people in recovery. Instead of taking the bait, and it's a pretty massive piece of bait being dangled in front of him, Moses instantly turns it over to God. God guides every nuance of Moses' response to Korach. God punishes Korach for his transgressions. If only we could be like this in our recovery: Turning our faces away from all manner of toxic bait being thrown at us by others, turning our difficulties over to God, letting God guide us through trouble. We would all be a lot healthier in recovery.

Questions to Ponder	
Are you prone to taking the bait from toxic people? I.e. Letting yourself get drawn into fights that hurt your sobriety?	
What would it take for you to become better at ignoring the bait and instead turning to God for help in resolving the problem?	
For Today: Can you stay away from toxic people who dangle "baited hooks," in front of you, so to speak?	

Step 8 - Made a list of all persons we had harmed, and became willing to make amends to them all.

Journaling Exercise: Ironically, the process of doing the eighth step can sometimes trigger us into anger and resentment. We think of a person we have harmed and then become resentful at the thought that the other person harmed us first! Can you think of examples of people like this on your eighth step list? What can do to avoid falling into this emotional trap?

Numbers 19:6 – "The Priest shall take cedar wood, hyssop, and crimson thread, and he shall throw them into the burning of the [red] cow."

As the Red Heifer was being burned on the Altar, the Priest would take cedar wood, hyssop (which is a low-growing shrub), and a red-dyed thread, and throw them onto the burning offering. This act adds to the symbolism of repentance inherent in the offering. The cedar is a tall tree. It represents the sinner, who once "stood tall" through lofty behavior, is brought low by being combined in the fire with the hyssop, which grows at ground level. The thread has been dyed with the blood of a worm, adding the imagery of being brought low. Haughty, arrogant behavior leads to a comeuppance and repentance. Addicts will recognize this transformation. Yet, for many addicts, the comeuppance does not lead to repentance. Without recovery, the inevitable collapse of the arrogant sinner begets more resentment and addictive acting out. Ultimately, it can even lead to jails, institutions and death. At the very least, it's a totally miserable way to live. The sacrifice of the red cow gives us a metaphor we can meditate on as we consider how our arrogant, self-serving ways have not worked for us in life and how we need to change if we want to experience true recovery.

Questions to Ponder	
Did you act in haughty and arrogant ways when you were drinking or using? What did you do? How do you think others felt about it?	
Have you changed in recovery? Are you less prone to acting arrogantly – or are you at least more aware of when the temptation to act arrogantly arises?	
For Today: Can you focus on being humble?	

Step 9 - Made direct amends to such people wherever possible, except when to do so would injure them or others.

Journaling Exercise: Making direct amends to others requires humility. In what ways does the ninth step force you to be humble and cease acting in a haughty or arrogant way, at least temporarily?

Day 66

Numbers 20:1 – 20:5 – "The Children of Israel, the whole assembly, arrived at the Wilderness of Zin in the first month and the people settled in Kadesh. Miriam died here and she was buried there. There was no water for the assembly, and they gathered against Moses and Aaron. The people quarreled with Moses and spoke up saying, 'If only we had perished as our brethren perished before God! ...Why have you brought us up from Egypt to bring us to this evil place? Not a place of seed, or fig, or grape or pomegranate; and there is no water to drink!'"

Miriam, the older sister of Moses and a great prophetess, dies. The Israelites have been in the desert for many years at this point. When Miriam dies, the wells run dry. Why is this? The miraculous well of water that followed the Israelites throughout the desert turned out to have been present in the honor of Miriam. The Sages teach us that when a righteous person dies, the community loses. Recovery has its righteous people. When we lose them, it is as if we are losing our sustenance, too. How do the people react? They panic and lash out at Moses. However, their complaint is much more subdued and reasonable than earlier rebellions. They are not asking to return to Egypt. They are not demanding meat or complaining about manna. They are terrified of dying of thirst. God is understanding about this criticism. How do we react when something goes wrong, when someone who gave us spiritual direction dies? That is a test of recovery. We need to learn to turn over our fears to God. Then, we will be able to handle the loss and grow from the experience.

Questions to Ponder	
Have you ever lost someone who gave you spiritual direction? How did you react? Is there someone you hope never to lose?	
What is an appropriate way to react to a crisis? How do you react but stay conscious of your recovery?	
For Today: Focus on people in your life now who give you spiritual direction. Who are they? What do you learn from them?	

Step 9 - Made direct amends to such people wherever possible, except when to do so would injure them or others.

Journaling Exercise: Can the process of doing the ninth step serve to restore the "wells of water" to your spiritual life? Will your recovery be helped by restoring relationships with people in your life who can help you grow in spiritual terms?

Day 67

Numbers 20:12 – 20:13 – "God said to Moses and to Aaron, 'Because you did not believe in Me to sanctify Me in the eyes of the Children of Israel, therefore you will not bring this congregation to the Land that I have given them.'"

Moses is punished for the sin of striking the rock – instead of talking to it as he was instructed by God – by being prohibited from entering the Land of Israel. To most observers, this seems like a very extreme punishment for a somewhat minor transgression. Moses' entire life's work was to lead the Children of Israel out of captivity and to the Promised Land. For not listening to God, or perhaps for letting his anger get the better of him for a few seconds, he is being punished by never getting to set foot in that land. It doesn't seem fair. One way to look at it is that for someone on the level of Moses, God has a much higher expectation of good behavior. You or I could get away with hitting the rock. Moses cannot. He is at such a high spiritual level that he is supposed to do better. Another perspective is that there are some heavenly decisions that we simply cannot understand with our human minds. This parallels the concept of the heavenly decree. It is a decree of The Torah that we sacrifice a completely red cow. Why? It's not obvious, but it is the decree nonetheless. Moses accepted his punishment. It was the decree of God.

Questions to Ponder	
As you grow in recovery, do you think you should be held to a higher standard of behavior?	
Have had experiences where life didn't seem fair but you accepted the situation as God's will?	
For Today: Are there aspects of your life that seem like heavenly decrees that defy easy understanding? What are they and what can you do about them?	

Step 10 - Continued to take personal inventory and when we were wrong promptly admitted it.

Journaling Exercise: As you work the tenth step, can you see items in your personal inventory that feel like "heavenly decrees" that are difficult to understand at face value?

Numbers 22:5 – 22:6 – "He [Balak, King of Moab] sent messengers to Balaam son of Beor to Pethor, which is by the River of the land of the members of his people, to summon him, saying, 'Behold! A people has come out of Egypt, behold! It has covered the surface of the earth and it sits opposite me. So now – please come and curse this people for me, for it is too powerful for me...'"

The Children of Israel are on the move now, heading toward the Land of Israel. To get there, they need to cross the land of Moab, which is approximately where the nation of Jordan is today. Balak, the king of Moab, panics and summons Balaam, a prophet who is known for his skill at placing effective curses on people. Balak wants Balaam to curse the Children of Israel so they will go away or die. He is frightened of their strength. It doesn't end well for Balak, of course, and there's a lesson in the story for those of us who react to the fear of sobriety with the urge to wish ill on others. Balak is a study in denial. He has watched as God miraculously frees the Israelites from Pharaoh, the most powerful king in the world. He has watched as this people miraculously survives and thrives in a barren wilderness. Yet, when it's his time to confront them, his instinct is to find someone evil who can curse them. If it wasn't obvious to Balak that he was dealing with a power greater than himself in the Children of Israel, he was severely deluded. You can't hide from God's will. Cursing others and wishing bad things to happen to people who bring you the word of God won't stop the word of God. It will only make your situation worse.

Questions to Ponder	
Have you ever been in denial about something you were afraid of or didn't understand? What happened?	
Have you ever lashed out in anger at something you were afraid of or didn't understand? i.e. Did you want to curse the situation or the person who caused it, per the verse? What happened?	
For Today: Is there a clear signal from your Higher Power that you wish you weren't receiving? What is it? What will you do about it? (If you don't think you're getting signals from your Higher Power, do you want to change that?)	

Step 10 - Continued to take personal inventory and when we were wrong promptly admitted it.

Journaling Exercise: In your tenth step, which is continuous (as in "continued to..."), have you ever found yourself getting angry and wanting to lash out before you admitted you were wrong about something?

Numbers 22:21 – 22:23 – "Balaam arose in the morning and saddled his she-donkey and went with the officers of Moab. God's wrath flared because he was going, and an angel of God stood on the road to impede him. He was riding on his she-donkey and his two young men were with him. The she-donkey saw the angel of God and turned away from the road and went into the field; then Balaam struck the she-donkey to turn it back onto the road."

God finally gave Balaam permission to go on his mission on the condition that Balaam only say the words that God will tell him — not a curse. Balaam can't wait one extra second to go do something bad. We've probably been there, right? Rushing out the door to drink and use. God is angry that Balaam is going, even though God gave permission. This is perplexing, of course, but it makes sense. God is telling Balaam that he has free will and can go if he likes, even though God thinks it is a bad idea. We've been here, too. We are told, "Go do it if you really want to, but I wouldn't if I were you." Yet, we dash out to do whatever self-destructive thing it is we want to try. Then we have the strange image of the donkey seeing the angel of God, which is invisible to Balaam. The disapproval of God and the wrongness of Balaam's choice are so obvious that even a donkey can see it, while Balaam cannot. This is a classic addict moment. Everyone in your life can see that you're destroying yourself. They warn you, but you ignore them. An animal could see it, but you know better.

Questions to Ponder	
Have you ever been told something like, "Go do it if you really want to, but I wouldn't if I were you."? What did you do?	
Did you ever hurry to do something that was bad for yourself?	
For Today: Can you find an aspect of your behavior that needs work — to the point where even a donkey could see it, so to speak, but you can't?	

Step 11 - Sought through prayer and meditation to improve our conscious contact with God as we understood Him, praying only for knowledge of His will for us and the power to carry that out.

Journaling Exercise: The eleventh step offers a chance to pray for self-awareness. In your eleventh step prayer and meditation work, have you been able to achieve any new insights into yourself? What are they? What will you do about them?

Numbers 25:10 – 25:12 – "God spoke to Moses, saying: 'Phinehas son of Elazar son of Aaron the Priest, turned back My wrath from upon the Children of Israel when he zealously avenged My vengeance among them, so I did not consume the Children of Israel in My vengeance.'"

Previously, the evil prophet Balaam is unable to deliver the curse on the Israelites that he planned. Instead, he prompts the women of Moab to seduce the men of Israel and get them to commit acts of sexual immorality and idol worship. Phinehas, grandson of Aaron the High Priest, takes action, killing a leading Israelite who is cohabiting with a Midianite woman in full view of Moses. His decisive action causes God to withhold the very serious punishment that He was about to mete out against the sinful Israelites in this disgraceful episode. There is much to say about this moment in The Torah. One aspect of the Phinehas story that is relevant to recovery is how highly toxic sexual attraction and lack of self-control can be to sobriety. There's a reason that most seasoned sponsors discourage newcomers from dating in early sobriety. They know that recovery is a demanding, all-consuming process early on, a fragile environment for important personal work – one that can easily be disrupted by the ups and downs of a fresh romantic relationship. There is also the potential for the addict to transpose addictions and start acting out sexually once he or she has stopped drinking or taking drugs. It happens all the time, with disastrous results.

Questions to Ponder	
Were you advised to avoid romantic and sexual relationships in early recovery? Do you think it was good advice? Why or why not?	
Have you ever experienced being romantically or sexually attracted to someone in recovery who might have been bad for your recovery?	
For Today: Can you identify behaviors where you might be transposing one type of addiction onto another, e.g. you don't drink any more but gambling looks awfully interesting all of a sudden?	

Step 11 - Sought through prayer and meditation to improve our conscious contact with God as we understood Him, praying only for knowledge of His will for us and the power to carry that out.

Journaling Exercise: How can the eleventh step, a recurring, permanent process of seeking conscious contact with your Higher Power, protect you against unwise relationships with toxic or risky people?

Numbers 31:3 – 31:4 – "Moses spoke to the people, saying, 'Arm men from among yourselves for the legion that may be against Midian to inflict God's vengeance against Midian. A thousand from a tribe, a thousand from a tribe, for all the tribes of Israel shall you send to the legion.'"

There is a slight disagreement among The Commentators about the size of the "army" that went to attack Midian. Depending on which tribes you include, it was either 12,000 or 13,000 men. What were these men to do? They were to go to war against *an entire country*. That's right. A group of untrained soldiers smaller than a modern army division went out and defeated an entire country and its whole army. It was a decisive victory, too. Extremely decisive. How was that possible? It's a reminder that anything is possible when God is on your side. You can vanquish any enemy when you are in the army of God, even an army of one. Yet, we surely all face moments of doubts about this truth when in recovery. Consider what the Israelites thought when Moses asked for 12,000 men to go to war against Midian. People must have thought, "That's a suicide mission. We can't win." Yet, we can. When the call comes to go to war against our addictions, we need to get into the fight, no matter how bad the odds look. God is on our side.

Questions to Ponder	
Have you ever felt in recovery that you were on a "suicide mission," facing a battle you couldn't possibly win? How did you handle the feeling?	
In recovery, can the program help you feel as if you are an army capable of defeating a vastly superior enemy?	
For Today: Will you "do battle" with your demons today?	

Step 12 - Having had a spiritual awakening as the result of these steps, we tried to carry this message to alcoholics and to practice these principles in all our affairs.

Journaling Exercise: In what ways might the spiritual awakening of the twelfth step relate to the idea that you must never stop fighting against the power of addiction in your life?

Day 72

Numbers 33:1 – "These are the journeys of the Children of Israel, who went forth from the land of Egypt according to their legions, under the hand of Moses and Aaron."

This section of The Bible records 42 places that the Israelites went during their wanderings in the Wilderness for 40 years. Some of the places listed in the chronology that follows were not mentioned earlier in The Bible. According to The Commentators, this is the complete list of where the Israelites traveled. Some of the places mentioned in these verses were not notable at the time, so they were not mentioned in earlier chapters. We can learn something from this. As we go through recovery, we will tell our stories again and again. In this spirit, our fourth steps should be exhaustive, listing our complete journeys through addiction. There may be "locations" that we forget to list initially. We can go back and add them to our stories. The significance of these places or experiences may elude us for a time, but eventually we may come to see that there was a reason we went to a certain place or did some particular thing. Later on, as we recover from addiction, the meaning of that place or experience will help us in sobriety. We need to create our own complete list of our "travels" through addiction in order to get sober.

Questions to Ponder	
As you progress in recovery, have you thought of "places" you visited along the way that perhaps you didn't remember or think were important before?	
Do you see your process of recovery as a journey consisting of "places" where you stopped and had experiences?	
For Today: Where are you on your journey of recovery? How will you remember today's place in your journey?	

Step 12 - Having had a spiritual awakening as the result of these steps, we tried to carry this message to alcoholics and to practice these principles in all our affairs.

Journaling Exercise: In what ways can your continuing journey in recovery include carrying this message to alcoholics and practicing these principles in all your affairs?

Suggested Instructor Prompts:

- *The twelfth step is not static. You do it continually and it will probably change for you as you progress in sobriety. Do you think you can advance in recovery by carrying the message to alcoholics and practicing these principles in all your affairs?*

- *What new "places" do you think you might visit on your continuing journey in recovery? What do you want to achieve when you get there?*

Deuteronomy Workbook

Deuteronomy 1:1 – "These are the words that Moses spoke to all Israel, on the other side of the Jordan, concerning the Wilderness, concerning the Arabah, opposite the Sea of Reeds, between Paran and Tophel and Laban, and Hazeroth, and Di-zahab..."

The Hebrew name of the book of Deuteronomy is "Devarim," which means "words." The Greeks called it Deuteronomy, which means "the second." Both names have a relevant meaning to us. The book is essentially one very long speech by Moses to all the Children of Israel on the last day of his life. It repeats many things that they have experienced and learned, along with most of the important laws they will need to observe when they move forward and take possession of the Promised Land. It was Moses' last chance to speak with the people he loved. Moses wanted to make sure that the Israelites would be strong and remember The Torah when they left the constant miracles and spiritual solitude of the Wilderness. In the Land of Israel, where they would be farmers, dealing with commerce and real-life issues, they might find it tempting to abandon the principles of The Torah. Thus, the people needed a reminder. That is Deuteronomy. We also need repetition of important concepts of sobriety to stay in recovery. We don't attend a single meeting, hear the steps one time, and pronounce ourselves recovered for life. (It's been tried, and believe me, it almost never ends well.) We need regular reminders of why we are doing what we're doing. We need a recharge of the important principles of the program as we make our way through the difficulties of everyday life.

Questions to Ponder	
Have you ever had to hear about an idea in recovery more than once to understand what it really meant?	
Has the process of attending multiple meetings enabled you to grasp recovery principles better over time?	
For Today: What important principle of the program do you need to recharge for yourself today?	

Step 1: We admitted we were powerless over alcohol - that our lives had become unmanageable.

Journaling Exercise: As the verse suggests, important lessons in life often take some repetition to sink in. In doing your first step, can you think of experiences where you had to see you were powerless over alcohol multiple times before you finally got the message that your life had become unmanageable?

Deuteronomy 1:1 – "These are the words that Moses spoke to all Israel, on the other side of the Jordan, concerning the Wilderness, concerning the Arabah, opposite the Sea of Reeds, between Paran and Tophel and Laban, and Hazeroth, and Di-zahab..."

Much of Deuteronomy can be viewed on one level as a rebuke to the Children of Israel. When Moses says, "concerning the Wilderness…," he is referring to the nation's many shortcomings and ungrateful acts of rebellion against him and God. The Commentators say that the places named in the verse are code words for various sins that the Israelites committed in the Wilderness. The people are supposed to think about what they did wrong in each place and understand the rebuke. We may inadvertently tell these types of stories about ourselves. Like, we might say, "Oh yeah, college was a crazy time." But, what we really mean is, "In college, I got drunk and injured someone else in a car crash." When we tell our stories and do the steps, we need to be rigorous in examining how we participated in bad experiences, so we can avoid them in the future.

Questions to Ponder	
Are there bad experiences from your drinking or using days that you don't talk about?	
Do you sugar-coat bad experiences and rationalize or minimize your actions? Would it help your recovery to be more honest about what happened?	
For today: Can you focus on living for today in a way that you will never be ashamed of later?	

Step 2 - Came to believe that a Power greater than ourselves could restore us to sanity.

Journaling Exercise: Reviewing your journey through addiction, in what ways can your experiences show that you need to believe that only a Power greater than yourself could restore you to sanity?

Deuteronomy 1:16 – 1:17 – "I [Moses] instructed your judges at that time, saying, 'Listen among your brethren and judge righteously between a man and his brother his litigant. You shall not show favoritism in judgment, small and great alike shall you hear; you shall not tremble before any man, for judgment is God's...'"

Moses tells the judges, "You shall not tremble before any man, for judgment is God's." He means that a judge should not be intimidated by someone wealthy or powerful. God will guide the decision of the judge and help him arrive at a just outcome. There are many people in recovery who are accustomed to being "trembled at." Recovery in Los Angeles presents a parade of movie stars, rock stars, sports legends, and so forth. They may be used to getting all kinds of attention and special treatment, but in reality they need help from you and me just like any other struggling addict. Years ago, I saw a famous actor at an AA meeting. This was a man who had his face posted on every billboard in town, the star of a hit TV series. Someone asked him how it felt to be famous and rich. He responded, "I'm the same. Now, I get to drink until I black out in a $10 million home, not an apartment." Wow. That was amazing honesty. This man knew that if he didn't get sober he was probably going to die before he turned 40. In his case, he did the work and got sober. As we know, unfortunately, this is not always the case. We should not tremble before important people in recovery. We are all the same in the eyes of God.

Questions to Ponder	
Have you ever encountered someone famous or important in recovery? How did you react?	
Have you ever felt that you were important and should be treated differently in recovery because of who you are?	
For Today: Can you focus on feeling special because God loves you and has a plan for you, not because you think you're important and everyone should treat you differently?	

Step 3- Made a decision to turn our will and our lives over to the care of God as we understood Him.

Journaling Exercise: The third step has a lot to do with humility. In what ways does it take humility to believe that you should turn your live and will over to the care of God – and not handle everything all by yourself?

Deuteronomy 5:7 – "You shall not recognize the gods of others in My presence."

Deuteronomy repeats The Ten Commandments. In this Commandment, God is telling the Israelites that they may not practice idolatry. They may not recognize the gods of others in His presence. While we may not be attracted to actual idol worship in our modern lives, we have no lack of idolatrous passions that threaten to lure us into their webs – money, power, sex, anger. All of these can become fixations that take us away from God. We are commanded not to recognize these false gods in the presence of the real God. But, what does it mean to be in "God's presence?" We are always in God's presence, so we should view this Commandment as being permanently in effect. If that seems excessive, perhaps think about it like this: If we are aware of God, then we are in God's presence. Being conscious of God in our lives and working on achieving conscious contact with God constitute being in the presence of God. That presence can be our barrier against becoming lost in destructive, self-seeking pursuits of modern idolatry.

Questions to Ponder	
Have you ever been fixated on something to the extent that it started to seem like an idol that needed to be worshipped, e.g. money, sex, status? How did it affect your life and consciousness of the true God?	
What does it mean to you that you should not worship idols, so to speak, in "God's presence"?	
For Today: Can you work on being aware of God's presence in all aspects of your life?	

Step 4 - Made a searching and fearless moral inventory of ourselves.

Journaling Exercise: In working on your fourth step, can you think of experiences where you were "worshipping idols," so to speak, in God's presence? What were they? How do you feel about it now?

Deuteronomy 9:1 – 9:2 – "Hear, O Israel, today you cross the Jordan, to come and drive out nations that are greater and mightier than you, cities that are great and fortified up to the Heavens, a great and lofty people, children of giants, that you knew of whom you have heard, 'Who can stand up against the children of a giant?'"

We sometimes forget, in the grand sweep of history and epic narrative that forms The Torah, that there was actually once a specific day when the Israelites woke up in the morning and crossed the Jordan River to begin their conquest of the Promised Land. What must that day have been like? "Ha-Yom" – the day, today, in Hebrew. It was surely a momentous day, a day of fear and courage, a day of immense faith. We also have such days. We might call it today or yesterday, perhaps tomorrow. Every day is special in recovery. Recovery is, as we say, a "day-at-a-time deal." We have today. Yesterday is history. Tomorrow's a mystery. Today is what matters. And, on some days, we will feel as if we are about to do battle with nations that are greater and mightier than us, against cities that are great and fortified. We battle with lofty people, children of giants, addictions, temptations, resentments – these are the great and lofty giants we slay every day in recovery. Who can stand up against the children of a giant? You can. We can. God will help us carry out this important mission one day at a time.

Questions to Ponder	
Can you relate to the idea of having to wake up one day and make a decision to cross your personal "Jordan River" into a personal promised land, no matter the risks?	
Have you battled with "giants" in your life – both in addiction and recovery? How did it go?	
For Today: What rivers do you need to cross today (not tomorrow)?	

Step 5 - Admitted to God, to ourselves and to another human being the exact nature of our wrongs.

Journaling Exercise: It takes a lot of guts to admit to God, to yourself and another human being the exact nature of your wrongs. In what ways is the fifth step like the instruction to rise up and do battle with giants, as per the verse?

Day 78

Deuteronomy 11:26 – "See, I present before you today a blessing and a curse."

This verse begins with the Hebrew word "re'eh," which means "see," as in, "Look at this." This sentence succinctly captures what is known as the Deuteronomic theology: If you follow the commandments of God, you will be blessed. If you stray from them, you will suffer a curse. The rest is detail. The main verb, though, "see," can tell us something important about recovery. Most people who have lived through an addiction problem will tell you that it robbed them of their ability to see what was really going on in their lives. Addiction is a form of blindness, both in moral and practical terms. In fact, many addicts finally wake up to what's going on in their lives when they either see themselves as they have truly become, or experience what they look like from someone else's perspective. I'm not necessarily talking about physical appearance, though addiction will destroy that, too. What do you look like, in general, when you're in the pit of addiction? It's not a pretty picture, but you probably won't be able to see it accurately if your live revolves around acquiring and using substances or self-destructive activities like gambling. In recovery, we can pray that God opens our eyes and gives us an accurate, complete visual of who we are, who we have been, as well as who we can become. That vision of the future can be the foundation for a successful path to recovery.

Questions to Ponder	
Have you ever experienced addiction as a form of blindness, so to speak, about who you were and what you were doing in your life? How so?	
Did you experience a moment when you woke up, so to speak, and saw what was really going on in your life?	
For Today: How do you visualize your future life in recovery? Is it easy or hard to do this?	

Step 6 - Were entirely ready to have God remove all these defects of character.

Journaling Exercise: In what ways can you connect the verse, "See, I present before you today a blessing and a curse," with the process of being ready to have God remove your defects of character? Do you feel as if the sixth step represents, at some level, a decision about accepting a blessing or curse in your life?

Deuteronomy 16:21 – "You shall not plant for yourselves an idolatrous tree – any tree – near the Altar of God, your God, that you shall make for yourself."

The Talmud[2] finds meaning in the fact that warning against planting an idolatrous tree immediately follows the caution about judges that may be unqualified. A potentially corrupt judge is like a toxic tree that can take root and ruin the holiness of God's Altar. We addicts are great at compartmentalizing our lives. We can keep our spiritual health in a meeting, but behave badly when we're outside. This eventually catches up with us. Like a tree that grows roots and becomes stronger over time, the bad behavior outside the meeting will ultimately become extremely difficult to remove. We have to guard against poisoning our spiritual well-being. When we are in a meeting, or in worship, we need to focus on keeping harmful outside influences at bay. When we leave that spiritual realm, we need to keep that holiness with us as we move around on the outside.

Questions to Ponder	
Can you relate to the idea that a toxic thought can take root and spread throughout your life?	
Do you compartmentalize your life, perhaps acting differently in meetings than you do outside? How does that affect your recovery?	
For Today: Can you focus on keeping harmful influences away from your life in recovery?	

[2] Avodah Zarah 52a

Step 7 - Humbly asked Him to remove our shortcomings.

Journaling Exercise: In what ways can humbly asking God to remove your shortcomings be likened to uprooting a "toxic" tree in your life, so to speak?

Deuteronomy 21:10 – 21:14 – "When you will go out to war against your enemies ... and you will see among its captivity a woman who is beautiful of form, and you will desire her, you may take her to yourself for a wife. You shall bring her to the midst of your house; she shall shave her head and let her nails grow. She shall remove the garment of her captivity from upon herself and sit in your house and she shall weep for her father and her mother for a full month; thereafter you may come to her and live with her, and she shall be a wife to you."

It is difficult to understand this verse without understanding that warfare was different in ancient times from the way it is today. Women prisoners were often "married" to victorious soldiers against their will. An Israelite soldier may adopt this practice, but if you read between the lines, it is discouraging it emphatically. He must let her grieve for her parents and homeland in his house for a full month, her head shaved and her finery removed. The soldier should let his passions cool down and let the woman go.

Recovery can be a bit like going to war. It's intense. We fight many battles. We get aroused, and we can make very bad decisions in the heat of the moment. The verse gives us a way to handle these situations. We need to calm down and cool down, avoiding making important decisions when we are in the "battle" of recovery. Whether we're on the "pink cloud" or falling into a pit of despair in the recovery process, we need to avoid instant gratification and stop ourselves from plunging head first into mistakes when we are in the wrong frame of mind for serious decisions.

Questions to Ponder	
Have you ever made a bad decision in the heat of the moment? What happened? How did it go for you?	
Can you relate to the idea of being either too happy, sad or angry to think clearly about life decisions?	
For Today: What decisions are you facing? How can you get yourself into a focused, calm state of mind to make the right choice?	

Step 7 - Humbly asked Him to remove our shortcomings.

Journaling Exercise: Doing the seventh step may involve working on your state of mind in order to focus properly on the task of humbly asking God to remove your shortcomings. What can you do to get yourself into the right state of mind to do the seventh step effectively?

Deuteronomy 21:22 – 21:23 – "If a man shall have committed a sin whose judgment is death, he shall be put to death, and you shall hang him on a gallows. His body shall not remain for the night on the gallows, rather you shall surely bury him on that day, for a hanging person is a curse of God, and you shall not contaminate your Land, which God, your God, gives you as an inheritance."

If a man is put to death by hanging, that is adequate punishment. The Torah is warning us not to compound the punishment on our own by allowing the body to hang overnight. When a murderer is hated, as they often are, it is tempting to humiliate him in death in this way. God is wise to tell us to exact the punishment and move on. Acts of revenge like this are not healthy, even if they feel good at the time. For most addicts, revenge excites resentments that are toxic to recovery. Good recovery happens when we can turn over a desire for revenge and focus on keeping ourselves in a positive recovery mindset. Another interpretation of this verse puts the issue in a different light. Man was made in God's image. If we hang a man and invite people to gawk at the dead body, we are letting people look unfavorably on God. A parable explains: There was once a murderer who was an identical twin to the king of a country. They caught him and hanged him. People saw the body and said, "Look, the king has been hanged." God is our king. Excessive punishment and revenge is a desecration of God's name.

Questions to Ponder	
Have you ever wanted to take revenge on someone? How did it feel to want revenge? Was it good for you?	
Can you relate to the idea that excessively punishing another human being is actually a desecration of God's name?	
For Today: Is there is a resentment you can rid yourself of?	

Step 8 - Made a list of all persons we had harmed, and became willing to make amends to them all.

Journaling Exercise: The eighth step sometimes has the opposite of its intended effect — allowing us to spin up a lot of old resentments against people whom we actually harmed ourselves. Have you had this experience while working on your eighth step? Toward whom did you feel resentments and desire for revenge, even though the point of the exercise is to figure out how to make your amends? What can you do about this conflicting feeling?

Deuteronomy 22:1 – "You shall not see the ox of your brother or his sheep or goat cast off, and hide yourself from them; you shall surely return them to your brother."

The literal meaning of this verse is that you should return a lost object to its rightful owner. It says "your brother," but it means every person. You should not turn away and pretend you didn't see it. Every other human being, in essence – is like a brother. Certainly, if we take the time to return a lost object to a person, even someone we don't know, that person will consider us as if we were a true brother. On a deeper level, the verse is telling us to help others when they are in need. We are supposed to stop ourselves from the entirely natural and common instinct to walk in the other direction when someone else needs help. Most of us have a tendency to "hide ourselves," as the verse says, when someone else is having a problem. Recovery is about taking opposite action with familiar, negative traits like this. If someone else in the program needs help, we need to move toward that person and offer help, even if we don't feel like it. The action will benefit them, as well as ourselves.

Questions to Ponder	
Have you ever "hidden yourself" from another person who is having a problem – because you didn't want to deal with it?	
Can you relate to the idea that helping someone in need makes you like a bit like a brother to that person?	
For Today: Is there someone who needs your help, to whom you can return something that was lost, so to speak?	

Step 8 - Made a list of all persons we had harmed, and became willing to make amends to them all.

Journaling Exercise: In what ways is the eighth step like returning a lost object to someone? What might you be "returning" to the people on your amends list? For instance, if you harmed someone by insulting them, perhaps you caused them to lose their self-respect. Can you return their "lost" self-respect to them in the amends process?

Deuteronomy 23:18 – "There shall not be a promiscuous woman among the daughters of Israel, and there shall not be a promiscuous man among the sons of Israel."

This commandment is clear and equal: Neither women nor men should act promiscuously. It's good advice that most of us would agree with in general. Promiscuity, putting aside moral issues, is not healthy in spiritual, psychological, or physical terms. Yet, we are vulnerable to it on many levels in recovery. True, we may not be hopping from bed to bed, but sexual compulsiveness and out-of-control romance in all its incarnations blossom when we get clean from other addictions. It's a classic pattern. A person stops drinking and remains sober. Life is good, but somehow, mysteriously, the sober person starts to have a totally dysfunctional, unbalanced love life. The addiction has shifted into the realm of physical pleasure caused by sex. This may not be the worst thing in the world, but it can be potentially very harmful for recovery. The emotional rollercoaster of romantic overindulgence has been shown to throw people off of sobriety time after time. In early recovery especially, it's wise to move slowly in the romance department.

Questions to Ponder	
Have you felt tempted to act out in terms of sex and romance during recovery? What did you do about the feeling?	
Were you drawn to a new romantic relationship early in recovery? What did you do about it? Did you seek advice from your sponsor about pursuing the relationship?	
For Today: Are you feeling attracted to any unhealthy compulsions today? What can you do to avoid falling under their spell?	

Step 9 - Made direct amends to such people wherever possible, except when to do so would injure them or others.

Journaling Exercise: The ninth step is hard, hard enough to be notorious for inviting procrastination. For a lot of us, there's almost anything we'd rather be doing than trying to start the ninth step. Does this sound familiar? What activities, including unhealthy ones, seem very appealing compared to getting started on making amends to people?

Deuteronomy 26:2 – "...you shall take of the first of every fruit of the ground that you bring in from your Land that God, your God, gives you, and you shall put it in a basket and go to the place that God, your God, will choose, to make His Name rest there."

Growing fruit trees is a lengthy, back-breaking process. It takes years of hard work to tend to young trees. Finally, after years of toil, the first fruit appears. This is a moment of true joy. All of your hard work has paid off. How should we celebrate this moment? The Torah tells us that we are to take those first fruits, put them in a basket, and take them up to Jerusalem, to the Temple, and offer them to the Priests as an offering to God.

When we achieve long sought-after objectives through our own hard work, we deserve praise and the right to feel good about ourselves. At the same time, we must acknowledge God's role in helping us accomplish our goals. As the verse says, the Israelites grew their first fruits on the Land that God gave them. God is the force that makes the wind blow, the rain fall, and the trees yield their fruits. The fruit is the product of a genuine partnership between people and God. Your hard work makes it happen, with God's help. If you don't pay tribute to God and just gobble up those first fruits without thanking God, you can slip into an egocentric mindset where you are the master of all things. The path to recovery takes the opposite direction. It urges us to be humble and thank God for giving us the ability to achieve what we have set out to do.

Questions to Ponder	
If you have achieved a goal in recovery, can you see it as the result of a partnership between you and God?	
Have you felt tempted to view your success as being entirely yours, without any help from God?	
For Today: What can you accomplish in partnership with God?	

Step 9 - Made direct amends to such people wherever possible, except when to do so would injure them or others.

Journaling Exercise: If you're feeling nervous about doing the ninth step, can you think of ways that being in a partnership with God can help you move forward and make your amends?

Deuteronomy 28:1 – 28:2 – "It shall be that if you hearken to the voice of Hashem, your God, to observe all of His commandments that I command you this day, then God, your God, will make you supreme over all the nations of the earth. All these blessings will come upon you and overtake you, if you hearken to the voice of God, your God."

What does it mean for blessings to "come upon you and overtake you?" Sforno, one of the great Commentators, says that this phrase means that God will be so generous with His blessings that you will be overwhelmed with blessing, blessings that may even defy logic and nature. The assumption, of course, is that you are following the first part of the verse. You are hearkening (listening) to the voice of God, your God. Why does it say "your God?" This is to emphasize that although God is universal, God is also personal. If you focus your life on God, God will focus back on you. You may experience unexpected blessings in return. We see this often in recovery: The person who has "great luck" in life after becoming sober. All of a sudden, the once drunken loser is happily married and successful in business. The once criminal drug addict is now a community leader. What happened? They have been overtaken by blessing.

Questions to Ponder	
Do you have a personal God? If you focus on God in recovery, can you feel God focusing back on you?	
Have you experienced unexpected blessings, e.g. being surprised by success and happiness that you didn't anticipate having in your life?	
For Today: Can you identify any new blessings in your life today?	

Step 10 - Continued to take personal inventory and when we were wrong promptly admitted it.

Journaling Exercise: Can you look at the ability to admit that you are wrong as a blessing? Are there examples in your life in recovery where your newfound capacity to take personal inventory was a blessing?

Deuteronomy 29:13 – 29:14 – "Not with you alone do I seal this covenant and this imprecation, but with whoever is here, standing with us today, and with whoever is not here with us today."

What does it mean that God is sealing the covenant with people who are not there? One interpretation is that God is sealing the covenant with all future generations of Israelites, who were not alive at that time. This was a somewhat important practical matter at the time. The grandchildren of the people who stood with Moses on the far side of the Jordan River might claim, "Hey, I wasn't there. I have no covenant or obligations to God." This statement includes them. On a more profound level, the verse shows that God's covenant is eternal. It is a permanent promise to the Israelites that the Land will be theirs if they adhere to the laws of The Torah. It's not an entitlement. It's an earned privilege, but it's accessible to every Jew.

The same idea applies to you even if you missed opportunities to understand God's covenant earlier in life due to addictive acting out or lack of education. It doesn't matter. The covenant still applies to you even if you were not present. That is another meaning of the verse. If you have a soul, you can be part of the covenant. Your soul was included in the covenant, whether or not you were alive at the time or aware of what was going on. This is a reason to be hopeful and to do the work of recovery.

Questions to Ponder	
How do you feel about that idea that there may be a covenant between yourself and God? Like, if you follow God's commandments, you will receive God's blessing?	
If you left the covenant with God (or never knew about it or understood it), can you return to it? How can you do that?	
For Today: What nourishment does your soul need today, to make yourself part of (or a bigger part of) God's covenant with humanity?	

Step 10 - Continued to take personal inventory and when we were wrong promptly admitted it.

Journaling Exercise: The covenant holds that the Promised Land will belong to the Israelites as long as they follow God's laws. If they cease to follow the Law, they will lose the right to live in the Promised Land. How might your tenth step personal inventory reflect situations where your behavior threatened to eject you from your personal "Promised Land"?

Deuteronomy 29:18 – "And it will be that when he hears the words of the imprecation [from 29:17 – Day 26], he will bless himself in his heart, saying, 'Peace will be with me, though I walk as my heart sees fit' – thereby adding the watered to the thirsty."

This verse presents us with a puzzling phrase, "thereby adding the watered to the thirsty." What does this mean? The context is that after 29:17, where Moses warns the people not to turn away from God and serve idols, we have an example of a person who does just that. The person described here has heard the warning but ignores it, blessing himself in his heart and saying, "Peace will be with me, though I walk as my heart sees fit." Unchecked, your heart can lead you astray, leading you to bless yourself and talk yourself into feeling as if you're totally fine. The "watered" refers to unintentional sin, i.e. things we do when we're drunk or high. The "thirsty" is the intentional sin, the stuff we do deliberately and that we know is wrong. The verse is saying that God will punish us for both the intentional and unintentional sins if we delude ourselves into thinking that we are in charge and that we can do as we please. This is not a good path for sobriety and conscious contact with a Higher Power.

Questions to Ponder	
Have you ever blessed yourself in your own heart, so to speak, thinking "I'm okay no matter what… I will do as my heart sees fit?" How did it go for you?	
Do you think your heart can lead you astray? What can you do about that?	
For Today: What does your heart want for you that perhaps your soul can't handle?	

Step 11 - Sought through prayer and meditation to improve our conscious contact with God as we understood Him, praying only for knowledge of His will for us and the power to carry that out.

Journaling Exercise: While working the eleventh step, can you identify feelings and situations where your heart is pulling you in one direction while your spiritual being is pulling in a different direction? How can the eleventh step process help you resolve this tension?

Day 88

Deuteronomy 29:18 – "And it will be that when he hears the words of the imprecation [from 29:17], he will bless himself in his heart, saying, 'Peace will be with me, though I walk as my heart sees fit' – thereby adding the watered to the thirsty."

According to The Commentators, the phrase "adding watered to the thirsty" is a cryptic reference to the difference between intentional and unintentional sin. A person who is absorbed in idol worship is at risk of piling unintentional sins on top of other, more obvious transgressions. Both, of course, are harmful to spiritual health and recovery. This topic should resonate with anyone (and honestly, it's all of us) who has ever tried to evade accountability for something done while intoxicated. "I was drunk," we say, washing our hands of responsibility for hurting someone's feelings, wrecking a car, or far worse things that we can do when under the influence of drugs or alcohol. Or, we may not even know what we did. We were drunk, we tell ourselves, when we ran over someone's foot and had no idea about it until we got arrested. Does that absolve us from accountability? No, of course not. Letting ourselves off the hook for unintentional transgressions is one of the worst delusions of addiction. If anything, it makes the sin worse. One of the purposes of the steps is to force us to examine ourselves and chronicle just this sort of thing. Knowing what we have done, we can set about making amends.

Questions to Ponder	
When you were drinking or using, did you ever do something wrong unintentionally, but upon later reflection realized that you were actually responsible for what happened? (e.g. you unintentionally injured someone but you would not have injured them if you had been sober?)	
Have you ever minimized something you did, or let yourself off the hook, because you were intoxicated at the time?	
For Today: Can you be aware of your actions and speech so that you will avoid unintentionally hurting others, as well as yourself?	

Step 11 - Sought through prayer and meditation to improve our conscious contact with God as we understood Him, praying only for knowledge of His will for us and the power to carry that out.

Journaling Exercise: In what ways can you use prayer and meditation in your eleventh step to become more aware of your actions and speech? Can improving your conscious contact with God help keep you away from unintentionally hurting others or yourself?

Deuteronomy 32:13 – "He would suckle him with honey from a stone, and oil from a flinty rock."

Being suckled with honey from a stone is an amazing double-edged metaphor of recovery. Finding spiritual sustenance in the seemingly harsh, unforgiving world is as miraculous as getting honey from a rock. The rock does not look as if it will produce honey, but the honey is there. God is our rock. If we do our work, we can get the "honey" that is in the rock. At the same time, getting honey from a stone, sort of like "getting blood from a stone," gives us a great image of the futility of trying to connect with active addicts or co-addicts. In Alanon, they say, "Don't try to buy oranges at the hardware store," meaning that we should not try to get emotional support or nurturing relationships with people who are incapacitated with addiction. Some stones have no honey in them. If we work on conscious contact with God, God can help us discern which stones are empty.

Questions to Ponder	
Have you ever had the miraculous experience of "getting honey from a rock," so to speak – accomplishing something that seemed impossible, in spiritual terms?	
On the other hand, have you ever tried to get "blood from a stone" or "buy oranges at the hardware store" – seeking spiritual wellness through people and places that were not capable of helping you?	
For Today: Can you identity which sources of emotional and spiritual nourishment in your life that are full and available to you, versus those that are empty?	

Step 12 - Having had a spiritual awakening as the result of these steps, we tried to carry this message to alcoholics and to practice these principles in all our affairs.

Journaling Exercise: In what ways is having a spiritual awakening as a result of these steps translating into a better sense of whom you can trust as an emotional or spiritual resource in your life?

Day 90

Deuteronomy 33:25 – "May your borders be sealed like iron and copper, and like the days of your prime, so may your old age be."

People with addiction problems are often said to have "poor boundaries," meaning they don't know quite where they end and other people begin. Their souls are open, like unlocked gates, vulnerable to toxic ideas and bad people who can easily invade. Here, Moses is offering his blessing that the Land of Israel have solid borders. We can interpret this to mean that we would do well to make our personal boundaries "like iron and copper." We must do the work and build up our boundaries to make us impenetrable to harmful ideas and people. It's a balancing act, of course, because at the same time we need to be open to hearing what others have to say. Learning Torah and focusing on conscious contact with God will help us form the kind of personal boundaries that are strong enough to keep us sober, while open to the right kind of thinking.

Questions to Ponder	
Has the program and the process of recovery helped you make your personal boundaries stronger? i.e. is it harder for toxic people and ideas to "invade" your spiritual being?	
Can you also relate to the opposite idea, which is that when your personal boundaries are too hardened, you may miss out on opportunities to grow along spiritual lines?	
For Today: How will you work on making your personal boundaries stronger and healthier?	

Step 12 - Having had a spiritual awakening as the result of these steps, we tried to carry this message to alcoholics and to practice these principles in all our affairs.

Journaling Exercise: In what ways does the "spiritual awakening" described in the twelfth step involve a strengthening of personal boundaries? Or, put another way, can you carry the message and practice these principles in all your affairs if you don't know where you end and others begin?

The Old Testament

The Book of Genesis

NOTE: This translation of the Bible varies slightly from the classic Hebrew-to-English translations used elsewhere in the book. In a very few places, the chapter and verse numbering is also different.

Genesis 1

1 In the beginning, God[3] created the heavens and the earth.

2 The earth was formless and empty. Darkness was on the surface of the deep and God's Spirit was hovering over the surface of the waters.

3 God said, "Let there be light," and there was light. 4 God saw the light, and saw that it was good. God divided the light from the darkness. 5 God called the light "day", and the darkness he called "night". There was evening and there was morning, the first day.

6 God said, "Let there be an expanse in the middle of the waters, and let it divide the waters from the waters." 7 God made the expanse, and divided the waters which were under the expanse from the waters which were above the expanse; and it was so.

8 God called the expanse "sky". There was evening and there was morning, a second day.

9 God said, "Let the waters under the sky be gathered together to one place, and let the dry land appear;" and it was so. 10 God called the dry land "earth", and the gathering together of the waters he called "seas". God saw that it was good. 11 God said, "Let the earth yield grass, herbs yielding seeds, and fruit trees bearing fruit after their kind, with their seeds in it, on the earth;" and it was so. 12 The earth yielded grass, herbs yielding seed after their kind, and trees bearing fruit, with their seeds in it, after their kind; and God saw that it was good. 13 There was evening and there was morning, a third day.

14 God said, "Let there be lights in the expanse of the sky to divide the day from the night; and let them be for signs to mark seasons, days, and years; 15 and let them be for lights in the expanse of the sky to give light on the earth;" and it was so.

16 God made the two great lights: the greater light to rule the day, and the lesser light to rule the night. He also made the stars.

17 God set them in the expanse of the sky to give light to the earth, 18 and to rule over the day and over the night, and to divide the light from the darkness. God saw that it was good.

19 There was evening and there was morning, a fourth day.

20 God said, "Let the waters abound with living creatures, and let birds fly above the earth in the open expanse of the sky."

21 God created the large sea creatures and every living creature that moves, with which the waters swarmed, after their kind, and every winged bird after its kind. God saw that it was good.

22 God blessed them, saying, "Be fruitful, and multiply, and fill the waters in the seas, and let birds multiply on the earth."

23 There was evening and there was morning, a fifth day.

24 God said, "Let the earth produce living creatures after their kind, livestock, creeping things, and animals of the earth after their kind;" and it was so. 25 God made the animals of the earth after their kind, and the livestock after their kind, and everything that creeps on the ground after its kind. God saw that it was good.

26 God said, "Let's make man in our image, after our likeness. Let them have dominion over the fish of the sea, and over the birds of the sky, and over the livestock, and over all the earth, and over every creeping thing that creeps on the earth." 27 God created man in his own image. In God's image he created him; male and female he created them. 28 God blessed them. God said to them, "Be fruitful, multiply, fill the earth, and subdue it. Have dominion over the fish of the sea, over the birds of the sky, and over every living thing that moves on the earth." 29 God said, "Behold,[4] I have given you every herb yielding seed, which is on the surface of all the earth, and every tree, which bears fruit yielding seed. It will be your food. 30 To every animal of the earth, and to every bird of the sky, and to everything that creeps on the earth, in which there is life, I have given every green herb for food;" and it was so.

31 God saw everything that he had made, and, behold, it was very good. There was evening and there was morning, a sixth day.

Genesis 2

1 The heavens, the earth, and all their vast array were finished.

2 On the seventh day God finished his work which he had done; and he rested on the seventh day from all his work which he had done. 3 God blessed the seventh day, and made it holy, because he rested in it from all his work of creation which he had done.

4 This is the history of the generations of the heavens and of the earth when they were created, in the day that God[5] God made the earth and the heavens. 5 No plant of the field was yet in the earth, and no herb of the field had yet sprung up; for God God had not caused it to rain on the earth. There was not a man to till the ground, 6 but a mist went up from the earth, and watered the whole surface of the ground. 7 God God formed man from the dust of the ground, and breathed into his nostrils the breath of life; and man became a living soul. 8 God God planted a garden eastward, in Eden, and there he put the man whom he had formed. 9 Out of the ground God God made every tree to grow that is pleasant to the sight, and good for food, including the tree of life in the middle of the garden and the tree of the knowledge of good and evil. 10 A river went out of Eden to water the garden; and from there it was parted, and became the source of four rivers. 11 The name of the first is Pishon: it flows through the whole land of Havilah, where there is gold; 12 and the gold of that land is good. Bdellium[6] and onyx stone are also there.

13 The name of the second river is Gihon. It is the same river that flows through the whole land of Cush. 14 The name of the third river is Hiddekel. This is the one which flows in front of Assyria. The fourth river is the Euphrates. 15 God God took the man, and put him into the garden of Eden to cultivate and keep it.

16 God God commanded the man, saying, "You may freely eat of every tree of the garden; 17 but you shall not eat of the tree of the knowledge of good and evil; for in the day that you eat of it, you will surely die."

18 God God said, "It is not good for the man to be alone. I will make him a helper comparable to[7] him." 19 Out of the ground God God formed every animal of the field, and every bird of the sky, and brought them to the man to see what he would call them. Whatever the man called every living creature became its name.

20 The man gave names to all livestock, and to the birds of the sky, and to every animal of the field; but for man there was not found a helper comparable to him. 21 God God caused the man to fall into a deep sleep. As the man slept, he took one of his ribs, and closed up the flesh in its place. 22 God God made a woman from the rib which he had taken from the man, and brought her to the man. 23 The man said, "This is now bone of my bones, and flesh of my flesh. She will be called 'woman,' because she was taken out of Man." 24 Therefore a man will leave his father and his mother, and will join with his wife, and they will be one flesh.

25 The man and his wife were both naked, and they were not ashamed.

Genesis 3

1 Now the serpent was more subtle than any animal of the field which God God had made. He said to the woman, "Has God really said, 'You shall not eat of any tree of the garden'?"

2 The woman said to the serpent, "We may eat fruit from the trees of the garden, 3 but not the fruit of the tree which is in the middle of the garden. God has said, 'You shall not eat of it. You shall not touch it, lest you die.'"

4 The serpent said to the woman, "You won't really die, 5 for God knows that in the day you eat it, your eyes will be opened, and you will be like God, knowing good and evil."

6 When the woman saw that the tree was good for food, and that it was a delight to the eyes, and that the tree was to be desired to make one wise, she took some of its fruit, and ate. Then she gave some to her husband with her, and he ate it, too. 7 Their eyes were opened, and they both knew that they were naked. They sewed fig leaves together, and made coverings for themselves.

8 They heard God God's voice walking in the garden in the cool of the day, and the man and his wife hid themselves from the presence of God God among the trees of the garden.

9 God God called to the man, and said to him, "Where are you?"

10 The man said, "I heard your voice in the garden, and I was afraid, because I was naked; so I hid myself."

11 God said, "Who told you that you were naked? Have you eaten from the tree that I commanded you not to eat from?"

12 The man said, "The woman whom you gave to be with me, she gave me fruit from the tree, and I ate it."

13 God God said to the woman, "What have you done?"
The woman said, "The serpent deceived me, and I ate."

14 God God said to the serpent,
"Because you have done this,
you are cursed above all livestock,
and above every animal of the field.
You shall go on your belly
and you shall eat dust all the days of your life.

15 I will put hostility between you and the woman,
and between your offspring and her offspring.
He will bruise your head,
and you will bruise his heel."

16 To the woman he said,
"I will greatly multiply your pain in childbirth.
You will bear children in pain.
Your desire will be for your husband,
and he will rule over you."

17 To Adam he said,
"Because you have listened to your wife's voice,
and ate from the tree,
about which I commanded you, saying, 'You shall not eat of it,'
the ground is cursed for your sake.
You will eat from it with much labor all the days of your life.

18 It will yield thorns and thistles to you;
and you will eat the herb of the field.

19 You will eat bread by the sweat of your face until you return to the ground,
for you were taken out of it.
For you are dust,
and you shall return to dust."

20 The man called his wife Eve because she would be the mother of all the living. 21 God God made garments of animal skins for Adam and for his wife, and clothed them.

22 God God said, "Behold, the man has become like one of us, knowing good and evil. Now, lest he reach out his hand, and also take of the tree of life, and eat, and live forever—" 23 Therefore God God sent him out from the garden of Eden, to till the ground from which he was taken. 24 So he drove out the man; and he placed cherubim [8] at the east of the garden of Eden, and a flaming sword which turned every way, to guard the way to the tree of life.

Genesis 4

1 The man knew[9] Eve his wife. She conceived,[10] and gave birth to Cain, and said, "I have gotten a man with God's help."

2 Again she gave birth, to Cain's brother Abel. Abel was a keeper of sheep, but Cain was a tiller of the ground. 3 As time passed, Cain brought an offering to God from the fruit of the ground. 4 Abel also brought some of the firstborn of his flock and of its fat. God respected Abel and his offering, 5 but he didn't respect Cain and his offering. Cain was very angry, and the expression on his face fell. 6 God said to Cain, "Why are you angry? Why has the expression of your face fallen? 7 If you do well, won't it be lifted up? If you don't do well, sin crouches at the door. Its desire is for you, but you are to rule over it." 8 Cain said to Abel, his brother, "Let's go into the field." While they were in the field, Cain rose up against Abel, his brother, and killed him.

---

[3] **1:1** *1:1* The Hebrew word rendered "God" is "אֱלֹהִים" (Elohim).

[4] **1:29** *1:29* "Behold", from "הִנֵּה", means look at, take notice, observe, see, or gaze at. It is often used as an interjection.

[5] **2:4** *2:4* "God" is God's proper Name, sometimes rendered "LORD" (all caps) in other translations.

[6] **2:12** *2:12* or, aromatic resin

[7] **2:18** *2:18* or, suitable for, or appropriate for.

[8] **3:24** *3:24* cherubim are powerful angelic creatures, messengers of God with wings. See Ezekiel 10.

[9] **4:1** *4:1* or, lay with, or, had relations with

[10] **4:1** *4:1* or, became pregnant

9 God said to Cain, "Where is Abel, your brother?"
He said, "I don't know. Am I my brother's keeper?"
10 God said, "What have you done? The voice of your brother's
blood cries to me from the ground. 11 Now you are cursed
because of the ground, which has opened its mouth to receive
your brother's blood from your hand. 12 From now on, when
you till the ground, it won't yield its strength to you. You will be
a fugitive and a wanderer in the earth."
13 Cain said to God, "My punishment is greater than I can bear.
14 Behold, you have driven me out today from the surface of the
ground. I will be hidden from your face, and I will be a fugitive
and a wanderer in the earth. Whoever finds me will kill me."
15 God said to him, "Therefore whoever slays Cain, vengeance
will be taken on him sevenfold." God appointed a sign for Cain,
so that anyone finding him would not strike him.
16 Cain left God's presence, and lived in the land of Nod, east of
Eden. 17 Cain knew his wife. She conceived, and gave birth to
Enoch. He built a city, and named the city after the name of his
son, Enoch. 18 Irad was born to Enoch. Irad became the father of
Mehujael. Mehujael became the father of Methushael.
Methushael became the father of Lamech. 19 Lamech took two
wives: the name of the first one was Adah, and the name of the
second one was Zillah. 20 Adah gave birth to Jabal, who was the
father of those who dwell in tents and have livestock. 21 His
brother's name was Jubal, who was the father of all who handle
the harp and pipe. 22 Zillah also gave birth to Tubal Cain, the
forger of every cutting instrument of bronze and iron. Tubal
Cain's sister was Naamah. 23 Lamech said to his wives,
"Adah and Zillah, hear my voice.
You wives of Lamech, listen to my speech,
for I have slain a man for wounding me,
a young man for bruising me.
24 If Cain will be avenged seven times,
truly Lamech seventy-seven times."
25 Adam knew his wife again. She gave birth to a son, and
named him Seth, saying, "for God has given me another child
instead of Abel, for Cain killed him." 26 A son was also born to
Seth, and he named him Enosh. At that time men began to call on
God's name.

Genesis 5

1 This is the book of the generations of Adam. In the day that
God created man, he made him in God's likeness. 2 He created
them male and female, and blessed them. On the day they were
created, he named them Adam.[11] 3 Adam lived one hundred
thirty years, and became the father of a son in his own likeness,
after his image, and named him Seth. 4 The days of Adam after
he became the father of Seth were eight hundred years, and he
became the father of other sons and daughters. 5 All the days
that Adam lived were nine hundred thirty years, then he died.
6 Seth lived one hundred five years, then became the father of
Enosh. 7 Seth lived after he became the father of Enosh eight
hundred seven years, and became the father of other sons and
daughters. 8 All of the days of Seth were nine hundred twelve
years, then he died.
9 Enosh lived ninety years, and became the father of Kenan.
10 Enosh lived after he became the father of Kenan eight
hundred fifteen years, and became the father of other sons and
daughters. 11 All of the days of Enosh were nine hundred five
years, then he died.
12 Kenan lived seventy years, then became the father of
Mahalalel. 13 Kenan lived after he became the father of
Mahalalel eight hundred forty years, and became the father of
other sons and daughters 14 and all of the days of Kenan were
nine hundred ten years, then he died.
15 Mahalalel lived sixty-five years, then became the father of
Jared. 16 Mahalalel lived after he became the father of Jared
eight hundred thirty years, and became the father of other sons
and daughters. 17 All of the days of Mahalalel were eight
hundred ninety-five years, then he died.
18 Jared lived one hundred sixty-two years, then became the
father of Enoch. 19 Jared lived after he became the father of
Enoch eight hundred years, and became the father of other sons
and daughters. 20 All of the days of Jared were nine hundred
sixty-two years, then he died.
21 Enoch lived sixty-five years, then became the father of
Methuselah. 22 After Methuselah's birth, Enoch walked with
God for three hundred years, and became the father of more sons
and daughters. 23 All the days of Enoch were three hundred
sixty-five years. 24 Enoch walked with God, and he was not
found, for God took him.
25 Methuselah lived one hundred eighty-seven years, then
became the father of Lamech. 26 Methuselah lived after he
became the father of Lamech seven hundred eighty-two years,
and became the father of other sons and daughters. 27 All the
days of Methuselah were nine hundred sixty-nine years, then he
died.
28 Lamech lived one hundred eighty-two years, then became the
father of a son. 29 He named him Noah, saying, "This one will
comfort us in our work and in the toil of our hands, caused by the
ground which God has cursed." 30 Lamech lived after he
became the father of Noah five hundred ninety-five years, and
became the father of other sons and daughters. 31 All the days of
Lamech were seven hundred seventy-seven years, then he died.
32 Noah was five hundred years old, then Noah became the
father of Shem, Ham, and Japheth.

Genesis 6

1 When men began to multiply on the surface of the ground, and
daughters were born to them, 2 God's sons saw that men's
daughters were beautiful, and they took any that they wanted for
themselves as wives. 3 God said, "My Spirit will not strive with
man forever, because he also is flesh; so his days will be one
hundred twenty years." 4 The Nephilim[12] were in the earth in
those days, and also after that, when God's sons came in to men's
daughters and had children with them. Those were the mighty
men who were of old, men of renown.
5 God saw that the wickedness of man was great in the earth,
and that every imagination of the thoughts of man's heart was
continually only evil. 6 God was sorry that he had made man on
the earth, and it grieved him in his heart. 7 God said, "I will
destroy man whom I have created from the surface of the
ground—man, along with animals, creeping things, and birds of
the sky—for I am sorry that I have made them." 8 But Noah
found favor in God's eyes.
9 This is the history of the generations of Noah: Noah was a
righteous man, blameless among the people of his time. Noah
walked with God. 10 Noah became the father of three sons:
Shem, Ham, and Japheth. 11 The earth was corrupt before God,
and the earth was filled with violence. 12 God saw the earth, and
saw that it was corrupt, for all flesh had corrupted their way on
the earth.
13 God said to Noah, "I will bring an end to all flesh, for the
earth is filled with violence through them. Behold, I will destroy
them and the earth. 14 Make a ship of gopher wood. You shall
make rooms in the ship, and shall seal it inside and outside with
pitch. 15 This is how you shall make it. The length of the ship
shall be three hundred cubits,[13] its width fifty cubits, and its
height thirty cubits. 16 You shall make a roof in the ship, and
you shall finish it to a cubit upward. You shall set the door of the
ship in its side. You shall make it with lower, second, and third
levels. 17 I, even I, will bring the flood of waters on this earth, to
destroy all flesh having the breath of life from under the sky.
Everything that is in the earth will die. 18 But I will establish my
covenant with you. You shall come into the ship, you, your sons,
your wife, and your sons' wives with you. 19 Of every living
thing of all flesh, you shall bring two of every sort into the ship,
to keep them alive with you. They shall be male and female.
20 Of the birds after their kind, of the livestock after their kind,
of every creeping thing of the ground after its kind, two of every
sort will come to you, to keep them alive. 21 Take with you
some of all food that is eaten, and gather it to yourself; and it will
be for food for you, and for them." 22 Thus Noah did. He did all
that God commanded him.

Genesis 7

1 God said to Noah, "Come with all of your household into the
ship, for I have seen your righteousness before me in this
generation. 2 You shall take seven pairs of every clean animal
with you, the male and his female. Of the animals that are not
clean, take two, the male and his female. 3 Also of the birds of
the sky, seven and seven, male and female, to keep seed alive on
the surface of all the earth. 4 In seven days, I will cause it to rain
on the earth for forty days and forty nights. I will destroy every
living thing that I have made from the surface of the ground."
5 Noah did everything that God commanded him.
6 Noah was six hundred years old when the flood of waters came
on the earth. 7 Noah went into the ship with his sons, his wife,
and his sons' wives, because of the floodwaters. 8 Clean
animals, unclean animals, birds, and everything that creeps on the
ground 9 went by pairs to Noah into the ship, male and female,
as God commanded Noah. 10 After the seven days, the
floodwaters came on the earth. 11 In the six hundredth year of
Noah's life, in the second month, on the seventeenth day of the
month, on that day all the fountains of the great deep burst open,
and the sky's windows opened. 12 It rained on the earth forty
days and forty nights.
13 In the same day Noah, and Shem, Ham, and Japheth—the
sons of Noah—and Noah's wife and the three wives of his sons
with them, entered into the ship— 14 they, and every animal
after its kind, all the livestock after their kind, every creeping
thing that creeps on the earth after its kind, and every bird after
its kind, every bird of every sort. 15 Pairs from all flesh with the
breath of life in them went into the ship to Noah. 16 Those who
went in, went in male and female of all flesh, as God commanded
him; then God shut him in. 17 The flood was forty days on the
earth. The waters increased, and lifted up the ship, and it was
lifted up above the earth. 18 The waters rose, and increased
greatly on the earth; and the ship floated on the surface of the
waters. 19 The waters rose very high on the earth. All the high
mountains that were under the whole sky were covered. 20 The
waters rose fifteen cubits[14] higher, and the mountains were
covered. 21 All flesh died that moved on the earth, including
birds, livestock, animals, every creeping thing that creeps on the
earth, and every man. 22 All on the dry land, in whose nostrils
was the breath of the spirit of life, died. 23 Every living thing
was destroyed that was on the surface of the ground, including
man, livestock, creeping things, and birds of the sky. They were
destroyed from the earth. Only Noah was left, and those who
were with him in the ship. 24 The waters flooded the earth one
hundred fifty days.

Genesis 8

1 God remembered Noah, all the animals, and all the livestock
that were with him in the ship; and God made a wind to pass over
the earth. The waters subsided. 2 The deep's fountains and the
sky's windows were also stopped, and the rain from the sky was
restrained. 3 The waters continually receded from the earth.
After the end of one hundred fifty days the waters receded.
4 The ship rested in the seventh month, on the seventeenth day
of the month, on Ararat's mountains. 5 The waters receded
continually until the tenth month. In the tenth month, on the first
day of the month, the tops of the mountains were visible.
6 At the end of forty days, Noah opened the window of the ship
which he had made, 7 and he sent out a raven. It went back and
forth, until the waters were dried up from the earth. 8 He himself
sent out a dove to see if the waters were abated from the surface
of the ground, 9 but the dove found no place to rest her foot, and
she returned into the ship to him, for the waters were on the
surface of the whole earth. He put out his hand, and took her, and
brought her to him into the ship. 10 He waited yet another seven
days; and again he sent the dove out of the ship. 11 The dove
came back to him at evening and, behold, in her mouth was a
freshly plucked olive leaf. So Noah knew that the waters were
abated from the earth. 12 He waited yet another seven days, and
sent out the dove; and she didn't return to him any more.
13 In the six hundred first year, in the first month, the first day of
the month, the waters were dried up from the earth. Noah
removed the covering of the ship, and looked. He saw that the

---

[11] **5:2** *5:2* **"Adam" and "Man" are spelled with the exact same consonants in Hebrew, so this can be correctly translated either way.**
[12] **6:4** *6:4* **or, giants**
[13] **6:15** *6:15* **A cubit is the length from the tip of the middle finger to the elbow on a man's arm, or about 18 inches or 46 centimeters.**
[14] **7:20** *7:20* **A cubit is the length from the tip of the middle finger to the elbow on a man's arm, or about 18 inches or 46 centimeters.**

surface of the ground was dry. 14 In the second month, on the
twenty-seventh day of the month, the earth was dry.
15 God spoke to Noah, saying, 16 "Go out of the ship, you,
your wife, your sons, and your sons' wives with you. 17 Bring
out with you every living thing that is with you of all flesh,
including birds, livestock, and every creeping thing that creeps on
the earth, that they may breed abundantly in the earth, and be
fruitful, and multiply on the earth."
18 Noah went out, with his sons, his wife, and his sons' wives
with him. 19 Every animal, every creeping thing, and every bird,
whatever moves on the earth, after their families, went out of the
ship.
20 Noah built an altar to God, and took of every clean animal,
and of every clean bird, and offered burnt offerings on the altar.
21 God smelled the pleasant aroma. God said in his heart, "I will
not again curse the ground any more for man's sake because the
imagination of man's heart is evil from his youth. I will never
again strike every living thing, as I have done. 22 While the
earth remains, seed time and harvest, and cold and heat, and
summer and winter, and day and night will not cease."

Genesis 9

1 God blessed Noah and his sons, and said to them, "Be fruitful,
multiply, and replenish the earth. 2 The fear of you and the dread
of you will be on every animal of the earth, and on every bird of
the sky. Everything that moves along the ground, and all the fish
of the sea, are delivered into your hand. 3 Every moving thing
that lives will be food for you. As I gave you the green herb, I
have given everything to you. 4 But flesh with its life, that is, its
blood, you shall not eat. 5 I will surely require accounting for
your life's blood. At the hand of every animal I will require it. At
the hand of man, even at the hand of every man's brother, I will
require the life of man. 6 Whoever sheds man's blood, his blood
will be shed by man, for God made man in his own image. 7 Be
fruitful and multiply. Increase abundantly in the earth, and
multiply in it."
8 God spoke to Noah and to his sons with him, saying, 9 "As for
me, behold, I establish my covenant with you, and with your
offspring after you, 10 and with every living creature that is with
you: the birds, the livestock, and every animal of the earth with
you, of all that go out of the ship, even every animal of the earth.
11 I will establish my covenant with you: All flesh will not be
cut off any more by the waters of the flood. There will never
again be a flood to destroy the earth." 12 God said, "This is the
token of the covenant which I make between me and you and
every living creature that is with you, for perpetual generations:
13 I set my rainbow in the cloud, and it will be a sign of a
covenant between me and the earth. 14 When I bring a cloud
over the earth, that the rainbow will be seen in the cloud, 15 I
will remember my covenant, which is between me and you and
every living creature of all flesh, and the waters will no more
become a flood to destroy all flesh. 16 The rainbow will be in
the cloud. I will look at it, that I may remember the everlasting
covenant between God and every living creature of all flesh that
is on the earth." 17 God said to Noah, "This is the token of the
covenant which I have established between me and all flesh that
is on the earth."
18 The sons of Noah who went out from the ship were Shem,
Ham, and Japheth. Ham is the father of Canaan. 19 These three
were the sons of Noah, and from these the whole earth was
populated.
20 Noah began to be a farmer, and planted a vineyard. 21 He
drank of the wine and got drunk. He was uncovered within his
tent. 22 Ham, the father of Canaan, saw the nakedness of his
father, and told his two brothers outside. 23 Shem and Japheth
took a garment, and laid it on both their shoulders, went in
backwards, and covered the nakedness of their father. Their faces
were backwards, and they didn't see their father's nakedness.
24 Noah awoke from his wine, and knew what his youngest son
had done to him. 25 He said,
"Canaan is cursed.
He will be a servant of servants to his brothers."
26 He said,
"Blessed be God, the God of Shem.
Let Canaan be his servant.
27 May God enlarge Japheth.
Let him dwell in the tents of Shem.
Let Canaan be his servant."
28 Noah lived three hundred fifty years after the flood. 29 All
the days of Noah were nine hundred fifty years, and then he died.

Genesis 10

1 Now this is the history of the generations of the sons of Noah
and of Shem, Ham, and Japheth. Sons were born to them after the
flood.
2 The sons of Japheth were: Gomer, Magog, Madai, Javan,
Tubal, Meshech, and Tiras. 3 The sons of Gomer were:
Ashkenaz, Riphath, and Togarmah. 4 The sons of Javan were:
Elishah, Tarshish, Kittim, and Dodanim. 5 Of these were the
islands of the nations divided in their lands, everyone after his
language, after their families, in their nations.
6 The sons of Ham were: Cush, Mizraim, Put, and Canaan.
7 The sons of Cush were: Seba, Havilah, Sabtah, Raamah, and
Sabteca. The sons of Raamah were: Sheba and Dedan. 8 Cush
became the father of Nimrod. He began to be a mighty one in the
earth. 9 He was a mighty hunter before God. Therefore it is
said, "like Nimrod, a mighty hunter before God". 10 The
beginning of his kingdom was Babel, Erech, Accad, and Calneh,
in the land of Shinar. 11 Out of that land he went into Assyria,
and built Nineveh, Rehoboth Ir, Calah, 12 and Resen between
Nineveh and the great city Calah. 13 Mizraim became the father
of Ludim, Anamim, Lehabim, Naphtuhim, 14 Pathrusim,
Casluhim (which the Philistines descended from), and
Caphtorim.
15 Canaan became the father of Sidon (his firstborn), Heth,
16 the Jebusites, the Amorites, the Girgashites, 17 the Hivites,
the Arkites, the Sinites, 18 the Arvadites, the Zemarites, and the
Hamathites. Afterward the families of the Canaanites were spread
abroad. 19 The border of the Canaanites was from Sidon—as
you go toward Gerar—to Gaza—as you go toward Sodom,
Gomorrah, Admah, and Zeboiim—to Lasha. 20 These are the
sons of Ham, after their families, according to their languages, in
their lands and their nations.
21 Children were also born to Shem (the elder brother of
Japheth), the father of all the children of Eber. 22 The sons of
Shem were: Elam, Asshur, Arpachshad, Lud, and Aram. 23 The
sons of Aram were: Uz, Hul, Gether, and Mash. 24 Arpachshad
became the father of Shelah. Shelah became the father of Eber.
25 To Eber were born two sons. The name of the one was
Peleg, for in his days the earth was divided. His brother's name
was Joktan. 26 Joktan became the father of Almodad, Sheleph,
Hazarmaveth, Jerah, 27 Hadoram, Uzal, Diklah, 28 Obal,
Abimael, Sheba, 29 Ophir, Havilah, and Jobab. All these were
the sons of Joktan. 30 Their dwelling extended from Mesha, as
you go toward Sephar, the mountain of the east. 31 These are
the sons of Shem, by their families, according to their languages,
lands, and nations.
32 These are the families of the sons of Noah, by their
generations, according to their nations. The nations divided from
these in the earth after the flood.

Genesis 11

1 The whole earth was of one language and of one speech.
2 As they traveled from the east, they found a plain in the land
of Shinar, and they lived there. 3 They said to one another,
"Come, let's make bricks, and burn them thoroughly." They had
brick for stone, and they used tar for mortar. 4 They said,
"Come, let's build ourselves a city, and a tower whose top
reaches to the sky, and let's make a name for ourselves, lest we
be scattered abroad on the surface of the whole earth."
5 God came down to see the city and the tower, which the
children of men built. 6 God said, "Behold, they are one people,
and they all have one language, and this is what they begin to do.
Now nothing will be withheld from them, which they intend to
do. 7 Come, let's go down, and there confuse their language,
that they may not understand one another's speech." 8 So God
scattered them abroad from there on the surface of all the earth.
They stopped building the city. 9 Therefore its name was called
Babel, because there God confused the language of all the earth.
From there, God scattered them abroad on the surface of all the
earth.
10 This is the history of the generations of Shem: Shem was one
hundred years old when he became the father of Arpachshad two
years after the flood. 11 Shem lived five hundred years after he
became the father of Arpachshad, and became the father of more
sons and daughters.
12 Arpachshad lived thirty-five years and became the father of
Shelah. 13 Arpachshad lived four hundred three years after he
became the father of Shelah, and became the father of more sons
and daughters.
14 Shelah lived thirty years, and became the father of Eber.
15 Shelah lived four hundred three years after he became the
father of Eber, and became the father of more sons and daughters.
16 Eber lived thirty-four years, and became the father of Peleg.
17 Eber lived four hundred thirty years after he became the
father of Peleg, and became the father of more sons and
daughters.
18 Peleg lived thirty years, and became the father of Reu.
19 Peleg lived two hundred nine years after he became the
father of Reu, and became the father of more sons and daughters.
20 Reu lived thirty-two years, and became the father of Serug.
21 Reu lived two hundred seven years after he became the
father of Serug, and became the father of more sons and
daughters.
22 Serug lived thirty years, and became the father of Nahor.
23 Serug lived two hundred years after he became the father of
Nahor, and became the father of more sons and daughters.
24 Nahor lived twenty-nine years, and became the father of
Terah. 25 Nahor lived one hundred nineteen years after he
became the father of Terah, and became the father of more sons
and daughters.
26 Terah lived seventy years, and became the father of Abram,
Nahor, and Haran.
27 Now this is the history of the generations of Terah. Terah
became the father of Abram, Nahor, and Haran. Haran became
the father of Lot. 28 Haran died in the land of his birth, in Ur of
the Chaldees, while his father Terah was still alive. 29 Abram
and Nahor married wives. The name of Abram's wife was Sarai,
and the name of Nahor's wife was Milcah, the daughter of Haran,
who was also the father of Iscah. 30 Sarai was barren. She had
no child. 31 Terah took Abram his son, Lot the son of Haran,
his son's son, and Sarai his daughter-in-law, his son Abram's
wife. They went from Ur of the Chaldees, to go into the land of
Canaan. They came to Haran and lived there. 32 The days of
Terah were two hundred five years. Terah died in Haran.

Genesis 12

1 Now God said to Abram, "Leave your country, and your
relatives, and your father's house, and go to the land that I will
show you. 2 I will make of you a great nation. I will bless you
and make your name great. You will be a blessing. 3 I will bless
those who bless you, and I will curse him who treats you with
contempt. All the families of the earth will be blessed through
you."
4 So Abram went, as God had told him. Lot went with him.
Abram was seventy-five years old when he departed from Haran.
5 Abram took Sarai his wife, Lot his brother's son, all their
possessions that they had gathered, and the people whom they
had acquired in Haran, and they went to go into the land of
Canaan. They entered into the land of Canaan. 6 Abram passed
through the land to the place of Shechem, to the oak of Moreh. At
that time, Canaanites were in the land.
7 God appeared to Abram and said, "I will give this land to your
offspring." [15]
He built an altar there to God, who had appeared to him. 8 He
left from there to go to the mountain on the east of Bethel and
pitched his tent, having Bethel on the west, and Ai on the east.
There he built an altar to God and called on God's name.
9 Abram traveled, still going on toward the South.
10 There was a famine in the land. Abram went down into
Egypt to live as a foreigner there, for the famine was severe in the
land. 11 When he had come near to enter Egypt, he said to Sarai
his wife, "See now, I know that you are a beautiful woman to
look at. 12 It will happen, when the Egyptians see you, that they
will say, 'This is his wife.' They will kill me, but they will save
you alive. 13 Please say that you are my sister, that it may be
well with me for your sake, and that my soul may live because of
you."
14 When Abram had come into Egypt, Egyptians saw that the
woman was very beautiful. 15 The princes of Pharaoh saw her,
and praised her to Pharaoh; and the woman was taken into
Pharaoh's house. 16 He dealt well with Abram for her sake. He

[15] **12:7** *12:7* or, seed

had sheep, cattle, male donkeys, male servants, female servants,
female donkeys, and camels. 17 God afflicted Pharaoh and his
house with great plagues because of Sarai, Abram's wife.
18 Pharaoh called Abram and said, "What is this that you have
done to me? Why didn't you tell me that she was your wife?
19 Why did you say, 'She is my sister,' so that I took her to be
my wife? Now therefore, see your wife, take her, and go your
way."
20 Pharaoh commanded men concerning him, and they escorted
him away with his wife and all that he had.

Genesis 13

1 Abram went up out of Egypt—he, his wife, all that he had,
and Lot with him—into the South. 2 Abram was very rich in
livestock, in silver, and in gold. 3 He went on his journeys from
the South as far as Bethel, to the place where his tent had been at
the beginning, between Bethel and Ai, 4 to the place of the
altar, which he had made there at the first. There Abram called on
God's name. 5 Lot also, who went with Abram, had flocks,
herds, and tents. 6 The land was not able to bear them, that they
might live together; for their possessions were so great that they
couldn't live together. 7 There was strife between the herdsmen
of Abram's livestock and the herdsmen of Lot's livestock. The
Canaanites and the Perizzites lived in the land at that time.
8 Abram said to Lot, "Please, let there be no strife between you
and me, and between your herdsmen and my herdsmen; for we
are relatives. 9 Isn't the whole land before you? Please separate
yourself from me. If you go to the left hand, then I will go to the
right. Or if you go to the right hand, then I will go to the left."
10 Lot lifted up his eyes, and saw all the plain of the Jordan,
that it was well-watered everywhere, before God destroyed
Sodom and Gomorrah, like the garden of God, like the land of
Egypt, as you go to Zoar. 11 So Lot chose the Plain of the
Jordan for himself. Lot traveled east, and they separated
themselves from one other. 12 Abram lived in the land of
Canaan, and Lot lived in the cities of the plain, and moved his
tent as far as Sodom. 13 Now the men of Sodom were
exceedingly wicked and sinners against God.
14 God said to Abram, after Lot was separated from him,
"Now, lift up your eyes, and look from the place where you are,
northward and southward and eastward and westward, 15 for I
will give all the land which you see to you and to your offspring
forever. 16 I will make your offspring as the dust of the earth,
so that if a man can count the dust of the earth, then your
offspring may also be counted. 17 Arise, walk through the land
in its length and in its width; for I will give it to you."
18 Abram moved his tent, and came and lived by the oaks of
Mamre, which are in Hebron, and built an altar there to God.

Genesis 14

1 In the days of Amraphel, king of Shinar; Arioch, king of
Ellasar; Chedorlaomer, king of Elam; and Tidal, king of Goiim,
2 they made war with Bera, king of Sodom; Birsha, king of
Gomorrah; Shinab, king of Admah; Shemeber, king of Zeboiim;
and the king of Bela (also called Zoar). 3 All these joined
together in the valley of Siddim (also called the Salt Sea).
4 They served Chedorlaomer for twelve years, and in the
thirteenth year they rebelled. 5 In the fourteenth year
Chedorlaomer came, and the kings who were with him, and
struck the Rephaim in Ashteroth Karnaim, the Zuzim in Ham, the
Emim in Shaveh Kiriathaim, 6 and the Horites in their Mount
Seir, to El Paran, which is by the wilderness. 7 They returned,
and came to En Mishpat (also called Kadesh), and struck all the
country of the Amalekites, and also the Amorites, that lived in
Hazazon Tamar. 8 The king of Sodom, and the king of
Gomorrah, the king of Admah, the king of Zeboiim, and the king
of Bela (also called Zoar) went out; and they set the battle in
array against them in the valley of Siddim 9 against
Chedorlaomer king of Elam, Tidal king of Goiim, Amraphel king
of Shinar, and Arioch king of Ellasar; four kings against the five.
10 Now the valley of Siddim was full of tar pits; and the kings
of Sodom and Gomorrah fled, and some fell there. Those who
remained fled to the hills. 11 They took all the goods of Sodom
and Gomorrah, and all their food, and went their way. 12 They
took Lot, Abram's brother's son, who lived in Sodom, and his
goods, and departed.
13 One who had escaped came and told Abram, the Hebrew. At
that time, he lived by the oaks of Mamre, the Amorite, brother of
Eshcol and brother of Aner. They were allies of Abram.
14 When Abram heard that his relative was taken captive, he
led out his three hundred eighteen trained men, born in his house,
and pursued as far as Dan. 15 He divided himself against them
by night, he and his servants, and struck them, and pursued them
to Hobah, which is on the left hand of Damascus. 16 He brought
back all the goods, and also brought back his relative Lot and his
goods, and the women also, and the other people.
17 The king of Sodom went out to meet him after his return
from the slaughter of Chedorlaomer and the kings who were with
him, at the valley of Shaveh (that is, the King's Valley).
18 Melchizedek king of Salem brought out bread and wine. He
was priest of God Most High. 19 He blessed him, and said,
"Blessed be Abram of God Most High, possessor of heaven and
earth. 20 Blessed be God Most High, who has delivered your
enemies into your hand."
Abram gave him a tenth of all.
21 The king of Sodom said to Abram, "Give me the people, and
take the goods for yourself."
22 Abram said to the king of Sodom, "I have lifted up my hand
to God, God Most High, possessor of heaven and earth, 23 that
I will not take a thread nor a sandal strap nor anything that is
yours, lest you should say, 'I have made Abram rich.' 24 I will
accept nothing from you except that which the young men have
eaten, and the portion of the men who went with me: Aner,
Eshcol, and Mamre. Let them take their portion."

Genesis 15

1 After these things God's word came to Abram in a vision,
saying, "Don't be afraid, Abram. I am your shield, your
exceedingly great reward."
2 Abram said, "Lord[16] God, what will you give me, since I go
childless, and he who will inherit my estate is Eliezer of
Damascus?" 3 Abram said, "Behold, you have given no
children to me: and, behold, one born in my house is my heir."
4 Behold, God's word came to him, saying, "This man will not
be your heir, but he who will come out of your own body will be
your heir." 5 God brought him outside, and said, "Look now
toward the sky, and count the stars, if you are able to count
them." He said to Abram, "So your offspring will be." 6 He
believed in God, who credited it to him for righteousness. 7 He
said to Abram, "I am God who brought you out of Ur of the
Chaldees, to give you this land to inherit it."
8 He said, "Lord God, how will I know that I will inherit it?"
9 He said to him, "Bring me a heifer three years old, a female
goat three years old, a ram three years old, a turtledove, and a
young pigeon." 10 He brought him all these, and divided them
in the middle, and laid each half opposite the other; but he didn't
divide the birds. 11 The birds of prey came down on the
carcasses, and Abram drove them away.
12 When the sun was going down, a deep sleep fell on Abram.
Now terror and great darkness fell on him. 13 He said to
Abram, "Know for sure that your offspring will live as foreigners
in a land that is not theirs, and will serve them. They will afflict
them four hundred years. 14 I will also judge that nation, whom
they will serve. Afterward they will come out with great wealth;
15 but you will go to your fathers in peace. You will be buried
at a good old age. 16 In the fourth generation they will come
here again, for the iniquity of the Amorite is not yet full." 17 It
came to pass that, when the sun went down, and it was dark,
behold, a smoking furnace and a flaming torch passed between
these pieces. 18 In that day God made a covenant with Abram,
saying, "I have given this land to your offspring, from the river of
Egypt to the great river, the river Euphrates: 19 the land of the
Kenites, the Kenizzites, the Kadmonites, 20 the Hittites, the
Perizzites, the Rephaim, 21 the Amorites, the Canaanites, the
Girgashites, and the Jebusites."

Genesis 16

1 Now Sarai, Abram's wife, bore him no children. She had a
servant, an Egyptian, whose name was Hagar. 2 Sarai said to
Abram, "See now, God has restrained me from bearing. Please go
in to my servant. It may be that I will obtain children by her."
Abram listened to the voice of Sarai. 3 Sarai, Abram's wife,
took Hagar the Egyptian, her servant, after Abram had lived ten
years in the land of Canaan, and gave her to Abram her husband
to be his wife. 4 He went in to Hagar, and she conceived. When
she saw that she had conceived, her mistress was despised in her
eyes. 5 Sarai said to Abram, "This wrong is your fault. I gave
my servant into your bosom, and when she saw that she had
conceived, she despised me. May God judge between me and
you."
6 But Abram said to Sarai, "Behold, your maid is in your hand.
Do to her whatever is good in your eyes." Sarai dealt harshly
with her, and she fled from her face.
7 God's angel found her by a fountain of water in the
wilderness, by the fountain on the way to Shur. 8 He said,
"Hagar, Sarai's servant, where did you come from? Where are
you going?"
She said, "I am fleeing from the face of my mistress Sarai."
9 God's angel said to her, "Return to your mistress, and submit
yourself under her hands." 10 God's angel said to her, "I will
greatly multiply your offspring, that they will not be counted for
multitude." 11 God's angel said to her, "Behold, you are with
child, and will bear a son. You shall call his name Ishmael,
because God has heard your affliction. 12 He will be like a wild
donkey among men. His hand will be against every man, and
every man's hand against him. He will live opposed to all of his
brothers."
13 She called the name of God who spoke to her, "You are a
God who sees," for she said, "Have I even stayed alive after
seeing him?" 14 Therefore the well was called Beer Lahai
Roi.[17] Behold, it is between Kadesh and Bered.
15 Hagar bore a son for Abram. Abram called the name of his
son, whom Hagar bore, Ishmael. 16 Abram was eighty-six years
old when Hagar bore Ishmael to Abram.

Genesis 17

1 When Abram was ninety-nine years old, God appeared to
Abram and said to him, "I am God Almighty. Walk before me
and be blameless. 2 I will make my covenant between me and
you, and will multiply you exceedingly."
3 Abram fell on his face. God talked with him, saying, 4 "As
for me, behold, my covenant is with you. You will be the father
of a multitude of nations. 5 Your name will no more be called
Abram, but your name will be Abraham; for I have made you the
father of a multitude of nations. 6 I will make you exceedingly
fruitful, and I will make nations of you. Kings will come out of
you. 7 I will establish my covenant between me and you and
your offspring after you throughout their generations for an
everlasting covenant, to be a God to you and to your offspring
after you. 8 I will give to you, and to your offspring after you,
the land where you are traveling, all the land of Canaan, for an
everlasting possession. I will be their God."
9 God said to Abraham, "As for you, you will keep my
covenant, you and your offspring after you throughout their
generations. 10 This is my covenant, which you shall keep,
between me and you and your offspring after you. Every male
among you shall be circumcised. 11 You shall be circumcised
in the flesh of your foreskin. It will be a token of the covenant
between me and you. 12 He who is eight days old will be
circumcised among you, every male throughout your generations,
he who is born in the house, or bought with money from any
foreigner who is not of your offspring. 13 He who is born in
your house, and he who is bought with your money, must be
circumcised. My covenant will be in your flesh for an everlasting
covenant. 14 The uncircumcised male who is not circumcised in
the flesh of his foreskin, that soul shall be cut off from his people.
He has broken my covenant."
15 God said to Abraham, "As for Sarai your wife, you shall not
call her name Sarai, but her name will be Sarah. 16 I will bless
her, and moreover I will give you a son by her. Yes, I will bless
her, and she will be a mother of nations. Kings of peoples will
come from her."
17 Then Abraham fell on his face, and laughed, and said in his
heart, "Will a child be born to him who is one hundred years old?
Will Sarah, who is ninety years old, give birth?" 18 Abraham
said to God, "Oh that Ishmael might live before you!"
19 God said, "No, but Sarah, your wife, will bear you a son.
You shall call his name Isaac.[18] I will establish my covenant with
him for an everlasting covenant for his offspring after him.
20 As for Ishmael, I have heard you. Behold, I have blessed
him, and will make him fruitful, and will multiply him
exceedingly. He will become the father of twelve princes, and I

---

[16] **15:2** *15:2* **The word translated "Lord" is "Adonai".**

[17] **16:14** *16:14* **Beer Lahai Roi means "well of the one who lives and sees me".**

[18] **17:19** *17:19* **Isaac means "he laughs".**

will make him a great nation. **21** But I will establish my
covenant with Isaac, whom Sarah will bear to you at this set time
next year."
22 When he finished talking with him, God went up from
Abraham. **23** Abraham took Ishmael his son, all who were born
in his house, and all who were bought with his money: every
male among the men of Abraham's house, and circumcised the
flesh of their foreskin in the same day, as God had said to him.
24 Abraham was ninety-nine years old when he was
circumcised in the flesh of his foreskin. **25** Ishmael, his son,
was thirteen years old when he was circumcised in the flesh of
his foreskin. **26** In the same day both Abraham and Ishmael, his
son, were circumcised. **27** All the men of his house, those born
in the house, and those bought with money from a foreigner,
were circumcised with him.

Genesis 18

1 God appeared to him by the oaks of Mamre, as he sat in the
tent door in the heat of the day. **2** He lifted up his eyes and
looked, and saw that three men stood near him. When he saw
them, he ran to meet them from the tent door, and bowed himself
to the earth, **3** and said, "My lord, if now I have found favor in
your sight, please don't go away from your servant. **4** Now let a
little water be fetched, wash your feet, and rest yourselves under
the tree. **5** I will get a piece of bread so you can refresh your
heart. After that you may go your way, now that you have come
to your servant."
They said, "Very well, do as you have said."
6 Abraham hurried into the tent to Sarah, and said, "Quickly
prepare three seahs[19] of fine meal, knead it, and make cakes."
7 Abraham ran to the herd, and fetched a tender and good calf,
and gave it to the servant. He hurried to dress it. **8** He took
butter, milk, and the calf which he had dressed, and set it before
them. He stood by them under the tree, and they ate.
9 They asked him, "Where is Sarah, your wife?"
He said, "There, in the tent."
10 He said, "I will certainly return to you at about this time next
year; and behold, Sarah your wife will have a son."
Sarah heard in the tent door, which was behind him. **11** Now
Abraham and Sarah were old, well advanced in age. Sarah had
passed the age of childbearing. **12** Sarah laughed within herself,
saying, "After I have grown old will I have pleasure, my lord
being old also?"
13 God said to Abraham, "Why did Sarah laugh, saying, 'Will I
really bear a child when I am old?' **14** Is anything too hard for
God? At the set time I will return to you, when the season comes
round, and Sarah will have a son."
15 Then Sarah denied it, saying, "I didn't laugh," for she was
afraid.
He said, "No, but you did laugh."
16 The men rose up from there, and looked toward Sodom.
Abraham went with them to see them on their way. **17** God
said, "Will I hide from Abraham what I do, **18** since Abraham
will surely become a great and mighty nation, and all the nations
of the earth will be blessed in him? **19** For I have known him, to
the end that he may command his children and his household
after him, that they may keep the way of God, to do righteousness
and justice; to the end that God may bring on Abraham that
which he has spoken of him." **20** God said, "Because the cry of
Sodom and Gomorrah is great, and because their sin is very
grievous, **21** I will go down now, and see whether their deeds
are as bad as the reports which have come to me. If not, I will
know."
22 The men turned from there, and went toward Sodom, but
Abraham stood yet before God. **23** Abraham came near, and
said, "Will you consume the righteous with the wicked?
24 What if there are fifty righteous within the city? Will you
consume and not spare the place for the fifty righteous who are in
it? **25** May it be far from you to do things like that, to kill the
righteous with the wicked, so that the righteous should be like the
wicked. May that be far from you. Shouldn't the Judge of all the
earth do right?"
26 God said, "If I find in Sodom fifty righteous within the city,
then I will spare the whole place for their sake." **27** Abraham
answered, "See now, I have taken it on myself to speak to the
Lord, although I am dust and ashes. **28** What if there will lack
five of the fifty righteous? Will you destroy all the city for lack of
five?"
He said, "I will not destroy it if I find forty-five there."
29 He spoke to him yet again, and said, "What if there are forty
found there?"
He said, "I will not do it for the forty's sake."
30 He said, "Oh don't let the Lord be angry, and I will speak.
What if there are thirty found there?"
He said, "I will not do it if I find thirty there."
31 He said, "See now, I have taken it on myself to speak to the
Lord. What if there are twenty found there?"
He said, "I will not destroy it for the twenty's sake."
32 He said, "Oh don't let the Lord be angry, and I will speak
just once more. What if ten are found there?"
He said, "I will not destroy it for the ten's sake."
33 God went his way, as soon as he had finished communing
with Abraham, and Abraham returned to his place.

Genesis 19

1 The two angels came to Sodom at evening. Lot sat in the gate
of Sodom. Lot saw them, and rose up to meet them. He bowed
himself with his face to the earth, **2** and he said, "See now, my
lords, please come into your servant's house, stay all night, wash
your feet, and you can rise up early, and go on your way."
They said, "No, but we will stay in the street all night."
3 He urged them greatly, and they came in with him, and
entered into his house. He made them a feast, and baked
unleavened bread, and they ate. **4** But before they lay down, the
men of the city, the men of Sodom, surrounded the house, both
young and old, all the people from every quarter. **5** They called
to Lot, and said to him, "Where are the men who came in to you
this night? Bring them out to us, that we may have sex with
them."
6 Lot went out to them through the door, and shut the door after
himself. **7** He said, "Please, my brothers, don't act so wickedly.
8 See now, I have two virgin daughters. Please let me bring
them out to you, and you may do to them what seems good to
you. Only don't do anything to these men, because they have
come under the shadow of my roof."
9 They said, "Stand back!" Then they said, "This one fellow
came in to live as a foreigner, and he appoints himself a judge.
Now we will deal worse with you than with them!" They pressed
hard on the man Lot, and came near to break the door. **10** But
the men reached out their hand, and brought Lot into the house to
them, and shut the door. **11** They struck the men who were at
the door of the house with blindness, both small and great, so that
they wearied themselves to find the door.
12 The men said to Lot, "Do you have anybody else here?
Sons-in-law, your sons, your daughters, and whomever you have
in the city, bring them out of the place: **13** for we will destroy
this place, because the outcry against them has grown so great
before God that God has sent us to destroy it."
14 Lot went out, and spoke to his sons-in-law, who were
pledged to marry his daughters, and said, "Get up! Get out of this
place, for God will destroy the city!"
But he seemed to his sons-in-law to be joking. **15** When the
morning came, then the angels hurried Lot, saying, "Get up! Take
your wife and your two daughters who are here, lest you be
consumed in the iniquity of the city." **16** But he lingered; and
the men grabbed his hand, his wife's hand, and his two
daughters' hands, God being merciful to him; and they took him
out, and set him outside of the city. **17** It came to pass, when
they had taken them out, that he said, "Escape for your life!
Don't look behind you, and don't stay anywhere in the plain.
Escape to the mountains, lest you be consumed!"
18 Lot said to them, "Oh, not so, my lord. **19** See now, your
servant has found favor in your sight, and you have magnified
your loving kindness, which you have shown to me in saving my
life. I can't escape to the mountain, lest evil overtake me, and I
die. **20** See now, this city is near to flee to, and it is a little one.
Oh let me escape there (isn't it a little one?), and my soul will
live."
21 He said to him, "Behold, I have granted your request
concerning this thing also, that I will not overthrow the city of
which you have spoken. **22** Hurry, escape there, for I can't do
anything until you get there." Therefore the name of the city was
called Zoar.[20]
23 The sun had risen on the earth when Lot came to Zoar.
24 Then God rained on Sodom and on Gomorrah sulfur and fire
from God out of the sky. **25** He overthrew those cities, all the
plain, all the inhabitants of the cities, and that which grew on the
ground. **26** But Lot's wife looked back from behind him, and
she became a pillar of salt.
27 Abraham went up early in the morning to the place where he
had stood before God. **28** He looked toward Sodom and
Gomorrah, and toward all the land of the plain, and saw that the
smoke of the land went up as the smoke of a furnace.
29 When God destroyed the cities of the plain, God
remembered Abraham, and sent Lot out of the middle of the
overthrow, when he overthrew the cities in which Lot lived.
30 Lot went up out of Zoar, and lived in the mountain, and his
two daughters with him; for he was afraid to live in Zoar. He
lived in a cave with his two daughters. **31** The firstborn said to
the younger, "Our father is old, and there is not a man in the earth
to come in to us in the way of all the earth. **32** Come, let's make
our father drink wine, and we will lie with him, that we may
preserve our father's family line." **33** They made their father
drink wine that night: and the firstborn went in, and lay with her
father. He didn't know when she lay down, nor when she arose.
34 It came to pass on the next day, that the firstborn said to the
younger, "Behold, I lay last night with my father. Let's make him
drink wine again tonight. You go in, and lie with him, that we
may preserve our father's family line." **35** They made their
father drink wine that night also. The younger went and lay with
him. He didn't know when she lay down, nor when she got up.
36 Thus both of Lot's daughters were with child by their father.
37 The firstborn bore a son, and named him Moab. He is the
father of the Moabites to this day. **38** The younger also bore a
son, and called his name Ben Ammi. He is the father of the
children of Ammon to this day.

Genesis 20

1 Abraham traveled from there toward the land of the South,
and lived between Kadesh and Shur. He lived as a foreigner in
Gerar. **2** Abraham said about Sarah his wife, "She is my sister."
Abimelech king of Gerar sent, and took Sarah. **3** But God came
to Abimelech in a dream of the night, and said to him, "Behold,
you are a dead man, because of the woman whom you have
taken; for she is a man's wife."
4 Now Abimelech had not come near her. He said, "Lord, will
you kill even a righteous nation? **5** Didn't he tell me, 'She is my
sister'? She, even she herself, said, 'He is my brother.' I have
done this in the integrity of my heart and the innocence of my
hands."
6 God said to him in the dream, "Yes, I know that in the
integrity of your heart you have done this, and I also withheld
you from sinning against me. Therefore I didn't allow you to
touch her. **7** Now therefore, restore the man's wife. For he is a
prophet, and he will pray for you, and you will live. If you don't
restore her, know for sure that you will die, you, and all who are
yours."
8 Abimelech rose early in the morning, and called all his
servants, and told all these things in their ear. The men were very
scared. **9** Then Abimelech called Abraham, and said to him,
"What have you done to us? How have I sinned against you, that
you have brought on me and on my kingdom a great sin? You
have done deeds to me that ought not to be done!"
10 Abimelech said to Abraham, "What did you see, that you
have done this thing?"
11 Abraham said, "Because I thought, 'Surely the fear of God is
not in this place. They will kill me for my wife's sake.'
12 Besides, she is indeed my sister, the daughter of my father,
but not the daughter of my mother; and she became my wife.
13 When God caused me to wander from my father's house, I
said to her, 'This is your kindness which you shall show to me.
Everywhere that we go, say of me, "He is my brother."'"
14 Abimelech took sheep and cattle, male servants and female
servants, and gave them to Abraham, and restored Sarah, his
wife, to him. **15** Abimelech said, "Behold, my land is before
you. Dwell where it pleases you." **16** To Sarah he said,
"Behold, I have given your brother a thousand pieces of silver.
Behold, it is for you a covering of the eyes to all that are with
you. In front of all you are vindicated."
17 Abraham prayed to God. God healed Abimelech, and his
wife, and his female servants, and they bore children. **18** For
God had closed up tight all the wombs of the house of
Abimelech, because of Sarah, Abraham's wife.

---

[19] **18:6** *18:6* 1 seah is about 7 liters or 1.9 gallons or 0.8 pecks

[20] **19:22** *19:22* Zoar means "little".

Genesis 21

1 God visited Sarah as he had said, and God did to Sarah as he
had spoken. 2 Sarah conceived, and bore Abraham a son in his
old age, at the set time of which God had spoken to him.
3 Abraham called his son who was born to him, whom Sarah
bore to him, Isaac.[21] 4 Abraham circumcised his son, Isaac,
when he was eight days old, as God had commanded him.
5 Abraham was one hundred years old when his son, Isaac, was
born to him. 6 Sarah said, "God has made me laugh. Everyone
who hears will laugh with me." 7 She said, "Who would have
said to Abraham that Sarah would nurse children? For I have
borne him a son in his old age."
8 The child grew and was weaned. Abraham made a great feast
on the day that Isaac was weaned. 9 Sarah saw the son of Hagar
the Egyptian, whom she had borne to Abraham, mocking.
10 Therefore she said to Abraham, "Cast out this servant and
her son! For the son of this servant will not be heir with my son,
Isaac."
11 The thing was very grievous in Abraham's sight on account
of his son. 12 God said to Abraham, "Don't let it be grievous in
your sight because of the boy, and because of your servant. In all
that Sarah says to you, listen to her voice. For your offspring will
be named through Isaac. 13 I will also make a nation of the son
of the servant, because he is your child." 14 Abraham rose up
early in the morning, and took bread and a container of water,
and gave it to Hagar, putting it on her shoulder; and gave her the
child, and sent her away. She departed, and wandered in the
wilderness of Beersheba. 15 The water in the container was
spent, and she put the child under one of the shrubs. 16 She
went and sat down opposite him, a good way off, about a bow
shot away. For she said, "Don't let me see the death of the child."
She sat opposite him, and lifted up her voice, and wept. 17 God
heard the voice of the boy.
The angel of God called to Hagar out of the sky, and said to her,
"What troubles you, Hagar? Don't be afraid. For God has heard
the voice of the boy where he is. 18 Get up, lift up the boy, and
hold him with your hand. For I will make him a great nation."
19 God opened her eyes, and she saw a well of water. She went,
filled the container with water, and gave the boy a drink.
20 God was with the boy, and he grew. He lived in the
wilderness, and as he grew up, became an archer. 21 He lived in
the wilderness of Paran. His mother got a wife for him out of the
land of Egypt.
22 At that time, Abimelech and Phicol the captain of his army
spoke to Abraham, saying, "God is with you in all that you do.
23 Now, therefore, swear to me here by God that you will not
deal falsely with me, nor with my son, nor with my son's son.
But according to the kindness that I have done to you, you shall
do to me, and to the land in which you have lived as a foreigner."
24 Abraham said, "I will swear." 25 Abraham complained to
Abimelech because of a water well, which Abimelech's servants
had violently taken away. 26 Abimelech said, "I don't know
who has done this thing. You didn't tell me, and I didn't hear of it
until today."
27 Abraham took sheep and cattle, and gave them to
Abimelech. Those two made a covenant. 28 Abraham set seven
ewe lambs of the flock by themselves. 29 Abimelech said to
Abraham, "What do these seven ewe lambs, which you have set
by themselves, mean?"
30 He said, "You shall take these seven ewe lambs from my
hand, that it may be a witness to me, that I have dug this well."
31 Therefore he called that place Beersheba,[22] because they
both swore an oath there. 32 So they made a covenant at
Beersheba. Abimelech rose up with Phicol, the captain of his
army, and they returned into the land of the Philistines.
33 Abraham planted a tamarisk tree in Beersheba, and called
there on the name of God, the Everlasting God. 34 Abraham
lived as a foreigner in the land of the Philistines many days.

Genesis 22

1 After these things, God tested Abraham, and said to him,
"Abraham!"
He said, "Here I am."
2 He said, "Now take your son, your only son, Isaac, whom you
love, and go into the land of Moriah. Offer him there as a burnt
offering on one of the mountains which I will tell you of."
3 Abraham rose early in the morning, and saddled his donkey;
and took two of his young men with him, and Isaac his son. He
split the wood for the burnt offering, and rose up, and went to the
place of which God had told him. 4 On the third day Abraham
lifted up his eyes, and saw the place far off. 5 Abraham said to
his young men, "Stay here with the donkey. The boy and I will
go over there. We will worship, and come back to you."
6 Abraham took the wood of the burnt offering and laid it on
Isaac his son. He took in his hand the fire and the knife. They
both went together. 7 Isaac spoke to Abraham his father, and
said, "My father?"
He said, "Here I am, my son."
He said, "Here is the fire and the wood, but where is the lamb for
a burnt offering?"
8 Abraham said, "God will provide himself the lamb for a burnt
offering, my son." So they both went together. 9 They came to
the place which God had told him of. Abraham built the altar
there, and laid the wood in order, bound Isaac his son, and laid
him on the altar, on the wood. 10 Abraham stretched out his
hand, and took the knife to kill his son.
11 God's angel called to him out of the sky, and said,
"Abraham, Abraham!"
He said, "Here I am."
12 He said, "Don't lay your hand on the boy or do anything to
him. For now I know that you fear God, since you have not
withheld your son, your only son, from me."
13 Abraham lifted up his eyes, and looked, and saw that behind
him was a ram caught in the thicket by his horns. Abraham went
and took the ram, and offered him up for a burnt offering instead
of his son. 14 Abraham called the name of that place "God Will
Provide".[23] As it is said to this day, "On God's mountain, it will
be provided."
15 God's angel called to Abraham a second time out of the sky,
16 and said, "'I have sworn by myself,' says God, 'because you
have done this thing, and have not withheld your son, your only
son, 17 that I will bless you greatly, and I will multiply your
offspring greatly like the stars of the heavens, and like the sand
which is on the seashore. Your offspring will possess the gate of
his enemies. 18 All the nations of the earth will be blessed by
your offspring, because you have obeyed my voice.'"
19 So Abraham returned to his young men, and they rose up
and went together to Beersheba. Abraham lived at Beersheba.
20 After these things, Abraham was told, "Behold, Milcah, she
also has borne children to your brother Nahor: 21 Uz his
firstborn, Buz his brother, Kemuel the father of Aram,
22 Chesed, Hazo, Pildash, Jidlaph, and Bethuel." 23 Bethuel
became the father of Rebekah. These eight Milcah bore to Nahor,
Abraham's brother. 24 His concubine, whose name was
Reumah, also bore Tebah, Gaham, Tahash, and Maacah.

Genesis 23

1 Sarah lived one hundred twenty-seven years. This was the
length of Sarah's life. 2 Sarah died in Kiriath Arba (also called
Hebron), in the land of Canaan. Abraham came to mourn for
Sarah, and to weep for her. 3 Abraham rose up from before his
dead and spoke to the children of Heth, saying, 4 "I am a
stranger and a foreigner living with you. Give me a possession of
a burying-place with you, that I may bury my dead out of my
sight."
5 The children of Heth answered Abraham, saying to him,
6 "Hear us, my lord. You are a prince of God among us. Bury
your dead in the best of our tombs. None of us will withhold from
you his tomb. Bury your dead."
7 Abraham rose up, and bowed himself to the people of the
land, to the children of Heth. 8 He talked with them, saying, "If
you agree that I should bury my dead out of my sight, hear me,
and entreat for me to Ephron the son of Zohar, 9 that he may
sell me the cave of Machpelah, which he has, which is in the end
of his field. For the full price let him sell it to me among you as a
possession for a burial place."
10 Now Ephron was sitting in the middle of the children of
Heth. Ephron the Hittite answered Abraham in the hearing of the
children of Heth, even of all who went in at the gate of his city,
saying, 11 "No, my lord, hear me. I give you the field, and I
give you the cave that is in it. In the presence of the children of
my people I give it to you. Bury your dead."
12 Abraham bowed himself down before the people of the land.
13 He spoke to Ephron in the audience of the people of the land,
saying, "But if you will, please hear me. I will give the price of
the field. Take it from me, and I will bury my dead there."
14 Ephron answered Abraham, saying to him, 15 "My lord,
listen to me. What is a piece of land worth four hundred shekels
of silver[24] between me and you? Therefore bury your dead."
16 Abraham listened to Ephron. Abraham weighed to Ephron
the silver which he had named in the hearing of the children of
Heth, four hundred shekels of silver, according to the current
merchants' standard.
17 So the field of Ephron, which was in Machpelah, which was
before Mamre, the field, the cave which was in it, and all the
trees that were in the field, that were in all of its borders, were
deeded 18 to Abraham for a possession in the presence of the
children of Heth, before all who went in at the gate of his city.
19 After this, Abraham buried Sarah his wife in the cave of the
field of Machpelah before Mamre (that is, Hebron), in the land of
Canaan. 20 The field, and the cave that is in it, were deeded to
Abraham by the children of Heth as a possession for a burial
place.

Genesis 24

1 Abraham was old, and well advanced in age. God had blessed
Abraham in all things. 2 Abraham said to his servant, the elder
of his house, who ruled over all that he had, "Please put your
hand under my thigh. 3 I will make you swear by God, the God
of heaven and the God of the earth, that you shall not take a wife
for my son of the daughters of the Canaanites, among whom I
live. 4 But you shall go to my country, and to my relatives, and
take a wife for my son Isaac."
5 The servant said to him, "What if the woman isn't willing to
follow me to this land? Must I bring your son again to the land
you came from?"
6 Abraham said to him, "Beware that you don't bring my son
there again. 7 God, the God of heaven—who took me from my
father's house, and from the land of my birth, who spoke to me,
and who swore to me, saying, 'I will give this land to your
offspring—he will send his angel before you, and you shall take a
wife for my son from there. 8 If the woman isn't willing to
follow you, then you shall be clear from this oath to me. Only
you shall not bring my son there again."
9 The servant put his hand under the thigh of Abraham his
master, and swore to him concerning this matter. 10 The servant
took ten of his master's camels, and departed, having a variety of
good things of his master's with him. He arose, and went to
Mesopotamia, to the city of Nahor. 11 He made the camels
kneel down outside the city by the well of water at the time of
evening, the time that women go out to draw water. 12 He said,
"God, the God of my master Abraham, please give me success
today, and show kindness to my master Abraham. 13 Behold, I
am standing by the spring of water. The daughters of the men of
the city are coming out to draw water. 14 Let it happen, that the
young lady to whom I will say, 'Please let down your pitcher,
that I may drink,' then she says, 'Drink, and I will also give your
camels a drink,'—let her be the one you have appointed for your
servant Isaac. By this I will know that you have shown kindness
to my master."
15 Before he had finished speaking, behold, Rebekah came out,
who was born to Bethuel the son of Milcah, the wife of Nahor,
Abraham's brother, with her pitcher on her shoulder. 16 The
young lady was very beautiful to look at, a virgin. No man had
known her. She went down to the spring, filled her pitcher, and
came up. 17 The servant ran to meet her, and said, "Please give
me a drink, a little water from your pitcher."
18 She said, "Drink, my lord." She hurried, and let down her
pitcher on her hand, and gave him a drink. 19 When she had
finished giving him a drink, she said, "I will also draw for your
camels, until they have finished drinking." 20 She hurried, and
emptied her pitcher into the trough, and ran again to the well to
draw, and drew for all his camels.
21 The man looked steadfastly at her, remaining silent, to know
whether God had made his journey prosperous or not. 22 As the
camels had done drinking, the man took a golden ring of half a
shekel[25] weight, and two bracelets for her hands of ten shekels

---

[21] **21:3** *21:3* Isaac means "He laughs".

[22] **21:31** *21:31* Beersheba can mean "well of the oath" or "well of seven".

[23] **22:14** *22:14* or, God-Jireh, or, God-Seeing

[24] **23:15** *23:15* A shekel is about 10 grams, so 400 shekels would be about 4 kg. or 8.8 pounds.

[25] **24:22** *24:22* A shekel is about 10 grams or about 0.35 ounces.

weight of gold, 23 and said, "Whose daughter are you? Please
tell me. Is there room in your father's house for us to stay?"

24 She said to him, "I am the daughter of Bethuel the son of
Milcah, whom she bore to Nahor." 25 She said moreover to
him, "We have both straw and feed enough, and room to lodge
in."

26 The man bowed his head, and worshiped God. 27 He said,
"Blessed be God, the God of my master Abraham, who has not
forsaken his loving kindness and his truth toward my master. As
for me, God has led me on the way to the house of my master's
relatives."

28 The young lady ran, and told her mother's house about these
words. 29 Rebekah had a brother, and his name was Laban.
Laban ran out to the man, to the spring. 30 When he saw the
ring, and the bracelets on his sister's hands, and when he heard
the words of Rebekah his sister, saying, "This is what the man
said to me," he came to the man. Behold, he was standing by the
camels at the spring. 31 He said, "Come in, you blessed of God.
Why do you stand outside? For I have prepared the house, and
room for the camels."

32 The man came into the house, and he unloaded the camels.
He gave straw and feed for the camels, and water to wash his feet
and the feet of the men who were with him. 33 Food was set
before him to eat, but he said, "I will not eat until I have told my
message."
Laban said, "Speak on."

34 He said, "I am Abraham's servant. 35 God has blessed my
master greatly. He has become great. God has given him flocks
and herds, silver and gold, male servants and female servants,
and camels and donkeys. 36 Sarah, my master's wife, bore a
son to my master when she was old. He has given all that he has
to him. 37 My master made me swear, saying, 'You shall not
take a wife for my son from the daughters of the Canaanites, in
whose land I live, 38 but you shall go to my father's house, and
to my relatives, and take a wife for my son.' 39 I asked my
master, 'What if the woman will not follow me?' 40 He said to
me, 'God, before whom I walk, will send his angel with you, and
prosper your way. You shall take a wife for my son from my
relatives, and of my father's house. 41 Then you will be clear
from my oath, when you come to my relatives. If they don't give
her to you, you shall be clear from my oath.' 42 I came today to
the spring, and said, 'God, the God of my master Abraham, if
now you do prosper my way which I go— 43 behold, I am
standing by this spring of water. Let it happen, that the maiden
who comes out to draw, to whom I will say, "Please give me a
little water from your pitcher to drink," 44 then she tells me,
"Drink, and I will also draw for your camels,"—let her be the
woman whom God has appointed for my master's son.'

45 Before I had finished speaking in my heart, behold, Rebekah
came out with her pitcher on her shoulder. She went down to the
spring, and drew. I said to her, 'Please let me drink.' 46 She
hurried and let down her pitcher from her shoulder, and said,
'Drink, and I will also give your camels a drink.' So I drank, and
she also gave the camels a drink. 47 I asked her, and said,
'Whose daughter are you?' She said, 'The daughter of Bethuel,
Nahor's son, whom Milcah bore to him.' I put the ring on her
nose, and the bracelets on her hands. 48 I bowed my head, and
worshiped God, and blessed God, the God of my master
Abraham, who had led me in the right way to take my master's
brother's daughter for his son. 49 Now if you will deal kindly
and truly with my master, tell me. If not, tell me, that I may turn
to the right hand, or to the left."

50 Then Laban and Bethuel answered, "The thing proceeds
from God. We can't speak to you bad or good. 51 Behold,
Rebekah is before you. Take her, and go, and let her be your
master's son's wife, as God has spoken."

52 When Abraham's servant heard their words, he bowed
himself down to the earth to God. 53 The servant brought out
jewels of silver, and jewels of gold, and clothing, and gave them
to Rebekah. He also gave precious things to her brother and her
mother. 54 They ate and drank, he and the men who were with
him, and stayed all night. They rose up in the morning, and he
said, "Send me away to my master."

55 Her brother and her mother said, "Let the young lady stay
with us a few days, at least ten. After that she will go."

56 He said to them, "Don't hinder me, since God has prospered
my way. Send me away that I may go to my master."

57 They said, "We will call the young lady, and ask her."

58 They called Rebekah, and said to her, "Will you go with this
man?"
She said, "I will go."

59 They sent away Rebekah, their sister, with her nurse,
Abraham's servant, and his men. 60 They blessed Rebekah, and
said to her, "Our sister, may you be the mother of thousands of
ten thousands, and let your offspring possess the gate of those
who hate them."

61 Rebekah arose with her ladies. They rode on the camels, and
followed the man. The servant took Rebekah, and went his way.

62 Isaac came from the way of Beer Lahai Roi, for he lived in
the land of the South. 63 Isaac went out to meditate in the field
at the evening. He lifted up his eyes and looked. Behold, there
were camels coming. 64 Rebekah lifted up her eyes, and when
she saw Isaac, she got off the camel. 65 She said to the servant,
"Who is the man who is walking in the field to meet us?"
The servant said, "It is my master."
She took her veil, and covered herself. 66 The servant told Isaac
all the things that he had done. 67 Isaac brought her into his
mother Sarah's tent, and took Rebekah, and she became his wife.
He loved her. So Isaac was comforted after his mother's death.

Genesis 25

1 Abraham took another wife, and her name was Keturah.

2 She bore him Zimran, Jokshan, Medan, Midian, Ishbak, and
Shuah. 3 Jokshan became the father of Sheba, and Dedan. The
sons of Dedan were Asshurim, Letushim, and Leummim. 4 The
sons of Midian were Ephah, Epher, Hanoch, Abida, and Eldaah.
All these were the children of Keturah. 5 Abraham gave all that
he had to Isaac, 6 but Abraham gave gifts to the sons of
Abraham's concubines. While he still lived, he sent them away
from Isaac his son, eastward, to the east country. 7 These are
the days of the years of Abraham's life which he lived: one
hundred seventy-five years. 8 Abraham gave up his spirit, and
died at a good old age, an old man, and full of years, and was
gathered to his people. 9 Isaac and Ishmael, his sons, buried him
in the cave of Machpelah, in the field of Ephron, the son of Zohar
the Hittite, which is near Mamre, 10 the field which Abraham
purchased from the children of Heth. Abraham was buried there
with Sarah, his wife. 11 After the death of Abraham, God
blessed Isaac, his son. Isaac lived by Beer Lahai Roi.

12 Now this is the history of the generations of Ishmael,
Abraham's son, whom Hagar the Egyptian, Sarah's servant, bore
to Abraham. 13 These are the names of the sons of Ishmael, by
their names, according to the order of their birth: the firstborn of
Ishmael, Nebaioth, then Kedar, Adbeel, Mibsam, 14 Mishma,
Dumah, Massa, 15 Hadad, Tema, Jetur, Naphish, and Kedemah.

16 These are the sons of Ishmael, and these are their names, by
their villages, and by their encampments: twelve princes,
according to their nations. 17 These are the years of the life of
Ishmael: one hundred thirty-seven years. He gave up his spirit
and died, and was gathered to his people. 18 They lived from
Havilah to Shur that is before Egypt, as you go toward Assyria.
He lived opposite all his relatives.

19 This is the history of the generations of Isaac, Abraham's
son. Abraham became the father of Isaac. 20 Isaac was forty
years old when he took Rebekah, the daughter of Bethuel the
Syrian of Paddan Aram, the sister of Laban the Syrian, to be his
wife. 21 Isaac entreated God for his wife, because she was
barren. God was entreated by him, and Rebekah his wife
conceived. 22 The children struggled together within her. She
said, "If it is like this, why do I live?" She went to inquire of
God. 23 God said to her,
"Two nations are in your womb.
Two peoples will be separated from your body.
The one people will be stronger than the other people.
The elder will serve the younger."

24 When her days to be delivered were fulfilled, behold, there
were twins in her womb. 25 The first came out red all over, like
a hairy garment. They named him Esau. 26 After that, his
brother came out, and his hand had hold on Esau's heel. He was
named Jacob. Isaac was sixty years old when she bore them.

27 The boys grew. Esau was a skillful hunter, a man of the
field. Jacob was a quiet man, living in tents. 28 Now Isaac
loved Esau, because he ate his venison. Rebekah loved Jacob.

29 Jacob boiled stew. Esau came in from the field, and he was
famished. 30 Esau said to Jacob, "Please feed me with some of
that red stew, for I am famished." Therefore his name was called
Edom.[26]

31 Jacob said, "First, sell me your birthright."

32 Esau said, "Behold, I am about to die. What good is the
birthright to me?"

33 Jacob said, "Swear to me first."
He swore to him. He sold his birthright to Jacob. 34 Jacob gave
Esau bread and lentil stew. He ate and drank, rose up, and went
his way. So Esau despised his birthright.

Genesis 26

1 There was a famine in the land, in addition to the first famine
that was in the days of Abraham. Isaac went to Abimelech king
of the Philistines, to Gerar. 2 God appeared to him, and said,
"Don't go down into Egypt. Live in the land I will tell you about.

3 Live in this land, and I will be with you, and will bless you.
For I will give to you, and to your offspring, all these lands, and I
will establish the oath which I swore to Abraham your father.

4 I will multiply your offspring as the stars of the sky, and will
give all these lands to your offspring. In your offspring all the
nations of the earth will be blessed, 5 because Abraham obeyed
my voice, and kept my requirements, my commandments, my
statutes, and my laws."

6 Isaac lived in Gerar. 7 The men of the place asked him about
his wife. He said, "She is my sister," for he was afraid to say,
"My wife", lest, he thought, "the men of the place might kill me
for Rebekah, because she is beautiful to look at." 8 When he
had been there a long time, Abimelech king of the Philistines
looked out at a window, and saw, and, behold, Isaac was
caressing Rebekah, his wife. 9 Abimelech called Isaac, and
said, "Behold, surely she is your wife. Why did you say, 'She is
my sister?'"
Isaac said to him, "Because I said, 'Lest I die because of her.'"

10 Abimelech said, "What is this you have done to us? One of
the people might easily have lain with your wife, and you would
have brought guilt on us!"

11 Abimelech commanded all the people, saying, "He who
touches this man or his wife will surely be put to death."

12 Isaac sowed in that land, and reaped in the same year one
hundred times what he planted. God blessed him. 13 The man
grew great, and grew more and more until he became very great.

14 He had possessions of flocks, possessions of herds, and a
great household. The Philistines envied him. 15 Now all the
wells which his father's servants had dug in the days of Abraham
his father, the Philistines had stopped, and filled with earth.

16 Abimelech said to Isaac, "Go away from us, for you are
much mightier than we."

17 Isaac departed from there, encamped in the valley of Gerar,
and lived there.

18 Isaac dug again the wells of water, which they had dug in the
days of Abraham his father, for the Philistines had stopped them
after the death of Abraham. He called their names after the names
by which his father had called them. 19 Isaac's servants dug in
the valley, and found there a well of springing water. 20 The
herdsmen of Gerar argued with Isaac's herdsmen, saying, "The
water is ours." He called the name of the well Esek, because they
contended with him. 21 They dug another well, and they argued
over that, also. He called its name Sitnah. 22 He left that place,
and dug another well. They didn't argue over that one. He called
it Rehoboth. He said, "For now God has made room for us, and
we will be fruitful in the land."

23 He went up from there to Beersheba. 24 God appeared to
him the same night, and said, "I am the God of Abraham your
father. Don't be afraid, for I am with you, and will bless you, and
multiply your offspring for my servant Abraham's sake."

25 He built an altar there, and called on God's name, and
pitched his tent there. There Isaac's servants dug a well.

26 Then Abimelech went to him from Gerar, and Ahuzzath his
friend, and Phicol the captain of his army. 27 Isaac said to them,
"Why have you come to me, since you hate me, and have sent me
away from you?"

28 They said, "We saw plainly that God was with you. We said,
'Let there now be an oath between us, even between us and you,
and let's make a covenant with you, 29 that you will do us no
harm, as we have not touched you, and as we have done to you
nothing but good, and have sent you away in peace.' You are
now the blessed of God."

[26] **25:30** *25:30* **"Edom" means "red".**

30 He made them a feast, and they ate and drank. **31** They rose up some time in the morning, and swore an oath to one another. Isaac sent them away, and they departed from him in peace. **32** The same day, Isaac's servants came, and told him concerning the well which they had dug, and said to him, "We have found water." **33** He called it "Shibah".[27] Therefore the name of the city is "Beersheba"[28] to this day.

34 When Esau was forty years old, he took as wife Judith, the daughter of Beeri the Hittite, and Basemath, the daughter of Elon the Hittite. **35** They grieved Isaac's and Rebekah's spirits.

Genesis 27

1 When Isaac was old, and his eyes were dim, so that he could not see, he called Esau his elder son, and said to him, "My son?" He said to him, "Here I am."

2 He said, "See now, I am old. I don't know the day of my death. **3** Now therefore, please take your weapons, your quiver and your bow, and go out to the field, and get me venison.

4 Make me savory food, such as I love, and bring it to me, that I may eat, and that my soul may bless you before I die."

5 Rebekah heard when Isaac spoke to Esau his son. Esau went to the field to hunt for venison, and to bring it. **6** Rebekah spoke to Jacob her son, saying, "Behold, I heard your father speak to Esau your brother, saying, **7** 'Bring me venison, and make me savory food, that I may eat, and bless you before God before my death.' **8** Now therefore, my son, obey my voice according to that which I command you. **9** Go now to the flock and get me two good young goats from there. I will make them savory food for your father, such as he loves. **10** You shall bring it to your father, that he may eat, so that he may bless you before his death."

11 Jacob said to Rebekah his mother, "Behold, Esau my brother is a hairy man, and I am a smooth man. **12** What if my father touches me? I will seem to him as a deceiver, and I would bring a curse on myself, and not a blessing."

13 His mother said to him, "Let your curse be on me, my son. Only obey my voice, and go get them for me."

14 He went, and got them, and brought them to his mother. His mother made savory food, such as his father loved. **15** Rebekah took the good clothes of Esau, her elder son, which were with her in the house, and put them on Jacob, her younger son. **16** She put the skins of the young goats on his hands, and on the smooth of his neck. **17** She gave the savory food and the bread, which she had prepared, into the hand of her son Jacob.

18 He came to his father, and said, "My father?"

He said, "Here I am. Who are you, my son?"

19 Jacob said to his father, "I am Esau your firstborn. I have done what you asked me to do. Please arise, sit and eat of my venison, that your soul may bless me."

20 Isaac said to his son, "How is it that you have found it so quickly, my son?"

He said, "Because God your God gave me success."

21 Isaac said to Jacob, "Please come near, that I may feel you, my son, whether you are really my son Esau or not."

22 Jacob went near to Isaac his father. He felt him, and said, "The voice is Jacob's voice, but the hands are the hands of Esau."

23 He didn't recognize him, because his hands were hairy, like his brother, Esau's hands. So he blessed him. **24** He said, "Are you really my son Esau?"

He said, "I am."

25 He said, "Bring it near to me, and I will eat of my son's venison, that my soul may bless you."

He brought it near to him, and he ate. He brought him wine, and he drank. **26** His father Isaac said to him, "Come near now, and kiss me, my son." **27** He came near, and kissed him. He smelled the smell of his clothing, and blessed him, and said,

"Behold, the smell of my son
is as the smell of a field which God has blessed.

28 God give you of the dew of the sky,
of the fatness of the earth,
and plenty of grain and new wine.

29 Let peoples serve you,
and nations bow down to you.
Be lord over your brothers.
Let your mother's sons bow down to you.
Cursed be everyone who curses you.
Blessed be everyone who blesses you."

30 As soon as Isaac had finished blessing Jacob, and Jacob had just gone out from the presence of Isaac his father, Esau his brother came in from his hunting. **31** He also made savory food, and brought it to his father. He said to his father, "Let my father arise, and eat of his son's venison, that your soul may bless me."

32 Isaac his father said to him, "Who are you?"

He said, "I am your son, your firstborn, Esau."

33 Isaac trembled violently, and said, "Who, then, is he who has taken venison, and brought it to me, and I have eaten of all before you came, and have blessed him? Yes, he will be blessed."

34 When Esau heard the words of his father, he cried with an exceedingly great and bitter cry, and said to his father, "Bless me, even me also, my father."

35 He said, "Your brother came with deceit, and has taken away your blessing."

36 He said, "Isn't he rightly named Jacob? For he has supplanted me these two times. He took away my birthright. See, now he has taken away my blessing." He said, "Haven't you reserved a blessing for me?"

37 Isaac answered Esau, "Behold, I have made him your lord, and all his brothers I have given to him for servants. I have sustained him with grain and new wine. What then will I do for you, my son?"

38 Esau said to his father, "Do you have just one blessing, my father? Bless me, even me also, my father." Esau lifted up his voice, and wept.

39 Isaac his father answered him,

"Behold, your dwelling will be of the fatness of the earth,
and of the dew of the sky from above.

40 You will live by your sword, and you will serve your brother.
It will happen, when you will break loose,
that you will shake his yoke from off your neck."

41 Esau hated Jacob because of the blessing with which his father blessed him. Esau said in his heart, "The days of mourning for my father are at hand. Then I will kill my brother Jacob."

42 The words of Esau, her elder son, were told to Rebekah. She sent and called Jacob, her younger son, and said to him, "Behold, your brother Esau comforts himself about you by planning to kill you. **43** Now therefore, my son, obey my voice. Arise, flee to Laban, my brother, in Haran. **44** Stay with him a few days, until your brother's fury turns away— **45** until your brother's anger turns away from you, and he forgets what you have done to him. Then I will send, and get you from there. Why should I be bereaved of you both in one day?"

46 Rebekah said to Isaac, "I am weary of my life because of the daughters of Heth. If Jacob takes a wife of the daughters of Heth, such as these, of the daughters of the land, what good will my life do me?"

Genesis 28

1 Isaac called Jacob, blessed him, and commanded him, "You shall not take a wife of the daughters of Canaan. **2** Arise, go to Paddan Aram, to the house of Bethuel your mother's father. Take a wife from there from the daughters of Laban, your mother's brother. **3** May God Almighty bless you, and make you fruitful, and multiply you, that you may be a company of peoples, **4** and give you the blessing of Abraham, to you and to your offspring with you, that you may inherit the land where you travel, which God gave to Abraham."

5 Isaac sent Jacob away. He went to Paddan Aram to Laban, son of Bethuel the Syrian, the brother of Rebekah, Jacob's and Esau's mother.

6 Now Esau saw that Isaac had blessed Jacob and sent him away to Paddan Aram, to take him a wife from there, and that as he blessed him he gave him a command, saying, "You shall not take a wife of the daughters of Canaan;" **7** and that Jacob obeyed his father and his mother, and was gone to Paddan Aram.

8 Esau saw that the daughters of Canaan didn't please Isaac, his father. **9** Esau went to Ishmael, and took, in addition to the wives that he had, Mahalath the daughter of Ishmael, Abraham's son, the sister of Nebaioth, to be his wife.

10 Jacob went out from Beersheba, and went toward Haran.

11 He came to a certain place, and stayed there all night, because the sun had set. He took one of the stones of the place, and put it under his head, and lay down in that place to sleep.

12 He dreamed and saw a stairway set upon the earth, and its top reached to heaven. Behold, the angels of God were ascending and descending on it. **13** Behold, God stood above it, and said,

"I am God, the God of Abraham your father, and the God of Isaac. I will give the land you lie on to you and to your offspring.

14 Your offspring will be as the dust of the earth, and you will spread abroad to the west, and to the east, and to the north, and to the south. In you and in your offspring, all the families of the earth will be blessed. **15** Behold, I am with you, and will keep you, wherever you go, and will bring you again into this land. For I will not leave you, until I have done that which I have spoken of to you."

16 Jacob awakened out of his sleep, and he said, "Surely God is in this place, and I didn't know it." **17** He was afraid, and said, "How awesome this place is! This is none other than God's house, and this is the gate of heaven."

18 Jacob rose up early in the morning, and took the stone that he had put under his head, and set it up for a pillar, and poured oil on its top. **19** He called the name of that place Bethel, but the name of the city was Luz at the first. **20** Jacob vowed a vow, saying, "If God will be with me, and will keep me in this way that I go, and will give me bread to eat, and clothing to put on, **21** so that I come again to my father's house in peace, and God will be my God, **22** then this stone, which I have set up for a pillar, will be God's house. Of all that you will give me I will surely give a tenth to you."

Genesis 29

1 Then Jacob went on his journey, and came to the land of the children of the east. **2** He looked, and behold, a well in the field, and saw three flocks of sheep lying there by it. For out of that well they watered the flocks. The stone on the well's mouth was large. **3** There all the flocks were gathered. They rolled the stone from the well's mouth, and watered the sheep, and put the stone again on the well's mouth in its place. **4** Jacob said to them, "My relatives, where are you from?"

They said, "We are from Haran."

5 He said to them, "Do you know Laban, the son of Nahor?"

They said, "We know him."

6 He said to them, "Is it well with him?"

They said, "It is well. See, Rachel, his daughter, is coming with the sheep."

7 He said, "Behold, it is still the middle of the day, not time to gather the livestock together. Water the sheep, and go and feed them."

8 They said, "We can't, until all the flocks are gathered together, and they roll the stone from the well's mouth. Then we water the sheep."

9 While he was yet speaking with them, Rachel came with her father's sheep, for she kept them. **10** When Jacob saw Rachel the daughter of Laban, his mother's brother, and the sheep of Laban, his mother's brother, Jacob went near, and rolled the stone from the well's mouth, and watered the flock of Laban his mother's brother. **11** Jacob kissed Rachel, and lifted up his voice, and wept. **12** Jacob told Rachel that he was her father's relative, and that he was Rebekah's son. She ran and told her father.

13 When Laban heard the news of Jacob, his sister's son, he ran to meet Jacob, and embraced him, and kissed him, and brought him to his house. Jacob told Laban all these things. **14** Laban said to him, "Surely you are my bone and my flesh." Jacob stayed with him for a month. **15** Laban said to Jacob, "Because you are my relative, should you therefore serve me for nothing? Tell me, what will your wages be?"

16 Laban had two daughters. The name of the elder was Leah, and the name of the younger was Rachel. **17** Leah's eyes were weak, but Rachel was beautiful in form and attractive. **18** Jacob loved Rachel. He said, "I will serve you seven years for Rachel, your younger daughter."

19 Laban said, "It is better that I give her to you, than that I should give her to another man. Stay with me."

20 Jacob served seven years for Rachel. They seemed to him but a few days, for the love he had for her.

21 Jacob said to Laban, "Give me my wife, for my days are fulfilled, that I may go in to her."

22 Laban gathered together all the men of the place, and made a feast. **23** In the evening, he took Leah his daughter, and brought her to Jacob. He went in to her. **24** Laban gave Zilpah his servant to his daughter Leah for a servant. **25** In the morning, behold, it was Leah! He said to Laban, "What is this you have

---

[27]**26:33** *26:33* Shibah means "oath" or "seven".

[28]**26:33** *26:33* Beersheba means "well of the oath" or "well of the seven"

done to me? Didn't I serve with you for Rachel? Why then have
you deceived me?"
26 Laban said, "It is not done so in our place, to give the
younger before the firstborn. 27 Fulfill the week of this one, and
we will give you the other also for the service which you will
serve with me for seven more years."
28 Jacob did so, and fulfilled her week. He gave him Rachel his
daughter as wife. 29 Laban gave Bilhah, his servant, to his
daughter Rachel to be her servant. 30 He went in also to Rachel,
and he loved also Rachel more than Leah, and served with him
seven more years.
31 God saw that Leah was hated, and he opened her womb, but
Rachel was barren. 32 Leah conceived, and bore a son, and she
named him Reuben. For she said, "Because God has looked at
my affliction; for now my husband will love me." 33 She
conceived again, and bore a son, and said, "Because God has
heard that I am hated, he has therefore given me this son also."
She named him Simeon. 34 She conceived again, and bore a
son. She said, "Now this time my husband will be joined to me,
because I have borne him three sons." Therefore his name was
called Levi. 35 She conceived again, and bore a son. She said,
"This time I will praise God." Therefore she named him Judah.
Then she stopped bearing.

Genesis 30

1 When Rachel saw that she bore Jacob no children, Rachel
envied her sister. She said to Jacob, "Give me children, or else I
will die."
2 Jacob's anger burned against Rachel, and he said, "Am I in
God's place, who has withheld from you the fruit of the womb?"
3 She said, "Behold, my maid Bilhah. Go in to her, that she may
bear on my knees, and I also may obtain children by her." 4 She
gave him Bilhah her servant as wife, and Jacob went in to her.
5 Bilhah conceived, and bore Jacob a son. 6 Rachel said, "God
has judged me, and has also heard my voice, and has given me a
son." Therefore she called his name Dan. 7 Bilhah, Rachel's
servant, conceived again, and bore Jacob a second son. 8 Rachel
said, "I have wrestled with my sister with mighty wrestlings, and
have prevailed." She named him Naphtali.
9 When Leah saw that she had finished bearing, she took
Zilpah, her servant, and gave her to Jacob as a wife. 10 Zilpah,
Leah's servant, bore Jacob a son. 11 Leah said, "How
fortunate!" She named him Gad. 12 Zilpah, Leah's servant, bore
Jacob a second son. 13 Leah said, "Happy am I, for the
daughters will call me happy." She named him Asher.
14 Reuben went in the days of wheat harvest, and found
mandrakes in the field, and brought them to his mother, Leah.
Then Rachel said to Leah, "Please give me some of your son's
mandrakes."
15 Leah said to her, "Is it a small matter that you have taken
away my husband? Would you take away my son's mandrakes,
also?"
Rachel said, "Therefore he will lie with you tonight for your
son's mandrakes."
16 Jacob came from the field in the evening, and Leah went out
to meet him, and said, "You must come in to me; for I have
surely hired you with my son's mandrakes."
He lay with her that night. 17 God listened to Leah, and she
conceived, and bore Jacob a fifth son. 18 Leah said, "God has
given me my hire, because I gave my servant to my husband."
She named him Issachar. 19 Leah conceived again, and bore a
sixth son to Jacob. 20 Leah said, "God has endowed me with a
good dowry. Now my husband will live with me, because I have
borne him six sons." She named him Zebulun. 21 Afterwards,
she bore a daughter, and named her Dinah.
22 God remembered Rachel, and God listened to her, and
opened her womb. 23 She conceived, bore a son, and said,
"God has taken away my reproach." 24 She named him
Joseph,[29] saying, "May God add another son to me."
25 When Rachel had borne Joseph, Jacob said to Laban, "Send
me away, that I may go to my own place, and to my country.
26 Give me my wives and my children for whom I have served
you, and let me go; for you know my service with which I have
served you."
27 Laban said to him, "If now I have found favor in your eyes,
stay here, for I have divined that God has blessed me for your
sake." 28 He said, "Appoint me your wages, and I will give it."
29 Jacob said to him, "You know how I have served you, and
how your livestock have fared with me. 30 For it was little
which you had before I came, and it has increased to a multitude.
God has blessed you wherever I turned. Now when will I provide
for my own house also?"
31 Laban said, "What shall I give you?"
Jacob said, "You shall not give me anything. If you will do this
thing for me, I will again feed your flock and keep it. 32 I will
pass through all your flock today, removing from there every
speckled and spotted one, and every black one among the sheep,
and the spotted and speckled among the goats. This will be my
hire. 33 So my righteousness will answer for me hereafter,
when you come concerning my hire that is before you. Every one
that is not speckled and spotted among the goats, and black
among the sheep, that might be with me, will be considered
stolen."
34 Laban said, "Behold, let it be according to your word."
35 That day, he removed the male goats that were streaked and
spotted, and all the female goats that were speckled and spotted,
every one that had white in it, and all the black ones among the
sheep, and gave them into the hand of his sons. 36 He set three
days' journey between himself and Jacob, and Jacob fed the rest
of Laban's flocks.
37 Jacob took to himself rods of fresh poplar, almond, and
plane tree, peeled white streaks in them, and made the white
appear which was in the rods. 38 He set the rods which he had
peeled opposite the flocks in the watering troughs where the
flocks came to drink. They conceived when they came to drink.
39 The flocks conceived before the rods, and the flocks
produced streaked, speckled, and spotted. 40 Jacob separated
the lambs, and set the faces of the flocks toward the streaked and
all the black in Laban's flock. He put his own droves apart, and
didn't put them into Laban's flock. 41 Whenever the stronger of
the flock conceived, Jacob laid the rods in front of the eyes of the
flock in the watering troughs, that they might conceive among the
rods; 42 but when the flock were feeble, he didn't put them in.
So the feebler were Laban's, and the stronger Jacob's. 43 The
man increased exceedingly, and had large flocks, female servants
and male servants, and camels and donkeys.

Genesis 31

1 Jacob heard Laban's sons' words, saying, "Jacob has taken
away all that was our father's. He has obtained all this wealth
from that which was our father's." 2 Jacob saw the expression
on Laban's face, and, behold, it was not toward him as before.
3 God said to Jacob, "Return to the land of your fathers, and to
your relatives, and I will be with you."
4 Jacob sent and called Rachel and Leah to the field to his flock,
5 and said to them, "I see the expression on your father's face,
that it is not toward me as before; but the God of my father has
been with me. 6 You know that I have served your father with
all of my strength. 7 Your father has deceived me, and changed
my wages ten times, but God didn't allow him to hurt me. 8 If
he said, 'The speckled will be your wages,' then all the flock bore
speckled. If he said, 'The streaked will be your wages,' then all
the flock bore streaked. 9 Thus God has taken away your
father's livestock, and given them to me. 10 During mating
season, I lifted up my eyes, and saw in a dream, and behold, the
male goats which leaped on the flock were streaked, speckled,
and grizzled. 11 The angel of God said to me in the dream,
'Jacob,' and I said, 'Here I am.' 12 He said, 'Now lift up your
eyes, and behold, all the male goats which leap on the flock are
streaked, speckled, and grizzled, for I have seen all that Laban
does to you. 13 I am the God of Bethel, where you anointed a
pillar, where you vowed a vow to me. Now arise, get out from
this land, and return to the land of your birth.'"
14 Rachel and Leah answered him, "Is there yet any portion or
inheritance for us in our father's house? 15 Aren't we
considered as foreigners by him? For he has sold us, and has also
used up our money. 16 For all the riches which God has taken
away from our father are ours and our children's. Now then,
whatever God has said to you, do."
17 Then Jacob rose up, and set his sons and his wives on the
camels, 18 and he took away all his livestock, and all his
possessions which he had gathered, including the livestock which
he had gained in Paddan Aram, to go to Isaac his father, to the
land of Canaan. 19 Now Laban had gone to shear his sheep; and
Rachel stole the teraphim [30] that were her father's.
20 Jacob deceived Laban the Syrian, in that he didn't tell him
that he was running away. 21 So he fled with all that he had. He
rose up, passed over the River, and set his face toward the
mountain of Gilead.
22 Laban was told on the third day that Jacob had fled. 23 He
took his relatives with him, and pursued him seven days' journey.
He overtook him in the mountain of Gilead. 24 God came to
Laban the Syrian in a dream of the night, and said to him, "Be
careful that you don't speak to Jacob either good or bad."
25 Laban caught up with Jacob. Now Jacob had pitched his tent
in the mountain, and Laban with his relatives encamped in the
mountain of Gilead. 26 Laban said to Jacob, "What have you
done, that you have deceived me, and carried away my daughters
like captives of the sword? 27 Why did you flee secretly, and
deceive me, and didn't tell me, that I might have sent you away
with mirth and with songs, with tambourine and with harp;
28 and didn't allow me to kiss my sons and my daughters? Now
have you done foolishly. 29 It is in the power of my hand to
hurt you, but the God of your father spoke to me last night,
saying, 'Be careful that you don't speak to Jacob either good or
bad.' 30 Now, you want to be gone, because you greatly longed
for your father's house, but why have you stolen my gods?"
31 Jacob answered Laban, "Because I was afraid, for I said,
'Lest you should take your daughters from me by force.'
32 Anyone you find your gods with shall not live. Before our
relatives, discern what is yours with me, and take it." For Jacob
didn't know that Rachel had stolen them.
33 Laban went into Jacob's tent, into Leah's tent, and into the
tent of the two female servants; but he didn't find them. He went
out of Leah's tent, and entered into Rachel's tent. 34 Now
Rachel had taken the teraphim, put them in the camel's saddle,
and sat on them. Laban felt around all the tent, but didn't find
them. 35 She said to her father, "Don't let my lord be angry that
I can't rise up before you; for I'm having my period." He
searched, but didn't find the teraphim.
36 Jacob was angry, and argued with Laban. Jacob answered
Laban, "What is my trespass? What is my sin, that you have hotly
pursued me? 37 Now that you have felt around in all my stuff,
what have you found of all your household stuff? Set it here
before my relatives and your relatives, that they may judge
between us two.
38 "These twenty years I have been with you. Your ewes and
your female goats have not cast their young, and I haven't eaten
the rams of your flocks. 39 That which was torn of animals, I
didn't bring to you. I bore its loss. Of my hand you required it,
whether stolen by day or stolen by night. 40 This was my
situation: in the day the drought consumed me, and the frost by
night; and my sleep fled from my eyes. 41 These twenty years I
have been in your house. I served you fourteen years for your two
daughters, and six years for your flock, and you have changed my
wages ten times. 42 Unless the God of my father, the God of
Abraham, and the fear of Isaac, had been with me, surely now
you would have sent me away empty. God has seen my affliction
and the labor of my hands, and rebuked you last night."
43 Laban answered Jacob, "The daughters are my daughters,
the children are my children, the flocks are my flocks, and all that
you see is mine! What can I do today to these my daughters, or to
their children whom they have borne? 44 Now come, let's make
a covenant, you and I. Let it be for a witness between me and
you."
45 Jacob took a stone, and set it up for a pillar. 46 Jacob said
to his relatives, "Gather stones." They took stones, and made a
heap. They ate there by the heap. 47 Laban called it Jegar
Sahadutha,[31] but Jacob called it Galeed.[32] 48 Laban said, "This
heap is witness between me and you today." Therefore it was
named Galeed 49 and Mizpah, for he said, "God watch between
me and you, when we are absent one from another. 50 If you
afflict my daughters, or if you take wives in addition to my
daughters, no man is with us; behold, God is witness between me
and you." 51 Laban said to Jacob, "See this heap, and see the
pillar, which I have set between me and you. 52 May this heap

---

[29] **30:24** *30:24* **Joseph means "may he add".**

[30] **31:19** *31:19* **teraphim were household idols that may have been associated with inheritance rights to the household property.**

[31] **31:47** *31:47* **"Jegar Sahadutha" means "Witness Heap" in Aramaic.**

[32] **31:47** *31:47* **"Galeed" means "Witness Heap" in Hebrew.**

be a witness, and the pillar be a witness, that I will not pass over
this heap to you, and that you will not pass over this heap and this
pillar to me, for harm. 53 The God of Abraham, and the God of
Nahor, the God of their father, judge between us." Then Jacob
swore by the fear of his father, Isaac. 54 Jacob offered a
sacrifice in the mountain, and called his relatives to eat bread.
They ate bread, and stayed all night in the mountain. 55 Early in
the morning, Laban rose up, and kissed his sons and his
daughters, and blessed them. Laban departed and returned to his
place.

Genesis 32

1 Jacob went on his way, and the angels of God met him.
2 When he saw them, Jacob said, "This is God's army." He
called the name of that place Mahanaim.
3 Jacob sent messengers in front of him to Esau, his brother, to
the land of Seir, the field of Edom. 4 He commanded them,
saying, "This is what you shall tell my lord, Esau: 'This is what
your servant, Jacob, says. I have lived as a foreigner with Laban,
and stayed until now. 5 I have cattle, donkeys, flocks, male
servants, and female servants. I have sent to tell my lord, that I
may find favor in your sight.'" 6 The messengers returned to
Jacob, saying, "We came to your brother Esau. He is coming to
meet you, and four hundred men are with him." 7 Then Jacob
was greatly afraid and was distressed. He divided the people who
were with him, and the flocks, and the herds, and the camels, into
two companies; 8 and he said, "If Esau comes to the one
company, and strikes it, then the company which is left will
escape." 9 Jacob said, "God of my father Abraham, and God of
my father Isaac, God, who said to me, 'Return to your country,
and to your relatives, and I will do you good,' 10 I am not
worthy of the least of all the loving kindnesses, and of all the
truth, which you have shown to your servant; for with just my
staff I crossed over this Jordan; and now I have become two
companies. 11 Please deliver me from the hand of my brother,
from the hand of Esau; for I fear him, lest he come and strike me
and the mothers with the children. 12 You said, 'I will surely do
you good, and make your offspring as the sand of the sea, which
can't be counted because there are so many.'"
13 He stayed there that night, and took from that which he had
with him a present for Esau, his brother: 14 two hundred female
goats and twenty male goats, two hundred ewes and twenty rams,
15 thirty milk camels and their colts, forty cows, ten bulls,
twenty female donkeys and ten foals. 16 He delivered them into
the hands of his servants, every herd by itself, and said to his
servants, "Pass over before me, and put a space between herd and
herd." 17 He commanded the foremost, saying, "When Esau,
my brother, meets you, and asks you, saying, 'Whose are you?
Where are you going? Whose are these before you?' 18 Then
you shall say, 'They are your servant, Jacob's. It is a present sent
to my lord, Esau. Behold, he also is behind us.'" 19 He
commanded also the second, and the third, and all that followed
the herds, saying, "This is how you shall speak to Esau, when
you find him. 20 You shall say, 'Not only that, but behold, your
servant, Jacob, is behind us.'" For, he said, "I will appease him
with the present that goes before me, and afterward I will see his
face. Perhaps he will accept me."
21 So the present passed over before him, and he himself stayed
that night in the camp.
22 He rose up that night, and took his two wives, and his two
servants, and his eleven sons, and crossed over the ford of the
Jabbok. 23 He took them, and sent them over the stream, and
sent over that which he had. 24 Jacob was left alone, and
wrestled with a man there until the breaking of the day.
25 When he saw that he didn't prevail against him, the man
touched the hollow of his thigh, and the hollow of Jacob's thigh
was strained as he wrestled. 26 The man said, "Let me go, for
the day breaks."
Jacob said, "I won't let you go unless you bless me."
27 He said to him, "What is your name?"
He said, "Jacob".
28 He said, "Your name will no longer be called Jacob, but
Israel; for you have fought with God and with men, and have
prevailed."
29 Jacob asked him, "Please tell me your name."
He said, "Why is it that you ask what my name is?" He blessed
him there.
30 Jacob called the name of the place Peniel;[33] for he said, "I
have seen God face to face, and my life is preserved." 31 The
sun rose on him as he passed over Peniel, and he limped because
of his thigh. 32 Therefore the children of Israel don't eat the
sinew of the hip, which is on the hollow of the thigh, to this day,
because he touched the hollow of Jacob's thigh in the sinew of
the hip.

Genesis 33

1 Jacob lifted up his eyes, and looked, and, behold, Esau was
coming, and with him four hundred men. He divided the children
between Leah, Rachel, and the two servants. 2 He put the
servants and their children in front, Leah and her children after,
and Rachel and Joseph at the rear. 3 He himself passed over in
front of them, and bowed himself to the ground seven times, until
he came near to his brother.
4 Esau ran to meet him, embraced him, fell on his neck, kissed
him, and they wept. 5 He lifted up his eyes, and saw the women
and the children; and said, "Who are these with you?"
He said, "The children whom God has graciously given your
servant." 6 Then the servants came near with their children, and
they bowed themselves. 7 Leah also and her children came near,
and bowed themselves. After them, Joseph came near with
Rachel, and they bowed themselves.
8 Esau said, "What do you mean by all this company which I
met?"
Jacob said, "To find favor in the sight of my lord."
9 Esau said, "I have enough, my brother; let that which you
have be yours."
10 Jacob said, "Please, no, if I have now found favor in your
sight, then receive my present at my hand, because I have seen
your face, as one sees the face of God, and you were pleased with
me. 11 Please take the gift that I brought to you, because God
has dealt graciously with me, and because I have enough." He
urged him, and he took it.
12 Esau said, "Let's take our journey, and let's go, and I will go
before you."
13 Jacob said to him, "My lord knows that the children are
tender, and that the flocks and herds with me have their young,
and if they overdrive them one day, all the flocks will die.
14 Please let my lord pass over before his servant, and I will
lead on gently, according to the pace of the livestock that are
before me and according to the pace of the children, until I come
to my lord to Seir."
15 Esau said, "Let me now leave with you some of the people
who are with me."
He said, "Why? Let me find favor in the sight of my lord."
16 So Esau returned that day on his way to Seir. 17 Jacob
traveled to Succoth, built himself a house, and made shelters for
his livestock. Therefore the name of the place is called Succoth.[34]
18 Jacob came in peace to the city of Shechem, which is in the
land of Canaan, when he came from Paddan Aram; and
encamped before the city. 19 He bought the parcel of ground
where he had spread his tent, at the hand of the children of
Hamor, Shechem's father, for one hundred pieces of money.
20 He erected an altar there, and called it El Elohe Israel. [35]

Genesis 34

1 Dinah, the daughter of Leah, whom she bore to Jacob, went
out to see the daughters of the land. 2 Shechem the son of
Hamor the Hivite, the prince of the land, saw her. He took her,
lay with her, and humbled her. 3 His soul joined to Dinah, the
daughter of Jacob, and he loved the young lady, and spoke kindly
to the young lady. 4 Shechem spoke to his father, Hamor,
saying, "Get me this young lady as a wife."
5 Now Jacob heard that he had defiled Dinah, his daughter; and
his sons were with his livestock in the field. Jacob held his peace
until they came. 6 Hamor the father of Shechem went out to
Jacob to talk with him. 7 The sons of Jacob came in from the
field when they heard it. The men were grieved, and they were
very angry, because he had done folly in Israel in lying with
Jacob's daughter, a thing ought not to be done. 8 Hamor talked
with them, saying, "The soul of my son, Shechem, longs for your
daughter. Please give her to him as a wife. 9 Make marriages
with us. Give your daughters to us, and take our daughters for
yourselves. 10 You shall dwell with us, and the land will be
before you. Live and trade in it, and get possessions in it."
11 Shechem said to her father and to her brothers, "Let me find
favor in your eyes, and whatever you will tell me I will give.
12 Ask me a great amount for a dowry, and I will give whatever
you ask of me, but give me the young lady as a wife."
13 The sons of Jacob answered Shechem and Hamor his father
with deceit when they spoke, because he had defiled Dinah their
sister, 14 and said to them, "We can't do this thing, to give our
sister to one who is uncircumcised; for that is a reproach to us.
15 Only on this condition will we consent to you. If you will be
as we are, that every male of you be circumcised, 16 then will
we give our daughters to you; and we will take your daughters to
us, and we will dwell with you, and we will become one people.
17 But if you will not listen to us and be circumcised, then we
will take our sister,[36] and we will be gone."
18 Their words pleased Hamor and Shechem, Hamor's son.
19 The young man didn't wait to do this thing, because he had
delight in Jacob's daughter, and he was honored above all the
house of his father. 20 Hamor and Shechem, his son, came to
the gate of their city, and talked with the men of their city,
saying, 21 "These men are peaceful with us. Therefore let them
live in the land and trade in it. For behold, the land is large
enough for them. Let's take their daughters to us for wives, and
let's give them our daughters. 22 Only on this condition will the
men consent to us to live with us, to become one people, if every
male among us is circumcised, as they are circumcised.
23 Won't their livestock and their possessions and all their
animals be ours? Only let's give our consent to them, and they
will dwell with us."
24 All who went out of the gate of his city listened to Hamor,
and to Shechem his son; and every male was circumcised, all
who went out of the gate of his city. 25 On the third day, when
they were sore, two of Jacob's sons, Simeon and Levi, Dinah's
brothers, each took his sword, came upon the unsuspecting city,
and killed all the males. 26 They killed Hamor and Shechem,
his son, with the edge of the sword, and took Dinah out of
Shechem's house, and went away. 27 Jacob's sons came on the
dead, and plundered the city, because they had defiled their sister.
28 They took their flocks, their herds, their donkeys, that which
was in the city, that which was in the field, 29 and all their
wealth. They took captive all their little ones and their wives, and
took as plunder everything that was in the house. 30 Jacob said
to Simeon and Levi, "You have troubled me, to make me odious
to the inhabitants of the land, among the Canaanites and the
Perizzites. I am few in number. They will gather themselves
together against me and strike me, and I will be destroyed, I and
my house."
31 They said, "Should he deal with our sister as with a
prostitute?"

Genesis 35

1 God said to Jacob, "Arise, go up to Bethel, and live there.
Make there an altar to God, who appeared to you when you fled
from the face of Esau your brother."
2 Then Jacob said to his household, and to all who were with
him, "Put away the foreign gods that are among you, purify
yourselves, change your garments. 3 Let's arise, and go up to
Bethel. I will make there an altar to God, who answered me in the
day of my distress, and was with me on the way which I went."
4 They gave to Jacob all the foreign gods which were in their
hands, and the rings which were in their ears; and Jacob hid them
under the oak which was by Shechem. 5 They traveled, and a
terror of God was on the cities that were around them, and they
didn't pursue the sons of Jacob. 6 So Jacob came to Luz (that is,
Bethel), which is in the land of Canaan, he and all the people who
were with him. 7 He built an altar there, and called the place El
Beth El; because there God was revealed to him, when he fled
from the face of his brother. 8 Deborah, Rebekah's nurse, died,
and she was buried below Bethel under the oak; and its name was
called Allon Bacuth.
9 God appeared to Jacob again, when he came from Paddan
Aram, and blessed him. 10 God said to him, "Your name is
Jacob. Your name shall not be Jacob any more, but your name
will be Israel." He named him Israel. 11 God said to him, "I am
God Almighty. Be fruitful and multiply. A nation and a company
of nations will be from you, and kings will come out of your
body. 12 The land which I gave to Abraham and Isaac, I will
give it to you, and to your offspring after you I will give the
land."

---

[33] **32:30** *32:30* Peniel means "face of God".

[34] **33:17** *33:17* succoth means shelters or booths.

[35] **33:20** *33:20* El Elohe Israel means "God, the God of Israel" or "The God of Israel is mighty".

[36] **34:17** *34:17* Hebrew has, literally, "daughter"

13 God went up from him in the place where he spoke with
him. 14 Jacob set up a pillar in the place where he spoke with
him, a pillar of stone. He poured out a drink offering on it, and
poured oil on it. 15 Jacob called the name of the place where
God spoke with him "Bethel".
16 They traveled from Bethel. There was still some distance to
come to Ephrath, and Rachel travailed. She had hard labor.
17 When she was in hard labor, the midwife said to her, "Don't
be afraid, for now you will have another son."
18 As her soul was departing (for she died), she named him
Benoni,[37] but his father named him Benjamin.[38] 19 Rachel died,
and was buried on the way to Ephrath (also called Bethlehem).
20 Jacob set up a pillar on her grave. The same is the Pillar of
Rachel's grave to this day. 21 Israel traveled, and spread his
tent beyond the tower of Eder. 22 While Israel lived in that
land, Reuben went and lay with Bilhah, his father's concubine,
and Israel heard of it.
Now the sons of Jacob were twelve. 23 The sons of Leah:
Reuben (Jacob's firstborn), Simeon, Levi, Judah, Issachar, and
Zebulun. 24 The sons of Rachel: Joseph and Benjamin. 25 The
sons of Bilhah (Rachel's servant): Dan and Naphtali. 26 The
sons of Zilpah (Leah's servant): Gad and Asher. These are the
sons of Jacob, who were born to him in Paddan Aram. 27 Jacob
came to Isaac his father, to Mamre, to Kiriath Arba (which is
Hebron), where Abraham and Isaac lived as foreigners.
28 The days of Isaac were one hundred eighty years. 29 Isaac
gave up the spirit and died, and was gathered to his people, old
and full of days. Esau and Jacob, his sons, buried him.

Genesis 36

1 Now this is the history of the generations of Esau (that is,
Edom). 2 Esau took his wives from the daughters of Canaan:
Adah the daughter of Elon, the Hittite; and Oholibamah the
daughter of Anah, the daughter of Zibeon, the Hivite; 3 and
Basemath, Ishmael's daughter, sister of Nebaioth. 4 Adah bore
to Esau Eliphaz. Basemath bore Reuel. 5 Oholibamah bore
Jeush, Jalam, and Korah. These are the sons of Esau, who were
born to him in the land of Canaan. 6 Esau took his wives, his
sons, his daughters, and all the members of his household, with
his livestock, all his animals, and all his possessions, which he
had gathered in the land of Canaan, and went into a land away
from his brother Jacob. 7 For their substance was too great for
them to dwell together, and the land of their travels couldn't bear
them because of their livestock. 8 Esau lived in the hill country
of Seir. Esau is Edom.
9 This is the history of the generations of Esau the father of the
Edomites in the hill country of Seir: 10 these are the names of
Esau's sons: Eliphaz, the son of Adah, the wife of Esau; and
Reuel, the son of Basemath, the wife of Esau. 11 The sons of
Eliphaz were Teman, Omar, Zepho, and Gatam, and Kenaz.
12 Timna was concubine to Eliphaz, Esau's son; and she bore to
Eliphaz Amalek. These are the descendants of Adah, Esau's wife.
13 These are the sons of Reuel: Nahath, Zerah, Shammah, and
Mizzah. These were the descendants of Basemath, Esau's wife.
14 These were the sons of Oholibamah, the daughter of Anah,
the daughter of Zibeon, Esau's wife: she bore to Esau Jeush,
Jalam, and Korah.
15 These are the chiefs of the sons of Esau: the sons of Eliphaz
the firstborn of Esau: chief Teman, chief Omar, chief Zepho,
chief Kenaz, 16 chief Korah, chief Gatam, chief Amalek. These
are the chiefs who came of Eliphaz in the land of Edom. These
are the sons of Adah. 17 These are the sons of Reuel, Esau's
son: chief Nahath, chief Zerah, chief Shammah, chief Mizzah.
These are the chiefs who came of Reuel in the land of Edom.
These are the sons of Basemath, Esau's wife. 18 These are the
sons of Oholibamah, Esau's wife: chief Jeush, chief Jalam, chief
Korah. These are the chiefs who came of Oholibamah the
daughter of Anah, Esau's wife. 19 These are the sons of Esau
(that is, Edom), and these are their chiefs.
20 These are the sons of Seir the Horite, the inhabitants of the
land: Lotan, Shobal, Zibeon, Anah, 21 Dishon, Ezer, and
Dishan. These are the chiefs who came of the Horites, the
children of Seir in the land of Edom. 22 The children of Lotan
were Hori and Heman. Lotan's sister was Timna. 23 These are
the children of Shobal: Alvan, Manahath, Ebal, Shepho, and
Onam. 24 These are the children of Zibeon: Aiah and Anah.
This is Anah who found the hot springs in the wilderness, as he
fed the donkeys of Zibeon his father. 25 These are the children
of Anah: Dishon and Oholibamah, the daughter of Anah.
26 These are the children of Dishon: Hemdan, Eshban, Ithran,
and Cheran. 27 These are the children of Ezer: Bilhan, Zaavan,
and Akan. 28 These are the children of Dishan: Uz and Aran.
29 These are the chiefs who came of the Horites: chief Lotan,
chief Shobal, chief Zibeon, chief Anah, 30 chief Dishon, chief
Ezer, and chief Dishan. These are the chiefs who came of the
Horites, according to their chiefs in the land of Seir.
31 These are the kings who reigned in the land of Edom, before
any king reigned over the children of Israel. 32 Bela, the son of
Beor, reigned in Edom. The name of his city was Dinhabah.
33 Bela died, and Jobab, the son of Zerah of Bozrah, reigned in
his place. 34 Jobab died, and Husham of the land of the
Temanites reigned in his place. 35 Husham died, and Hadad,
the son of Bedad, who struck Midian in the field of Moab,
reigned in his place. The name of his city was Avith. 36 Hadad
died, and Samlah of Masrekah reigned in his place. 37 Samlah
died, and Shaul of Rehoboth by the river, reigned in his place.
38 Shaul died, and Baal Hanan the son of Achbor reigned in his
place. 39 Baal Hanan the son of Achbor died, and Hadar
reigned in his place. The name of his city was Pau. His wife's
name was Mehetabel, the daughter of Matred, the daughter of
Mezahab.
40 These are the names of the chiefs who came from Esau,
according to their families, after their places, and by their names:
chief Timna, chief Alvah, chief Jetheth, 41 chief Oholibamah,
chief Elah, chief Pinon, 42 chief Kenaz, chief Teman, chief
Mibzar, 43 chief Magdiel, and chief Iram. These are the chiefs
of Edom, according to their habitations in the land of their
possession. This is Esau, the father of the Edomites.

Genesis 37

1 Jacob lived in the land of his father's travels, in the land of
Canaan. 2 This is the history of the generations of Jacob.
Joseph, being seventeen years old, was feeding the flock with his
brothers. He was a boy with the sons of Bilhah and Zilpah, his
father's wives. Joseph brought an evil report of them to their
father. 3 Now Israel loved Joseph more than all his children,
because he was the son of his old age, and he made him a tunic of
many colors. 4 His brothers saw that their father loved him
more than all his brothers, and they hated him, and couldn't
speak peaceably to him.
5 Joseph dreamed a dream, and he told it to his brothers, and
they hated him all the more. 6 He said to them, "Please hear this
dream which I have dreamed: 7 for behold, we were binding
sheaves in the field, and behold, my sheaf arose and also stood
upright; and behold, your sheaves came around, and bowed down
to my sheaf."
8 His brothers asked him, "Will you indeed reign over us? Will
you indeed have dominion over us?" They hated him all the more
for his dreams and for his words. 9 He dreamed yet another
dream, and told it to his brothers, and said, "Behold, I have
dreamed yet another dream: and behold, the sun and the moon
and eleven stars bowed down to me." 10 He told it to his father
and to his brothers. His father rebuked him, and said to him,
"What is this dream that you have dreamed? Will I and your
mother and your brothers indeed come to bow ourselves down to
you to the earth?" 11 His brothers envied him, but his father
kept this saying in mind.
12 His brothers went to feed their father's flock in Shechem.
13 Israel said to Joseph, "Aren't your brothers feeding the flock
in Shechem? Come, and I will send you to them." He said to him,
"Here I am."
14 He said to him, "Go now, see whether it is well with your
brothers, and well with the flock; and bring me word again." So
he sent him out of the valley of Hebron, and he came to
Shechem. 15 A certain man found him, and behold, he was
wandering in the field. The man asked him, "What are you
looking for?"
16 He said, "I am looking for my brothers. Tell me, please,
where they are feeding the flock."
17 The man said, "They have left here, for I heard them say,
'Let's go to Dothan.'"
Joseph went after his brothers, and found them in Dothan.
18 They saw him afar off, and before he came near to them,
they conspired against him to kill him. 19 They said to one
another, "Behold, this dreamer comes. 20 Come now therefore,
and let's kill him, and cast him into one of the pits, and we will
say, 'An evil animal has devoured him.' We will see what will
become of his dreams."
21 Reuben heard it, and delivered him out of their hand, and
said, "Let's not take his life." 22 Reuben said to them, "Shed no
blood. Throw him into this pit that is in the wilderness, but lay no
hand on him"—that he might deliver him out of their hand, to
restore him to his father. 23 When Joseph came to his brothers,
they stripped Joseph of his tunic, the tunic of many colors that
was on him; 24 and they took him, and threw him into the pit.
The pit was empty. There was no water in it.
25 They sat down to eat bread, and they lifted up their eyes and
looked, and saw a caravan of Ishmaelites was coming from
Gilead, with their camels bearing spices and balm and myrrh,
going to carry it down to Egypt. 26 Judah said to his brothers,
"What profit is it if we kill our brother and conceal his blood?
27 Come, and let's sell him to the Ishmaelites, and not let our
hand be on him; for he is our brother, our flesh." His brothers
listened to him. 28 Midianites who were merchants passed by,
and they drew and lifted up Joseph out of the pit, and sold Joseph
to the Ishmaelites for twenty pieces of silver. The merchants
brought Joseph into Egypt.
29 Reuben returned to the pit, and saw that Joseph wasn't in the
pit; and he tore his clothes. 30 He returned to his brothers, and
said, "The child is no more; and I, where will I go?" 31 They
took Joseph's tunic, and killed a male goat, and dipped the tunic
in the blood. 32 They took the tunic of many colors, and they
brought it to their father, and said, "We have found this. Examine
it, now, and see if it is your son's tunic or not."
33 He recognized it, and said, "It is my son's tunic. An evil
animal has devoured him. Joseph is without doubt torn in pieces."
34 Jacob tore his clothes, and put sackcloth on his waist, and
mourned for his son many days. 35 All his sons and all his
daughters rose up to comfort him, but he refused to be comforted.
He said, "For I will go down to Sheol[39] to my son, mourning."
His father wept for him. 36 The Midianites sold him into Egypt
to Potiphar, an officer of Pharaoh's, the captain of the guard.

Genesis 38

1 At that time, Judah went down from his brothers, and visited a
certain Adullamite, whose name was Hirah. 2 There, Judah saw
the daughter of a certain Canaanite man named Shua. He took
her, and went in to her. 3 She conceived, and bore a son; and he
named him Er. 4 She conceived again, and bore a son; and she
named him Onan. 5 She yet again bore a son, and named him
Shelah. He was at Chezib when she bore him. 6 Judah took a
wife for Er, his firstborn, and her name was Tamar. 7 Er,
Judah's firstborn, was wicked in God's sight. So God killed him.
8 Judah said to Onan, "Go in to your brother's wife, and
perform the duty of a husband's brother to her, and raise up
offspring for your brother." 9 Onan knew that the offspring
wouldn't be his; and when he went in to his brother's wife, he
spilled his semen on the ground, lest he should give offspring to
his brother. 10 The thing which he did was evil in God's sight,
and he killed him also. 11 Then Judah said to Tamar, his
daughter-in-law, "Remain a widow in your father's house, until
Shelah, my son, is grown up;" for he said, "Lest he also die, like
his brothers." Tamar went and lived in her father's house.
12 After many days, Shua's daughter, the wife of Judah, died.
Judah was comforted, and went up to his sheep shearers to
Timnah, he and his friend Hirah, the Adullamite. 13 Tamar was
told, "Behold, your father-in-law is going up to Timnah to shear
his sheep." 14 She took off the garments of her widowhood, and
covered herself with her veil, and wrapped herself, and sat in the
gate of Enaim, which is on the way to Timnah; for she saw that
Shelah was grown up, and she wasn't given to him as a wife.
15 When Judah saw her, he thought that she was a prostitute,
for she had covered her face. 16 He turned to her by the way,
and said, "Please come, let me come in to you," for he didn't
know that she was his daughter-in-law.
She said, "What will you give me, that you may come in to me?"
17 He said, "I will send you a young goat from the flock."
She said, "Will you give me a pledge, until you send it?"
18 He said, "What pledge will I give you?"
She said, "Your signet and your cord, and your staff that is in
your hand."

---

[37]**35:18** *35:18* "Benoni" means "son of my trouble".

[38]**35:18** *35:18* "Benjamin" means "son of my right hand".

[39]**37:35** *37:35* Sheol is the place of the dead.

He gave them to her, and came in to her, and she conceived by
him. 19 She arose, and went away, and put off her veil from
her, and put on the garments of her widowhood. 20 Judah sent
the young goat by the hand of his friend, the Adullamite, to
receive the pledge from the woman's hand, but he didn't find her.
21 Then he asked the men of her place, saying, "Where is the
prostitute, that was at Enaim by the road?"
They said, "There has been no prostitute here."
22 He returned to Judah, and said, "I haven't found her; and
also the men of the place said, 'There has been no prostitute
here.'" 23 Judah said, "Let her keep it, lest we be shamed.
Behold, I sent this young goat, and you haven't found her."
24 About three months later, Judah was told, "Tamar, your
daughter-in-law, has played the prostitute. Moreover, behold, she
is with child by prostitution."
Judah said, "Bring her out, and let her be burned." 25 When she
was brought out, she sent to her father-in-law, saying, "I am with
child by the man who owns these." She also said, "Please discern
whose these are—the signet, and the cords, and the staff."
26 Judah acknowledged them, and said, "She is more righteous
than I, because I didn't give her to Shelah, my son."
He knew her again no more. 27 In the time of her travail,
behold, twins were in her womb. 28 When she travailed, one
put out a hand, and the midwife took and tied a scarlet thread on
his hand, saying, "This came out first." 29 As he drew back his
hand, behold, his brother came out, and she said, "Why have you
made a breach for yourself?" Therefore his name was called
Perez.[40] 30 Afterward his brother came out, who had the scarlet
thread on his hand, and his name was called Zerah. [41]

Genesis 39

1 Joseph was brought down to Egypt. Potiphar, an officer of
Pharaoh's, the captain of the guard, an Egyptian, bought him
from the hand of the Ishmaelites that had brought him down
there. 2 God was with Joseph, and he was a prosperous man. He
was in the house of his master the Egyptian. 3 His master saw
that God was with him, and that God made all that he did prosper
in his hand. 4 Joseph found favor in his sight. He ministered to
him, and Potiphar made him overseer over his house, and all that
he had he put into his hand. 5 From the time that he made him
overseer in his house, and over all that he had, God blessed the
Egyptian's house for Joseph's sake. God's blessing was on all
that he had, in the house and in the field. 6 He left all that he
had in Joseph's hand. He didn't concern himself with anything,
except for the food which he ate.
Joseph was well-built and handsome. 7 After these things, his
master's wife set her eyes on Joseph; and she said, "Lie with
me."
8 But he refused, and said to his master's wife, "Behold, my
master doesn't know what is with me in the house, and he has put
all that he has into my hand. 9 No one is greater in this house
than I am, and he has not kept back anything from me but you,
because you are his wife. How then can I do this great
wickedness, and sin against God?"
10 As she spoke to Joseph day by day, he didn't listen to her, to
lie by her, or to be with her. 11 About this time, he went into the
house to do his work, and there were none of the men of the
house inside. 12 She caught him by his garment, saying, "Lie
with me!"
He left his garment in her hand, and ran outside. 13 When she
saw that he had left his garment in her hand, and had run outside,
14 she called to the men of her house, and spoke to them,
saying, "Behold, he has brought a Hebrew in to us to mock us.
He came in to me to lie with me, and I cried with a loud voice.
15 When he heard that I lifted up my voice and cried, he left his
garment by me, and ran outside." 16 She laid up his garment by
her, until his master came home. 17 She spoke to him according
to these words, saying, "The Hebrew servant, whom you have
brought to us, came in to me to mock me, 18 and as I lifted up
my voice and cried, he left his garment by me, and ran outside."
19 When his master heard the words of his wife, which she
spoke to him, saying, "This is what your servant did to me," his
wrath was kindled. 20 Joseph's master took him, and put him
into the prison, the place where the king's prisoners were bound,
and he was there in custody. 21 But God was with Joseph, and
showed kindness to him, and gave him favor in the sight of the
keeper of the prison. 22 The keeper of the prison committed to
Joseph's hand all the prisoners who were in the prison. Whatever
they did there, he was responsible for it. 23 The keeper of the
prison didn't look after anything that was under his hand, because
God was with him; and that which he did, God made it prosper.

Genesis 40

1 After these things, the butler of the king of Egypt and his
baker offended their lord, the king of Egypt. 2 Pharaoh was
angry with his two officers, the chief cup bearer and the chief
baker. 3 He put them in custody in the house of the captain of
the guard, into the prison, the place where Joseph was bound.
4 The captain of the guard assigned them to Joseph, and he took
care of them. They stayed in prison many days. 5 They both
dreamed a dream, each man his dream, in one night, each man
according to the interpretation of his dream, the cup bearer and
the baker of the king of Egypt, who were bound in the prison.
6 Joseph came in to them in the morning, and saw them, and
saw that they were sad. 7 He asked Pharaoh's officers who were
with him in custody in his master's house, saying, "Why do you
look so sad today?"
8 They said to him, "We have dreamed a dream, and there is no
one who can interpret it."
Joseph said to them, "Don't interpretations belong to God? Please
tell it to me."
9 The chief cup bearer told his dream to Joseph, and said to
him, "In my dream, behold, a vine was in front of me, 10 and in
the vine were three branches. It was as though it budded, it
blossomed, and its clusters produced ripe grapes. 11 Pharaoh's
cup was in my hand; and I took the grapes, and pressed them into
Pharaoh's cup, and I gave the cup into Pharaoh's hand."
12 Joseph said to him, "This is its interpretation: the three
branches are three days. 13 Within three more days, Pharaoh
will lift up your head, and restore you to your office. You will
give Pharaoh's cup into his hand, the way you did when you were
his cup bearer. 14 But remember me when it is well with you.
Please show kindness to me, and make mention of me to
Pharaoh, and bring me out of this house. 15 For indeed, I was
stolen away out of the land of the Hebrews, and here also I have
done nothing that they should put me into the dungeon."
16 When the chief baker saw that the interpretation was good,
he said to Joseph, "I also was in my dream, and behold, three
baskets of white bread were on my head. 17 In the uppermost
basket there were all kinds of baked food for Pharaoh, and the
birds ate them out of the basket on my head."
18 Joseph answered, "This is its interpretation. The three
baskets are three days. 19 Within three more days, Pharaoh will
lift up your head from off you, and will hang you on a tree; and
the birds will eat your flesh from off you." 20 On the third day,
which was Pharaoh's birthday, he made a feast for all his
servants, and he lifted up the head of the chief cup bearer and the
head of the chief baker among his servants. 21 He restored the
chief cup bearer to his position again, and he gave the cup into
Pharaoh's hand; 22 but he hanged the chief baker, as Joseph had
interpreted to them. 23 Yet the chief cup bearer didn't
remember Joseph, but forgot him.

Genesis 41

1 At the end of two full years, Pharaoh dreamed, and behold, he
stood by the river. 2 Behold, seven cattle came up out of the
river. They were sleek and fat, and they fed in the marsh grass.
3 Behold, seven other cattle came up after them out of the river,
ugly and thin, and stood by the other cattle on the brink of the
river. 4 The ugly and thin cattle ate up the seven sleek and fat
cattle. So Pharaoh awoke. 5 He slept and dreamed a second
time; and behold, seven heads of grain came up on one stalk,
healthy and good. 6 Behold, seven heads of grain, thin and
blasted with the east wind, sprung up after them. 7 The thin
heads of grain swallowed up the seven healthy and full ears.
Pharaoh awoke, and behold, it was a dream. 8 In the morning,
his spirit was troubled, and he sent and called for all of Egypt's
magicians and wise men. Pharaoh told them his dreams, but there
was no one who could interpret them to Pharaoh.
9 Then the chief cup bearer spoke to Pharaoh, saying, "I
remember my faults today. 10 Pharaoh was angry with his
servants, and put me in custody in the house of the captain of the
guard, with the chief baker. 11 We dreamed a dream in one
night, he and I. Each man dreamed according to the interpretation
of his dream. 12 There was with us there a young man, a
Hebrew, servant to the captain of the guard, and we told him, and
he interpreted to us our dreams. He interpreted to each man
according to his dream. 13 As he interpreted to us, so it was. He
restored me to my office, and he hanged him."
14 Then Pharaoh sent and called Joseph, and they brought him
hastily out of the dungeon. He shaved himself, changed his
clothing, and came in to Pharaoh. 15 Pharaoh said to Joseph, "I
have dreamed a dream, and there is no one who can interpret it. I
have heard it said of you, that when you hear a dream you can
interpret it."
16 Joseph answered Pharaoh, saying, "It isn't in me. God will
give Pharaoh an answer of peace."
17 Pharaoh spoke to Joseph, "In my dream, behold, I stood on
the brink of the river; 18 and behold, there came up out of the
river seven cattle, fat and sleek. They fed in the marsh grass;
19 and behold, seven other cattle came up after them, poor and
very ugly and thin, such as I never saw in all the land of Egypt
for ugliness. 20 The thin and ugly cattle ate up the first seven fat
cattle; 21 and when they had eaten them up, it couldn't be
known that they had eaten them, but they were still ugly, as at the
beginning. So I awoke. 22 I saw in my dream, and behold,
seven heads of grain came up on one stalk, full and good;
23 and behold, seven heads of grain, withered, thin, and blasted
with the east wind, sprung up after them. 24 The thin heads of
grain swallowed up the seven good heads of grain. I told it to the
magicians, but there was no one who could explain it to me."
25 Joseph said to Pharaoh, "The dream of Pharaoh is one. What
God is about to do he has declared to Pharaoh. 26 The seven
good cattle are seven years; and the seven good heads of grain are
seven years. The dream is one. 27 The seven thin and ugly
cattle that came up after them are seven years, and also the seven
empty heads of grain blasted with the east wind; they will be
seven years of famine. 28 That is the thing which I have spoken
to Pharaoh. God has shown Pharaoh what he is about to do.
29 Behold, seven years of great plenty throughout all the land of
Egypt are coming. 30 Seven years of famine will arise after
them, and all the plenty will be forgotten in the land of Egypt.
The famine will consume the land, 31 and the plenty will not be
known in the land by reason of that famine which follows; for it
will be very grievous. 32 The dream was doubled to Pharaoh,
because the thing is established by God, and God will shortly
bring it to pass.
33 "Now therefore let Pharaoh look for a discreet and wise man,
and set him over the land of Egypt. 34 Let Pharaoh do this, and
let him appoint overseers over the land, and take up the fifth part
of the land of Egypt's produce in the seven plenteous years.
35 Let them gather all the food of these good years that come,
and store grain under the hand of Pharaoh for food in the cities,
and let them keep it. 36 The food will be to supply the land
against the seven years of famine, which will be in the land of
Egypt; so that the land will not perish through the famine."
37 The thing was good in the eyes of Pharaoh, and in the eyes
of all his servants. 38 Pharaoh said to his servants, "Can we find
such a one as this, a man in whom is the Spirit of God?"
39 Pharaoh said to Joseph, "Because God has shown you all of
this, there is no one so discreet and wise as you. 40 You shall be
over my house. All my people will be ruled according to your
word. Only in the throne I will be greater than you." 41 Pharaoh
said to Joseph, "Behold, I have set you over all the land of
Egypt." 42 Pharaoh took off his signet ring from his hand, and
put it on Joseph's hand, and arrayed him in robes of fine linen,
and put a gold chain about his neck. 43 He made him ride in the
second chariot which he had. They cried before him, "Bow the
knee!" He set him over all the land of Egypt. 44 Pharaoh said to
Joseph, "I am Pharaoh. Without you, no man shall lift up his
hand or his foot in all the land of Egypt." 45 Pharaoh called
Joseph's name Zaphenath-Paneah. He gave him Asenath, the
daughter of Potiphera priest of On as a wife. Joseph went out
over the land of Egypt.
46 Joseph was thirty years old when he stood before Pharaoh
king of Egypt. Joseph went out from the presence of Pharaoh,
and went throughout all the land of Egypt. 47 In the seven
plenteous years the earth produced abundantly. 48 He gathered
up all the food of the seven years which were in the land of
Egypt, and laid up the food in the cities. He stored food in each
city from the fields around that city. 49 Joseph laid up grain as
the sand of the sea, very much, until he stopped counting, for it
was without number. 50 To Joseph were born two sons before
the year of famine came, whom Asenath, the daughter of
Potiphera priest of On, bore to him. 51 Joseph called the name

[40] **38:29** *38:29* **Perez means "breaking out".**

[41] **38:30** *38:30* **Zerah means "scarlet" or "brightness".**

of the firstborn Manasseh,[42] “For”, he said, “God has made me
forget all my toil, and all my father’s house.” 52 The name of
the second, he called Ephraim:[43] “For God has made me fruitful
in the land of my affliction.”
53 The seven years of plenty, that were in the land of Egypt,
came to an end. 54 The seven years of famine began to come,
just as Joseph had said. There was famine in all lands, but in all
the land of Egypt there was bread. 55 When all the land of
Egypt was famished, the people cried to Pharaoh for bread, and
Pharaoh said to all the Egyptians, “Go to Joseph. What he says to
you, do.” 56 The famine was over all the surface of the earth.
Joseph opened all the store houses, and sold to the Egyptians.
The famine was severe in the land of Egypt. 57 All countries
came into Egypt, to Joseph, to buy grain, because the famine was
severe in all the earth.

Genesis 42

1 Now Jacob saw that there was grain in Egypt, and Jacob said
to his sons, “Why do you look at one another?” 2 He said,
“Behold, I have heard that there is grain in Egypt. Go down there,
and buy for us from there, so that we may live, and not die.”
3 Joseph’s ten brothers went down to buy grain from Egypt.
4 But Jacob didn’t send Benjamin, Joseph’s brother, with his
brothers; for he said, “Lest perhaps harm happen to him.” 5 The
sons of Israel came to buy among those who came, for the famine
was in the land of Canaan. 6 Joseph was the governor over the
land. It was he who sold to all the people of the land. Joseph’s
brothers came, and bowed themselves down to him with their
faces to the earth. 7 Joseph saw his brothers, and he recognized
them, but acted like a stranger to them, and spoke roughly with
them. He said to them, “Where did you come from?”
They said, “From the land of Canaan, to buy food.”
8 Joseph recognized his brothers, but they didn’t recognize him.
9 Joseph remembered the dreams which he dreamed about
them, and said to them, “You are spies! You have come to see the
nakedness of the land.”
10 They said to him, “No, my lord, but your servants have come
to buy food. 11 We are all one man’s sons; we are honest men.
Your servants are not spies.”
12 He said to them, “No, but you have come to see the
nakedness of the land!”
13 They said, “We, your servants, are twelve brothers, the sons
of one man in the land of Canaan; and behold, the youngest is
today with our father, and one is no more.”
14 Joseph said to them, “It is like I told you, saying, ‘You are
spies!’ 15 By this you shall be tested. By the life of Pharaoh,
you shall not go out from here, unless your youngest brother
comes here. 16 Send one of you, and let him get your brother,
and you shall be bound, that your words may be tested, whether
there is truth in you, or else by the life of Pharaoh surely you are
spies.” 17 He put them all together into custody for three days.
18 Joseph said to them the third day, “Do this, and live, for I
fear God. 19 If you are honest men, then let one of your
brothers be bound in your prison; but you go, carry grain for the
famine of your houses. 20 Bring your youngest brother to me;
so will your words be verified, and you won’t die.”
They did so. 21 They said to one another, “We are certainly
guilty concerning our brother, in that we saw the distress of his
soul, when he begged us, and we wouldn’t listen. Therefore this
distress has come upon us.” 22 Reuben answered them, saying,
“Didn’t I tell you, saying, ‘Don’t sin against the child,’ and you
wouldn’t listen? Therefore also, behold, his blood is required.”
23 They didn’t know that Joseph understood them; for there
was an interpreter between them. 24 He turned himself away
from them, and wept. Then he returned to them, and spoke to
them, and took Simeon from among them, and bound him before
their eyes. 25 Then Joseph gave a command to fill their bags
with grain, and to restore each man’s money into his sack, and to
give them food for the way. So it was done to them.
26 They loaded their donkeys with their grain, and departed
from there. 27 As one of them opened his sack to give his
donkey food in the lodging place, he saw his money. Behold, it
was in the mouth of his sack. 28 He said to his brothers, “My
money is restored! Behold, it is in my sack!” Their hearts failed
them, and they turned trembling to one another, saying, “What is
this that God has done to us?” 29 They came to Jacob their
father, to the land of Canaan, and told him all that had happened
to them, saying, 30 “The man, the lord of the land, spoke
roughly with us, and took us for spies of the country. 31 We
said to him, ‘We are honest men. We are no spies. 32 We are
twelve brothers, sons of our father; one is no more, and the
youngest is today with our father in the land of Canaan.’ 33 The
man, the lord of the land, said to us, ‘By this I will know that you
are honest men: leave one of your brothers with me, and take
grain for the famine of your houses, and go your way. 34 Bring
your youngest brother to me. Then I will know that you are not
spies, but that you are honest men. So I will deliver your brother
to you, and you shall trade in the land.’”
35 As they emptied their sacks, behold, each man’s bundle of
money was in his sack. When they and their father saw their
bundles of money, they were afraid. 36 Jacob, their father, said
to them, “You have bereaved me of my children! Joseph is no
more, Simeon is no more, and you want to take Benjamin away.
All these things are against me.”
37 Reuben spoke to his father, saying, “Kill my two sons, if I
don’t bring him to you. Entrust him to my care, and I will bring
him to you again.”
38 He said, “My son shall not go down with you; for his brother
is dead, and he only is left. If harm happens to him along the way
in which you go, then you will bring down my gray hairs with
sorrow to Sheol.”[44]

Genesis 43

1 The famine was severe in the land. 2 When they had eaten
up the grain which they had brought out of Egypt, their father
said to them, “Go again, buy us a little more food.”
3 Judah spoke to him, saying, “The man solemnly warned us,
saying, ‘You shall not see my face, unless your brother is with
you.’ 4 If you’ll send our brother with us, we’ll go down and
buy you food; 5 but if you don’t send him, we won’t go down,
for the man said to us, ‘You shall not see my face, unless your
brother is with you.’”
6 Israel said, “Why did you treat me so badly, telling the man
that you had another brother?”
7 They said, “The man asked directly concerning ourselves, and
concerning our relatives, saying, ‘Is your father still alive? Have
you another brother?’ We just answered his questions. Is there
any way we could know that he would say, ‘Bring your brother
down?’”
8 Judah said to Israel, his father, “Send the boy with me, and
we’ll get up and go, so that we may live, and not die, both we,
and you, and also our little ones. 9 I’ll be collateral for him.
From my hand will you require him. If I don’t bring him to you,
and set him before you, then let me bear the blame forever;
10 for if we hadn’t delayed, surely we would have returned a
second time by now.”
11 Their father, Israel, said to them, “If it must be so, then do
this: Take from the choice fruits of the land in your bags, and
carry down a present for the man, a little balm, a little honey,
spices and myrrh, nuts, and almonds; 12 and take double money
in your hand, and take back the money that was returned in the
mouth of your sacks. Perhaps it was an oversight. 13 Take your
brother also, get up, and return to the man. 14 May God
Almighty give you mercy before the man, that he may release to
you your other brother and Benjamin. If I am bereaved of my
children, I am bereaved.”
15 The men took that present, and they took double money in
their hand, and Benjamin; and got up, went down to Egypt, and
stood before Joseph. 16 When Joseph saw Benjamin with them,
he said to the steward of his house, “Bring the men into the
house, and butcher an animal, and prepare; for the men will dine
with me at noon.”
17 The man did as Joseph commanded, and the man brought the
men to Joseph’s house. 18 The men were afraid, because they
were brought to Joseph’s house; and they said, “Because of the
money that was returned in our sacks the first time, we’re brought
in; that he may seek occasion against us, attack us, and seize us
as slaves, along with our donkeys.” 19 They came near to the
steward of Joseph’s house, and they spoke to him at the door of
the house, 20 and said, “Oh, my lord, we indeed came down the
first time to buy food. 21 When we came to the lodging place,
we opened our sacks, and behold, each man’s money was in the
mouth of his sack, our money in full weight. We have brought it
back in our hand. 22 We have brought down other money in our
hand to buy food. We don’t know who put our money in our
sacks.”
23 He said, “Peace be to you. Don’t be afraid. Your God, and
the God of your father, has given you treasure in your sacks. I
received your money.” He brought Simeon out to them. 24 The
man brought the men into Joseph’s house, and gave them water,
and they washed their feet. He gave their donkeys fodder.
25 They prepared the present for Joseph’s coming at noon, for
they heard that they should eat bread there.
26 When Joseph came home, they brought him the present
which was in their hand into the house, and bowed themselves
down to the earth before him. 27 He asked them of their
welfare, and said, “Is your father well, the old man of whom you
spoke? Is he yet alive?”
28 They said, “Your servant, our father, is well. He is still
alive.” They bowed down humbly. 29 He lifted up his eyes, and
saw Benjamin, his brother, his mother’s son, and said, “Is this
your youngest brother, of whom you spoke to me?” He said,
“God be gracious to you, my son.” 30 Joseph hurried, for his
heart yearned over his brother; and he sought a place to weep. He
entered into his room, and wept there. 31 He washed his face,
and came out. He controlled himself, and said, “Serve the meal.”
32 They served him by himself, and them by themselves, and
the Egyptians who ate with him by themselves, because the
Egyptians don’t eat with the Hebrews, for that is an abomination
to the Egyptians. 33 They sat before him, the firstborn
according to his birthright, and the youngest according to his
youth, and the men marveled with one another. 34 He sent
portions to them from before him, but Benjamin’s portion was
five times as much as any of theirs. They drank, and were merry
with him.

Genesis 44

1 He commanded the steward of his house, saying, “Fill the
men’s sacks with food, as much as they can carry, and put each
man’s money in his sack’s mouth. 2 Put my cup, the silver cup,
in the sack’s mouth of the youngest, with his grain money.” He
did according to the word that Joseph had spoken. 3 As soon as
the morning was light, the men were sent away, they and their
donkeys. 4 When they had gone out of the city, and were not
yet far off, Joseph said to his steward, “Up, follow after the men.
When you overtake them, ask them, ‘Why have you rewarded
evil for good? 5 Isn’t this that from which my lord drinks, and
by which he indeed divines? You have done evil in so doing.’”
6 He overtook them, and he spoke these words to them.
7 They said to him, “Why does my lord speak such words as
these? Far be it from your servants that they should do such a
thing! 8 Behold, the money, which we found in our sacks’
mouths, we brought again to you out of the land of Canaan. How
then should we steal silver or gold out of your lord’s house?
9 With whomever of your servants it is found, let him die, and
we also will be my lord’s slaves.”
10 He said, “Now also let it be according to your words. He
with whom it is found will be my slave; and you will be
blameless.”
11 Then they hurried, and each man took his sack down to the
ground, and each man opened his sack. 12 He searched,
beginning with the oldest, and ending at the youngest. The cup
was found in Benjamin’s sack. 13 Then they tore their clothes,
and each man loaded his donkey, and returned to the city.
14 Judah and his brothers came to Joseph’s house, and he was
still there. They fell on the ground before him. 15 Joseph said to
them, “What deed is this that you have done? Don’t you know
that such a man as I can indeed do divination?”
16 Judah said, “What will we tell my lord? What will we speak?
How will we clear ourselves? God has found out the iniquity of
your servants. Behold, we are my lord’s slaves, both we and he
also in whose hand the cup is found.”
17 He said, “Far be it from me that I should do so. The man in
whose hand the cup is found, he will be my slave; but as for you,
go up in peace to your father.”
18 Then Judah came near to him, and said, “Oh, my lord, please
let your servant speak a word in my lord’s ears, and don’t let your
anger burn against your servant; for you are even as Pharaoh.
19 My lord asked his servants, saying, ‘Have you a father, or a
brother?’ 20 We said to my lord, ‘We have a father, an old man,
and a child of his old age, a little one; and his brother is dead, and
he alone is left of his mother; and his father loves him.’ 21 You
said to your servants, ‘Bring him down to me, that I may set my
eyes on him.’ 22 We said to my lord, ‘The boy can’t leave his

---

[42] **41:51** *41:51* **“Manasseh” sounds like the Hebrew for “forget”.**

[43] **41:52** *41:52* **“Ephraim” sounds like the Hebrew for “twice fruitful”.**

[44] **42:38** *42:38* **Sheol is the place of the dead.**

father, for if he should leave his father, his father would die.'
23 You said to your servants, 'Unless your youngest brother
comes down with you, you will see my face no more.' 24 When
we came up to your servant my father, we told him the words of
my lord. 25 Our father said, 'Go again and buy us a little food.'
26 We said, 'We can't go down. If our youngest brother is with
us, then we will go down: for we may not see the man's face,
unless our youngest brother is with us.' 27 Your servant, my
father, said to us, 'You know that my wife bore me two sons.
28 One went out from me, and I said, "Surely he is torn in
pieces;" and I haven't seen him since. 29 If you take this one
also from me, and harm happens to him, you will bring down my
gray hairs with sorrow to Sheol.'[45] 30 Now therefore when I
come to your servant my father, and the boy is not with us; since
his life is bound up in the boy's life; 31 it will happen, when he
sees that the boy is no more, that he will die. Your servants will
bring down the gray hairs of your servant, our father, with sorrow
to Sheol.[46] 32 For your servant became collateral for the boy to
my father, saying, 'If I don't bring him to you, then I will bear
the blame to my father forever.' 33 Now therefore, please let
your servant stay instead of the boy, my lord's slave; and let the
boy go up with his brothers. 34 For how will I go up to my
father, if the boy isn't with me?—lest I see the evil that will come
on my father."

Genesis 45

1 Then Joseph couldn't control himself before all those who
stood before him, and he called out, "Cause everyone to go out
from me!" No one else stood with him, while Joseph made
himself known to his brothers. 2 He wept aloud. The Egyptians
heard, and the house of Pharaoh heard. 3 Joseph said to his
brothers, "I am Joseph! Does my father still live?"
His brothers couldn't answer him; for they were terrified at his
presence. 4 Joseph said to his brothers, "Come near to me,
please."
They came near. He said, "I am Joseph, your brother, whom you
sold into Egypt. 5 Now don't be grieved, nor angry with
yourselves, that you sold me here, for God sent me before you to
preserve life. 6 For these two years the famine has been in the
land, and there are yet five years, in which there will be no
plowing and no harvest. 7 God sent me before you to preserve
for you a remnant in the earth, and to save you alive by a great
deliverance. 8 So now it wasn't you who sent me here, but God,
and he has made me a father to Pharaoh, lord of all his house, and
ruler over all the land of Egypt. 9 Hurry, and go up to my
father, and tell him, 'This is what your son Joseph says, "God has
made me lord of all Egypt. Come down to me. Don't wait.
10 You shall dwell in the land of Goshen, and you will be near
to me, you, your children, your children's children, your flocks,
your herds, and all that you have. 11 There I will provide for
you; for there are yet five years of famine; lest you come to
poverty, you, and your household, and all that you have."'
12 Behold, your eyes see, and the eyes of my brother Benjamin,
that it is my mouth that speaks to you. 13 You shall tell my
father of all my glory in Egypt, and of all that you have seen. You
shall hurry and bring my father down here." 14 He fell on his
brother Benjamin's neck and wept, and Benjamin wept on his
neck. 15 He kissed all his brothers, and wept on them. After that
his brothers talked with him.
16 The report of it was heard in Pharaoh's house, saying,
"Joseph's brothers have come." It pleased Pharaoh well, and his
servants. 17 Pharaoh said to Joseph, "Tell your brothers, 'Do
this: Load your animals, and go, travel to the land of Canaan.
18 Take your father and your households, and come to me, and
I will give you the good of the land of Egypt, and you will eat the
fat of the land.' 19 Now you are commanded to do this: Take
wagons out of the land of Egypt for your little ones, and for your
wives, and bring your father, and come. 20 Also, don't concern
yourselves about your belongings, for the good of all the land of
Egypt is yours."
21 The sons of Israel did so. Joseph gave them wagons,
according to the commandment of Pharaoh, and gave them
provision for the way. 22 He gave each one of them changes of
clothing, but to Benjamin he gave three hundred pieces of silver
and five changes of clothing. 23 He sent the following to his
father: ten donkeys loaded with the good things of Egypt, and ten
female donkeys loaded with grain and bread and provision for his
father by the way. 24 So he sent his brothers away, and they
departed. He said to them, "See that you don't quarrel on the
way."
25 They went up out of Egypt, and came into the land of
Canaan, to Jacob their father. 26 They told him, saying, "Joseph
is still alive, and he is ruler over all the land of Egypt." His heart
fainted, for he didn't believe them. 27 They told him all the
words of Joseph, which he had said to them. When he saw the
wagons which Joseph had sent to carry him, the spirit of Jacob,
their father, revived. 28 Israel said, "It is enough. Joseph my
son is still alive. I will go and see him before I die."

Genesis 46

1 Israel traveled with all that he had, and came to Beersheba,
and offered sacrifices to the God of his father, Isaac. 2 God
spoke to Israel in the visions of the night, and said, "Jacob,
Jacob!"
He said, "Here I am."
3 He said, "I am God, the God of your father. Don't be afraid to
go down into Egypt, for there I will make of you a great nation.
4 I will go down with you into Egypt. I will also surely bring
you up again. Joseph's hand will close your eyes."
5 Jacob rose up from Beersheba, and the sons of Israel carried
Jacob, their father, their little ones, and their wives, in the wagons
which Pharaoh had sent to carry him. 6 They took their
livestock, and their goods, which they had gotten in the land of
Canaan, and came into Egypt—Jacob, and all his offspring with
him, 7 his sons, and his sons' sons with him, his daughters, and
his sons' daughters, and he brought all his offspring with him into
Egypt.
8 These are the names of the children of Israel, who came into
Egypt, Jacob and his sons: Reuben, Jacob's firstborn. 9 The
sons of Reuben: Hanoch, Pallu, Hezron, and Carmi. 10 The
sons of Simeon: Jemuel, Jamin, Ohad, Jachin, Zohar, and Shaul
the son of a Canaanite woman. 11 The sons of Levi: Gershon,
Kohath, and Merari. 12 The sons of Judah: Er, Onan, Shelah,
Perez, and Zerah; but Er and Onan died in the land of Canaan.
The sons of Perez were Hezron and Hamul. 13 The sons of
Issachar: Tola, Puvah, Iob, and Shimron. 14 The sons of
Zebulun: Sered, Elon, and Jahleel. 15 These are the sons of
Leah, whom she bore to Jacob in Paddan Aram, with his daughter
Dinah. All the souls of his sons and his daughters were thirty-
three. 16 The sons of Gad: Ziphion, Haggi, Shuni, Ezbon, Eri,
Arodi, and Areli. 17 The sons of Asher: Imnah, Ishvah, Ishvi,
Beriah, and Serah their sister. The sons of Beriah: Heber and
Malchiel. 18 These are the sons of Zilpah, whom Laban gave to
Leah, his daughter, and these she bore to Jacob, even sixteen
souls. 19 The sons of Rachel, Jacob's wife: Joseph and
Benjamin. 20 To Joseph in the land of Egypt were born
Manasseh and Ephraim, whom Asenath, the daughter of
Potiphera, priest of On, bore to him. 21 The sons of Benjamin:
Bela, Becher, Ashbel, Gera, Naaman, Ehi, Rosh, Muppim,
Huppim, and Ard. 22 These are the sons of Rachel, who were
born to Jacob: all the souls were fourteen. 23 The son of Dan:
Hushim. 24 The sons of Naphtali: Jahzeel, Guni, Jezer, and
Shillem. 25 These are the sons of Bilhah, whom Laban gave to
Rachel, his daughter, and these she bore to Jacob: all the souls
were seven. 26 All the souls who came with Jacob into Egypt,
who were his direct offspring, in addition to Jacob's sons' wives,
all the souls were sixty-six. 27 The sons of Joseph, who were
born to him in Egypt, were two souls. All the souls of the house
of Jacob, who came into Egypt, were seventy.
28 Jacob sent Judah before him to Joseph, to show the way
before him to Goshen, and they came into the land of Goshen.
29 Joseph prepared his chariot, and went up to meet Israel, his
father, in Goshen. He presented himself to him, and fell on his
neck, and wept on his neck a good while. 30 Israel said to
Joseph, "Now let me die, since I have seen your face, that you are
still alive."
31 Joseph said to his brothers, and to his father's house, "I will
go up, and speak with Pharaoh, and will tell him, 'My brothers,
and my father's house, who were in the land of Canaan, have
come to me. 32 These men are shepherds, for they have been
keepers of livestock, and they have brought their flocks, and their
herds, and all that they have.' 33 It will happen, when Pharaoh
summons you, and will say, 'What is your occupation?' 34 that
you shall say, 'Your servants have been keepers of livestock from
our youth even until now, both we, and our fathers:' that you may
dwell in the land of Goshen; for every shepherd is an
abomination to the Egyptians."

Genesis 47

1 Then Joseph went in and told Pharaoh, and said, "My father
and my brothers, with their flocks, their herds, and all that they
own, have come out of the land of Canaan; and behold, they are
in the land of Goshen." 2 From among his brothers he took five
men, and presented them to Pharaoh. 3 Pharaoh said to his
brothers, "What is your occupation?"
They said to Pharaoh, "Your servants are shepherds, both we, and
our fathers." 4 They also said to Pharaoh, "We have come to
live as foreigners in the land, for there is no pasture for your
servants' flocks. For the famine is severe in the land of Canaan.
Now therefore, please let your servants dwell in the land of
Goshen."
5 Pharaoh spoke to Joseph, saying, "Your father and your
brothers have come to you. 6 The land of Egypt is before you.
Make your father and your brothers dwell in the best of the land.
Let them dwell in the land of Goshen. If you know any able men
among them, then put them in charge of my livestock."
7 Joseph brought in Jacob, his father, and set him before
Pharaoh; and Jacob blessed Pharaoh. 8 Pharaoh said to Jacob,
"How old are you?"
9 Jacob said to Pharaoh, "The years of my pilgrimage are one
hundred thirty years. The days of the years of my life have been
few and evil. They have not attained to the days of the years of
the life of my fathers in the days of their pilgrimage." 10 Jacob
blessed Pharaoh, and went out from the presence of Pharaoh.
11 Joseph placed his father and his brothers, and gave them a
possession in the land of Egypt, in the best of the land, in the land
of Rameses, as Pharaoh had commanded. 12 Joseph provided
his father, his brothers, and all of his father's household with
bread, according to the sizes of their families.
13 There was no bread in all the land; for the famine was very
severe, so that the land of Egypt and the land of Canaan fainted
by reason of the famine. 14 Joseph gathered up all the money
that was found in the land of Egypt, and in the land of Canaan,
for the grain which they bought: and Joseph brought the money
into Pharaoh's house. 15 When the money was all spent in the
land of Egypt, and in the land of Canaan, all the Egyptians came
to Joseph, and said, "Give us bread, for why should we die in
your presence? For our money fails."
16 Joseph said, "Give me your livestock; and I will give you
food for your livestock, if your money is gone."
17 They brought their livestock to Joseph, and Joseph gave
them bread in exchange for the horses, and for the flocks, and for
the herds, and for the donkeys: and he fed them with bread in
exchange for all their livestock for that year. 18 When that year
was ended, they came to him the second year, and said to him,
"We will not hide from my lord how our money is all spent, and
the herds of livestock are my lord's. There is nothing left in the
sight of my lord, but our bodies, and our lands. 19 Why should
we die before your eyes, both we and our land? Buy us and our
land for bread, and we and our land will be servants to Pharaoh.
Give us seed, that we may live, and not die, and that the land
won't be desolate."
20 So Joseph bought all the land of Egypt for Pharaoh, for
every man of the Egyptians sold his field, because the famine was
severe on them, and the land became Pharaoh's. 21 As for the
people, he moved them to the cities from one end of the border of
Egypt even to the other end of it. 22 Only he didn't buy the land
of the priests, for the priests had a portion from Pharaoh, and ate
their portion which Pharaoh gave them. That is why they didn't
sell their land. 23 Then Joseph said to the people, "Behold, I
have bought you and your land today for Pharaoh. Behold, here is
seed for you, and you shall sow the land. 24 It will happen at
the harvests, that you shall give a fifth to Pharaoh, and four parts
will be your own, for seed of the field, for your food, for them of
your households, and for food for your little ones."
25 They said, "You have saved our lives! Let us find favor in
the sight of my lord, and we will be Pharaoh's servants."
26 Joseph made it a statute concerning the land of Egypt to this
day, that Pharaoh should have the fifth. Only the land of the
priests alone didn't become Pharaoh's.
27 Israel lived in the land of Egypt, in the land of Goshen; and
they got themselves possessions therein, and were fruitful, and
multiplied exceedingly. 28 Jacob lived in the land of Egypt
seventeen years. So the days of Jacob, the years of his life, were
one hundred forty-seven years. 29 The time came near that

---

[45] **44:29** *44:29* **Sheol is the place of the dead.**

[46] **44:31** *44:31* **Sheol is the place of the dead.**

Israel must die, and he called his son Joseph, and said to him, "If now I have found favor in your sight, please put your hand under my thigh, and deal kindly and truly with me. Please don't bury me in Egypt, **30** but when I sleep with my fathers, you shall carry me out of Egypt, and bury me in their burying place." Joseph said, "I will do as you have said."

31 Israel said, "Swear to me," and he swore to him. Then Israel bowed himself on the bed's head.

Genesis 48

1 After these things, someone said to Joseph, "Behold, your father is sick." He took with him his two sons, Manasseh and Ephraim. **2** Someone told Jacob, and said, "Behold, your son Joseph comes to you," and Israel strengthened himself, and sat on the bed. **3** Jacob said to Joseph, "God Almighty appeared to me at Luz in the land of Canaan, and blessed me, **4** and said to me, 'Behold, I will make you fruitful, and multiply you, and I will make of you a company of peoples, and will give this land to your offspring after you for an everlasting possession.' **5** Now your two sons, who were born to you in the land of Egypt before I came to you into Egypt, are mine; Ephraim and Manasseh, even as Reuben and Simeon, will be mine. **6** Your offspring, whom you become the father of after them, will be yours. They will be called after the name of their brothers in their inheritance. **7** As for me, when I came from Paddan, Rachel died beside me in the land of Canaan on the way, when there was still some distance to come to Ephrath, and I buried her there on the way to Ephrath (also called Bethlehem)."

8 Israel saw Joseph's sons, and said, "Who are these?"

9 Joseph said to his father, "They are my sons, whom God has given me here."

He said, "Please bring them to me, and I will bless them."

10 Now the eyes of Israel were dim for age, so that he couldn't see well. Joseph brought them near to him; and he kissed them, and embraced them. **11** Israel said to Joseph, "I didn't think I would see your face, and behold, God has let me see your offspring also." **12** Joseph brought them out from between his knees, and he bowed himself with his face to the earth. **13** Joseph took them both, Ephraim in his right hand toward Israel's left hand, and Manasseh in his left hand toward Israel's right hand, and brought them near to him. **14** Israel stretched out his right hand, and laid it on Ephraim's head, who was the younger, and his left hand on Manasseh's head, guiding his hands knowingly, for Manasseh was the firstborn. **15** He blessed Joseph, and said,

"The God before whom my fathers Abraham and Isaac walked, the God who has fed me all my life long to this day,

16 the angel who has redeemed me from all evil, bless the lads, and let my name be named on them, and the name of my fathers Abraham and Isaac. Let them grow into a multitude upon the earth."

17 When Joseph saw that his father laid his right hand on the head of Ephraim, it displeased him. He held up his father's hand, to remove it from Ephraim's head to Manasseh's head. **18** Joseph said to his father, "Not so, my father, for this is the firstborn. Put your right hand on his head."

19 His father refused, and said, "I know, my son, I know. He also will become a people, and he also will be great. However, his younger brother will be greater than he, and his offspring will become a multitude of nations." **20** He blessed them that day, saying, "Israel will bless in you, saying, 'God make you as Ephraim and as Manasseh'" He set Ephraim before Manasseh.

21 Israel said to Joseph, "Behold, I am dying, but God will be with you, and bring you again to the land of your fathers. **22** Moreover I have given to you one portion above your brothers, which I took out of the hand of the Amorite with my sword and with my bow."

Genesis 49

1 Jacob called to his sons, and said: "Gather yourselves together, that I may tell you that which will happen to you in the days to come.

2 Assemble yourselves, and hear, you sons of Jacob. Listen to Israel, your father.

3 "Reuben, you are my firstborn, my might, and the beginning of my strength;
excelling in dignity, and excelling in power.

4 Boiling over like water, you shall not excel;
because you went up to your father's bed,
then defiled it. He went up to my couch.

5 "Simeon and Levi are brothers.
Their swords are weapons of violence.

6 My soul, don't come into their council.
My glory, don't be united to their assembly;
for in their anger they killed men.
In their self-will they hamstrung cattle.

7 Cursed be their anger, for it was fierce;
and their wrath, for it was cruel.
I will divide them in Jacob,
and scatter them in Israel.

8 "Judah, your brothers will praise you.
Your hand will be on the neck of your enemies.
Your father's sons will bow down before you.

9 Judah is a lion's cub.
From the prey, my son, you have gone up.
He stooped down, he crouched as a lion,
as a lioness.
Who will rouse him up?

10 The scepter will not depart from Judah,
nor the ruler's staff from between his feet,
until he comes to whom it belongs.
To him will the obedience of the peoples be.

11 Binding his foal to the vine,
his donkey's colt to the choice vine;
he has washed his garments in wine,
his robes in the blood of grapes.

12 His eyes will be red with wine,
his teeth white with milk.

13 "Zebulun will dwell at the haven of the sea.
He will be for a haven of ships.
His border will be on Sidon.

14 "Issachar is a strong donkey,
lying down between the saddlebags.

15 He saw a resting place, that it was good,
the land, that it was pleasant.
He bows his shoulder to the burden,
and becomes a servant doing forced labor.

16 "Dan will judge his people,
as one of the tribes of Israel.

17 Dan will be a serpent on the trail,
an adder in the path,
That bites the horse's heels,
so that his rider falls backward.

18 I have waited for your salvation, God.

19 "A troop will press on Gad,
but he will press on their heel.

20 "Asher's food will be rich.
He will produce royal dainties.

21 "Naphtali is a doe set free,
who bears beautiful fawns.

22 "Joseph is a fruitful vine,
a fruitful vine by a spring.
His branches run over the wall.

23 The archers have severely grieved him,
shot at him, and persecuted him:

24 But his bow remained strong.
The arms of his hands were made strong,
by the hands of the Mighty One of Jacob,
(from there is the shepherd, the stone of Israel),

25 even by the God of your father, who will help you,
by the Almighty, who will bless you,
with blessings of heaven above,
blessings of the deep that lies below,
blessings of the breasts, and of the womb.

26 The blessings of your father have prevailed above the blessings of your ancestors,
above the boundaries of the ancient hills.
They will be on the head of Joseph,
on the crown of the head of him who is separated from his brothers.

27 "Benjamin is a ravenous wolf.
In the morning he will devour the prey.
At evening he will divide the plunder."

28 All these are the twelve tribes of Israel, and this is what their father spoke to them, and blessed them. He blessed everyone according to his own blessing. **29** He instructed them, and said to them, "I am to be gathered to my people. Bury me with my fathers in the cave that is in the field of Ephron the Hittite, **30** in the cave that is in the field of Machpelah, which is before Mamre, in the land of Canaan, which Abraham bought with the field from Ephron the Hittite as a burial place. **31** There they buried Abraham and Sarah, his wife. There they buried Isaac and Rebekah, his wife, and there I buried Leah: **32** the field and the cave that is therein, which was purchased from the children of Heth." **33** When Jacob finished charging his sons, he gathered up his feet into the bed, breathed his last breath, and was gathered to his people.

Genesis 50

1 Joseph fell on his father's face, wept on him, and kissed him.

2 Joseph commanded his servants, the physicians, to embalm his father; and the physicians embalmed Israel. **3** Forty days were used for him, for that is how many the days it takes to embalm. The Egyptians wept for Israel for seventy days.

4 When the days of weeping for him were past, Joseph spoke to Pharaoh's staff, saying, "If now I have found favor in your eyes, please speak in the ears of Pharaoh, saying, **5** 'My father made me swear, saying, "Behold, I am dying. Bury me in my grave which I have dug for myself in the land of Canaan." Now therefore, please let me go up and bury my father, and I will come again.'"

6 Pharaoh said, "Go up, and bury your father, just like he made you swear."

7 Joseph went up to bury his father; and with him went up all the servants of Pharaoh, the elders of his house, all the elders of the land of Egypt, **8** All the house of Joseph, his brothers, and his father's house. Only their little ones, their flocks, and their herds, they left in the land of Goshen. **9** There went up with him both chariots and horsemen. It was a very great company.

10 They came to the threshing floor of Atad, which is beyond the Jordan, and there they lamented with a very great and severe lamentation. He mourned for his father seven days. **11** When the inhabitants of the land, the Canaanites, saw the mourning in the floor of Atad, they said, "This is a grievous mourning by the Egyptians." Therefore its name was called Abel Mizraim, which is beyond the Jordan. **12** His sons did to him just as he commanded them, **13** for his sons carried him into the land of Canaan, and buried him in the cave of the field of Machpelah, which Abraham bought with the field, as a possession for a burial site, from Ephron the Hittite, near Mamre. **14** Joseph returned into Egypt—he, and his brothers, and all that went up with him to bury his father, after he had buried his father.

15 When Joseph's brothers saw that their father was dead, they said, "It may be that Joseph will hate us, and will fully pay us back for all the evil which we did to him." **16** They sent a message to Joseph, saying, "Your father commanded before he died, saying, **17** 'You shall tell Joseph, "Now please forgive the disobedience of your brothers, and their sin, because they did evil to you."' Now, please forgive the disobedience of the servants of the God of your father." Joseph wept when they spoke to him.

18 His brothers also went and fell down before his face; and they said, "Behold, we are your servants." **19** Joseph said to them, "Don't be afraid, for am I in the place of God? **20** As for you, you meant evil against me, but God meant it for good, to save many people alive, as is happening today. **21** Now therefore don't be afraid. I will provide for you and your little ones." He comforted them, and spoke kindly to them.

22 Joseph lived in Egypt, he, and his father's house. Joseph lived one hundred ten years. **23** Joseph saw Ephraim's children to the third generation. The children also of Machir, the son of Manasseh, were born on Joseph's knees. **24** Joseph said to his brothers, "I am dying, but God will surely visit you, and bring you up out of this land to the land which he swore to Abraham, to Isaac, and to Jacob." **25** Joseph took an oath from the children of Israel, saying, "God will surely visit you, and you shall carry up my bones from here." **26** So Joseph died, being one hundred ten years old, and they embalmed him, and he was put in a coffin in Egypt.

The Book of Exodus

Exodus 1

1 Now these are the names of the sons of Israel, who came into
Egypt (every man and his household came with Jacob):
2 Reuben, Simeon, Levi, and Judah, 3 Issachar, Zebulun, and
Benjamin, 4 Dan and Naphtali, Gad and Asher. 5 All the souls
who came out of Jacob's body were seventy souls, and Joseph
was in Egypt already. 6 Joseph died, as did all his brothers, and
all that generation. 7 The children of Israel were fruitful, and
increased abundantly, and multiplied, and grew exceedingly
mighty; and the land was filled with them.
8 Now there arose a new king over Egypt, who didn't know
Joseph. 9 He said to his people, "Behold,[47] the people of the
children of Israel are more and mightier than we. 10 Come, let's
deal wisely with them, lest they multiply, and it happen that when
any war breaks out, they also join themselves to our enemies and
fight against us, and escape out of the land." 11 Therefore they
set taskmasters over them to afflict them with their burdens. They
built storage cities for Pharaoh: Pithom and Raamses. 12 But the
more they afflicted them, the more they multiplied and the more
they spread out. They started to dread the children of Israel.
13 The Egyptians ruthlessly made the children of Israel serve,
14 and they made their lives bitter with hard service in mortar
and in brick, and in all kinds of service in the field, all their
service, in which they ruthlessly made them serve.
15 The king of Egypt spoke to the Hebrew midwives, of whom
the name of the one was Shiphrah, and the name of the other
Puah, 16 and he said, "When you perform the duty of a midwife
to the Hebrew women, and see them on the birth stool, if it is a
son, then you shall kill him; but if it is a daughter, then she shall
live." 17 But the midwives feared God,[48] and didn't do what the
king of Egypt commanded them, but saved the baby boys alive.
18 The king of Egypt called for the midwives, and said to them,
"Why have you done this thing and saved the boys alive?"
19 The midwives said to Pharaoh, "Because the Hebrew women
aren't like the Egyptian women; for they are vigorous and give
birth before the midwife comes to them."
20 God dealt well with the midwives, and the people multiplied,
and grew very mighty. 21 Because the midwives feared God, he
gave them families. 22 Pharaoh commanded all his people,
saying, "You shall cast every son who is born into the river, and
every daughter you shall save alive."

Exodus 2

1 A man of the house of Levi went and took a daughter of Levi
as his wife. 2 The woman conceived and bore a son. When she
saw that he was a fine child, she hid him three months. 3 When
she could no longer hide him, she took a papyrus basket for him,
and coated it with tar and with pitch. She put the child in it, and
laid it in the reeds by the river's bank. 4 His sister stood far off,
to see what would be done to him. 5 Pharaoh's daughter came
down to bathe at the river. Her maidens walked along by the
riverside. She saw the basket among the reeds, and sent her
servant to get it. 6 She opened it, and saw the child, and behold,
the baby cried. She had compassion on him, and said, "This is
one of the Hebrews' children."
7 Then his sister said to Pharaoh's daughter, "Should I go and
call a nurse for you from the Hebrew women, that she may nurse
the child for you?"
8 Pharaoh's daughter said to her, "Go."
The young woman went and called the child's mother.
9 Pharaoh's daughter said to her, "Take this child away, and
nurse him for me, and I will give you your wages."
The woman took the child, and nursed it. 10 The child grew, and
she brought him to Pharaoh's daughter, and he became her son.
She named him Moses,[49] and said, "Because I drew him out of
the water."
11 In those days, when Moses had grown up, he went out to his
brothers and saw their burdens. He saw an Egyptian striking a
Hebrew, one of his brothers. 12 He looked this way and that
way, and when he saw that there was no one, he killed the
Egyptian, and hid him in the sand.
13 He went out the second day, and behold, two men of the
Hebrews were fighting with each other. He said to him who did
the wrong, "Why do you strike your fellow?"
14 He said, "Who made you a prince and a judge over us? Do
you plan to kill me, as you killed the Egyptian?"
Moses was afraid, and said, "Surely this thing is known."
15 Now when Pharaoh heard this thing, he sought to kill Moses.
But Moses fled from the face of Pharaoh, and lived in the land of
Midian, and he sat down by a well.
16 Now the priest of Midian had seven daughters. They came
and drew water, and filled the troughs to water their father's
flock. 17 The shepherds came and drove them away; but Moses
stood up and helped them, and watered their flock. 18 When
they came to Reuel, their father, he said, "How is it that you have
returned so early today?"
19 They said, "An Egyptian delivered us out of the hand of the
shepherds, and moreover he drew water for us, and watered the
flock."
20 He said to his daughters, "Where is he? Why is it that you
have left the man? Call him, that he may eat bread."
21 Moses was content to dwell with the man. He gave Moses
Zipporah, his daughter. 22 She bore a son, and he named him
Gershom,[50] for he said, "I have lived as a foreigner in a foreign
land."
23 In the course of those many days, the king of Egypt died, and
the children of Israel sighed because of the bondage, and they
cried, and their cry came up to God because of the bondage.
24 God heard their groaning, and God remembered his covenant
with Abraham, with Isaac, and with Jacob. 25 God saw the
children of Israel, and God was concerned about them.

Exodus 3

1 Now Moses was keeping the flock of Jethro, his father-in-law,
the priest of Midian, and he led the flock to the back of the
wilderness, and came to God's mountain, to Horeb. 2 God's[51]
angel appeared to him in a flame of fire out of the middle of a
bush. He looked, and behold, the bush burned with fire, and the
bush was not consumed. 3 Moses said, "I will go now, and see
this great sight, why the bush is not burned."
4 When God saw that he came over to see, God called to him out
of the middle of the bush, and said, "Moses! Moses!"
He said, "Here I am."
5 He said, "Don't come close. Take off your sandals, for the
place you are standing on is holy ground." 6 Moreover he said,
"I am the God of your father, the God of Abraham, the God of
Isaac, and the God of Jacob."
Moses hid his face because he was afraid to look at God.
7 God said, "I have surely seen the affliction of my people who
are in Egypt, and have heard their cry because of their
taskmasters, for I know their sorrows. 8 I have come down to
deliver them out of the hand of the Egyptians, and to bring them
up out of that land to a good and large land, to a land flowing
with milk and honey; to the place of the Canaanite, the Hittite,
the Amorite, the Perizzite, the Hivite, and the Jebusite. 9 Now,
behold, the cry of the children of Israel has come to me.
Moreover I have seen the oppression with which the Egyptians
oppress them. 10 Come now therefore, and I will send you to
Pharaoh, that you may bring my people, the children of Israel, out
of Egypt."
11 Moses said to God, "Who am I, that I should go to Pharaoh,
and that I should bring the children of Israel out of Egypt?"
12 He said, "Certainly I will be with you. This will be the token
to you, that I have sent you: when you have brought the people
out of Egypt, you shall serve God on this mountain."
13 Moses said to God, "Behold, when I come to the children of
Israel, and tell them, 'The God of your fathers has sent me to
you,' and they ask me, 'What is his name?' what should I tell
them?"
14 God said to Moses, "I AM WHO I AM," and he said, "You
shall tell the children of Israel this: 'I AM has sent me to you.'"
15 God said moreover to Moses, "You shall tell the children of
Israel this, 'God, the God of your fathers, the God of Abraham,
the God of Isaac, and the God of Jacob, has sent me to you.' This
is my name forever, and this is my memorial to all generations.
16 Go and gather the elders of Israel together, and tell them,
'God, the God of your fathers, the God of Abraham, of Isaac, and
of Jacob, has appeared to me, saying, "I have surely visited you,
and seen that which is done to you in Egypt. 17 I have said, I
will bring you up out of the affliction of Egypt to the land of the
Canaanite, the Hittite, the Amorite, the Perizzite, the Hivite, and
the Jebusite, to a land flowing with milk and honey."' 18 They
will listen to your voice. You shall come, you and the elders of
Israel, to the king of Egypt, and you shall tell him, 'God, the God
of the Hebrews, has met with us. Now please let us go three days'
journey into the wilderness, that we may sacrifice to God, our
God.' 19 I know that the king of Egypt won't give you
permission to go, no, not by a mighty hand. 20 I will reach out
my hand and strike Egypt with all my wonders which I will do
among them, and after that he will let you go. 21 I will give this
people favor in the sight of the Egyptians, and it will happen that
when you go, you shall not go empty-handed. 22 But every
woman shall ask of her neighbor, and of her who visits her house,
jewels of silver, jewels of gold, and clothing. You shall put them
on your sons, and on your daughters. You shall plunder the
Egyptians."

Exodus 4

1 Moses answered, "But, behold, they will not believe me, nor
listen to my voice; for they will say, 'God has not appeared to
you.'"
2 God said to him, "What is that in your hand?"
He said, "A rod."
3 He said, "Throw it on the ground."
He threw it on the ground, and it became a snake; and Moses ran
away from it.
4 God said to Moses, "Stretch out your hand, and take it by the
tail."
He stretched out his hand, and took hold of it, and it became a rod
in his hand.
5 "This is so that they may believe that God, the God of their
fathers, the God of Abraham, the God of Isaac, and the God of
Jacob, has appeared to you." 6 God said furthermore to him,
"Now put your hand inside your cloak."
He put his hand inside his cloak, and when he took it out, behold,
his hand was leprous, as white as snow.
7 He said, "Put your hand inside your cloak again."
He put his hand inside his cloak again, and when he took it out of
his cloak, behold, it had turned again as his other flesh.
8 "It will happen, if they will not believe you or listen to the
voice of the first sign, that they will believe the voice of the latter
sign. 9 It will happen, if they will not believe even these two
signs or listen to your voice, that you shall take of the water of
the river, and pour it on the dry land. The water which you take
out of the river will become blood on the dry land."
10 Moses said to God, "O Lord,[52] I am not eloquent, neither
before now, nor since you have spoken to your servant; for I am
slow of speech, and of a slow tongue."
11 God said to him, "Who made man's mouth? Or who makes
one mute, or deaf, or seeing, or blind? Isn't it I, God? 12 Now
therefore go, and I will be with your mouth, and teach you what
you shall speak."
13 Moses said, "Oh, Lord, please send someone else."
14 God's anger burned against Moses, and he said, "What about
Aaron, your brother, the Levite? I know that he can speak well.
Also, behold, he is coming out to meet you. When he sees you,
he will be glad in his heart. 15 You shall speak to him, and put
the words in his mouth. I will be with your mouth, and with his
mouth, and will teach you what you shall do. 16 He will be your
spokesman to the people. It will happen that he will be to you a

---

[47] **1:9** *1:9* **"Behold", from "הִנֵּה", means look at, take notice, observe, see, or gaze at. It is often used as an interjection.**

[48] **1:17** *1:17* **The Hebrew word rendered "God" is "אֱלֹהִים" (Elohim).**

[49] **2:10** *2:10* **"Moses" sounds like the Hebrew for "draw out".**

[50] **2:22** *2:22* **"Gershom" sounds like the Hebrew for "an alien there".**

[51] **3:2** *3:2* **"God" is God's proper Name, sometimes rendered "LORD" (all caps) in other translations.**

[52] **4:10** *4:10* **The word translated "Lord" is "Adonai".**

mouth, and you will be to him as God. **17** You shall take this rod in your hand, with which you shall do the signs."

18 Moses went and returned to Jethro his father-in-law, and said to him, "Please let me go and return to my brothers who are in Egypt, and see whether they are still alive."

Jethro said to Moses, "Go in peace."

19 God said to Moses in Midian, "Go, return into Egypt; for all the men who sought your life are dead."

20 Moses took his wife and his sons, and set them on a donkey, and he returned to the land of Egypt. Moses took God's rod in his hand. **21** God said to Moses, "When you go back into Egypt, see that you do before Pharaoh all the wonders which I have put in your hand, but I will harden his heart and he will not let the people go. **22** You shall tell Pharaoh, 'God says, Israel is my son, my firstborn, **23** and I have said to you, "Let my son go, that he may serve me;" and you have refused to let him go. Behold, I will kill your firstborn son.'"

24 On the way at a lodging place, God met Moses and wanted to kill him. **25** Then Zipporah took a flint, and cut off the foreskin of her son, and cast it at his feet; and she said, "Surely you are a bridegroom of blood to me."

26 So he let him alone. Then she said, "You are a bridegroom of blood," because of the circumcision.

27 God said to Aaron, "Go into the wilderness to meet Moses." He went, and met him on God's mountain, and kissed him.

28 Moses told Aaron all God's words with which he had sent him, and all the signs with which he had instructed him.

29 Moses and Aaron went and gathered together all the elders of the children of Israel. **30** Aaron spoke all the words which God had spoken to Moses, and did the signs in the sight of the people.

31 The people believed, and when they heard that God had visited the children of Israel, and that he had seen their affliction, then they bowed their heads and worshiped.

Exodus 5

1 Afterward Moses and Aaron came, and said to Pharaoh, "This is what God, the God of Israel, says, 'Let my people go, that they may hold a feast to me in the wilderness.'"

2 Pharaoh said, "Who is God, that I should listen to his voice to let Israel go? I don't know God, and moreover I will not let Israel go."

3 They said, "The God of the Hebrews has met with us. Please let us go three days' journey into the wilderness, and sacrifice to God, our God, lest he fall on us with pestilence, or with the sword."

4 The king of Egypt said to them, "Why do you, Moses and Aaron, take the people from their work? Get back to your burdens!" **5** Pharaoh said, "Behold, the people of the land are now many, and you make them rest from their burdens." **6** The same day Pharaoh commanded the taskmasters of the people and their officers, saying, **7** "You shall no longer give the people straw to make brick, as before. Let them go and gather straw for themselves. **8** You shall require from them the number of the bricks which they made before. You shall not diminish anything of it, for they are idle. Therefore they cry, saying, 'Let's go and sacrifice to our God.' **9** Let heavier work be laid on the men, that they may labor in it. Don't let them pay any attention to lying words."

10 The taskmasters of the people went out, and their officers, and they spoke to the people, saying, "This is what Pharaoh says: 'I will not give you straw. **11** Go yourselves, get straw where you can find it, for nothing of your work shall be diminished.'"

12 So the people were scattered abroad throughout all the land of Egypt to gather stubble for straw. **13** The taskmasters were urgent saying, "Fulfill your work quota daily, as when there was straw!" **14** The officers of the children of Israel, whom Pharaoh's taskmasters had set over them, were beaten, and were asked, "Why haven't you fulfilled your quota both yesterday and today, in making brick as before?"

15 Then the officers of the children of Israel came and cried to Pharaoh, saying, "Why do you deal this way with your servants? **16** No straw is given to your servants, and they tell us, 'Make brick!' and behold, your servants are beaten; but the fault is in your own people."

17 But Pharaoh said, "You are idle! You are idle! Therefore you say, 'Let's go and sacrifice to God.' **18** Go therefore now, and work; for no straw shall be given to you; yet you shall deliver the same number of bricks!"

19 The officers of the children of Israel saw that they were in trouble when it was said, "You shall not diminish anything from your daily quota of bricks!"

20 They met Moses and Aaron, who stood along the way, as they came out from Pharaoh. **21** They said to them, "May God

look at you and judge, because you have made us a stench to be abhorred in the eyes of Pharaoh, and in the eyes of his servants, to put a sword in their hand to kill us!"

22 Moses returned to God, and said, "Lord, why have you brought trouble on this people? Why is it that you have sent me?

23 For since I came to Pharaoh to speak in your name, he has brought trouble on this people. You have not rescued your people at all!"

Exodus 6

1 God said to Moses, "Now you shall see what I will do to Pharaoh, for by a strong hand he shall let them go, and by a strong hand he shall drive them out of his land."

2 God spoke to Moses, and said to him, "I am God. **3** I appeared to Abraham, to Isaac, and to Jacob, as God Almighty; but by my name God I was not known to them. **4** I have also established my covenant with them, to give them the land of Canaan, the land of their travels, in which they lived as aliens. **5** Moreover I have heard the groaning of the children of Israel, whom the Egyptians keep in bondage, and I have remembered my covenant.

6 Therefore tell the children of Israel, 'I am God, and I will bring you out from under the burdens of the Egyptians, and I will rid you out of their bondage, and I will redeem you with an outstretched arm, and with great judgments. **7** I will take you to myself for a people. I will be your God; and you shall know that I am God your God, who brings you out from under the burdens of the Egyptians. **8** I will bring you into the land which I swore to give to Abraham, to Isaac, and to Jacob; and I will give it to you for a heritage: I am God.'"

9 Moses spoke so to the children of Israel, but they didn't listen to Moses for anguish of spirit, and for cruel bondage.

10 God spoke to Moses, saying, **11** "Go in, speak to Pharaoh king of Egypt, that he let the children of Israel go out of his land."

12 Moses spoke before God, saying, "Behold, the children of Israel haven't listened to me. How then shall Pharaoh listen to me, when I have uncircumcised lips?" **13** God spoke to Moses and to Aaron, and gave them a command to the children of Israel, and to Pharaoh king of Egypt, to bring the children of Israel out of the land of Egypt.

14 These are the heads of their fathers' houses. The sons of Reuben the firstborn of Israel: Hanoch, and Pallu, Hezron, and Carmi; these are the families of Reuben. **15** The sons of Simeon: Jemuel, and Jamin, and Ohad, and Jachin, and Zohar, and Shaul the son of a Canaanite woman; these are the families of Simeon.

16 These are the names of the sons of Levi according to their generations: Gershon, and Kohath, and Merari; and the years of the life of Levi were one hundred thirty-seven years. **17** The sons of Gershon: Libni and Shimei, according to their families.

18 The sons of Kohath: Amram, and Izhar, and Hebron, and Uzziel; and the years of the life of Kohath were one hundred thirty-three years. **19** The sons of Merari: Mahli and Mushi. These are the families of the Levites according to their generations. **20** Amram took Jochebed his father's sister to himself as wife; and she bore him Aaron and Moses. The years of the life of Amram were one hundred thirty-seven years. **21** The sons of Izhar: Korah, and Nepheg, and Zichri. **22** The sons of Uzziel: Mishael, and Elzaphan, and Sithri. **23** Aaron took Elisheba, the daughter of Amminadab, the sister of Nahshon, as his wife; and she bore him Nadab and Abihu, Eleazar and Ithamar. **24** The sons of Korah: Assir, and Elkanah, and Abiasaph; these are the families of the Korahites. **25** Eleazar Aaron's son took one of the daughters of Putiel as his wife; and she bore him Phinehas. These are the heads of the fathers' houses of the Levites according to their families. **26** These are that Aaron and Moses to whom God said, "Bring out the children of Israel from the land of Egypt according to their armies."

27 These are those who spoke to Pharaoh king of Egypt, to bring out the children of Israel from Egypt. These are that Moses and Aaron.

28 On the day when God spoke to Moses in the land of Egypt,

29 God said to Moses, "I am God. Tell Pharaoh king of Egypt all that I tell you."

30 Moses said before God, "Behold, I am of uncircumcised lips, and how shall Pharaoh listen to me?"

Exodus 7

1 God said to Moses, "Behold, I have made you as God to Pharaoh; and Aaron your brother shall be your prophet. **2** You shall speak all that I command you; and Aaron your brother shall speak to Pharaoh, that he let the children of Israel go out of his

land. **3** I will harden Pharaoh's heart, and multiply my signs and my wonders in the land of Egypt. **4** But Pharaoh will not listen to you, so I will lay my hand on Egypt, and bring out my armies, my people the children of Israel, out of the land of Egypt by great judgments. **5** The Egyptians shall know that I am God when I stretch out my hand on Egypt, and bring the children of Israel out from among them."

6 Moses and Aaron did so. As God commanded them, so they did. **7** Moses was eighty years old, and Aaron eighty-three years old, when they spoke to Pharaoh.

8 God spoke to Moses and to Aaron, saying, **9** "When Pharaoh speaks to you, saying, 'Perform a miracle!' then you shall tell Aaron, 'Take your rod, and cast it down before Pharaoh, and it will become a serpent.'"

10 Moses and Aaron went in to Pharaoh, and they did so, as God had commanded. Aaron cast down his rod before Pharaoh and before his servants, and it became a serpent. **11** Then Pharaoh also called for the wise men and the sorcerers. They also, the magicians of Egypt, did the same thing with their enchantments.

12 For they each cast down their rods, and they became serpents; but Aaron's rod swallowed up their rods. **13** Pharaoh's heart was hardened, and he didn't listen to them, as God had spoken.

14 God said to Moses, "Pharaoh's heart is stubborn. He refuses to let the people go. **15** Go to Pharaoh in the morning. Behold, he is going out to the water. You shall stand by the river's bank to meet him. You shall take the rod which was turned to a serpent in your hand. **16** You shall tell him, 'God, the God of the Hebrews, has sent me to you, saying, "Let my people go, that they may serve me in the wilderness. Behold, until now you haven't listened." **17** God says, "In this you shall know that I am God. Behold: I will strike with the rod that is in my hand on the waters which are in the river, and they shall be turned to blood.

18 The fish that are in the river will die and the river will become foul. The Egyptians will loathe to drink water from the river."'" **19** God said to Moses, "Tell Aaron, 'Take your rod, and stretch out your hand over the waters of Egypt, over their rivers, over their streams, and over their pools, and over all their ponds of water, that they may become blood. There will be blood throughout all the land of Egypt, both in vessels of wood and in vessels of stone.'"

20 Moses and Aaron did so, as God commanded; and he lifted up the rod, and struck the waters that were in the river, in the sight of Pharaoh, and in the sight of his servants; and all the waters that were in the river were turned to blood. **21** The fish that were in the river died. The river became foul. The Egyptians couldn't drink water from the river. The blood was throughout all the land of Egypt. **22** The magicians of Egypt did the same thing with their enchantments. So Pharaoh's heart was hardened, and he didn't listen to them, as God had spoken. **23** Pharaoh turned and went into his house, and he didn't even take this to heart.

24 All the Egyptians dug around the river for water to drink; for they couldn't drink the river water. **25** Seven days were fulfilled, after God had struck the river.

Exodus 8

1 God spoke to Moses, "Go in to Pharaoh, and tell him, 'This is what God says, "Let my people go, that they may serve me. **2** If you refuse to let them go, behold, I will plague all your borders with frogs. **3** The river will swarm with frogs, which will go up and come into your house, and into your bedroom, and on your bed, and into the house of your servants, and on your people, and into your ovens, and into your kneading troughs. **4** The frogs shall come up both on you, and on your people, and on all your servants."'" **5** God said to Moses, "Tell Aaron, 'Stretch out your hand with your rod over the rivers, over the streams, and over the pools, and cause frogs to come up on the land of Egypt.'"

6 Aaron stretched out his hand over the waters of Egypt; and the frogs came up, and covered the land of Egypt. **7** The magicians did the same thing with their enchantments, and brought up frogs on the land of Egypt.

8 Then Pharaoh called for Moses and Aaron, and said, "Entreat God, that he take away the frogs from me and from my people; and I will let the people go, that they may sacrifice to God."

9 Moses said to Pharaoh, "I give you the honor of setting the time that I should pray for you, and for your servants, and for your people, that the frogs be destroyed from you and your houses, and remain in the river only."

10 Pharaoh said, "Tomorrow."

Moses said, "Let it be according to your word, that you may know that there is no one like God our God. **11** The frogs shall depart from you, and from your houses, and from your servants, and from your people. They shall remain in the river only."

12 Moses and Aaron went out from Pharaoh, and Moses cried to
God concerning the frogs which he had brought on Pharaoh.
13 God did according to the word of Moses, and the frogs died
out of the houses, out of the courts, and out of the fields.
14 They gathered them together in heaps, and the land stank.
15 But when Pharaoh saw that there was a respite, he hardened
his heart, and didn't listen to them, as God had spoken.
16 God said to Moses, "Tell Aaron, 'Stretch out your rod, and
strike the dust of the earth, that it may become lice throughout all
the land of Egypt.'" 17 They did so; and Aaron stretched out his
hand with his rod, and struck the dust of the earth, and there were
lice on man, and on animal; all the dust of the earth became lice
throughout all the land of Egypt. 18 The magicians tried with
their enchantments to produce lice, but they couldn't. There were
lice on man, and on animal. 19 Then the magicians said to
Pharaoh, "This is God's finger;" but Pharaoh's heart was
hardened, and he didn't listen to them, as God had spoken.
20 God said to Moses, "Rise up early in the morning, and stand
before Pharaoh; behold, he comes out to the water; and tell him,
'This is what God says, "Let my people go, that they may serve
me. 21 Else, if you will not let my people go, behold, I will send
swarms of flies on you, and on your servants, and on your people,
and into your houses. The houses of the Egyptians shall be full of
swarms of flies, and also the ground they are on. 22 I will set
apart in that day the land of Goshen, in which my people dwell,
that no swarms of flies shall be there, to the end you may know
that I am God on the earth. 23 I will put a division between my
people and your people. This sign shall happen by tomorrow."'"
24 God did so; and there came grievous swarms of flies into the
house of Pharaoh, and into his servants' houses. In all the land of
Egypt the land was corrupted by reason of the swarms of flies.
25 Pharaoh called for Moses and for Aaron, and said, "Go,
sacrifice to your God in the land!"
26 Moses said, "It isn't appropriate to do so; for we shall
sacrifice the abomination of the Egyptians to God our God.
Behold, if we sacrifice the abomination of the Egyptians before
their eyes, won't they stone us? 27 We will go three days'
journey into the wilderness, and sacrifice to God our God, as he
shall command us."
28 Pharaoh said, "I will let you go, that you may sacrifice to God
your God in the wilderness, only you shall not go very far away.
Pray for me."
29 Moses said, "Behold, I am going out from you. I will pray to
God that the swarms of flies may depart from Pharaoh, from his
servants, and from his people, tomorrow; only don't let Pharaoh
deal deceitfully any more in not letting the people go to sacrifice
to God." 30 Moses went out from Pharaoh, and prayed to God.
31 God did according to the word of Moses, and he removed the
swarms of flies from Pharaoh, from his servants, and from his
people. There remained not one. 32 Pharaoh hardened his heart
this time also, and he didn't let the people go.

Exodus 9

1 Then God said to Moses, "Go in to Pharaoh, and tell him,
'This is what God, the God of the Hebrews, says: "Let my people
go, that they may serve me. 2 For if you refuse to let them go,
and hold them still, 3 behold, God's hand is on your livestock
which are in the field, on the horses, on the donkeys, on the
camels, on the herds, and on the flocks with a very grievous
pestilence. 4 God will make a distinction between the livestock
of Israel and the livestock of Egypt; and nothing shall die of all
that belongs to the children of Israel."'" 5 God appointed a set
time, saying, "Tomorrow God shall do this thing in the land."
6 God did that thing on the next day; and all the livestock of
Egypt died, but of the livestock of the children of Israel, not one
died. 7 Pharaoh sent, and, behold, there was not so much as one
of the livestock of the Israelites dead. But the heart of Pharaoh
was stubborn, and he didn't let the people go.
8 God said to Moses and to Aaron, "Take handfuls of ashes of
the furnace, and let Moses sprinkle it toward the sky in the sight
of Pharaoh. 9 It shall become small dust over all the land of
Egypt, and shall be a boils and blisters breaking out on man and
on animal, throughout all the land of Egypt."
10 They took ashes of the furnace, and stood before Pharaoh;
and Moses sprinkled it up toward the sky; and it became boils
and blisters breaking on man and on animal. 11 The magicians
couldn't stand before Moses because of the boils; for the boils
were on the magicians and on all the Egyptians. 12 God
hardened the heart of Pharaoh, and he didn't listen to them, as
God had spoken to Moses.
13 God said to Moses, "Rise up early in the morning, and stand
before Pharaoh, and tell him, 'This is what God, the God of the
Hebrews, says: "Let my people go, that they may serve me.
14 For this time I will send all my plagues against your heart,
against your officials, and against your people; that you may
know that there is no one like me in all the earth. 15 For now I
would have stretched out my hand, and struck you and your
people with pestilence, and you would have been cut off from the
earth; 16 but indeed for this cause I have made you stand: to
show you my power, and that my name may be declared
throughout all the earth, 17 because you still exalt yourself
against my people, that you won't let them go. 18 Behold,
tomorrow about this time I will cause it to rain a very grievous
hail, such as has not been in Egypt since the day it was founded
even until now. 19 Now therefore command that all of your
livestock and all that you have in the field be brought into shelter.
The hail will come down on every man and animal that is found
in the field, and isn't brought home, and they will die."'"
20 Those who feared God's word among the servants of Pharaoh
made their servants and their livestock flee into the houses.
21 Whoever didn't respect God's word left his servants and his
livestock in the field.
22 God said to Moses, "Stretch out your hand toward the sky,
that there may be hail in all the land of Egypt, on man, and on
animal, and on every herb of the field, throughout the land of
Egypt."
23 Moses stretched out his rod toward the heavens, and God sent
thunder and hail; and lightning flashed down to the earth. God
rained hail on the land of Egypt. 24 So there was very severe
hail, and lightning mixed with the hail, such as had not been in all
the land of Egypt since it became a nation. 25 The hail struck
throughout all the land of Egypt all that was in the field, both
man and animal; and the hail struck every herb of the field, and
broke every tree of the field. 26 Only in the land of Goshen,
where the children of Israel were, there was no hail.
27 Pharaoh sent and called for Moses and Aaron, and said to
them, "I have sinned this time. God is righteous, and I and my
people are wicked. 28 Pray to God; for there has been enough of
mighty thunderings and hail. I will let you go, and you shall stay
no longer."
29 Moses said to him, "As soon as I have gone out of the city, I
will spread out my hands to God. The thunders shall cease, and
there will not be any more hail; that you may know that the earth
is God's. 30 But as for you and your servants, I know that you
don't yet fear God God."
31 The flax and the barley were struck, for the barley had
ripened and the flax was blooming. 32 But the wheat and the
spelt were not struck, for they had not grown up. 33 Moses went
out of the city from Pharaoh, and spread out his hands to God;
and the thunders and hail ceased, and the rain was not poured on
the earth. 34 When Pharaoh saw that the rain and the hail and the
thunders had ceased, he sinned yet more, and hardened his heart,
he and his servants. 35 The heart of Pharaoh was hardened, and
he didn't let the children of Israel go, just as God had spoken
through Moses.

Exodus 10

1 God said to Moses, "Go in to Pharaoh, for I have hardened his
heart and the heart of his servants, that I may show these my
signs among them; 2 and that you may tell in the hearing of
your son, and of your son's son, what things I have done to
Egypt, and my signs which I have done among them; that you
may know that I am God."
3 Moses and Aaron went in to Pharaoh, and said to him, "This
is what God, the God of the Hebrews, says: 'How long will you
refuse to humble yourself before me? Let my people go, that they
may serve me. 4 Or else, if you refuse to let my people go,
behold, tomorrow I will bring locusts into your country, 5 and
they shall cover the surface of the earth, so that one won't be able
to see the earth. They shall eat the residue of that which has
escaped, which remains to you from the hail, and shall eat every
tree which grows for you out of the field. 6 Your houses shall
be filled, and the houses of all your servants, and the houses of all
the Egyptians, as neither your fathers nor your fathers' fathers
have seen, since the day that they were on the earth to this day.'"
He turned, and went out from Pharaoh.
7 Pharaoh's servants said to him, "How long will this man be a
snare to us? Let the men go, that they may serve God, their God.
Don't you yet know that Egypt is destroyed?"
8 Moses and Aaron were brought again to Pharaoh, and he said
to them, "Go, serve God your God; but who are those who will
go?"
9 Moses said, "We will go with our young and with our old. We
will go with our sons and with our daughters, with our flocks and
with our herds; for we must hold a feast to God."
10 He said to them, "God be with you if I let you go with your
little ones! See, evil is clearly before your faces. 11 Not so! Go
now you who are men, and serve God; for that is what you
desire!" Then they were driven out from Pharaoh's presence.
12 God said to Moses, "Stretch out your hand over the land of
Egypt for the locusts, that they may come up on the land of
Egypt, and eat every herb of the land, even all that the hail has
left." 13 Moses stretched out his rod over the land of Egypt, and
God brought an east wind on the land all that day, and all night;
and when it was morning, the east wind brought the locusts.
14 The locusts went up over all the land of Egypt, and rested in
all the borders of Egypt. They were very grievous. Before them
there were no such locusts as they, nor will there ever be again.
15 For they covered the surface of the whole earth, so that the
land was darkened, and they ate every herb of the land, and all
the fruit of the trees which the hail had left. There remained
nothing green, either tree or herb of the field, through all the land
of Egypt. 16 Then Pharaoh called for Moses and Aaron in haste,
and he said, "I have sinned against God your God, and against
you. 17 Now therefore please forgive my sin again, and pray to
God your God, that he may also take away from me this death."
18 Moses went out from Pharaoh, and prayed to God. 19 God
sent an exceedingly strong west wind, which took up the locusts,
and drove them into the Red Sea.[53] There remained not one locust
in all the borders of Egypt. 20 But God hardened Pharaoh's
heart, and he didn't let the children of Israel go.
21 God said to Moses, "Stretch out your hand toward the sky,
that there may be darkness over the land of Egypt, even darkness
which may be felt." 22 Moses stretched out his hand toward the
sky, and there was a thick darkness in all the land of Egypt for
three days. 23 They didn't see one another, and nobody rose
from his place for three days; but all the children of Israel had
light in their dwellings.
24 Pharaoh called to Moses, and said, "Go, serve God. Only let
your flocks and your herds stay behind. Let your little ones also
go with you."
25 Moses said, "You must also give into our hand sacrifices and
burnt offerings, that we may sacrifice to God our God. 26 Our
livestock also shall go with us. Not a hoof shall be left behind, for
of it we must take to serve God our God; and we don't know with
what we must serve God, until we come there."
27 But God hardened Pharaoh's heart, and he wouldn't let them
go. 28 Pharaoh said to him, "Get away from me! Be careful to
see my face no more; for in the day you see my face you shall
die!"
29 Moses said, "You have spoken well. I will see your face
again no more."

Exodus 11

1 God said to Moses, "I will bring yet one more plague on
Pharaoh, and on Egypt; afterwards he will let you go. When he
lets you go, he will surely thrust you out altogether. 2 Speak
now in the ears of the people, and let every man ask of his
neighbor, and every woman of her neighbor, jewels of silver, and
jewels of gold." 3 God gave the people favor in the sight of the
Egyptians. Moreover, the man Moses was very great in the land
of Egypt, in the sight of Pharaoh's servants, and in the sight of
the people.
4 Moses said, "This is what God says: 'About midnight I will
go out into the middle of Egypt, 5 and all the firstborn in the
land of Egypt shall die, from the firstborn of Pharaoh who sits on
his throne, even to the firstborn of the female servant who is
behind the mill, and all the firstborn of livestock. 6 There will
be a great cry throughout all the land of Egypt, such as there has
not been, nor will be any more. 7 But against any of the
children of Israel a dog won't even bark or move its tongue,
against man or animal, that you may know that God makes a

---

[53] **10:19** *10:19* **"Red Sea" is the translation for the Hebrew "Yam Suf", which could be more literally translated "Sea of Reeds" or "Sea of Cattails". It refers to the body of water currently known as the Red Sea, or possibly to one of the bodies of water connected to it or near it.**

distinction between the Egyptians and Israel. 8 All these
servants of yours will come down to me, and bow down
themselves to me, saying, "Get out, with all the people who
follow you;" and after that I will go out.'" He went out from
Pharaoh in hot anger.
9 God said to Moses, "Pharaoh won't listen to you, that my
wonders may be multiplied in the land of Egypt." 10 Moses and
Aaron did all these wonders before Pharaoh, but God hardened
Pharaoh's heart, and he didn't let the children of Israel go out of
his land.

Exodus 12

1 God spoke to Moses and Aaron in the land of Egypt, saying,
2 "This month shall be to you the beginning of months. It shall
be the first month of the year to you. 3 Speak to all the
congregation of Israel, saying, 'On the tenth day of this month,
they shall take to them every man a lamb, according to their
fathers' houses, a lamb for a household; 4 and if the household
is too little for a lamb, then he and his neighbor next to his house
shall take one according to the number of the souls. You shall
make your count for the lamb according to what everyone can
eat. 5 Your lamb shall be without defect, a male a year old. You
shall take it from the sheep, or from the goats. 6 You shall keep
it until the fourteenth day of the same month; and the whole
assembly of the congregation of Israel shall kill it at evening.
7 They shall take some of the blood, and put it on the two door
posts and on the lintel, on the houses in which they shall eat it.
8 They shall eat the meat in that night, roasted with fire, and
unleavened bread. They shall eat it with bitter herbs. 9 Don't eat
it raw, nor boiled at all with water, but roasted with fire; with its
head, its legs and its inner parts. 10 You shall let nothing of it
remain until the morning; but that which remains of it until the
morning you shall burn with fire. 11 This is how you shall eat
it: with your belt on your waist, your sandals on your feet, and
your staff in your hand; and you shall eat it in haste: it is God's
Passover. 12 For I will go through the land of Egypt in that
night, and will strike all the firstborn in the land of Egypt, both
man and animal. I will execute judgments against all the gods of
Egypt. I am God. 13 The blood shall be to you for a token on
the houses where you are. When I see the blood, I will pass over
you, and no plague will be on you to destroy you when I strike
the land of Egypt. 14 This day shall be a memorial for you. You
shall keep it as a feast to God. You shall keep it as a feast
throughout your generations by an ordinance forever.
15 "'Seven days you shall eat unleavened bread; even the first
day you shall put away yeast out of your houses, for whoever eats
leavened bread from the first day until the seventh day, that soul
shall be cut off from Israel. 16 In the first day there shall be to
you a holy convocation, and in the seventh day a holy
convocation; no kind of work shall be done in them, except that
which every man must eat, only that may be done by you.
17 You shall observe the feast of unleavened bread; for in this
same day I have brought your armies out of the land of Egypt.
Therefore you shall observe this day throughout your generations
by an ordinance forever. 18 In the first month, on the fourteenth
day of the month at evening, you shall eat unleavened bread, until
the twenty first day of the month at evening. 19 There shall be
no yeast found in your houses for seven days, for whoever eats
that which is leavened, that soul shall be cut off from the
congregation of Israel, whether he is a foreigner, or one who is
born in the land. 20 You shall eat nothing leavened. In all your
habitations you shall eat unleavened bread.'"
21 Then Moses called for all the elders of Israel, and said to
them, "Draw out, and take lambs according to your families, and
kill the Passover. 22 You shall take a bunch of hyssop, and dip
it in the blood that is in the basin, and strike the lintel and the two
door posts with the blood that is in the basin. None of you shall
go out of the door of his house until the morning. 23 For God
will pass through to strike the Egyptians; and when he sees the
blood on the lintel, and on the two door posts, God will pass over
the door, and will not allow the destroyer to come in to your
houses to strike you. 24 You shall observe this thing for an
ordinance to you and to your sons forever. 25 It shall happen
when you have come to the land which God will give you, as he
has promised, that you shall keep this service. 26 It will happen,
when your children ask you, 'What do you mean by this service?'
27 that you shall say, 'It is the sacrifice of God's Passover, who
passed over the houses of the children of Israel in Egypt, when he
struck the Egyptians, and spared our houses.'"
The people bowed their heads and worshiped. 28 The children
of Israel went and did so; as God had commanded Moses and
Aaron, so they did.
29 At midnight, God struck all the firstborn in the land of
Egypt, from the firstborn of Pharaoh who sat on his throne to the
firstborn of the captive who was in the dungeon, and all the
firstborn of livestock. 30 Pharaoh rose up in the night, he, and
all his servants, and all the Egyptians; and there was a great cry in
Egypt, for there was not a house where there was not one dead.
31 He called for Moses and Aaron by night, and said, "Rise up,
get out from among my people, both you and the children of
Israel; and go, serve God, as you have said! 32 Take both your
flocks and your herds, as you have said, and be gone; and bless
me also!"
33 The Egyptians were urgent with the people, to send them out
of the land in haste, for they said, "We are all dead men."
34 The people took their dough before it was leavened, their
kneading troughs being bound up in their clothes on their
shoulders. 35 The children of Israel did according to the word
of Moses; and they asked of the Egyptians jewels of silver, and
jewels of gold, and clothing. 36 God gave the people favor in
the sight of the Egyptians, so that they let them have what they
asked. They plundered the Egyptians.
37 The children of Israel traveled from Rameses to Succoth,
about six hundred thousand on foot who were men, in addition to
children. 38 A mixed multitude went up also with them, with
flocks, herds, and even very much livestock. 39 They baked
unleavened cakes of the dough which they brought out of Egypt;
for it wasn't leavened, because they were thrust out of Egypt, and
couldn't wait, and they had not prepared any food for themselves.
40 Now the time that the children of Israel lived in Egypt was
four hundred thirty years. 41 At the end of four hundred thirty
years, to the day, all of God's armies went out from the land of
Egypt. 42 It is a night to be much observed to God for bringing
them out from the land of Egypt. This is that night of God, to be
much observed by all the children of Israel throughout their
generations.
43 God said to Moses and Aaron, "This is the ordinance of the
Passover. No foreigner shall eat of it, 44 but every man's
servant who is bought for money, when you have circumcised
him, then shall he eat of it. 45 A foreigner and a hired servant
shall not eat of it. 46 It must be eaten in one house. You shall
not carry any of the meat outside of the house. Do not break any
of its bones. 47 All the congregation of Israel shall keep it.
48 When a stranger lives as a foreigner with you, and would
like to keep the Passover to God, let all his males be circumcised,
and then let him come near and keep it. He shall be as one who is
born in the land; but no uncircumcised person shall eat of it.
49 One law shall be to him who is born at home, and to the
stranger who lives as a foreigner among you." 50 All the
children of Israel did so. As God commanded Moses and Aaron,
so they did. 51 That same day, God brought the children of
Israel out of the land of Egypt by their armies.

Exodus 13

1 God spoke to Moses, saying, 2 "Sanctify to me all the
firstborn, whatever opens the womb among the children of Israel,
both of man and of animal. It is mine."
3 Moses said to the people, "Remember this day, in which you
came out of Egypt, out of the house of bondage; for by strength
of hand God brought you out from this place. No leavened bread
shall be eaten. 4 Today you go out in the month Abib. 5 It
shall be, when God brings you into the land of the Canaanite, and
the Hittite, and the Amorite, and the Hivite, and the Jebusite,
which he swore to your fathers to give you, a land flowing with
milk and honey, that you shall keep this service in this month.
6 Seven days you shall eat unleavened bread, and in the seventh
day shall be a feast to God. 7 Unleavened bread shall be eaten
throughout the seven days; and no leavened bread shall be seen
with you. No yeast shall be seen with you, within all your
borders. 8 You shall tell your son in that day, saying, 'It is
because of that which God did for me when I came out of Egypt.'
9 It shall be for a sign to you on your hand, and for a memorial
between your eyes, that God's law may be in your mouth; for
with a strong hand God has brought you out of Egypt. 10 You
shall therefore keep this ordinance in its season from year to year.
11 "It shall be, when God brings you into the land of the
Canaanite, as he swore to you and to your fathers, and will give it
you, 12 that you shall set apart to God all that opens the womb,
and every firstborn that comes from an animal which you have.
The males shall be God's. 13 Every firstborn of a donkey you
shall redeem with a lamb; and if you will not redeem it, then you
shall break its neck; and you shall redeem all the firstborn of man
among your sons. 14 It shall be, when your son asks you in time
to come, saying, 'What is this?' that you shall tell him, 'By
strength of hand God brought us out from Egypt, from the house
of bondage. 15 When Pharaoh stubbornly refused to let us go,
God killed all the firstborn in the land of Egypt, both the firstborn
of man, and the firstborn of livestock. Therefore I sacrifice to
God all that opens the womb, being males; but all the firstborn of
my sons I redeem.' 16 It shall be for a sign on your hand, and
for symbols between your eyes; for by strength of hand God
brought us out of Egypt."
17 When Pharaoh had let the people go, God didn't lead them
by the way of the land of the Philistines, although that was near;
for God said, "Lest perhaps the people change their minds when
they see war, and they return to Egypt"; 18 but God led the
people around by the way of the wilderness by the Red Sea; and
the children of Israel went up armed out of the land of Egypt.
19 Moses took the bones of Joseph with him, for he had made
the children of Israel swear, saying, "God will surely visit you,
and you shall carry up my bones away from here with you."
20 They took their journey from Succoth, and encamped in
Etham, in the edge of the wilderness. 21 God went before them
by day in a pillar of cloud, to lead them on their way, and by
night in a pillar of fire, to give them light, that they might go by
day and by night: 22 the pillar of cloud by day, and the pillar of
fire by night, didn't depart from before the people.

Exodus 14

1 God spoke to Moses, saying, 2 "Speak to the children of
Israel, that they turn back and encamp before Pihahiroth, between
Migdol and the sea, before Baal Zephon. You shall encamp
opposite it by the sea. 3 Pharaoh will say of the children of
Israel, 'They are entangled in the land. The wilderness has shut
them in.' 4 I will harden Pharaoh's heart, and he will follow
after them; and I will get honor over Pharaoh, and over all his
armies; and the Egyptians shall know that I am God." They did
so.
5 The king of Egypt was told that the people had fled; and the
heart of Pharaoh and of his servants was changed toward the
people, and they said, "What is this we have done, that we have
let Israel go from serving us?" 6 He prepared his chariot, and
took his army with him; 7 and he took six hundred chosen
chariots, and all the chariots of Egypt, with captains over all of
them. 8 God hardened the heart of Pharaoh king of Egypt, and
he pursued the children of Israel; for the children of Israel went
out with a high hand.[54] 9 The Egyptians pursued them. All the
horses and chariots of Pharaoh, his horsemen, and his army
overtook them encamping by the sea, beside Pihahiroth, before
Baal Zephon.
10 When Pharaoh came near, the children of Israel lifted up
their eyes, and behold, the Egyptians were marching after them;
and they were very afraid. The children of Israel cried out to God.
11 They said to Moses, "Because there were no graves in
Egypt, have you taken us away to die in the wilderness? Why
have you treated us this way, to bring us out of Egypt? 12 Isn't
this the word that we spoke to you in Egypt, saying, 'Leave us
alone, that we may serve the Egyptians?' For it would have been
better for us to serve the Egyptians than to die in the wilderness."
13 Moses said to the people, "Don't be afraid. Stand still, and
see the salvation of God, which he will work for you today; for
you will never again see the Egyptians whom you have seen
today. 14 God will fight for you, and you shall be still."
15 God said to Moses, "Why do you cry to me? Speak to the
children of Israel, that they go forward. 16 Lift up your rod, and
stretch out your hand over the sea and divide it. Then the children
of Israel shall go into the middle of the sea on dry ground.
17 Behold, I myself will harden the hearts of the Egyptians, and
they will go in after them. I will get myself honor over Pharaoh,
and over all his armies, over his chariots, and over his horsemen.
18 The Egyptians shall know that I am God when I have gotten
myself honor over Pharaoh, over his chariots, and over his
horsemen." 19 The angel of God, who went before the camp of
Israel, moved and went behind them; and the pillar of cloud
moved from before them, and stood behind them. 20 It came
between the camp of Egypt and the camp of Israel. There was the
cloud and the darkness, yet gave it light by night. One didn't
come near the other all night.

---

[54] **14:8** *14:8* or, defiantly.

21 Moses stretched out his hand over the sea, and God caused
the sea to go back by a strong east wind all night, and made the
sea dry land, and the waters were divided. 22 The children of
Israel went into the middle of the sea on the dry ground, and the
waters were a wall to them on their right hand, and on their left.
23 The Egyptians pursued, and went in after them into the
middle of the sea: all of Pharaoh's horses, his chariots, and his
horsemen. 24 In the morning watch, God looked out on the
Egyptian army through the pillar of fire and of cloud, and
confused the Egyptian army. 25 He took off their chariot
wheels, and they drove them heavily; so that the Egyptians said,
"Let's flee from the face of Israel, for God fights for them against
the Egyptians!"
26 God said to Moses, "Stretch out your hand over the sea, that
the waters may come again on the Egyptians, on their chariots,
and on their horsemen." 27 Moses stretched out his hand over
the sea, and the sea returned to its strength when the morning
appeared; and the Egyptians fled against it. God overthrew the
Egyptians in the middle of the sea. 28 The waters returned, and
covered the chariots and the horsemen, even all Pharaoh's army
that went in after them into the sea. There remained not so much
as one of them. 29 But the children of Israel walked on dry land
in the middle of the sea, and the waters were a wall to them on
their right hand, and on their left. 30 Thus God saved Israel that
day out of the hand of the Egyptians; and Israel saw the
Egyptians dead on the seashore. 31 Israel saw the great work
which God did to the Egyptians, and the people feared God; and
they believed in God and in his servant Moses.

Exodus 15

1 Then Moses and the children of Israel sang this song to God,
and said,
"I will sing to God, for he has triumphed gloriously.
He has thrown the horse and his rider into the sea.
2 Yah is my strength and song.
He has become my salvation.
This is my God, and I will praise him;
my father's God, and I will exalt him.
3 God is a man of war.
God is his name.
4 He has cast Pharaoh's chariots and his army into the sea.
His chosen captains are sunk in the Red Sea.
5 The deeps cover them.
They went down into the depths like a stone.
6 Your right hand, God, is glorious in power.
Your right hand, God, dashes the enemy in pieces.
7 In the greatness of your excellency, you overthrow those who
rise up against you.
You send out your wrath. It consumes them as stubble.
8 With the blast of your nostrils, the waters were piled up.
The floods stood upright as a heap.
The deeps were congealed in the heart of the sea.
9 The enemy said, 'I will pursue. I will overtake. I will divide
the plunder.
My desire will be satisfied on them.
I will draw my sword. My hand will destroy them.'
10 You blew with your wind.
The sea covered them.
They sank like lead in the mighty waters.
11 Who is like you, God, among the gods?
Who is like you, glorious in holiness,
fearful in praises, doing wonders?
12 You stretched out your right hand.
The earth swallowed them.
13 "You, in your loving kindness, have led the people that you
have redeemed.
You have guided them in your strength to your holy habitation.
14 The peoples have heard.
They tremble.
Pangs have taken hold of the inhabitants of Philistia.
15 Then the chiefs of Edom were dismayed.
Trembling takes hold of the mighty men of Moab.
All the inhabitants of Canaan have melted away.
16 Terror and dread falls on them.
By the greatness of your arm they are as still as a stone,
until your people pass over, God,
until the people you have purchased pass over.
17 You will bring them in, and plant them in the mountain of
your inheritance,
the place, God, which you have made for yourself to dwell in;
the sanctuary, Lord, which your hands have established.
18 God will reign forever and ever."
19 For the horses of Pharaoh went in with his chariots and with
his horsemen into the sea, and God brought back the waters of
the sea on them; but the children of Israel walked on dry land in
the middle of the sea. 20 Miriam the prophetess, the sister of
Aaron, took a tambourine in her hand; and all the women went
out after her with tambourines and with dances. 21 Miriam
answered them,
"Sing to God, for he has triumphed gloriously.
The horse and his rider he has thrown into the sea."
22 Moses led Israel onward from the Red Sea, and they went
out into the wilderness of Shur; and they went three days in the
wilderness, and found no water. 23 When they came to Marah,
they couldn't drink from the waters of Marah, for they were
bitter. Therefore its name was called Marah.[55] 24 The people
murmured against Moses, saying, "What shall we drink?"
25 Then he cried to God. God showed him a tree, and he threw
it into the waters, and the waters were made sweet. There he
made a statute and an ordinance for them, and there he tested
them. 26 He said, "If you will diligently listen to God your
God's voice, and will do that which is right in his eyes, and will
pay attention to his commandments, and keep all his statutes, I
will put none of the diseases on you, which I have put on the
Egyptians; for I am God who heals you."
27 They came to Elim, where there were twelve springs of
water, and seventy palm trees. They encamped there by the
waters.

Exodus 16

1 They took their journey from Elim, and all the congregation
of the children of Israel came to the wilderness of Sin, which is
between Elim and Sinai, on the fifteenth day of the second month
after their departing out of the land of Egypt. 2 The whole
congregation of the children of Israel murmured against Moses
and against Aaron in the wilderness; 3 and the children of Israel
said to them, "We wish that we had died by God's hand in the
land of Egypt, when we sat by the meat pots, when we ate our fill
of bread, for you have brought us out into this wilderness to kill
this whole assembly with hunger."
4 Then God said to Moses, "Behold, I will rain bread from the
sky for you, and the people shall go out and gather a day's
portion every day, that I may test them, whether they will walk in
my law or not. 5 It shall come to pass on the sixth day, that they
shall prepare that which they bring in, and it shall be twice as
much as they gather daily."
6 Moses and Aaron said to all the children of Israel, "At
evening, you shall know that God has brought you out from the
land of Egypt. 7 In the morning, you shall see God's glory;
because he hears your murmurings against God. Who are we, that
you murmur against us?" 8 Moses said, "Now God will give
you meat to eat in the evening, and in the morning bread to
satisfy you, because God hears your murmurings which you
murmur against him. And who are we? Your murmurings are not
against us, but against God." 9 Moses said to Aaron, "Tell all
the congregation of the children of Israel, 'Come close to God,
for he has heard your murmurings.'" 10 As Aaron spoke to the
whole congregation of the children of Israel, they looked toward
the wilderness, and behold, God's glory appeared in the cloud.
11 God spoke to Moses, saying, 12 "I have heard the
murmurings of the children of Israel. Speak to them, saying, 'At
evening you shall eat meat, and in the morning you shall be filled
with bread. Then you will know that I am God your God.'"
13 In the evening, quail came up and covered the camp; and in
the morning the dew lay around the camp. 14 When the dew
that lay had gone, behold, on the surface of the wilderness was a
small round thing, small as the frost on the ground. 15 When the
children of Israel saw it, they said to one another, "What is it?"
For they didn't know what it was. Moses said to them, "It is the
bread which God has given you to eat. 16 "This is the thing
which God has commanded: 'Gather of it everyone according to
his eating; an omer[56] a head, according to the number of your
persons, you shall take it, every man for those who are in his
tent.'" 17 The children of Israel did so, and some gathered
more, some less. 18 When they measured it with an omer, he
who gathered much had nothing over, and he who gathered little
had no lack. They each gathered according to his eating.
19 Moses said to them, "Let no one leave of it until the
morning." 20 Notwithstanding they didn't listen to Moses, but
some of them left of it until the morning, so it bred worms and
became foul; and Moses was angry with them. 21 They
gathered it morning by morning, everyone according to his
eating. When the sun grew hot, it melted. 22 On the sixth day,
they gathered twice as much bread, two omers for each one; and
all the rulers of the congregation came and told Moses. 23 He
said to them, "This is that which God has spoken, 'Tomorrow is a
solemn rest, a holy Sabbath to God. Bake that which you want to
bake, and boil that which you want to boil; and all that remains
over lay up for yourselves to be kept until the morning.'"
24 They laid it up until the morning, as Moses ordered, and it
didn't become foul, and there were no worms in it. 25 Moses
said, "Eat that today, for today is a Sabbath to God. Today you
shall not find it in the field. 26 Six days you shall gather it, but
on the seventh day is the Sabbath. In it there shall be none."
27 On the seventh day, some of the people went out to gather,
and they found none. 28 God said to Moses, "How long do you
refuse to keep my commandments and my laws? 29 Behold,
because God has given you the Sabbath, therefore he gives you
on the sixth day the bread of two days. Everyone stay in his
place. Let no one go out of his place on the seventh day." 30 So
the people rested on the seventh day.
31 The house of Israel called its name "Manna",[57] and it was
like coriander seed, white; and its taste was like wafers with
honey. 32 Moses said, "This is the thing which God has
commanded, 'Let an omer-full of it be kept throughout your
generations, that they may see the bread with which I fed you in
the wilderness, when I brought you out of the land of Egypt.'"
33 Moses said to Aaron, "Take a pot, and put an omer-full of
manna in it, and lay it up before God, to be kept throughout your
generations." 34 As God commanded Moses, so Aaron laid it
up before the Testimony, to be kept. 35 The children of Israel
ate the manna forty years, until they came to an inhabited land.
They ate the manna until they came to the borders of the land of
Canaan. 36 Now an omer is one tenth of an ephah. [58]

Exodus 17

1 All the congregation of the children of Israel traveled from the
wilderness of Sin, starting according to God's commandment,
and encamped in Rephidim; but there was no water for the people
to drink. 2 Therefore the people quarreled with Moses, and said,
"Give us water to drink."
Moses said to them, "Why do you quarrel with me? Why do you
test God?"
3 The people were thirsty for water there; so the people
murmured against Moses, and said, "Why have you brought us
up out of Egypt, to kill us, our children, and our livestock with
thirst?"
4 Moses cried to God, saying, "What shall I do with these
people? They are almost ready to stone me."
5 God said to Moses, "Walk on before the people, and take the
elders of Israel with you, and take the rod in your hand with
which you struck the Nile, and go. 6 Behold, I will stand before
you there on the rock in Horeb. You shall strike the rock, and
water will come out of it, that the people may drink." Moses did
so in the sight of the elders of Israel. 7 He called the name of
the place Massah,[59] and Meribah,[60] because the children of Israel
quarreled, and because they tested God, saying, "Is God among
us, or not?"
8 Then Amalek came and fought with Israel in Rephidim.
9 Moses said to Joshua, "Choose men for us, and go out, fight
with Amalek. Tomorrow I will stand on the top of the hill with
God's rod in my hand." 10 So Joshua did as Moses had told
him, and fought with Amalek; and Moses, Aaron, and Hur went
up to the top of the hill. 11 When Moses held up his hand, Israel
prevailed. When he let down his hand, Amalek prevailed.
12 But Moses' hands were heavy; so they took a stone, and put
it under him, and he sat on it. Aaron and Hur held up his hands,
the one on the one side, and the other on the other side. His hands
were steady until sunset. 13 Joshua defeated Amalek and his
people with the edge of the sword. 14 God said to Moses,
"Write this for a memorial in a book, and rehearse it in the ears of
Joshua: that I will utterly blot out the memory of Amalek from

---

[55]**15:23** *15:23* **Marah means bitter.**

[56]**16:16** *16:16* **An omer is about 2.2 liters or about 2.3 quarts**

[57]**16:31** *16:31* **"Manna" means "What is it?"**

[58]**16:36** *16:36* **1 ephah is about 22 liters or about 2/3 of a bushel**

[59]**17:7** *17:7* **Massah means testing.**

[60]**17:7** *17:7* **Meribah means quarreling.**

under the sky." 15 Moses built an altar, and called its name
"God our Banner".[61] 16 He said, "Yah has sworn: 'God will
have war with Amalek from generation to generation.'"

Exodus 18

1 Now Jethro, the priest of Midian, Moses' father-in-law, heard
of all that God had done for Moses, and for Israel his people, how
God had brought Israel out of Egypt. 2 Jethro, Moses' father-in-
law, received Zipporah, Moses' wife, after he had sent her away,
3 and her two sons. The name of one son was Gershom,[62] for
Moses said, "I have lived as a foreigner in a foreign land".
4 The name of the other was Eliezer,[63] for he said, "My father's
God was my help and delivered me from Pharaoh's sword."
5 Jethro, Moses' father-in-law, came with Moses' sons and his
wife to Moses into the wilderness where he was encamped, at the
Mountain of God. 6 He said to Moses, "I, your father-in-law
Jethro, have come to you with your wife, and her two sons with
her."
7 Moses went out to meet his father-in-law, and bowed and
kissed him. They asked each other of their welfare, and they
came into the tent. 8 Moses told his father-in-law all that God
had done to Pharaoh and to the Egyptians for Israel's sake, all the
hardships that had come on them on the way, and how God
delivered them. 9 Jethro rejoiced for all the goodness which
God had done to Israel, in that he had delivered them out of the
hand of the Egyptians. 10 Jethro said, "Blessed be God, who
has delivered you out of the hand of the Egyptians, and out of the
hand of Pharaoh; who has delivered the people from under the
hand of the Egyptians. 11 Now I know that God is greater than
all gods because of the way that they treated people arrogantly."
12 Jethro, Moses' father-in-law, took a burnt offering and
sacrifices for God. Aaron came with all the elders of Israel, to eat
bread with Moses' father-in-law before God.
13 On the next day, Moses sat to judge the people, and the
people stood around Moses from the morning to the evening.
14 When Moses' father-in-law saw all that he did to the people,
he said, "What is this thing that you do for the people? Why do
you sit alone, and all the people stand around you from morning
to evening?"
15 Moses said to his father-in-law, "Because the people come to
me to inquire of God. 16 When they have a matter, they come
to me, and I judge between a man and his neighbor, and I make
them know the statutes of God, and his laws." 17 Moses' father-
in-law said to him, "The thing that you do is not good. 18 You
will surely wear away, both you, and this people that is with you;
for the thing is too heavy for you. You are not able to perform it
yourself alone. 19 Listen now to my voice. I will give you
counsel, and God be with you. You represent the people before
God, and bring the causes to God. 20 You shall teach them the
statutes and the laws, and shall show them the way in which they
must walk, and the work that they must do. 21 Moreover you
shall provide out of all the people able men which fear God: men
of truth, hating unjust gain; and place such over them, to be rulers
of thousands, rulers of hundreds, rulers of fifties, and rulers of
tens. 22 Let them judge the people at all times. It shall be that
every great matter they shall bring to you, but every small matter
they shall judge themselves. So shall it be easier for you, and they
shall share the load with you. 23 If you will do this thing, and
God commands you so, then you will be able to endure, and all
these people also will go to their place in peace."
24 So Moses listened to the voice of his father-in-law, and did
all that he had said. 25 Moses chose able men out of all Israel,
and made them heads over the people, rulers of thousands, rulers
of hundreds, rulers of fifties, and rulers of tens. 26 They judged
the people at all times. They brought the hard cases to Moses, but
every small matter they judged themselves. 27 Moses let his
father-in-law depart, and he went his way into his own land.

Exodus 19

1 In the third month after the children of Israel had gone out of
the land of Egypt, on that same day they came into the wilderness
of Sinai. 2 When they had departed from Rephidim, and had
come to the wilderness of Sinai, they encamped in the
wilderness; and there Israel encamped before the mountain.
3 Moses went up to God, and God called to him out of the
mountain, saying, "This is what you shall tell the house of Jacob,
and tell the children of Israel: 4 'You have seen what I did to
the Egyptians, and how I bore you on eagles' wings, and brought
you to myself. 5 Now therefore, if you will indeed obey my
voice, and keep my covenant, then you shall be my own
possession from among all peoples; for all the earth is mine;
6 and you shall be to me a kingdom of priests, and a holy
nation.' These are the words which you shall speak to the
children of Israel."
7 Moses came and called for the elders of the people, and set
before them all these words which God commanded him. 8 All
the people answered together, and said, "All that God has spoken
we will do."
Moses reported the words of the people to God. 9 God said to
Moses, "Behold, I come to you in a thick cloud, that the people
may hear when I speak with you, and may also believe you
forever." Moses told the words of the people to God. 10 God
said to Moses, "Go to the people, and sanctify them today and
tomorrow, and let them wash their garments, 11 and be ready
for the third day; for on the third day God will come down in the
sight of all the people on Mount Sinai. 12 You shall set bounds
to the people all around, saying, 'Be careful that you don't go up
onto the mountain, or touch its border. Whoever touches the
mountain shall be surely put to death. 13 No hand shall touch
him, but he shall surely be stoned or shot through; whether it is
animal or man, he shall not live.' When the trumpet sounds long,
they shall come up to the mountain."
14 Moses went down from the mountain to the people, and
sanctified the people; and they washed their clothes. 15 He said
to the people, "Be ready by the third day. Don't have sexual
relations with a woman."
16 On the third day, when it was morning, there were thunders
and lightnings, and a thick cloud on the mountain, and the sound
of an exceedingly loud trumpet; and all the people who were in
the camp trembled. 17 Moses led the people out of the camp to
meet God; and they stood at the lower part of the mountain.
18 All of Mount Sinai smoked, because God descended on it in
fire; and its smoke ascended like the smoke of a furnace, and the
whole mountain quaked greatly. 19 When the sound of the
trumpet grew louder and louder, Moses spoke, and God answered
him by a voice. 20 God came down on Mount Sinai, to the top
of the mountain. God called Moses to the top of the mountain,
and Moses went up.
21 God said to Moses, "Go down, warn the people, lest they
break through to God to gaze, and many of them perish. 22 Let
the priests also, who come near to God, sanctify themselves, lest
God break out on them."
23 Moses said to God, "The people can't come up to Mount
Sinai, for you warned us, saying, 'Set bounds around the
mountain, and sanctify it.'"
24 God said to him, "Go down! You shall bring Aaron up with
you, but don't let the priests and the people break through to
come up to God, lest he break out against them."
25 So Moses went down to the people, and told them.

Exodus 20

1 God[64] spoke all these words, saying, 2 "I am God your God,
who brought you out of the land of Egypt, out of the house of
bondage.
3 "You shall have no other gods before me.
4 "You shall not make for yourselves an idol, nor any image of
anything that is in the heavens above, or that is in the earth
beneath, or that is in the water under the earth: 5 you shall not
bow yourself down to them, nor serve them, for I, God your God,
am a jealous God, visiting the iniquity of the fathers on the
children, on the third and on the fourth generation of those who
hate me, 6 and showing loving kindness to thousands of those
who love me and keep my commandments.
7 "You shall not misuse the name of God your God,[65] for God
will not hold him guiltless who misuses his name.
8 "Remember the Sabbath day, to keep it holy. 9 You shall
labor six days, and do all your work, 10 but the seventh day is a
Sabbath to God your God. You shall not do any work in it, you,
nor your son, nor your daughter, your male servant, nor your
female servant, nor your livestock, nor your stranger who is
within your gates; 11 for in six days God made heaven and
earth, the sea, and all that is in them, and rested the seventh day;
therefore God blessed the Sabbath day, and made it holy.
12 "Honor your father and your mother, that your days may be
long in the land which God your God gives you.
13 "You shall not murder.
14 "You shall not commit adultery.
15 "You shall not steal.
16 "You shall not give false testimony against your neighbor.
17 "You shall not covet your neighbor's house. You shall not
covet your neighbor's wife, nor his male servant, nor his female
servant, nor his ox, nor his donkey, nor anything that is your
neighbor's."
18 All the people perceived the thunderings, the lightnings, the
sound of the trumpet, and the mountain smoking. When the
people saw it, they trembled, and stayed at a distance. 19 They
said to Moses, "Speak with us yourself, and we will listen; but
don't let God speak with us, lest we die."
20 Moses said to the people, "Don't be afraid, for God has
come to test you, and that his fear may be before you, that you
won't sin." 21 The people stayed at a distance, and Moses came
near to the thick darkness where God was.
22 God said to Moses, "This is what you shall tell the children
of Israel: 'You yourselves have seen that I have talked with you
from heaven. 23 You shall most certainly not make gods of
silver or gods of gold for yourselves to be alongside me. 24 You
shall make an altar of earth for me, and shall sacrifice on it your
burnt offerings and your peace offerings, your sheep and your
cattle. In every place where I record my name I will come to you
and I will bless you. 25 If you make me an altar of stone, you
shall not build it of cut stones; for if you lift up your tool on it,
you have polluted it. 26 You shall not go up by steps to my
altar, that your nakedness may not be exposed to it.'

Exodus 21

1 "Now these are the ordinances which you shall set before
them:
2 "If you buy a Hebrew servant, he shall serve six years, and in
the seventh he shall go out free without paying anything. 3 If he
comes in by himself, he shall go out by himself. If he is married,
then his wife shall go out with him. 4 If his master gives him a
wife and she bears him sons or daughters, the wife and her
children shall be her master's, and he shall go out by himself.
5 But if the servant shall plainly say, 'I love my master, my
wife, and my children. I will not go out free;' 6 then his master
shall bring him to God, and shall bring him to the door or to the
doorpost, and his master shall bore his ear through with an awl,
and he shall serve him forever.
7 "If a man sells his daughter to be a female servant, she shall
not go out as the male servants do. 8 If she doesn't please her
master, who has married her to himself, then he shall let her be
redeemed. He shall have no right to sell her to a foreign people,
since he has dealt deceitfully with her. 9 If he marries her to his
son, he shall deal with her as a daughter. 10 If he takes another
wife to himself, he shall not diminish her food, her clothing, and
her marital rights. 11 If he doesn't do these three things for her,
she may go free without paying any money.
12 "One who strikes a man so that he dies shall surely be put to
death, 13 but not if it is unintentional, but God allows it to
happen; then I will appoint you a place where he shall flee. 14 If
a man schemes and comes presumptuously on his neighbor to kill
him, you shall take him from my altar, that he may die.
15 "Anyone who attacks his father or his mother shall be surely
put to death.
16 "Anyone who kidnaps someone and sells him, or if he is
found in his hand, he shall surely be put to death.
17 "Anyone who curses his father or his mother shall surely be
put to death.
18 "If men quarrel and one strikes the other with a stone, or
with his fist, and he doesn't die, but is confined to bed; 19 if he
rises again and walks around with his staff, then he who struck
him shall be cleared; only he shall pay for the loss of his time,
and shall provide for his healing until he is thoroughly healed.
20 "If a man strikes his servant or his maid with a rod, and he
dies under his hand, the man shall surely be punished.

[61] **17:15** *17:15* Hebrew, God Nissi

[62] **18:3** *18:3* "Gershom" sounds like the Hebrew for "an alien there".

[63] **18:4** *18:4* Eliezer means "God is my helper".

[64] **20:1** *20:1* After "God", the Hebrew has the two letters "Aleph Tav" (the first and last letters of the Hebrew alphabet), not as a word, but as a grammatical marker.

[65] **20:7** *20:7* or, You shall not take the name of God your God in vain

21 Notwithstanding, if his servant gets up after a day or two, he
shall not be punished, for the servant is his property.
22 "If men fight and hurt a pregnant woman so that she gives
birth prematurely, and yet no harm follows, he shall be surely
fined as much as the woman's husband demands and the judges
allow. 23 But if any harm follows, then you must take life for
life, 24 eye for eye, tooth for tooth, hand for hand, foot for foot,
25 burning for burning, wound for wound, and bruise for bruise.
26 "If a man strikes his servant's eye, or his maid's eye, and
destroys it, he shall let him go free for his eye's sake. 27 If he
strikes out his male servant's tooth, or his female servant's tooth,
he shall let the servant go free for his tooth's sake.
28 "If a bull gores a man or a woman to death, the bull shall
surely be stoned, and its meat shall not be eaten; but the owner of
the bull shall not be held responsible. 29 But if the bull had a
habit of goring in the past, and this has been testified to its owner,
and he has not kept it in, but it has killed a man or a woman, the
bull shall be stoned, and its owner shall also be put to death.
30 If a ransom is imposed on him, then he shall give for the
redemption of his life whatever is imposed. 31 Whether it has
gored a son or has gored a daughter, according to this judgment it
shall be done to him. 32 If the bull gores a male servant or a
female servant, thirty shekels[66] of silver shall be given to their
master, and the ox shall be stoned.
33 "If a man opens a pit, or if a man digs a pit and doesn't cover
it, and a bull or a donkey falls into it, 34 the owner of the pit
shall make it good. He shall give money to its owner, and the
dead animal shall be his.
35 "If one man's bull injures another's, so that it dies, then they
shall sell the live bull, and divide its price; and they shall also
divide the dead animal. 36 Or if it is known that the bull was in
the habit of goring in the past, and its owner has not kept it in, he
shall surely pay bull for bull, and the dead animal shall be his
own.

Exodus 22

1 "If a man steals an ox or a sheep, and kills it or sells it, he
shall pay five oxen for an ox, and four sheep for a sheep. 2 If
the thief is found breaking in, and is struck so that he dies, there
shall be no guilt of bloodshed for him. 3 If the sun has risen on
him, he is guilty of bloodshed. He shall make restitution. If he
has nothing, then he shall be sold for his theft. 4 If the stolen
property is found in his hand alive, whether it is ox, donkey, or
sheep, he shall pay double.
5 "If a man causes a field or vineyard to be eaten by letting his
animal loose, and it grazes in another man's field, he shall make
restitution from the best of his own field, and from the best of his
own vineyard.
6 "If fire breaks out, and catches in thorns so that the shocks of
grain, or the standing grain, or the field are consumed; he who
kindled the fire shall surely make restitution.
7 "If a man delivers to his neighbor money or stuff to keep, and
it is stolen out of the man's house, if the thief is found, he shall
pay double. 8 If the thief isn't found, then the master of the
house shall come near to God, to find out whether or not he has
put his hand on his neighbor's goods. 9 For every matter of
trespass, whether it is for ox, for donkey, for sheep, for clothing,
or for any kind of lost thing, about which one says, 'This is
mine,' the cause of both parties shall come before God. He whom
God condemns shall pay double to his neighbor.
10 "If a man delivers to his neighbor a donkey, an ox, a sheep,
or any animal to keep, and it dies or is injured, or driven away, no
man seeing it; 11 the oath of God shall be between them both,
he has not put his hand on his neighbor's goods; and its owner
shall accept it, and he shall not make restitution. 12 But if it is
stolen from him, the one who stole shall make restitution to its
owner. 13 If it is torn in pieces, let him bring it for evidence. He
shall not make good that which was torn.
14 "If a man borrows anything of his neighbor's, and it is
injured, or dies, its owner not being with it, he shall surely make
restitution. 15 If its owner is with it, he shall not make it good.
If it is a leased thing, it came for its lease.
16 "If a man entices a virgin who isn't pledged to be married,
and lies with her, he shall surely pay a dowry for her to be his
wife. 17 If her father utterly refuses to give her to him, he shall
pay money according to the dowry of virgins.
18 "You shall not allow a sorceress to live.
19 "Whoever has sex with an animal shall surely be put to
death.
20 "He who sacrifices to any god, except to God only, shall be
utterly destroyed.
21 "You shall not wrong an alien or oppress him, for you were
aliens in the land of Egypt.
22 "You shall not take advantage of any widow or fatherless
child. 23 If you take advantage of them at all, and they cry at all
to me, I will surely hear their cry; 24 and my wrath will grow
hot, and I will kill you with the sword; and your wives shall be
widows, and your children fatherless.
25 "If you lend money to any of my people with you who is
poor, you shall not be to him as a creditor. You shall not charge
him interest. 26 If you take your neighbor's garment as
collateral, you shall restore it to him before the sun goes down,
27 for that is his only covering, it is his garment for his skin.
What would he sleep in? It will happen, when he cries to me, that
I will hear, for I am gracious.
28 "You shall not blaspheme God, nor curse a ruler of your
people.
29 "You shall not delay to offer from your harvest and from the
outflow of your presses.
"You shall give the firstborn of your sons to me. 30 You shall
do likewise with your cattle and with your sheep. It shall be with
its mother seven days, then on the eighth day you shall give it to
me.
31 "You shall be holy men to me, therefore you shall not eat
any meat that is torn by animals in the field. You shall cast it to
the dogs.

Exodus 23

1 "You shall not spread a false report. Don't join your hand
with the wicked to be a malicious witness.
2 "You shall not follow a crowd to do evil. You shall not testify
in court to side with a multitude to pervert justice. 3 You shall
not favor a poor man in his cause.
4 "If you meet your enemy's ox or his donkey going astray, you
shall surely bring it back to him again. 5 If you see the donkey
of him who hates you fallen down under his burden, don't leave
him. You shall surely help him with it.
6 "You shall not deny justice to your poor people in their
lawsuits.
7 "Keep far from a false charge, and don't kill the innocent and
righteous; for I will not justify the wicked.
8 "You shall take no bribe, for a bribe blinds those who have
sight and perverts the words of the righteous.
9 "You shall not oppress an alien, for you know the heart of an
alien, since you were aliens in the land of Egypt.
10 "For six years you shall sow your land, and shall gather in its
increase, 11 but the seventh year you shall let it rest and lie
fallow, that the poor of your people may eat; and what they leave
the animal of the field shall eat. In the same way, you shall deal
with your vineyard and with your olive grove.
12 "Six days you shall do your work, and on the seventh day
you shall rest, that your ox and your donkey may have rest, and
the son of your servant, and the alien may be refreshed.
13 "Be careful to do all things that I have said to you; and don't
invoke the name of other gods or even let them be heard out of
your mouth.
14 "You shall observe a feast to me three times a year. 15 You
shall observe the feast of unleavened bread. Seven days you shall
eat unleavened bread, as I commanded you, at the time appointed
in the month Abib (for in it you came out of Egypt), and no one
shall appear before me empty. 16 And the feast of harvest, the
first fruits of your labors, which you sow in the field; and the
feast of ingathering, at the end of the year, when you gather in
your labors out of the field. 17 Three times in the year all your
males shall appear before the Lord God.
18 "You shall not offer the blood of my sacrifice with leavened
bread. The fat of my feast shall not remain all night until the
morning.
19 You shall bring the first of the first fruits of your ground into
the house of God your God.
"You shall not boil a young goat in its mother's milk.
20 "Behold, I send an angel before you, to keep you by the way,
and to bring you into the place which I have prepared. 21 Pay
attention to him, and listen to his voice. Don't provoke him, for
he will not pardon your disobedience, for my name is in him.
22 But if you indeed listen to his voice, and do all that I speak,
then I will be an enemy to your enemies, and an adversary to
your adversaries. 23 For my angel shall go before you, and
bring you in to the Amorite, the Hittite, the Perizzite, the
Canaanite, the Hivite, and the Jebusite; and I will cut them off.
24 You shall not bow down to their gods, nor serve them, nor
follow their practices, but you shall utterly overthrow them and
demolish their pillars. 25 You shall serve God your God, and he
will bless your bread and your water, and I will take sickness
away from among you. 26 No one will miscarry or be barren in
your land. I will fulfill the number of your days. 27 I will send
my terror before you, and will confuse all the people to whom
you come, and I will make all your enemies turn their backs to
you. 28 I will send the hornet before you, which will drive out
the Hivite, the Canaanite, and the Hittite, from before you. 29 I
will not drive them out from before you in one year, lest the land
become desolate, and the animals of the field multiply against
you. 30 Little by little I will drive them out from before you,
until you have increased and inherit the land. 31 I will set your
border from the Red Sea even to the sea of the Philistines, and
from the wilderness to the River; for I will deliver the inhabitants
of the land into your hand, and you shall drive them out before
you. 32 You shall make no covenant with them, nor with their
gods. 33 They shall not dwell in your land, lest they make you
sin against me, for if you serve their gods, it will surely be a snare
to you."

Exodus 24

1 He said to Moses, "Come up to God, you, and Aaron, Nadab,
and Abihu, and seventy of the elders of Israel; and worship from
a distance. 2 Moses alone shall come near to God, but they shall
not come near. The people shall not go up with him."
3 Moses came and told the people all God's words, and all the
ordinances; and all the people answered with one voice, and said,
"All the words which God has spoken will we do."
4 Moses wrote all God's words, then rose up early in the
morning and built an altar at the base of the mountain, with
twelve pillars for the twelve tribes of Israel. 5 He sent young
men of the children of Israel, who offered burnt offerings and
sacrificed peace offerings of cattle to God. 6 Moses took half of
the blood and put it in basins, and half of the blood he sprinkled
on the altar. 7 He took the book of the covenant and read it in
the hearing of the people, and they said, "We will do all that God
has said, and be obedient."
8 Moses took the blood, and sprinkled it on the people, and
said, "Look, this is the blood of the covenant, which God has
made with you concerning all these words."
9 Then Moses, Aaron, Nadab, Abihu, and seventy of the elders
of Israel went up. 10 They saw the God of Israel. Under his feet
was like a paved work of sapphire [67] stone, like the skies for
clearness. 11 He didn't lay his hand on the nobles of the
children of Israel. They saw God, and ate and drank.
12 God said to Moses, "Come up to me on the mountain, and
stay here, and I will give you the stone tablets with the law and
the commands that I have written, that you may teach them."
13 Moses rose up with Joshua, his servant, and Moses went up
onto God's Mountain. 14 He said to the elders, "Wait here for
us, until we come again to you. Behold, Aaron and Hur are with
you. Whoever is involved in a dispute can go to them."
15 Moses went up on the mountain, and the cloud covered the
mountain. 16 God's glory settled on Mount Sinai, and the cloud
covered it six days. The seventh day he called to Moses out of the
middle of the cloud. 17 The appearance of God's glory was like
devouring fire on the top of the mountain in the eyes of the
children of Israel. 18 Moses entered into the middle of the
cloud, and went up on the mountain; and Moses was on the
mountain forty days and forty nights.

Exodus 25

1 God spoke to Moses, saying, 2 "Speak to the children of
Israel, that they take an offering for me. From everyone whose
heart makes him willing you shall take my offering. 3 This is
the offering which you shall take from them: gold, silver, bronze,
4 blue, purple, scarlet, fine linen, goats' hair, 5 rams' skins
dyed red, sea cow hides,[68] acacia wood, 6 oil for the light,

---

[66]**21:32** *21:32* **A shekel is about 10 grams or about 0.35 ounces, so 30 shekels is about 300 grams or about 10.6 ounces.**

[67]**24:10** *24:10* **or, lapis lazuli**

[68]**25:5** *25:5* **or, fine leather**

spices for the anointing oil and for the sweet incense. 7 onyx
stones, and stones to be set for the ephod and for the breastplate.
8 Let them make me a sanctuary, that I may dwell among them.
9 According to all that I show you, the pattern of the tabernacle,
and the pattern of all of its furniture, even so you shall make it.
10 "They shall make an ark of acacia wood. Its length shall be
two and a half cubits,[69] its width a cubit and a half, and a cubit
and a half its height. 11 You shall overlay it with pure gold.
You shall overlay it inside and outside, and you shall make a gold
molding around it. 12 You shall cast four rings of gold for it,
and put them in its four feet. Two rings shall be on the one side of
it, and two rings on the other side of it. 13 You shall make poles
of acacia wood, and overlay them with gold. 14 You shall put
the poles into the rings on the sides of the ark to carry the ark.
15 The poles shall be in the rings of the ark. They shall not be
taken from it. 16 You shall put the covenant which I shall give
you into the ark. 17 You shall make a mercy seat of pure gold.
Two and a half cubits shall be its length, and a cubit and a half its
width. 18 You shall make two cherubim of hammered gold.
You shall make them at the two ends of the mercy seat.
19 Make one cherub at the one end, and one cherub at the other
end. You shall make the cherubim on its two ends of one piece
with the mercy seat. 20 The cherubim shall spread out their
wings upward, covering the mercy seat with their wings, with
their faces toward one another. The faces of the cherubim shall be
toward the mercy seat. 21 You shall put the mercy seat on top
of the ark, and in the ark you shall put the covenant that I will
give you. 22 There I will meet with you, and I will tell you from
above the mercy seat, from between the two cherubim which are
on the ark of the covenant, all that I command you for the
children of Israel.
23 "You shall make a table of acacia wood. Its length shall be
two cubits, and its width a cubit, and its height one and a half
cubits. 24 You shall overlay it with pure gold, and make a gold
molding around it. 25 You shall make a rim of a hand width
around it. You shall make a golden molding on its rim around it.
26 You shall make four rings of gold for it, and put the rings in
the four corners that are on its four feet. 27 the rings shall be
close to the rim, for places for the poles to carry the table.
28 You shall make the poles of acacia wood, and overlay them
with gold, that the table may be carried with them. 29 You shall
make its dishes, its spoons, its ladles, and its bowls to pour out
offerings with. You shall make them of pure gold. 30 You shall
set bread of the presence on the table before me always.
31 "You shall make a lamp stand of pure gold. The lamp stand
shall be made of hammered work. Its base, its shaft, its cups, its
buds, and its flowers shall be of one piece with it. 32 There
shall be six branches going out of its sides: three branches of the
lamp stand out of its one side, and three branches of the lamp
stand out of its other side; 33 three cups made like almond
blossoms in one branch, a bud and a flower; and three cups made
like almond blossoms in the other branch, a bud and a flower, so
for the six branches going out of the lamp stand; 34 and in the
lamp stand four cups made like almond blossoms, its buds and its
flowers; 35 and a bud under two branches of one piece with it,
and a bud under two branches of one piece with it, and a bud
under two branches of one piece with it, for the six branches
going out of the lamp stand. 36 Their buds and their branches
shall be of one piece with it, all of it one beaten work of pure
gold. 37 You shall make its lamps seven, and they shall light its
lamps to give light to the space in front of it. 38 Its snuffers and
its snuff dishes shall be of pure gold. 39 It shall be made of a
talent[70] of pure gold, with all these accessories. 40 See that you
make them after their pattern, which has been shown to you on
the mountain.

Exodus 26

1 "Moreover you shall make the tabernacle with ten curtains of
fine twined linen, and blue, and purple, and scarlet, with
cherubim. You shall make them with the work of a skillful
workman. 2 The length of each curtain shall be twenty-eight
cubits,[71] and the width of each curtain four cubits: all the curtains
shall have one measure. 3 Five curtains shall be coupled
together to one another, and the other five curtains shall be
coupled to one another. 4 You shall make loops of blue on the
edge of the one curtain from the edge in the coupling, and you
shall do likewise on the edge of the curtain that is outermost in
the second coupling. 5 You shall make fifty loops in the one
curtain, and you shall make fifty loops in the edge of the curtain
that is in the second coupling. The loops shall be opposite one
another. 6 You shall make fifty clasps of gold, and couple the
curtains to one another with the clasps. The tabernacle shall be a
unit.
7 "You shall make curtains of goats' hair for a covering over
the tabernacle. You shall make eleven curtains. 8 The length of
each curtain shall be thirty cubits, and the width of each curtain
four cubits: the eleven curtains shall have one measure. 9 You
shall couple five curtains by themselves, and six curtains by
themselves, and shall double over the sixth curtain in the
forefront of the tent. 10 You shall make fifty loops on the edge
of the one curtain that is outermost in the coupling, and fifty
loops on the edge of the curtain which is outermost in the second
coupling. 11 You shall make fifty clasps of bronze, and put the
clasps into the loops, and couple the tent together, that it may be
one. 12 The overhanging part that remains of the curtains of the
tent—the half curtain that remains—shall hang over the back of
the tabernacle. 13 The cubit on the one side and the cubit on the
other side, of that which remains in the length of the curtains of
the tent, shall hang over the sides of the tabernacle on this side
and on that side, to cover it. 14 You shall make a covering for
the tent of rams' skins dyed red, and a covering of sea cow hides
above.
15 "You shall make the boards for the tabernacle of acacia
wood, standing upright. 16 Ten cubits shall be the length of a
board, and one and a half cubits the width of each board.
17 There shall be two tenons in each board, joined to one
another: thus you shall make for all the boards of the tabernacle.
18 You shall make twenty boards for the tabernacle, for the
south side southward. 19 You shall make forty sockets of silver
under the twenty boards; two sockets under one board for its two
tenons, and two sockets under another board for its two tenons.
20 For the second side of the tabernacle, on the north side,
twenty boards, 21 and their forty sockets of silver; two sockets
under one board, and two sockets under another board. 22 For
the far side of the tabernacle westward you shall make six boards.
23 You shall make two boards for the corners of the tabernacle
in the far side. 24 They shall be double beneath, and in the same
way they shall be whole to its top to one ring: thus shall it be for
them both; they shall be for the two corners. 25 There shall be
eight boards, and their sockets of silver, sixteen sockets; two
sockets under one board, and two sockets under another board.
26 "You shall make bars of acacia wood: five for the boards of
the one side of the tabernacle, 27 and five bars for the boards of
the other side of the tabernacle, and five bars for the boards of the
side of the tabernacle, for the far side westward. 28 The middle
bar in the middle of the boards shall pass through from end to
end. 29 You shall overlay the boards with gold, and make their
rings of gold for places for the bars. You shall overlay the bars
with gold. 30 You shall set up the tabernacle according to the
way that it was shown to you on the mountain.
31 "You shall make a veil of blue, and purple, and scarlet, and
fine twined linen, with cherubim. It shall be the work of a skillful
workman. 32 You shall hang it on four pillars of acacia overlaid
with gold; their hooks shall be of gold, on four sockets of silver.
33 You shall hang up the veil under the clasps, and shall bring
the ark of the covenant in there within the veil. The veil shall
separate the holy place from the most holy for you. 34 You
shall put the mercy seat on the ark of the covenant in the most
holy place. 35 You shall set the table outside the veil, and the
lamp stand opposite the table on the side of the tabernacle toward
the south. You shall put the table on the north side.
36 "You shall make a screen for the door of the Tent, of blue,
and purple, and scarlet, and fine twined linen, the work of the
embroiderer. 37 You shall make for the screen five pillars of
acacia, and overlay them with gold. Their hooks shall be of gold.
You shall cast five sockets of bronze for them.

Exodus 27

1 "You shall make the altar of acacia wood, five cubits[72] long,
and five cubits wide. The altar shall be square. Its height shall be
three cubits.[73] 2 You shall make its horns on its four corners. Its
horns shall be of one piece with it. You shall overlay it with
bronze. 3 You shall make its pots to take away its ashes; and its
shovels, its basins, its meat hooks, and its fire pans. You shall
make all its vessels of bronze. 4 You shall make a grating for it
of network of bronze. On the net you shall make four bronze
rings in its four corners. 5 You shall put it under the ledge
around the altar beneath, that the net may reach halfway up the
altar. 6 You shall make poles for the altar, poles of acacia wood,
and overlay them with bronze. 7 Its poles shall be put into the
rings, and the poles shall be on the two sides of the altar when
carrying it. 8 You shall make it hollow with planks. They shall
make it as it has been shown you on the mountain.
9 "You shall make the court of the tabernacle: for the south side
southward there shall be hangings for the court of fine twined
linen one hundred cubits long for one side. 10 Its pillars shall be
twenty, and their sockets twenty, of bronze. The hooks of the
pillars and their fillets shall be of silver. 11 Likewise for the
length of the north side, there shall be hangings one hundred
cubits long, and its pillars twenty, and their sockets twenty, of
bronze; the hooks of the pillars, and their fillets, of silver.
12 For the width of the court on the west side shall be hangings
of fifty cubits; their pillars ten, and their sockets ten. 13 The
width of the court on the east side eastward shall be fifty cubits.
14 The hangings for the one side of the gate shall be fifteen
cubits; their pillars three, and their sockets three. 15 For the
other side shall be hangings of fifteen cubits; their pillars three,
and their sockets three. 16 For the gate of the court shall be a
screen of twenty cubits, of blue, and purple, and scarlet, and fine
twined linen, the work of the embroiderer; their pillars four, and
their sockets four. 17 All the pillars of the court around shall be
filleted with silver; their hooks of silver, and their sockets of
bronze. 18 The length of the court shall be one hundred cubits,
and the width fifty throughout, and the height five cubits, of fine
twined linen, and their sockets of bronze. 19 All the instruments
of the tabernacle in all its service, and all its pins, and all the pins
of the court, shall be of bronze.
20 "You shall command the children of Israel, that they bring to
you pure olive oil beaten for the light, to cause a lamp to burn
continually. 21 In the Tent of Meeting, outside the veil which is
before the covenant, Aaron and his sons shall keep it in order
from evening to morning before God: it shall be a statute forever
throughout their generations on the behalf of the children of
Israel.

Exodus 28

1 "Bring Aaron your brother, and his sons with him, near to you
from among the children of Israel, that he may minister to me in
the priest's office: Aaron, Nadab and Abihu, Eleazar and Ithamar,
Aaron's sons. 2 You shall make holy garments for Aaron your
brother, for glory and for beauty. 3 You shall speak to all who
are wise-hearted, whom I have filled with the spirit of wisdom,
that they make Aaron's garments to sanctify him, that he may
minister to me in the priest's office. 4 These are the garments
which they shall make: a breastplate, an ephod, a robe, a fitted
tunic, a turban, and a sash. They shall make holy garments for
Aaron your brother and his sons, that he may minister to me in
the priest's office. 5 They shall use the gold, and the blue, and
the purple, and the scarlet, and the fine linen.
6 "They shall make the ephod of gold, blue, purple, scarlet, and
fine twined linen, the work of the skillful workman. 7 It shall
have two shoulder straps joined to the two ends of it, that it may
be joined together. 8 The skillfully woven band, which is on it,
shall be like its work and of the same piece; of gold, blue, purple,
scarlet, and fine twined linen. 9 You shall take two onyx stones,
and engrave on them the names of the children of Israel. 10 Six
of their names on the one stone, and the names of the six that
remain on the other stone, in the order of their birth. 11 With
the work of an engraver in stone, like the engravings of a signet,
you shall engrave the two stones, according to the names of the
children of Israel. You shall make them to be enclosed in settings

---

[69]**25:10** *25:10* A cubit is the length from the tip of the middle finger to the elbow on a man's arm, or about 18 inches or 46 centimeters.

[70]**25:39** *25:39* A talent is about 30 kilograms or 66 pounds or 965 Troy ounces

[71]**26:2** *26:2* A cubit is the length from the tip of the middle finger to the elbow on a man's arm, or about 18 inches or 46 centimeters.

[72]**27:1** *27:1* A cubit is the length from the tip of the middle finger to the elbow on a man's arm, or about 18 inches or 46 centimeters.

[73]**27:1** *27:1* The altar was to be about 2.3×2.3×1.4 meters or about 7½×7½×4½ feet.

of gold. **12** You shall put the two stones on the shoulder straps of the ephod, to be stones of memorial for the children of Israel. Aaron shall bear their names before God on his two shoulders for a memorial. **13** You shall make settings of gold, **14** and two chains of pure gold; you shall make them like cords of braided work. You shall put the braided chains on the settings.

15 "You shall make a breastplate of judgment, the work of the skillful workman; like the work of the ephod you shall make it; of gold, of blue, and purple, and scarlet, and fine twined linen, you shall make it. **16** It shall be square and folded double; a span[74] shall be its length, and a span its width. **17** You shall set in it settings of stones, four rows of stones: a row of ruby, topaz, and beryl shall be the first row; **18** and the second row a turquoise, a sapphire,[75] and an emerald; **19** and the third row a jacinth, an agate, and an amethyst; **20** and the fourth row a chrysolite, an onyx, and a jasper. They shall be enclosed in gold in their settings. **21** The stones shall be according to the names of the children of Israel, twelve, according to their names; like the engravings of a signet, everyone according to his name, they shall be for the twelve tribes. **22** You shall make on the breastplate chains like cords, of braided work of pure gold. **23** You shall make on the breastplate two rings of gold, and shall put the two rings on the two ends of the breastplate. **24** You shall put the two braided chains of gold in the two rings at the ends of the breastplate. **25** The other two ends of the two braided chains you shall put on the two settings, and put them on the shoulder straps of the ephod in its forepart. **26** You shall make two rings of gold, and you shall put them on the two ends of the breastplate, on its edge, which is toward the side of the ephod inward. **27** You shall make two rings of gold, and shall put them on the two shoulder straps of the ephod underneath, in its forepart, close by its coupling, above the skillfully woven band of the ephod. **28** They shall bind the breastplate by its rings to the rings of the ephod with a lace of blue, that it may be on the skillfully woven band of the ephod, and that the breastplate may not swing out from the ephod. **29** Aaron shall bear the names of the children of Israel in the breastplate of judgment on his heart, when he goes in to the holy place, for a memorial before God continually. **30** You shall put in the breastplate of judgment the Urim and the Thummim; and they shall be on Aaron's heart, when he goes in before God. Aaron shall bear the judgment of the children of Israel on his heart before God continually.

31 "You shall make the robe of the ephod all of blue. **32** It shall have a hole for the head in the middle of it. It shall have a binding of woven work around its hole, as it were the hole of a coat of mail, that it not be torn. **33** On its hem you shall make pomegranates of blue, and of purple, and of scarlet, all around its hem; with bells of gold between and around them: **34** a golden bell and a pomegranate, a golden bell and a pomegranate, around the hem of the robe. **35** It shall be on Aaron to minister: and its sound shall be heard when he goes in to the holy place before God, and when he comes out, that he not die.

36 "You shall make a plate of pure gold, and engrave on it, like the engravings of a signet, 'HOLY TO YAHWEH.' **37** You shall put it on a lace of blue, and it shall be on the sash. It shall be on the front of the sash. **38** It shall be on Aaron's forehead, and Aaron shall bear the iniquity of the holy things, which the children of Israel shall make holy in all their holy gifts; and it shall be always on his forehead, that they may be accepted before God. **39** You shall weave the tunic with fine linen. You shall make a turban of fine linen. You shall make a sash, the work of the embroiderer.

40 "You shall make tunics for Aaron's sons. You shall make sashes for them. You shall make headbands for them, for glory and for beauty. **41** You shall put them on Aaron your brother, and on his sons with him, and shall anoint them, and consecrate them, and sanctify them, that they may minister to me in the priest's office. **42** You shall make them linen pants to cover their naked flesh. They shall reach from the waist even to the thighs. **43** They shall be on Aaron and on his sons, when they go in to the Tent of Meeting, or when they come near to the altar to minister in the holy place, that they don't bear iniquity, and

die. This shall be a statute forever to him and to his offspring after him.

Exodus 29

1 "This is the thing that you shall do to them to make them holy, to minister to me in the priest's office: take one young bull and two rams without defect, **2** unleavened bread, unleavened cakes mixed with oil, and unleavened wafers anointed with oil. You shall make them of fine wheat flour. **3** You shall put them into one basket, and bring them in the basket, with the bull and the two rams. **4** You shall bring Aaron and his sons to the door of the Tent of Meeting, and shall wash them with water. **5** You shall take the garments, and put on Aaron the tunic, the robe of the ephod, the ephod, and the breastplate, and clothe him with the skillfully woven band of the ephod. **6** You shall set the turban on his head, and put the holy crown on the turban. **7** Then you shall take the anointing oil, and pour it on his head, and anoint him. **8** You shall bring his sons, and put tunics on them. **9** You shall clothe them with belts, Aaron and his sons, and bind headbands on them. They shall have the priesthood by a perpetual statute. You shall consecrate Aaron and his sons.

10 "You shall bring the bull before the Tent of Meeting; and Aaron and his sons shall lay their hands on the head of the bull. **11** You shall kill the bull before God at the door of the Tent of Meeting. **12** You shall take of the blood of the bull, and put it on the horns of the altar with your finger; and you shall pour out all the blood at the base of the altar. **13** You shall take all the fat that covers the innards, the cover of the liver, the two kidneys, and the fat that is on them, and burn them on the altar. **14** But the meat of the bull, and its skin, and its dung, you shall burn with fire outside of the camp. It is a sin offering.

15 "You shall also take the one ram, and Aaron and his sons shall lay their hands on the head of the ram. **16** You shall kill the ram, and you shall take its blood, and sprinkle it around on the altar. **17** You shall cut the ram into its pieces, and wash its innards, and its legs, and put them with its pieces, and with its head. **18** You shall burn the whole ram on the altar: it is a burnt offering to God; it is a pleasant aroma, an offering made by fire to God.

19 "You shall take the other ram, and Aaron and his sons shall lay their hands on the head of the ram. **20** Then you shall kill the ram, and take some of its blood, and put it on the tip of the right ear of Aaron, and on the tip of the right ear of his sons, and on the thumb of their right hand, and on the big toe of their right foot; and sprinkle the blood around on the altar. **21** You shall take of the blood that is on the altar, and of the anointing oil, and sprinkle it on Aaron, and on his garments, and on his sons, and on the garments of his sons with him: and he shall be made holy, and his garments, and his sons, and his sons' garments with him.

22 Also you shall take some of the ram's fat, the fat tail, the fat that covers the innards, the cover of the liver, the two kidneys, the fat that is on them, and the right thigh (for it is a ram of consecration), **23** and one loaf of bread, one cake of oiled bread, and one wafer out of the basket of unleavened bread that is before God. **24** You shall put all of this in Aaron's hands, and in his sons' hands, and shall wave them for a wave offering before God. **25** You shall take them from their hands, and burn them on the altar on the burnt offering, for a pleasant aroma before God: it is an offering made by fire to God.

26 "You shall take the breast of Aaron's ram of consecration, and wave it for a wave offering before God. It shall be your portion. **27** You shall sanctify the breast of the wave offering and the thigh of the wave offering, which is waved, and which is raised up, of the ram of consecration, even of that which is for Aaron, and of that which is for his sons. **28** It shall be for Aaron and his sons as their portion forever from the children of Israel; for it is a wave offering. It shall be a wave offering from the children of Israel of the sacrifices of their peace offerings, even their wave offering to God.

29 "The holy garments of Aaron shall be for his sons after him, to be anointed in them, and to be consecrated in them. **30** Seven days shall the son who is priest in his place put them on, when he comes into the Tent of Meeting to minister in the holy place.

31 "You shall take the ram of consecration and boil its meat in a holy place. **32** Aaron and his sons shall eat the meat of the ram, and the bread that is in the basket, at the door of the Tent of Meeting. **33** They shall eat those things with which atonement was made, to consecrate and sanctify them; but a stranger shall not eat of it, because they are holy. **34** If anything of the meat of the consecration, or of the bread, remains to the morning, then you shall burn the remainder with fire. It shall not be eaten, because it is holy.

35 "You shall do so to Aaron and to his sons, according to all that I have commanded you. You shall consecrate them seven days. **36** Every day you shall offer the bull of sin offering for atonement. You shall cleanse the altar when you make atonement for it. You shall anoint it, to sanctify it. **37** Seven days you shall make atonement for the altar, and sanctify it; and the altar shall be most holy. Whatever touches the altar shall be holy.

38 "Now this is that which you shall offer on the altar: two lambs a year old day by day continually. **39** The one lamb you shall offer in the morning; and the other lamb you shall offer at evening; **40** and with the one lamb a tenth part of an ephah[76] of fine flour mixed with the fourth part of a hin[77] of beaten oil, and the fourth part of a hin of wine for a drink offering. **41** The other lamb you shall offer at evening, and shall do to it according to the meal offering of the morning and according to its drink offering, for a pleasant aroma, an offering made by fire to God. **42** It shall be a continual burnt offering throughout your generations at the door of the Tent of Meeting before God, where I will meet with you, to speak there to you. **43** There I will meet with the children of Israel; and the place shall be sanctified by my glory. **44** I will sanctify the Tent of Meeting and the altar. I will also sanctify Aaron and his sons to minister to me in the priest's office. **45** I will dwell among the children of Israel, and will be their God. **46** They shall know that I am God their God, who brought them out of the land of Egypt, that I might dwell among them: I am God their God.

Exodus 30

1 "You shall make an altar to burn incense on. You shall make it of acacia wood. **2** Its length shall be a cubit,[78] and its width a cubit. It shall be square, and its height shall be two cubits. Its horns shall be of one piece with it. **3** You shall overlay it with pure gold, its top, its sides around it, and its horns; and you shall make a gold molding around it. **4** You shall make two golden rings for it under its molding; on its two ribs, on its two sides you shall make them; and they shall be for places for poles with which to bear it. **5** You shall make the poles of acacia wood, and overlay them with gold. **6** You shall put it before the veil that is by the ark of the covenant, before the mercy seat that is over the covenant, where I will meet with you. **7** Aaron shall burn incense of sweet spices on it every morning. When he tends the lamps, he shall burn it. **8** When Aaron lights the lamps at evening, he shall burn it, a perpetual incense before God throughout your generations. **9** You shall offer no strange incense on it, nor burnt offering, nor meal offering; and you shall pour no drink offering on it. **10** Aaron shall make atonement on its horns once in the year; with the blood of the sin offering of atonement once in the year he shall make atonement for it throughout your generations. It is most holy to God."

11 God spoke to Moses, saying, **12** "When you take a census of the children of Israel, according to those who are counted among them, then each man shall give a ransom for his soul to God, when you count them; that there be no plague among them when you count them. **13** They shall give this, everyone who passes over to those who are counted, half a shekel according to the shekel[79] of the sanctuary (the shekel is twenty gerahs[80]); half a shekel for an offering to God. **14** Everyone who passes over to those who are counted, from twenty years old and upward, shall give the offering to God. **15** The rich shall not give more, and the poor shall not give less, than the half shekel,[81] when they give the offering of God, to make atonement for your souls. **16** You shall take the atonement money from the children of Israel, and shall appoint it for the service of the Tent of Meeting; that it may

---

[74]**28:16** *28:16* A span is the length from the tip of a man's thumb to the tip of his little finger when his hand is stretched out (about half a cubit, or 9 inches, or 22.8 cm.)

[75]**28:18** *28:18* or, lapis lazuli

[76]**29:40** *29:40* 1 ephah is about 22 liters or about 2/3 of a bushel

[77]**29:40** *29:40* A hin is about 6.5 liters or 1.7 gallons, so a fourth of a hin is about 1.6 liters.

[78]**30:2** *30:2* A cubit is the length from the tip of the middle finger to the elbow on a man's arm, or about 18 inches or 46 centimeters.

[79]**30:13** *30:13* A shekel is about 10 grams or about 0.35 ounces.

[80]**30:13** *30:13* a gerah is about 0.5 grams or about 7.7 grains

[81]**30:15** *30:15* A shekel is about 10 grams or about 0.35 ounces.

be a memorial for the children of Israel before God, to make
atonement for your souls."
17 God spoke to Moses, saying, 18 "You shall also make a
basin of bronze, and its base of bronze, in which to wash. You
shall put it between the Tent of Meeting and the altar, and you
shall put water in it. 19 Aaron and his sons shall wash their
hands and their feet in it. 20 When they go into the Tent of
Meeting, they shall wash with water, that they not die; or when
they come near to the altar to minister, to burn an offering made
by fire to God. 21 So they shall wash their hands and their feet,
that they not die. This shall be a statute forever to them, even to
him and to his descendants throughout their generations."
22 Moreover God spoke to Moses, saying, 23 "Also take fine
spices: of liquid myrrh, five hundred shekels;[82] and of fragrant
cinnamon half as much, even two hundred and fifty; and of
fragrant cane, two hundred and fifty; 24 and of cassia five
hundred, according to the shekel of the sanctuary; and a hin[83] of
olive oil. 25 You shall make it into a holy anointing oil, a
perfume compounded after the art of the perfumer: it shall be a
holy anointing oil. 26 You shall use it to anoint the Tent of
Meeting, the ark of the covenant, 27 the table and all its articles,
the lamp stand and its accessories, the altar of incense, 28 the
altar of burnt offering with all its utensils, and the basin with its
base. 29 You shall sanctify them, that they may be most holy.
Whatever touches them shall be holy. 30 You shall anoint
Aaron and his sons, and sanctify them, that they may minister to
me in the priest's office. 31 You shall speak to the children of
Israel, saying, 'This shall be a holy anointing oil to me
throughout your generations. 32 It shall not be poured on man's
flesh, and do not make any like it, according to its composition. It
is holy. It shall be holy to you. 33 Whoever compounds any like
it, or whoever puts any of it on a stranger, he shall be cut off from
his people.'"
34 God said to Moses, "Take to yourself sweet spices, gum
resin, onycha, and galbanum; sweet spices with pure
frankincense. There shall be an equal weight of each. 35 You
shall make incense of it, a perfume after the art of the perfumer,
seasoned with salt, pure and holy. 36 You shall beat some of it
very small, and put some of it before the covenant in the Tent of
Meeting, where I will meet with you. It shall be to you most holy.
37 The incense which you shall make, according to its
composition you shall not make for yourselves: it shall be to you
holy for God. 38 Whoever shall make any like that, to smell of
it, he shall be cut off from his people."
Exodus 31
1 God spoke to Moses, saying, 2 "Behold, I have called by
name Bezalel the son of Uri, the son of Hur, of the tribe of Judah.
3 I have filled him with the Spirit of God, in wisdom, and in
understanding, and in knowledge, and in all kinds of
workmanship, 4 to devise skillful works, to work in gold, and in
silver, and in bronze, 5 and in cutting of stones for setting, and
in carving of wood, to work in all kinds of workmanship.
6 Behold, I myself have appointed with him Oholiab, the son of
Ahisamach, of the tribe of Dan; and in the heart of all who are
wise-hearted I have put wisdom, that they may make all that I
have commanded you: 7 the Tent of Meeting, the ark of the
covenant, the mercy seat that is on it, all the furniture of the Tent,
8 the table and its vessels, the pure lamp stand with all its
vessels, the altar of incense, 9 the altar of burnt offering with all
its vessels, the basin and its base, 10 the finely worked
garments—the holy garments for Aaron the priest, the garments
of his sons to minister in the priest's office— 11 the anointing
oil, and the incense of sweet spices for the holy place: according
to all that I have commanded you they shall do."
12 God spoke to Moses, saying, 13 "Speak also to the children
of Israel, saying, 'Most certainly you shall keep my Sabbaths; for
it is a sign between me and you throughout your generations, that
you may know that I am God who sanctifies you. 14 You shall
keep the Sabbath therefore, for it is holy to you. Everyone who
profanes it shall surely be put to death; for whoever does any
work therein, that soul shall be cut off from among his people.
15 Six days shall work be done, but on the seventh day is a
Sabbath of solemn rest, holy to God. Whoever does any work on
the Sabbath day shall surely be put to death. 16 Therefore the
children of Israel shall keep the Sabbath, to observe the Sabbath
throughout their generations, for a perpetual covenant. 17 It is a
sign between me and the children of Israel forever; for in six days
God made heaven and earth, and on the seventh day he rested,
and was refreshed.'"
18 When he finished speaking with him on Mount Sinai, he
gave Moses the two tablets of the covenant, stone tablets, written
with God's finger.

Exodus 32

1 When the people saw that Moses delayed coming down from
the mountain, the people gathered themselves together to Aaron,
and said to him, "Come, make us gods, which shall go before us;
for as for this Moses, the man who brought us up out of the land
of Egypt, we don't know what has become of him."
2 Aaron said to them, "Take off the golden rings, which are in
the ears of your wives, of your sons, and of your daughters, and
bring them to me."
3 All the people took off the golden rings which were in their
ears, and brought them to Aaron. 4 He received what they
handed him, fashioned it with an engraving tool, and made it a
molded calf. Then they said, "These are your gods, Israel, which
brought you up out of the land of Egypt."
5 When Aaron saw this, he built an altar before it; and Aaron
made a proclamation, and said, "Tomorrow shall be a feast to
God."
6 They rose up early on the next day, and offered burnt
offerings, and brought peace offerings; and the people sat down
to eat and to drink, and rose up to play.
7 God spoke to Moses, "Go, get down; for your people, who
you brought up out of the land of Egypt, have corrupted
themselves! 8 They have turned away quickly out of the way
which I commanded them. They have made themselves a molded
calf, and have worshiped it, and have sacrificed to it, and said,
'These are your gods, Israel, which brought you up out of the
land of Egypt.'"
9 God said to Moses, "I have seen these people, and behold,
they are a stiff-necked people. 10 Now therefore leave me
alone, that my wrath may burn hot against them, and that I may
consume them; and I will make of you a great nation."
11 Moses begged God his God, and said, "God, why does your
wrath burn hot against your people, that you have brought out of
the land of Egypt with great power and with a mighty hand?
12 Why should the Egyptians talk, saying, 'He brought them
out for evil, to kill them in the mountains, and to consume them
from the surface of the earth?' Turn from your fierce wrath, and
turn away from this evil against your people. 13 Remember
Abraham, Isaac, and Israel, your servants, to whom you swore by
your own self, and said to them, 'I will multiply your offspring[84]
as the stars of the sky, and all this land that I have spoken of I
will give to your offspring, and they shall inherit it forever.'"
14 So God turned away from the evil which he said he would
do to his people.
15 Moses turned, and went down from the mountain, with the
two tablets of the covenant in his hand; tablets that were written
on both their sides. They were written on one side and on the
other. 16 The tablets were the work of God, and the writing was
the writing of God, engraved on the tablets.
17 When Joshua heard the noise of the people as they shouted,
he said to Moses, "There is the noise of war in the camp."
18 He said, "It isn't the voice of those who shout for victory. It
is not the voice of those who cry for being overcome; but the
noise of those who sing that I hear." 19 As soon as he came
near to the camp, he saw the calf and the dancing. Then Moses'
anger grew hot, and he threw the tablets out of his hands, and
broke them beneath the mountain. 20 He took the calf which
they had made, and burned it with fire, ground it to powder, and
scattered it on the water, and made the children of Israel drink it.
21 Moses said to Aaron, "What did these people do to you, that
you have brought a great sin on them?"
22 Aaron said, "Don't let the anger of my lord grow hot. You
know the people, that they are set on evil. 23 For they said to
me, 'Make us gods, which shall go before us. As for this Moses,
the man who brought us up out of the land of Egypt, we don't
know what has become of him.' 24 I said to them, 'Whoever
has any gold, let them take it off.' So they gave it to me; and I
threw it into the fire, and out came this calf."
25 When Moses saw that the people were out of control, (for
Aaron had let them lose control, causing derision among their
enemies), 26 then Moses stood in the gate of the camp, and
said, "Whoever is on God's side, come to me!"
All the sons of Levi gathered themselves together to him. 27 He
said to them, "God, the God of Israel, says, 'Every man put his
sword on his thigh, and go back and forth from gate to gate
throughout the camp, and every man kill his brother, and every
man his companion, and every man his neighbor.'" 28 The sons
of Levi did according to the word of Moses. About three
thousand men fell of the people that day. 29 Moses said,
"Consecrate yourselves today to God, for every man was against
his son and against his brother, that he may give you a blessing
today."
30 On the next day, Moses said to the people, "You have sinned
a great sin. Now I will go up to God. Perhaps I shall make
atonement for your sin."
31 Moses returned to God, and said, "Oh, this people have
sinned a great sin, and have made themselves gods of gold.
32 Yet now, if you will, forgive their sin—and if not, please
blot me out of your book which you have written."
33 God said to Moses, "Whoever has sinned against me, I will
blot him out of my book. 34 Now go, lead the people to the
place of which I have spoken to you. Behold, my angel shall go
before you. Nevertheless, in the day when I punish, I will punish
them for their sin." 35 God struck the people, because of what
they did with the calf, which Aaron made.

Exodus 33

1 God spoke to Moses, "Depart, go up from here, you and the
people that you have brought up out of the land of Egypt, to the
land of which I swore to Abraham, to Isaac, and to Jacob, saying,
'I will give it to your offspring.' 2 I will send an angel before
you; and I will drive out the Canaanite, the Amorite, and the
Hittite, and the Perizzite, the Hivite, and the Jebusite. 3 Go to a
land flowing with milk and honey; but I will not go up among
you, for you are a stiff-necked people, lest I consume you on the
way."
4 When the people heard this evil news, they mourned; and no
one put on his jewelry.
5 God had said to Moses, "Tell the children of Israel, 'You are a
stiff-necked people. If I were to go up among you for one
moment, I would consume you. Therefore now take off your
jewelry from you, that I may know what to do to you.'"
6 The children of Israel stripped themselves of their jewelry
from Mount Horeb onward.
7 Now Moses used to take the tent and pitch it outside the
camp, far away from the camp, and he called it "The Tent of
Meeting." Everyone who sought God went out to the Tent of
Meeting, which was outside the camp. 8 When Moses went out
to the Tent, all the people rose up, and stood, everyone at their
tent door, and watched Moses, until he had gone into the Tent.
9 When Moses entered into the Tent, the pillar of cloud
descended, stood at the door of the Tent, and God spoke with
Moses. 10 All the people saw the pillar of cloud stand at the
door of the Tent, and all the people rose up and worshiped,
everyone at their tent door. 11 God spoke to Moses face to face,
as a man speaks to his friend. He turned again into the camp, but
his servant Joshua, the son of Nun, a young man, didn't depart
from the Tent.
12 Moses said to God, "Behold, you tell me, 'Bring up this
people;' and you haven't let me know whom you will send with
me. Yet you have said, 'I know you by name, and you have also
found favor in my sight.' 13 Now therefore, if I have found
favor in your sight, please show me your way, now, that I may
know you, so that I may find favor in your sight; and consider
that this nation is your people."
14 He said, "My presence will go with you, and I will give you
rest."
15 Moses said to him, "If your presence doesn't go with me,
don't carry us up from here. 16 For how would people know
that I have found favor in your sight, I and your people? Isn't it
that you go with us, so that we are separated, I and your people,
from all the people who are on the surface of the earth?"
17 God said to Moses, "I will do this thing also that you have
spoken; for you have found favor in my sight, and I know you by
name."
18 Moses said, "Please show me your glory."
19 He said, "I will make all my goodness pass before you, and
will proclaim God's name before you. I will be gracious to whom
I will be gracious, and will show mercy on whom I will show
mercy." 20 He said, "You cannot see my face, for man may not

---

[82] **30:23** *30:23* **A shekel is about 10 grams or about 0.35 ounces, so 500 shekels is about 5 kilograms or about 11 pounds.**

[83] **30:24** *30:24* **A hin is about 6.5 liters or 1.7 gallons.**

[84] **32:13** *32:13* **or, seed**

see me and live." 21 God also said, "Behold, there is a place by me, and you shall stand on the rock. 22 It will happen, while my glory passes by, that I will put you in a cleft of the rock, and will cover you with my hand until I have passed by; 23 then I will take away my hand, and you will see my back; but my face shall not be seen."

Exodus 34

1 God said to Moses, "Chisel two stone tablets like the first. I will write on the tablets the words that were on the first tablets, which you broke. 2 Be ready by the morning, and come up in the morning to Mount Sinai, and present yourself there to me on the top of the mountain. 3 No one shall come up with you or be seen anywhere on the mountain. Do not let the flocks or herds graze in front of that mountain."

4 He chiseled two tablets of stone like the first; then Moses rose up early in the morning, and went up to Mount Sinai, as God had commanded him, and took in his hand two stone tablets. 5 God descended in the cloud, and stood with him there, and proclaimed God's name. 6 God passed by before him, and proclaimed, "God! God, a merciful and gracious God, slow to anger, and abundant in loving kindness and truth, 7 keeping loving kindness for thousands, forgiving iniquity and disobedience and sin; and who will by no means clear the guilty, visiting the iniquity of the fathers on the children, and on the children's children, on the third and on the fourth generation."

8 Moses hurried and bowed his head toward the earth, and worshiped. 9 He said, "If now I have found favor in your sight, Lord, please let the Lord go among us, even though this is a stiff-necked people; pardon our iniquity and our sin, and take us for your inheritance."

10 He said, "Behold, I make a covenant: before all your people I will do marvels, such as have not been worked in all the earth, nor in any nation; and all the people among whom you are shall see the work of God; for it is an awesome thing that I do with you. 11 Observe that which I command you today. Behold, I will drive out before you the Amorite, the Canaanite, the Hittite, the Perizzite, the Hivite, and the Jebusite. 12 Be careful, lest you make a covenant with the inhabitants of the land where you are going, lest it be for a snare among you; 13 but you shall break down their altars, and dash in pieces their pillars, and you shall cut down their Asherah poles; 14 for you shall worship no other god; for God, whose name is Jealous, is a jealous God.

15 "Don't make a covenant with the inhabitants of the land, lest they play the prostitute after their gods, and sacrifice to their gods, and one call you and you eat of his sacrifice; 16 and you take of their daughters to your sons, and their daughters play the prostitute after their gods, and make your sons play the prostitute after their gods.

17 "You shall make no cast idols for yourselves.

18 "You shall keep the feast of unleavened bread. Seven days you shall eat unleavened bread, as I commanded you, at the time appointed in the month Abib; for in the month Abib you came out of Egypt.

19 "All that opens the womb is mine; and all your livestock that is male, the firstborn of cow and sheep. 20 You shall redeem the firstborn of a donkey with a lamb. If you will not redeem it, then you shall break its neck. You shall redeem all the firstborn of your sons. No one shall appear before me empty.

21 "Six days you shall work, but on the seventh day you shall rest: in plowing time and in harvest you shall rest.

22 "You shall observe the feast of weeks with the first fruits of wheat harvest, and the feast of harvest at the year's end.

23 Three times in the year all your males shall appear before the Lord God, the God of Israel. 24 For I will drive out nations before you and enlarge your borders; neither shall any man desire your land when you go up to appear before God, your God, three times in the year.

25 "You shall not offer the blood of my sacrifice with leavened bread. The sacrifice of the feast of the Passover shall not be left to the morning.

26 "You shall bring the first of the first fruits of your ground to the house of God your God.
"You shall not boil a young goat in its mother's milk."

27 God said to Moses, "Write these words; for in accordance with these words I have made a covenant with you and with Israel."

28 He was there with God forty days and forty nights; he neither ate bread, nor drank water. He wrote on the tablets the words of the covenant, the ten commandments.

29 When Moses came down from Mount Sinai with the two tablets of the covenant in Moses' hand, when he came down from the mountain, Moses didn't know that the skin of his face shone by reason of his speaking with him. 30 When Aaron and all the children of Israel saw Moses, behold, the skin of his face shone; and they were afraid to come near him. 31 Moses called to them, and Aaron and all the rulers of the congregation returned to him; and Moses spoke to them. 32 Afterward all the children of Israel came near, and he gave them all the commandments that God had spoken with him on Mount Sinai. 33 When Moses was done speaking with them, he put a veil on his face. 34 But when Moses went in before God to speak with him, he took the veil off, until he came out; and he came out, and spoke to the children of Israel that which he was commanded. 35 The children of Israel saw Moses' face, that the skin of Moses' face shone; so Moses put the veil on his face again, until he went in to speak with him.

Exodus 35

1 Moses assembled all the congregation of the children of Israel, and said to them, "These are the words which God has commanded, that you should do them. 2 'Six days shall work be done, but on the seventh day there shall be a holy day for you, a Sabbath of solemn rest to God: whoever does any work in it shall be put to death. 3 You shall kindle no fire throughout your habitations on the Sabbath day.'"

4 Moses spoke to all the congregation of the children of Israel, saying, "This is the thing which God commanded, saying,

5 'Take from among you an offering to God. Whoever is of a willing heart, let him bring it as God's offering: gold, silver, bronze, 6 blue, purple, scarlet, fine linen, goats' hair, 7 rams' skins dyed red, sea cow hides, acacia wood, 8 oil for the light, spices for the anointing oil and for the sweet incense, 9 onyx stones, and stones to be set for the ephod and for the breastplate.

10 "'Let every wise-hearted man among you come, and make all that God has commanded: 11 the tabernacle, its outer covering, its roof, its clasps, its boards, its bars, its pillars, and its sockets; 12 the ark, and its poles, the mercy seat, the veil of the screen; 13 the table with its poles and all its vessels, and the show bread; 14 the lamp stand also for the light, with its vessels, its lamps, and the oil for the light; 15 and the altar of incense with its poles, the anointing oil, the sweet incense, the screen for the door, at the door of the tabernacle; 16 the altar of burnt offering, with its grating of bronze, its poles, and all its vessels, the basin and its base; 17 the hangings of the court, its pillars, their sockets, and the screen for the gate of the court;

18 the pins of the tabernacle, the pins of the court, and their cords; 19 the finely worked garments for ministering in the holy place—the holy garments for Aaron the priest, and the garments of his sons—to minister in the priest's office.'"

20 All the congregation of the children of Israel departed from the presence of Moses. 21 They came, everyone whose heart stirred him up, and everyone whom his spirit made willing, and brought God's offering for the work of the Tent of Meeting, and for all of its service, and for the holy garments. 22 They came, both men and women, as many as were willing-hearted, and brought brooches, earrings, signet rings, and armlets, all jewels of gold; even every man who offered an offering of gold to God.

23 Everyone with whom was found blue, purple, scarlet, fine linen, goats' hair, rams' skins dyed red, and sea cow hides, brought them. 24 Everyone who offered an offering of silver and bronze brought God's offering; and everyone with whom was found acacia wood for any work of the service, brought it.

25 All the women who were wise-hearted spun with their hands, and brought that which they had spun: the blue, the purple, the scarlet, and the fine linen. 26 All the women whose heart stirred them up in wisdom spun the goats' hair. 27 The rulers brought the onyx stones and the stones to be set for the ephod and for the breastplate; 28 with the spice and the oil for the light, for the anointing oil, and for the sweet incense. 29 The children of Israel brought a free will offering to God; every man and woman whose heart made them willing to bring for all the work, which God had commanded to be made by Moses.

30 Moses said to the children of Israel, "Behold, God has called by name Bezalel the son of Uri, the son of Hur, of the tribe of Judah. 31 He has filled him with the Spirit of God, in wisdom, in understanding, in knowledge, and in all kinds of workmanship;

32 and to make skillful works, to work in gold, in silver, in bronze, 33 in cutting of stones for setting, and in carving of wood, to work in all kinds of skillful workmanship. 34 He has put in his heart that he may teach, both he and Oholiab, the son of Ahisamach, of the tribe of Dan. 35 He has filled them with wisdom of heart to work all kinds of workmanship, of the engraver, of the skillful workman, and of the embroiderer, in blue, in purple, in scarlet, and in fine linen, and of the weaver, even of those who do any workmanship, and of those who make skillful works.

Exodus 36

1 "Bezalel and Oholiab shall work with every wise-hearted man, in whom God has put wisdom and understanding to know how to do all the work for the service of the sanctuary, according to all that God has commanded."

2 Moses called Bezalel and Oholiab, and every wise-hearted man, in whose heart God had put wisdom, even everyone whose heart stirred him up to come to the work to do it. 3 They received from Moses all the offering which the children of Israel had brought for the work of the service of the sanctuary, with which to make it. They kept bringing free will offerings to him every morning. 4 All the wise men, who performed all the work of the sanctuary, each came from his work which he did. 5 They spoke to Moses, saying, "The people have brought much more than enough for the service of the work which God commanded to make."

6 Moses gave a commandment, and they caused it to be proclaimed throughout the camp, saying, "Let neither man nor woman make anything else for the offering for the sanctuary." So the people were restrained from bringing. 7 For the stuff they had was sufficient to do all the work, and too much.

8 All the wise-hearted men among those who did the work made the tabernacle with ten curtains of fine twined linen, blue, purple, and scarlet. They made them with cherubim, the work of a skillful workman. 9 The length of each curtain was twenty-eight cubits,[85] and the width of each curtain four cubits. All the curtains had one measure. 10 He coupled five curtains to one another, and the other five curtains he coupled to one another.

11 He made loops of blue on the edge of the one curtain from the edge in the coupling. Likewise he made in the edge of the curtain that was outermost in the second coupling. 12 He made fifty loops in the one curtain, and he made fifty loops in the edge of the curtain that was in the second coupling. The loops were opposite to one another. 13 He made fifty clasps of gold, and coupled the curtains to one another with the clasps: so the tabernacle was a unit.

14 He made curtains of goats' hair for a covering over the tabernacle. He made them eleven curtains. 15 The length of each curtain was thirty cubits, and four cubits the width of each curtain. The eleven curtains had one measure. 16 He coupled five curtains by themselves, and six curtains by themselves.

17 He made fifty loops on the edge of the curtain that was outermost in the coupling, and he made fifty loops on the edge of the curtain which was outermost in the second coupling. 18 He made fifty clasps of bronze to couple the tent together, that it might be a unit. 19 He made a covering for the tent of rams' skins dyed red, and a covering of sea cow hides above.

20 He made the boards for the tabernacle of acacia wood, standing up. 21 Ten cubits was the length of a board, and a cubit and a half the width of each board. 22 Each board had two tenons, joined to one another. He made all the boards of the tabernacle this way. 23 He made the boards for the tabernacle, twenty boards for the south side southward. 24 He made forty sockets of silver under the twenty boards: two sockets under one board for its two tenons, and two sockets under another board for its two tenons. 25 For the second side of the tabernacle, on the north side, he made twenty boards 26 and their forty sockets of silver: two sockets under one board, and two sockets under another board. 27 For the far part of the tabernacle westward he made six boards. 28 He made two boards for the corners of the tabernacle in the far part. 29 They were double beneath, and in

---

[85] **36:9** *36:9* **A cubit is the length from the tip of the middle finger to the elbow on a man's arm, or about 18 inches or 46 centimeters.**

the same way they were all the way to its top to one ring. He did
this to both of them in the two corners. 30 There were eight
boards and their sockets of silver, sixteen sockets—under every
board two sockets.
31 He made bars of acacia wood: five for the boards of the one
side of the tabernacle, 32 and five bars for the boards of the
other side of the tabernacle, and five bars for the boards of the
tabernacle for the hinder part westward. 33 He made the middle
bar to pass through in the middle of the boards from the one end
to the other. 34 He overlaid the boards with gold, and made
their rings of gold as places for the bars, and overlaid the bars
with gold.
35 He made the veil of blue, purple, scarlet, and fine twined
linen, with cherubim. He made it the work of a skillful workman.
36 He made four pillars of acacia for it, and overlaid them with
gold. Their hooks were of gold. He cast four sockets of silver for
them. 37 He made a screen for the door of the tent, of blue,
purple, scarlet, and fine twined linen, the work of an embroiderer;
38 and the five pillars of it with their hooks. He overlaid their
capitals and their fillets with gold, and their five sockets were of
bronze.

Exodus 37

1 Bezalel made the ark of acacia wood. Its length was two and a
half cubits,[86] and its width a cubit and a half, and a cubit and a
half its height. 2 He overlaid it with pure gold inside and
outside, and made a molding of gold for it around it. 3 He cast
four rings of gold for it, in its four feet—two rings on its one side,
and two rings on its other side. 4 He made poles of acacia
wood, and overlaid them with gold. 5 He put the poles into the
rings on the sides of the ark, to bear the ark. 6 He made a mercy
seat of pure gold. Its length was two and a half cubits, and a cubit
and a half its width. 7 He made two cherubim of gold. He made
them of beaten work, at the two ends of the mercy seat: 8 one
cherub at the one end, and one cherub at the other end. He made
the cherubim of one piece with the mercy seat at its two ends.
9 The cherubim spread out their wings above, covering the
mercy seat with their wings, with their faces toward one another.
The faces of the cherubim were toward the mercy seat.
10 He made the table of acacia wood. Its length was two cubits,
and its width was a cubit, and its height was a cubit and a half.
11 He overlaid it with pure gold, and made a gold molding
around it. 12 He made a border of a hand's width around it, and
made a golden molding on its border around it. 13 He cast four
rings of gold for it, and put the rings in the four corners that were
on its four feet. 14 The rings were close by the border, the
places for the poles to carry the table. 15 He made the poles of
acacia wood, and overlaid them with gold, to carry the table.
16 He made the vessels which were on the table, its dishes, its
spoons, its bowls, and its pitchers with which to pour out, of pure
gold.
17 He made the lamp stand of pure gold. He made the lamp
stand of beaten work. Its base, its shaft, its cups, its buds, and its
flowers were of one piece with it. 18 There were six branches
going out of its sides: three branches of the lamp stand out of its
one side, and three branches of the lamp stand out of its other
side: 19 three cups made like almond blossoms in one branch, a
bud and a flower, and three cups made like almond blossoms in
the other branch, a bud and a flower; so for the six branches
going out of the lamp stand. 20 In the lamp stand were four
cups made like almond blossoms, its buds and its flowers;
21 and a bud under two branches of one piece with it, and a bud
under two branches of one piece with it, and a bud under two
branches of one piece with it, for the six branches going out of it.
22 Their buds and their branches were of one piece with it. The
whole thing was one beaten work of pure gold. 23 He made its
seven lamps, and its snuffers, and its snuff dishes, of pure gold.
24 He made it of a talent[87] of pure gold, with all its vessels.
25 He made the altar of incense of acacia wood. It was square:
its length was a cubit, and its width a cubit. Its height was two
cubits. Its horns were of one piece with it. 26 He overlaid it
with pure gold: its top, its sides around it, and its horns. He made
a gold molding around it. 27 He made two golden rings for it
under its molding crown, on its two ribs, on its two sides, for
places for poles with which to carry it. 28 He made the poles of
acacia wood, and overlaid them with gold. 29 He made the holy
anointing oil and the pure incense of sweet spices, after the art of
the perfumer.

Exodus 38

1 He made the altar of burnt offering of acacia wood. It was
square. Its length was five cubits,[88] its width was five cubits, and
its height was three cubits. 2 He made its horns on its four
corners. Its horns were of one piece with it, and he overlaid it
with bronze. 3 He made all the vessels of the altar: the pots, the
shovels, the basins, the forks, and the fire pans. He made all its
vessels of bronze. 4 He made for the altar a grating of a network
of bronze, under the ledge around it beneath, reaching halfway
up. 5 He cast four rings for the four corners of bronze grating,
to be places for the poles. 6 He made the poles of acacia wood,
and overlaid them with bronze. 7 He put the poles into the rings
on the sides of the altar, with which to carry it. He made it hollow
with planks.
8 He made the basin of bronze, and its base of bronze, out of the
mirrors of the ministering women who ministered at the door of
the Tent of Meeting.
9 He made the court: for the south side southward the hangings
of the court were of fine twined linen, one hundred cubits;
10 their pillars were twenty, and their sockets twenty, of bronze;
the hooks of the pillars and their fillets were of silver. 11 For
the north side one hundred cubits, their pillars twenty, and their
sockets twenty, of bronze; the hooks of the pillars, and their
fillets, of silver. 12 For the west side were hangings of fifty
cubits, their pillars ten, and their sockets ten; the hooks of the
pillars, and their fillets, of silver. 13 For the east side eastward
fifty cubits, 14 the hangings for the one side were fifteen cubits;
their pillars three, and their sockets three; 15 and so for the
other side: on this hand and that hand by the gate of the court
were hangings of fifteen cubits; their pillars three, and their
sockets three. 16 All the hangings around the court were of fine
twined linen. 17 The sockets for the pillars were of bronze. The
hooks of the pillars and their fillets were of silver. Their capitals
were overlaid with silver. All the pillars of the court had silver
bands. 18 The screen for the gate of the court was the work of
the embroiderer, of blue, purple, scarlet, and fine twined linen.
Twenty cubits was the length, and the height along the width was
five cubits, like the hangings of the court. 19 Their pillars were
four, and their sockets four, of bronze; their hooks of silver, and
the overlaying of their capitals, and their fillets, of silver. 20 All
the pins of the tabernacle, and around the court, were of bronze.
21 These are the amounts of materials used for the tabernacle,
even the Tabernacle of the Testimony, as they were counted,
according to the commandment of Moses, for the service of the
Levites, by the hand of Ithamar, the son of Aaron the priest.
22 Bezalel the son of Uri, the son of Hur, of the tribe of Judah,
made all that God commanded Moses. 23 With him was
Oholiab, the son of Ahisamach, of the tribe of Dan, an engraver,
and a skillful workman, and an embroiderer in blue, in purple, in
scarlet, and in fine linen.
24 All the gold that was used for the work in all the work of the
sanctuary, even the gold of the offering, was twenty-nine talents[89]
and seven hundred thirty shekels, according to the shekel[90] of the
sanctuary. 25 The silver of those who were counted of the
congregation was one hundred talents[91] and one thousand seven
hundred seventy-five shekels,[92] according to the shekel of the
sanctuary: 26 a beka[93] a head, that is, half a shekel, according to
the shekel[94] of the sanctuary, for everyone who passed over to
those who were counted, from twenty years old and upward, for
six hundred three thousand five hundred fifty men. 27 The one
hundred talents[95] of silver were for casting the sockets of the
sanctuary and the sockets of the veil: one hundred sockets for the
one hundred talents, one talent per socket. 28 From the one
thousand seven hundred seventy-five shekels[96] he made hooks for
the pillars, overlaid their capitals, and made fillets for them.
29 The bronze of the offering was seventy talents[97] and two
thousand four hundred shekels.[98] 30 With this he made the
sockets to the door of the Tent of Meeting, the bronze altar, the
bronze grating for it, all the vessels of the altar, 31 the sockets
around the court, the sockets of the gate of the court, all the pins
of the tabernacle, and all the pins around the court.

Exodus 39

1 Of the blue, purple, and scarlet, they made finely worked
garments for ministering in the holy place, and made the holy
garments for Aaron, as God commanded Moses.
2 He made the ephod of gold, blue, purple, scarlet, and fine
twined linen. 3 They beat the gold into thin plates, and cut it
into wires, to work it in with the blue, the purple, the scarlet, and
the fine linen, the work of the skillful workman. 4 They made
shoulder straps for it, joined together. It was joined together at
the two ends. 5 The skillfully woven band that was on it, with
which to fasten it on, was of the same piece, like its work: of
gold, of blue, purple, scarlet, and fine twined linen, as God
commanded Moses.
6 They worked the onyx stones, enclosed in settings of gold,
engraved with the engravings of a signet, according to the names
of the children of Israel. 7 He put them on the shoulder straps of
the ephod, to be stones of memorial for the children of Israel, as
God commanded Moses.
8 He made the breastplate, the work of a skillful workman, like
the work of the ephod: of gold, of blue, purple, scarlet, and fine
twined linen. 9 It was square. They made the breastplate double.
Its length was a span,[99] and its width a span, being double.
10 They set in it four rows of stones. A row of ruby, topaz, and
beryl was the first row; 11 and the second row, a turquoise, a
sapphire,[100] and an emerald; 12 and the third row, a jacinth, an
agate, and an amethyst; 13 and the fourth row, a chrysolite, an
onyx, and a jasper. They were enclosed in gold settings. 14 The
stones were according to the names of the children of Israel,
twelve, according to their names; like the engravings of a signet,
everyone according to his name, for the twelve tribes. 15 They
made on the breastplate chains like cords, of braided work of
pure gold. 16 They made two settings of gold, and two gold
rings, and put the two rings on the two ends of the breastplate.
17 They put the two braided chains of gold in the two rings at
the ends of the breastplate. 18 The other two ends of the two
braided chains they put on the two settings, and put them on the
shoulder straps of the ephod, in its front. 19 They made two
rings of gold, and put them on the two ends of the breastplate, on
its edge, which was toward the side of the ephod inward.
20 They made two more rings of gold, and put them on the two
shoulder straps of the ephod underneath, in its front, close by its
coupling, above the skillfully woven band of the ephod.
21 They bound the breastplate by its rings to the rings of the
ephod with a lace of blue, that it might be on the skillfully woven
band of the ephod, and that the breastplate might not come loose
from the ephod, as God commanded Moses.
22 He made the robe of the ephod of woven work, all of blue.
23 The opening of the robe in the middle of it was like the
opening of a coat of mail, with a binding around its opening, that
it should not be torn. 24 They made on the skirts of the robe
pomegranates of blue, purple, scarlet, and twined linen. 25 They
made bells of pure gold, and put the bells between the
pomegranates around the skirts of the robe, between the

[86] **37:1** *37:1* A cubit is the length from the tip of the middle finger to the elbow on a man's arm, or about 18 inches or 46 centimeters.

[87] **37:24** *37:24* A talent is about 30 kilograms or 66 pounds or 965 Troy ounces

[88] **38:1** *38:1* A cubit is the length from the tip of the middle finger to the elbow on a man's arm, or about 18 inches or 46 centimeters.

[89] **38:24** *38:24* A talent is about 30 kilograms or 66 pounds or 965 Troy ounces.

[90] **38:24** *38:24* A shekel is about 10 grams or about 0.32 Troy ounces.

[91] **38:25** *38:25* A talent is about 30 kilograms or 66 pounds

[92] **38:25** *38:25* A shekel is about 10 grams or about 0.35 ounces.

[93] **38:26** *38:26* a beka is about 5 grams or about 0.175 ounces

[94] **38:26** *38:26* A shekel is about 10 grams or about 0.35 ounces.

[95] **38:27** *38:27* A talent is about 30 kilograms or 66 pounds.

[96] **38:28** *38:28* A shekel is about 10 grams or about 0.35 ounces, so 1775 shekels is about 17.75 kilograms or about 39 pounds.

[97] **38:29** *38:29* A talent is about 30 kilograms or 66 pounds

[98] **38:29** *38:29* 70 talents + 2400 shekels is about 2124 kilograms, or 2.124 metric tons.

[99] **39:9** *39:9* A span is the length from the tip of a man's thumb to the tip of his little finger when his hand is stretched out (about half a cubit, or 9 inches, or 22.8 cm.)

[100] **39:11** *39:11* or, lapis lazuli

pomegranates; **26** a bell and a pomegranate, a bell and a pomegranate, around the skirts of the robe, to minister in, as God commanded Moses.

27 They made the tunics of fine linen of woven work for Aaron and for his sons, **28** the turban of fine linen, the linen headbands of fine linen, the linen trousers of fine twined linen, **29** the sash of fine twined linen, blue, purple, and scarlet, the work of the embroiderer, as God commanded Moses.

30 They made the plate of the holy crown of pure gold, and wrote on it an inscription, like the engravings of a signet: "HOLY TO YAHWEH". **31** They tied to it a lace of blue, to fasten it on the turban above, as God commanded Moses.

32 Thus all the work of the tabernacle of the Tent of Meeting was finished. The children of Israel did according to all that God commanded Moses; so they did. **33** They brought the tabernacle to Moses: the tent, with all its furniture, its clasps, its boards, its bars, its pillars, its sockets, **34** the covering of rams' skins dyed red, the covering of sea cow hides, the veil of the screen, **35** the ark of the covenant with its poles, the mercy seat, **36** the table, all its vessels, the show bread, **37** the pure lamp stand, its lamps, even the lamps to be set in order, all its vessels, the oil for the light, **38** the golden altar, the anointing oil, the sweet incense, the screen for the door of the Tent, **39** the bronze altar, its grating of bronze, its poles, all of its vessels, the basin and its base, **40** the hangings of the court, its pillars, its sockets, the screen for the gate of the court, its cords, its pins, and all the instruments of the service of the tabernacle, for the Tent of Meeting, **41** the finely worked garments for ministering in the holy place, the holy garments for Aaron the priest, and the garments of his sons, to minister in the priest's office.

42 According to all that God commanded Moses, so the children of Israel did all the work. **43** Moses saw all the work, and behold, they had done it as God had commanded. They had done so; and Moses blessed them.

cloud by night, in the sight of all the house of Israel, throughout all their journeys.

Exodus 40

1 God spoke to Moses, saying, **2** "On the first day of the first month you shall raise up the tabernacle of the Tent of Meeting.

3 You shall put the ark of the covenant in it, and you shall screen the ark with the veil. **4** You shall bring in the table, and set in order the things that are on it. You shall bring in the lamp stand, and light its lamps. **5** You shall set the golden altar for incense before the ark of the covenant, and put the screen of the door to the tabernacle.

6 "You shall set the altar of burnt offering before the door of the tabernacle of the Tent of Meeting. **7** You shall set the basin between the Tent of Meeting and the altar, and shall put water therein. **8** You shall set up the court around it, and hang up the screen of the gate of the court.

9 "You shall take the anointing oil, and anoint the tabernacle and all that is in it, and shall make it holy, and all its furniture, and it will be holy. **10** You shall anoint the altar of burnt offering, with all its vessels, and sanctify the altar, and the altar will be most holy. **11** You shall anoint the basin and its base, and sanctify it.

12 "You shall bring Aaron and his sons to the door of the Tent of Meeting, and shall wash them with water. **13** You shall put on Aaron the holy garments; and you shall anoint him, and sanctify him, that he may minister to me in the priest's office. **14** You shall bring his sons, and put tunics on them. **15** You shall anoint them, as you anointed their father, that they may minister to me in the priest's office. Their anointing shall be to them for an everlasting priesthood throughout their generations."

16 Moses did so. According to all that God commanded him, so he did.

17 In the first month in the second year, on the first day of the month, the tabernacle was raised up. **18** Moses raised up the tabernacle, and laid its sockets, and set up its boards, and put in its bars, and raised up its pillars. **19** He spread the covering over the tent, and put the roof of the tabernacle above on it, as God

commanded Moses. **20** He took and put the covenant into the ark, and set the poles on the ark, and put the mercy seat above on the ark. **21** He brought the ark into the tabernacle, and set up the veil of the screen, and screened the ark of the covenant, as God commanded Moses. **22** He put the table in the Tent of Meeting, on the north side of the tabernacle, outside of the veil. **23** He set the bread in order on it before God, as God commanded Moses.

24 He put the lamp stand in the Tent of Meeting, opposite the table, on the south side of the tabernacle. **25** He lit the lamps before God, as God commanded Moses. **26** He put the golden altar in the Tent of Meeting before the veil; **27** and he burned incense of sweet spices on it, as God commanded Moses. **28** He put up the screen of the door to the tabernacle. **29** He set the altar of burnt offering at the door of the tabernacle of the Tent of Meeting, and offered on it the burnt offering and the meal offering, as God commanded Moses. **30** He set the basin between the Tent of Meeting and the altar, and put water therein, with which to wash. **31** Moses, Aaron, and his sons washed their hands and their feet there. **32** When they went into the Tent of Meeting, and when they came near to the altar, they washed, as God commanded Moses. **33** He raised up the court around the tabernacle and the altar, and set up the screen of the gate of the court. So Moses finished the work.

34 Then the cloud covered the Tent of Meeting, and God's glory filled the tabernacle. **35** Moses wasn't able to enter into the Tent of Meeting, because the cloud stayed on it, and God's glory filled the tabernacle. **36** When the cloud was taken up from over the tabernacle, the children of Israel went onward, throughout all their journeys; **37** but if the cloud wasn't taken up, then they didn't travel until the day that it was taken up.

38 For the cloud of God was on the tabernacle by day, and there was fire in the sight of all the house of Israel, throughout all their journeys.

The Book of Leviticus

Leviticus 1

1 God called to Moses, and spoke to him from the Tent of Meeting, saying, **2** "Speak to the children of Israel, and tell them, 'When anyone of you offers an offering to God, you shall offer your offering of the livestock, from the herd and from the flock.

3 "'If his offering is a burnt offering from the herd, he shall offer a male without defect. He shall offer it at the door of the Tent of Meeting, that he may be accepted before God. **4** He shall lay his hand on the head of the burnt offering, and it shall be accepted for him to make atonement for him. **5** He shall kill the bull before God. Aaron's sons, the priests, shall present the blood and sprinkle the blood around on the altar that is at the door of the Tent of Meeting. **6** He shall skin the burnt offering, and cut it into pieces. **7** The sons of Aaron the priest shall put fire on the altar, and lay wood in order on the fire; **8** and Aaron's sons, the priests, shall lay the pieces, the head, and the fat in order on the wood that is on the fire which is on the altar; **9** but he shall wash its innards and its legs with water. The priest shall burn all of it on the altar, for a burnt offering, an offering made by fire, of a pleasant aroma to God.

10 "'If his offering is from the flock, from the sheep or from the goats, for a burnt offering, he shall offer a male without defect. **11** He shall kill it on the north side of the altar before God. Aaron's sons, the priests, shall sprinkle its blood around on the altar. **12** He shall cut it into its pieces, with its head and its fat. The priest shall lay them in order on the wood that is on the fire which is on the altar, **13** but the innards and the legs he shall wash with water. The priest shall offer the whole, and burn it on the altar. It is a burnt offering, an offering made by fire, of a pleasant aroma to God.

14 "'If his offering to God is a burnt offering of birds, then he shall offer his offering from turtledoves or of young pigeons. **15** The priest shall bring it to the altar, and wring off its head, and burn it on the altar; and its blood shall be drained out on the side of the altar; **16** and he shall take away its crop and its feathers, and cast it beside the altar on the east part, in the place of the ashes. **17** He shall tear it by its wings, but shall not divide it apart. The priest shall burn it on the altar, on the wood that is on the fire. It is a burnt offering, an offering made by fire, of a pleasant aroma to God.

Leviticus 2

1 "'When anyone offers an offering of a meal offering to God, his offering shall be of fine flour. He shall pour oil on it, and put frankincense on it. **2** He shall bring it to Aaron's sons, the priests. He shall take his handful of its fine flour, and of its oil, with all its frankincense, and the priest shall burn its memorial on the altar, an offering made by fire, of a pleasant aroma to God. **3** That which is left of the meal offering shall be Aaron's and his sons'. It is a most holy part of the offerings of God made by fire.

4 "'When you offer an offering of a meal offering baked in the oven, it shall be unleavened cakes of fine flour mixed with oil, or unleavened wafers anointed with oil. **5** If your offering is a meal offering made on a griddle, it shall be of unleavened fine flour, mixed with oil. **6** You shall cut it in pieces, and pour oil on it. It is a meal offering. **7** If your offering is a meal offering of the pan, it shall be made of fine flour with oil. **8** You shall bring the meal offering that is made of these things to God. It shall be presented to the priest, and he shall bring it to the altar. **9** The priest shall take from the meal offering its memorial, and shall burn it on the altar, an offering made by fire, of a pleasant aroma to God. **10** That which is left of the meal offering shall be Aaron's and his sons'. It is a most holy part of the offerings of God made by fire.

11 "'No meal offering which you shall offer to God shall be made with yeast; for you shall burn no yeast, nor any honey, as an offering made by fire to God. **12** As an offering of first fruits you shall offer them to God, but they shall not rise up as a pleasant aroma on the altar. **13** Every offering of your meal offering you shall season with salt. You shall not allow the salt of the covenant of your God[101] to be lacking from your meal offering. With all your offerings you shall offer salt.

14 "'If you offer a meal offering of first fruits to God, you shall offer for the meal offering of your first fruits fresh heads of grain parched with fire and crushed. **15** You shall put oil on it and lay frankincense on it. It is a meal offering. **16** The priest shall burn as its memorial part of its crushed grain and part of its oil, along with all its frankincense. It is an offering made by fire to God.

Leviticus 3

1 "'If his offering is a sacrifice of peace offerings, if he offers it from the herd, whether male or female, he shall offer it without defect before God. **2** He shall lay his hand on the head of his offering, and kill it at the door of the Tent of Meeting. Aaron's sons, the priests, shall sprinkle the blood around on the altar. **3** He shall offer of the sacrifice of peace offerings an offering made by fire to God. The fat that covers the innards, and all the fat that is on the innards, **4** and the two kidneys, and the fat that is on them, which is by the loins, and the cover on the liver, with the kidneys, he shall take away. **5** Aaron's sons shall burn it on the altar on the burnt offering, which is on the wood that is on the fire: it is an offering made by fire, of a pleasant aroma to God.

6 "'If his offering for a sacrifice of peace offerings to God is from the flock, either male or female, he shall offer it without defect. **7** If he offers a lamb for his offering, then he shall offer it before God; **8** and he shall lay his hand on the head of his offering, and kill it before the Tent of Meeting. Aaron's sons shall sprinkle its blood around on the altar. **9** He shall offer from the sacrifice of peace offerings an offering made by fire to God; its fat, the entire tail fat, he shall take away close to the backbone; and the fat that covers the entrails, and all the fat that is on the entrails, **10** and the two kidneys, and the fat that is on them, which is by the loins, and the cover on the liver, with the kidneys, he shall take away. **11** The priest shall burn it on the altar: it is the food of the offering made by fire to God.

12 "'If his offering is a goat, then he shall offer it before God. **13** He shall lay his hand on its head, and kill it before the Tent of Meeting; and the sons of Aaron shall sprinkle its blood around on the altar. **14** He shall offer from it as his offering, an offering made by fire to God; the fat that covers the innards, and all the fat that is on the innards, **15** and the two kidneys, and the fat that is on them, which is by the loins, and the cover on the liver, with the kidneys, he shall take away. **16** The priest shall burn them on the altar: it is the food of the offering made by fire, for a pleasant aroma; all the fat is God's.

17 "'It shall be a perpetual statute throughout your generations in all your dwellings, that you shall eat neither fat nor blood.'"

Leviticus 4

1 God spoke to Moses, saying, **2** "Speak to the children of Israel, saying, 'If anyone sins unintentionally, in any of the things which God has commanded not to be done, and does any one of them, **3** if the anointed priest sins so as to bring guilt on the people, then let him offer for his sin which he has sinned a young bull without defect to God for a sin offering. **4** He shall bring the bull to the door of the Tent of Meeting before God; and he shall lay his hand on the head of the bull, and kill the bull before God. **5** The anointed priest shall take some of the blood of the bull, and bring it to the Tent of Meeting. **6** The priest shall dip his finger in the blood, and sprinkle some of the blood seven times before God, before the veil of the sanctuary. **7** The priest shall put some of the blood on the horns of the altar of sweet incense before God, which is in the Tent of Meeting; and he shall pour out the rest of the blood of the bull at the base of the altar of burnt offering, which is at the door of the Tent of Meeting. **8** He shall take all the fat of the bull of the sin offering from it: the fat that covers the innards, and all the fat that is on the innards, **9** and the two kidneys, and the fat that is on them, which is by the loins, and the cover on the liver, with the kidneys, he shall remove, **10** as it is removed from the bull of the sacrifice of peace offerings. The priest shall burn them on the altar of burnt offering. **11** He shall carry the bull's skin, all its meat, with its head, and with its legs, its innards, and its dung **12** —all the rest of the bull—outside of the camp to a clean place where the ashes are poured out, and burn it on wood with fire. It shall be burned where the ashes are poured out.

13 "'If the whole congregation of Israel sins, and the thing is hidden from the eyes of the assembly, and they have done any of the things which God has commanded not to be done, and are guilty; **14** when the sin in which they have sinned is known, then the assembly shall offer a young bull for a sin offering, and bring it before the Tent of Meeting. **15** The elders of the congregation shall lay their hands on the head of the bull before God; and the bull shall be killed before God. **16** The anointed priest shall bring some of the blood of the bull to the Tent of Meeting. **17** The priest shall dip his finger in the blood and sprinkle it seven times before God, before the veil. **18** He shall put some of the blood on the horns of the altar which is before God, that is in the Tent of Meeting; and the rest of the blood he shall pour out at the base of the altar of burnt offering, which is at the door of the Tent of Meeting. **19** All its fat he shall take from it, and burn it on the altar. **20** Thus shall he do with the bull; as he did with the bull of the sin offering, so shall he do with this; and the priest shall make atonement for them, and they shall be forgiven. **21** He shall carry the bull outside the camp, and burn it as he burned the first bull. It is the sin offering for the assembly.

22 "'When a ruler sins, and unwittingly does any one of all the things which God his God has commanded not to be done, and is guilty, **23** if his sin in which he has sinned is made known to him, he shall bring as his offering a goat, a male without defect. **24** He shall lay his hand on the head of the goat, and kill it in the place where they kill the burnt offering before God. It is a sin offering. **25** The priest shall take some of the blood of the sin offering with his finger, and put it on the horns of the altar of burnt offering. He shall pour out the rest of its blood at the base of the altar of burnt offering. **26** All its fat he shall burn on the altar, like the fat of the sacrifice of peace offerings; and the priest shall make atonement for him concerning his sin, and he will be forgiven.

27 "'If anyone of the common people sins unwittingly, in doing any of the things which God has commanded not to be done, and is guilty, **28** if his sin which he has sinned is made known to him, then he shall bring for his offering a goat, a female without defect, for his sin which he has sinned. **29** He shall lay his hand on the head of the sin offering, and kill the sin offering in the place of burnt offering. **30** The priest shall take some of its blood with his finger, and put it on the horns of the altar of burnt offering; and the rest of its blood he shall pour out at the base of the altar. **31** All its fat he shall take away, like the fat is taken away from the sacrifice of peace offerings; and the priest shall burn it on the altar for a pleasant

[101] **2:13** *2:13* **The Hebrew word rendered "God" is "אֱלֹהִים" (Elohim).**

aroma to God; and the priest shall make atonement for
him, and he will be forgiven.
32 "'If he brings a lamb as his offering for a sin offering,
he shall bring a female without defect. **33** He shall lay his
hand on the head of the sin offering, and kill it for a sin
offering in the place where they kill the burnt offering.
34 The priest shall take some of the blood of the sin
offering with his finger, and put it on the horns of the altar
of burnt offering; and all the rest of its blood he shall pour
out at the base of the altar. **35** He shall remove all its fat,
like the fat of the lamb is removed from the sacrifice of
peace offerings. The priest shall burn them on the altar, on
the offerings of God made by fire. The priest shall make
atonement for him concerning his sin that he has sinned,
and he will be forgiven.

Leviticus 5

1 "'If anyone sins, in that he hears a public adjuration to
testify, he being a witness, whether he has seen or known,
if he doesn't report it, then he shall bear his iniquity.
2 "'Or if anyone touches any unclean thing, whether it is
the carcass of an unclean animal, or the carcass of unclean
livestock, or the carcass of unclean creeping things, and it
is hidden from him, and he is unclean, then he shall be
guilty.
3 "'Or if he touches the uncleanness of man, whatever his
uncleanness is with which he is unclean, and it is hidden
from him; when he knows of it, then he shall be guilty.
4 "'Or if anyone swears rashly with his lips to do evil or
to do good—whatever it is that a man might utter rashly
with an oath, and it is hidden from him—when he knows
of it, then he will be guilty of one of these. **5** It shall be,
when he is guilty of one of these, he shall confess that in
which he has sinned; **6** and he shall bring his trespass
offering to God for his sin which he has sinned: a female
from the flock, a lamb or a goat, for a sin offering; and the
priest shall make atonement for him concerning his sin.
7 "'If he can't afford a lamb, then he shall bring his
trespass offering for that in which he has sinned, two
turtledoves, or two young pigeons, to God; one for a sin
offering, and the other for a burnt offering. **8** He shall
bring them to the priest, who shall first offer the one
which is for the sin offering. He shall wring off its head
from its neck, but shall not sever it completely. **9** He shall
sprinkle some of the blood of the sin offering on the side
of the altar; and the rest of the blood shall be drained out
at the base of the altar. It is a sin offering. **10** He shall
offer the second for a burnt offering, according to the
ordinance; and the priest shall make atonement for him
concerning his sin which he has sinned, and he shall be
forgiven.
11 "'But if he can't afford two turtledoves or two young
pigeons, then he shall bring as his offering for that in
which he has sinned, one tenth of an ephah[102] of fine flour
for a sin offering. He shall put no oil on it, and he shall
not put any frankincense on it, for it is a sin offering.
12 He shall bring it to the priest, and the priest shall take
his handful of it as the memorial portion, and burn it on
the altar, on the offerings of God made by fire. It is a sin
offering. **13** The priest shall make atonement for him
concerning his sin that he has sinned in any of these
things, and he will be forgiven; and the rest shall be the
priest's, as the meal offering.'"
14 God spoke to Moses, saying, **15** "If anyone commits
a trespass, and sins unwittingly regarding God's holy
things, then he shall bring his trespass offering to God: a
ram without defect from the flock, according to your
estimation in silver by shekels, according to the shekel[103]
of the sanctuary, for a trespass offering. **16** He shall make
restitution for that which he has done wrong regarding the
holy thing, and shall add a fifth part to it, and give it to the
priest; and the priest shall make atonement for him with
the ram of the trespass offering, and he will be forgiven.
17 "If anyone sins, doing any of the things which God
has commanded not to be done, though he didn't know it,
he is still guilty, and shall bear his iniquity. **18** He shall
bring a ram without defect from of the flock, according to
your estimation, for a trespass offering, to the priest; and
the priest shall make atonement for him concerning the
thing in which he sinned and didn't know it, and he will
be forgiven. **19** It is a trespass offering. He is certainly
guilty before God."

Leviticus 6

1 God spoke to Moses, saying, **2** "If anyone sins, and
commits a trespass against God, and deals falsely with his
neighbor in a matter of deposit, or of bargain, or of
robbery, or has oppressed his neighbor, **3** or has found
that which was lost, and lied about it, and swearing to a
lie—in any of these things that a man sins in his actions—
4 then it shall be, if he has sinned, and is guilty, he shall
restore that which he took by robbery, or the thing which
he has gotten by oppression, or the deposit which was
committed to him, or the lost thing which he found, **5** or
any thing about which he has sworn falsely: he shall
restore it in full, and shall add a fifth part more to it. He
shall return it to him to whom it belongs in the day of his
being found guilty. **6** He shall bring his trespass offering
to God: a ram without defect from the flock, according to
your estimation, for a trespass offering, to the priest.
7 The priest shall make atonement for him before God,
and he will be forgiven concerning whatever he does to
become guilty."
8 God spoke to Moses, saying, **9** "Command Aaron and
his sons, saying, 'This is the law of the burnt offering: the
burnt offering shall be on the hearth on the altar all night
until the morning; and the fire of the altar shall be kept
burning on it. **10** The priest shall put on his linen
garment, and he shall put on his linen trousers upon his
body; and he shall remove the ashes from where the fire
has consumed the burnt offering on the altar, and he shall
put them beside the altar. **11** He shall take off his
garments, and put on other garments, and carry the ashes
outside the camp to a clean place. **12** The fire on the altar
shall be kept burning on it, it shall not go out; and the
priest shall burn wood on it every morning. He shall lay
the burnt offering in order upon it, and shall burn on it the
fat of the peace offerings. **13** Fire shall be kept burning
on the altar continually; it shall not go out.
14 "'This is the law of the meal offering: the sons of
Aaron shall offer it before God, before the altar. **15** He
shall take from there his handful of the fine flour of the
meal offering, and of its oil, and all the frankincense
which is on the meal offering, and shall burn it on the
altar for a pleasant aroma, as its memorial portion, to God.
16 That which is left of it Aaron and his sons shall eat. It
shall be eaten without yeast in a holy place. They shall eat
it in the court of the Tent of Meeting. **17** It shall not be
baked with yeast. I have given it as their portion of my
offerings made by fire. It is most holy, as are the sin
offering and the trespass offering. **18** Every male among
the children of Aaron shall eat of it, as their portion
forever throughout your generations, from the offerings of
God made by fire. Whoever touches them shall be holy.'"
19 God spoke to Moses, saying, **20** "This is the offering
of Aaron and of his sons, which they shall offer to God in
the day when he is anointed: one tenth of an ephah[104] of
fine flour for a meal offering perpetually, half of it in the
morning, and half of it in the evening. **21** It shall be made
with oil in a griddle. When it is soaked, you shall bring it
in. You shall offer the meal offering in baked pieces for a
pleasant aroma to God. **22** The anointed priest that will
be in his place from among his sons shall offer it. By a
statute forever, it shall be wholly burned to God.
23 Every meal offering of a priest shall be wholly
burned. It shall not be eaten."
24 God spoke to Moses, saying, **25** "Speak to Aaron and
to his sons, saying, 'This is the law of the sin offering: in
the place where the burnt offering is killed, the sin
offering shall be killed before God. It is most holy.
26 The priest who offers it for sin shall eat it. It shall be
eaten in a holy place, in the court of the Tent of Meeting.
27 Whatever shall touch its flesh shall be holy. When
there is any of its blood sprinkled on a garment, you shall
wash that on which it was sprinkled in a holy place.
28 But the earthen vessel in which it is boiled shall be
broken; and if it is boiled in a bronze vessel, it shall be
scoured, and rinsed in water. **29** Every male among the
priests shall eat of it. It is most holy. **30** No sin offering,
of which any of the blood is brought into the Tent of
Meeting to make atonement in the Holy Place, shall be
eaten. It shall be burned with fire.

Leviticus 7

1 "'This is the law of the trespass offering: It is most
holy. **2** In the place where they kill the burnt offering, he
shall kill the trespass offering; and its blood he shall
sprinkle around on the altar. **3** He shall offer all of its fat:
the fat tail, and the fat that covers the innards, **4** and he
shall take away the two kidneys, and the fat that is on
them, which is by the loins, and the cover on the liver,
with the kidneys; **5** and the priest shall burn them on the
altar for an offering made by fire to God: it is a trespass
offering. **6** Every male among the priests may eat of it. It
shall be eaten in a holy place. It is most holy.
7 "'As is the sin offering, so is the trespass offering; there
is one law for them. The priest who makes atonement
with them shall have it. **8** The priest who offers any
man's burnt offering shall have for himself the skin of the
burnt offering which he has offered. **9** Every meal
offering that is baked in the oven, and all that is prepared
in the pan and on the griddle, shall be the priest's who
offers it. **10** Every meal offering, mixed with oil or dry,
belongs to all the sons of Aaron, one as well as another.
11 "'This is the law of the sacrifice of peace offerings,
which one shall offer to God: **12** If he offers it for a
thanksgiving, then he shall offer with the sacrifice of
thanksgiving unleavened cakes mixed with oil, and
unleavened wafers anointed with oil, and cakes mixed
with oil. **13** He shall offer his offering with the sacrifice
of his peace offerings for thanksgiving with cakes of
leavened bread. **14** Of it he shall offer one out of each
offering for a heave offering to God. It shall be the
priest's who sprinkles the blood of the peace offerings.
15 The flesh of the sacrifice of his peace offerings for
thanksgiving shall be eaten on the day of his offering. He
shall not leave any of it until the morning.
16 "'But if the sacrifice of his offering is a vow, or a free
will offering, it shall be eaten on the day that he offers his
sacrifice. On the next day what remains of it shall be
eaten, **17** but what remains of the meat of the sacrifice on
the third day shall be burned with fire. **18** If any of the
meat of the sacrifice of his peace offerings is eaten on the
third day, it will not be accepted, and it shall not be
credited to him who offers it. It will be an abomination,
and the soul who eats any of it will bear his iniquity.
19 "'The meat that touches any unclean thing shall not be
eaten. It shall be burned with fire. As for the meat,
everyone who is clean may eat it; **20** but the soul who
eats of the meat of the sacrifice of peace offerings that
belongs to God, having his uncleanness on him, that soul
shall be cut off from his people. **21** When anyone touches
any unclean thing, the uncleanness of man, or an unclean
animal, or any unclean abomination, and eats some of the
meat of the sacrifice of peace offerings which belong to
God, that soul shall be cut off from his people.'"
22 God spoke to Moses, saying, **23** "Speak to the
children of Israel, saying, 'You shall eat no fat, of bull, or
sheep, or goat. **24** The fat of that which dies of itself, and
the fat of that which is torn of animals, may be used for
any other service, but you shall in no way eat of it. **25** For
whoever eats the fat of the animal which men offer as an
offering made by fire to God, even the soul who eats it
shall be cut off from his people. **26** You shall not eat any
blood, whether it is of bird or of animal, in any of your
dwellings. **27** Whoever it is who eats any blood, that soul
shall be cut off from his people.'"
28 God spoke to Moses, saying, **29** "Speak to the
children of Israel, saying, 'He who offers the sacrifice of
his peace offerings to God shall bring his offering to God
out of the sacrifice of his peace offerings. **30** With his
own hands he shall bring the offerings of God made by
fire. He shall bring the fat with the breast, that the breast
may be waved for a wave offering before God. **31** The
priest shall burn the fat on the altar, but the breast shall be
Aaron's and his sons'. **32** The right thigh you shall give
to the priest for a heave offering out of the sacrifices of
your peace offerings. **33** He among the sons of Aaron
who offers the blood of the peace offerings, and the fat,

[102] **5:11** *5:11* 1 ephah is about 22 liters or about 2/3 of a bushel

[103] **5:15** *5:15* A shekel is about 10 grams or about 0.35 ounces.

[104] **6:20** *6:20* 1 ephah is about 22 liters or about 2/3 of a bushel

shall have the right thigh for a portion. **34** For the waved breast and the heaved thigh I have taken from the children of Israel out of the sacrifices of their peace offerings, and have given them to Aaron the priest and to his sons as their portion forever from the children of Israel.'"

35 This is the consecrated portion of Aaron, and the consecrated portion of his sons, out of the offerings of God made by fire, in the day when he presented them to minister to God in the priest's office; **36** which God commanded to be given them of the children of Israel, in the day that he anointed them. It is their portion forever throughout their generations. **37** This is the law of the burnt offering, the meal offering, the sin offering, the trespass offering, the consecration, and the sacrifice of peace offerings **38** which God commanded Moses in Mount Sinai in the day that he commanded the children of Israel to offer their offerings to God, in the wilderness of Sinai.

Leviticus 8

1 God spoke to Moses, saying, **2** "Take Aaron and his sons with him, and the garments, and the anointing oil, and the bull of the sin offering, and the two rams, and the basket of unleavened bread; **3** and assemble all the congregation at the door of the Tent of Meeting."

4 Moses did as God commanded him; and the congregation was assembled at the door of the Tent of Meeting. **5** Moses said to the congregation, "This is the thing which God has commanded to be done." **6** Moses brought Aaron and his sons, and washed them with water.

7 He put the tunic on him, tied the sash on him, clothed him with the robe, put the ephod on him, and he tied the skillfully woven band of the ephod on him and fastened it to him with it. **8** He placed the breastplate on him. He put the Urim and Thummim in the breastplate. **9** He set the turban on his head. He set the golden plate, the holy crown, on the front of the turban, as God commanded Moses. **10** Moses took the anointing oil, and anointed the tabernacle and all that was in it, and sanctified them.

11 He sprinkled it on the altar seven times, and anointed the altar and all its vessels, and the basin and its base, to sanctify them. **12** He poured some of the anointing oil on Aaron's head, and anointed him, to sanctify him.

13 Moses brought Aaron's sons, and clothed them with tunics, and tied sashes on them, and put headbands on them, as God commanded Moses.

14 He brought the bull of the sin offering, and Aaron and his sons laid their hands on the head of the bull of the sin offering. **15** He killed it; and Moses took the blood, and put it around on the horns of the altar with his finger, and purified the altar, and poured out the blood at the base of the altar, and sanctified it, to make atonement for it.

16 He took all the fat that was on the innards, and the cover of the liver, and the two kidneys, and their fat; and Moses burned it on the altar. **17** But the bull, and its skin, and its meat, and its dung, he burned with fire outside the camp, as God commanded Moses. **18** He presented the ram of the burnt offering. Aaron and his sons laid their hands on the head of the ram. **19** He killed it; and Moses sprinkled the blood around on the altar. **20** He cut the ram into its pieces; and Moses burned the head, and the pieces, and the fat. **21** He washed the innards and the legs with water; and Moses burned the whole ram on the altar. It was a burnt offering for a pleasant aroma. It was an offering made by fire to God, as God commanded Moses.

22 He presented the other ram, the ram of consecration. Aaron and his sons laid their hands on the head of the ram. **23** He killed it; and Moses took some of its blood, and put it on the tip of Aaron's right ear, and on the thumb of his right hand, and on the great toe of his right foot. **24** He brought Aaron's sons; and Moses put some of the blood on the tip of their right ear, and on the thumb of their right hand, and on the great toe of their right foot; and Moses sprinkled the blood around on the altar. **25** He took the fat, the fat tail, all the fat that was on the innards, the cover of the liver, the two kidneys and their fat, and the right thigh; **26** and out of the basket of unleavened bread that was before God, he took one unleavened cake,

one cake of oiled bread, and one wafer, and placed them on the fat and on the right thigh. **27** He put all these in Aaron's hands and in his sons' hands, and waved them for a wave offering before God. **28** Moses took them from their hands, and burned them on the altar on the burnt offering. They were a consecration offering for a pleasant aroma. It was an offering made by fire to God. **29** Moses took the breast, and waved it for a wave offering before God. It was Moses' portion of the ram of consecration, as God commanded Moses. **30** Moses took some of the anointing oil, and some of the blood which was on the altar, and sprinkled it on Aaron, on his garments, and on his sons, and on his sons' garments with him, and sanctified Aaron, his garments, and his sons, and his sons' garments with him.

31 Moses said to Aaron and to his sons, "Boil the meat at the door of the Tent of Meeting, and there eat it and the bread that is in the basket of consecration, as I commanded, saying, 'Aaron and his sons shall eat it.' **32** What remains of the meat and of the bread you shall burn with fire. **33** You shall not go out from the door of the Tent of Meeting for seven days, until the days of your consecration are fulfilled: for he shall consecrate you seven days. **34** What has been done today, so God has commanded to do, to make atonement for you. **35** You shall stay at the door of the Tent of Meeting day and night seven days, and keep God's command, that you don't die: for so I am commanded." **36** Aaron and his sons did all the things which God commanded by Moses.

Leviticus 9

1 On the eighth day, Moses called Aaron and his sons, and the elders of Israel; **2** and he said to Aaron, "Take a calf from the herd for a sin offering, and a ram for a burnt offering, without defect, and offer them before God.

3 You shall speak to the children of Israel, saying, 'Take a male goat for a sin offering; and a calf and a lamb, both a year old, without defect, for a burnt offering; **4** and a bull and a ram for peace offerings, to sacrifice before God; and a meal offering mixed with oil: for today God appears to you.'"

5 They brought what Moses commanded before the Tent of Meeting. All the congregation came near and stood before God. **6** Moses said, "This is the thing which God commanded that you should do; and God's glory shall appear to you." **7** Moses said to Aaron, "Draw near to the altar, and offer your sin offering, and your burnt offering, and make atonement for yourself, and for the people; and offer the offering of the people, and make atonement for them, as God commanded."

8 So Aaron came near to the altar, and killed the calf of the sin offering, which was for himself. **9** The sons of Aaron presented the blood to him; and he dipped his finger in the blood, and put it on the horns of the altar, and poured out the blood at the base of the altar; **10** but the fat, and the kidneys, and the cover from the liver of the sin offering, he burned upon the altar, as God commanded Moses. **11** The meat and the skin he burned with fire outside the camp. **12** He killed the burnt offering; and Aaron's sons delivered the blood to him, and he sprinkled it around on the altar. **13** They delivered the burnt offering to him, piece by piece, and the head. He burned them upon the altar. **14** He washed the innards and the legs, and burned them on the burnt offering on the altar.

15 He presented the people's offering, and took the goat of the sin offering which was for the people, and killed it, and offered it for sin, like the first. **16** He presented the burnt offering, and offered it according to the ordinance.

17 He presented the meal offering, and filled his hand from there, and burned it upon the altar, in addition to the burnt offering of the morning. **18** He also killed the bull and the ram, the sacrifice of peace offerings, which was for the people. Aaron's sons delivered to him the blood, which he sprinkled around on the altar; **19** and the fat of the bull and of the ram, the fat tail, and that which covers the innards, and the kidneys, and the cover of the liver; **20** and they put the fat upon the breasts, and he burned

the fat on the altar. **21** Aaron waved the breasts and the right thigh for a wave offering before God, as Moses commanded. **22** Aaron lifted up his hands toward the people, and blessed them; and he came down from offering the sin offering, and the burnt offering, and the peace offerings.

23 Moses and Aaron went into the Tent of Meeting, and came out, and blessed the people; and God's glory appeared to all the people. **24** Fire came out from before God, and consumed the burnt offering and the fat upon the altar. When all the people saw it, they shouted, and fell on their faces.

Leviticus 10

1 Nadab and Abihu, the sons of Aaron, each took his censer, and put fire in it, and laid incense on it, and offered strange fire before God, which he had not commanded them. **2** Fire came out from before God, and devoured them, and they died before God.

3 Then Moses said to Aaron, "This is what God spoke of, saying,
'I will show myself holy to those who come near me,
and before all the people I will be glorified.'"
Aaron held his peace. **4** Moses called Mishael and Elzaphan, the sons of Uzziel the uncle of Aaron, and said to them, "Draw near, carry your brothers from before the sanctuary out of the camp." **5** So they came near, and carried them in their tunics out of the camp, as Moses had said.

6 Moses said to Aaron, and to Eleazar and to Ithamar, his sons, "Don't let the hair of your heads go loose, and don't tear your clothes, so that you don't die, and so that he will not be angry with all the congregation; but let your brothers, the whole house of Israel, bewail the burning which God has kindled. **7** You shall not go out from the door of the Tent of Meeting, lest you die; for the anointing oil of God is on you." They did according to the word of Moses. **8** Then God said to Aaron, **9** "You and your sons are not to drink wine or strong drink whenever you go into the Tent of Meeting, or you will die. This shall be a statute forever throughout your generations.

10 You are to make a distinction between the holy and the common, and between the unclean and the clean.

11 You are to teach the children of Israel all the statutes which God has spoken to them by Moses."

12 Moses spoke to Aaron, and to Eleazar and to Ithamar, his sons who were left, "Take the meal offering that remains of the offerings of God made by fire, and eat it without yeast beside the altar; for it is most holy; **13** and you shall eat it in a holy place, because it is your portion, and your sons' portion, of the offerings of God made by fire; for so I am commanded. **14** The waved breast and the heaved thigh you shall eat in a clean place, you, and your sons, and your daughters with you: for they are given as your portion, and your sons' portion, out of the sacrifices of the peace offerings of the children of Israel.

15 The heaved thigh and the waved breast they shall bring with the offerings made by fire of the fat, to wave it for a wave offering before God. It shall be yours, and your sons' with you, as a portion forever, as God has commanded."

16 Moses diligently inquired about the goat of the sin offering, and, behold,[105] it was burned. He was angry with Eleazar and with Ithamar, the sons of Aaron who were left, saying, **17** "Why haven't you eaten the sin offering in the place of the sanctuary, since it is most holy, and he has given it to you to bear the iniquity of the congregation, to make atonement for them before God?

18 Behold, its blood was not brought into the inner part of the sanctuary. You certainly should have eaten it in the sanctuary, as I commanded."

19 Aaron spoke to Moses, "Behold, today they have offered their sin offering and their burnt offering before God; and such things as these have happened to me. If I had eaten the sin offering today, would it have been pleasing in God's sight?"

20 When Moses heard that, it was pleasing in his sight.

---

[105]**10:16** *10:16* "Behold", from "הִנֵּה", means look at, take notice, observe, see, or gaze at. It is often used as an interjection.

Leviticus 11
1 God spoke to Moses and to Aaron, saying to them,
2 "Speak to the children of Israel, saying, 'These are the
living things which you may eat among all the animals
that are on the earth. 3 Whatever parts the hoof, and is
cloven-footed, and chews the cud among the animals, that
you may eat.
4 "'Nevertheless these you shall not eat of those that
chew the cud, or of those who part the hoof: the camel,
because it chews the cud but doesn't have a parted hoof,
is unclean to you. 5 The hyrax,[106] because it chews the
cud but doesn't have a parted hoof, is unclean to you.
6 The hare, because it chews the cud but doesn't have a
parted hoof, is unclean to you. 7 The pig, because it has
a split hoof, and is cloven-footed, but doesn't chew the
cud, is unclean to you. 8 You shall not eat their meat.
You shall not touch their carcasses. They are unclean to
you.
9 "'These you may eat of all that are in the waters:
whatever has fins and scales in the waters, in the seas, and
in the rivers, that you may eat. 10 All that don't have
fins and scales in the seas and rivers, all that move in the
waters, and all the living creatures that are in the waters,
they are an abomination to you, 11 and you shall detest
them. You shall not eat of their meat, and you shall detest
their carcasses. 12 Whatever has no fins nor scales in the
waters is an abomination to you.
13 "'You shall detest these among the birds; they shall
not be eaten because they are an abomination: the eagle,
the vulture, the black vulture, 14 the red kite, any kind
of black kite, 15 any kind of raven, 16 the horned owl,
the screech owl, the gull, any kind of hawk, 17 the little
owl, the cormorant, the great owl, 18 the white owl, the
desert owl, the osprey, 19 the stork, any kind of heron,
the hoopoe, and the bat.
20 "'All flying insects that walk on all fours are an
abomination to you. 21 Yet you may eat these: of all
winged creeping things that go on all fours, which have
long, jointed legs for hopping on the earth. 22 Even of
these you may eat: any kind of locust, any kind of
katydid, any kind of cricket, and any kind of grasshopper.
23 But all winged creeping things which have four feet
are an abomination to you.
24 "'By these you will become unclean: whoever
touches their carcass shall be unclean until the evening.
25 Whoever carries any part of their carcass shall wash
his clothes, and be unclean until the evening.
26 "'Every animal which has a split hoof that isn't
completely divided, or doesn't chew the cud, is unclean to
you. Everyone who touches them shall be unclean.
27 Whatever goes on its paws, among all animals that go
on all fours, they are unclean to you. Whoever touches
their carcass shall be unclean until the evening. 28 He
who carries their carcass shall wash his clothes, and be
unclean until the evening. They are unclean to you.
29 "'These are they which are unclean to you among the
creeping things that creep on the earth: the weasel, the rat,
any kind of great lizard, 30 the gecko, and the monitor
lizard, the wall lizard, the skink, and the chameleon.
31 These are they which are unclean to you among all
that creep. Whoever touches them when they are dead
shall be unclean until the evening. 32 Anything they fall
on when they are dead shall be unclean; whether it is any
vessel of wood, or clothing, or skin, or sack, whatever
vessel it is, with which any work is done, it must be put
into water, and it shall be unclean until the evening. Then
it will be clean. 33 Every earthen vessel into which any
of them falls and all that is in it shall be unclean. You
shall break it. 34 All food which may be eaten which is
soaked in water shall be unclean. All drink that may be
drunk in every such vessel shall be unclean.
35 Everything whereupon part of their carcass falls shall
be unclean; whether oven, or range for pots, it shall be
broken in pieces. They are unclean, and shall be unclean
to you. 36 Nevertheless a spring or a cistern in which
water is gathered shall be clean, but that which touches
their carcass shall be unclean. 37 If part of their carcass
falls on any sowing seed which is to be sown, it is clean.
38 But if water is put on the seed, and part of their
carcass falls on it, it is unclean to you.
39 "'If any animal of which you may eat dies, he who
touches its carcass shall be unclean until the evening.
40 He who eats of its carcass shall wash his clothes, and
be unclean until the evening. He also who carries its
carcass shall wash his clothes, and be unclean until the
evening.
41 "'Every creeping thing that creeps on the earth is an
abomination. It shall not be eaten. 42 Whatever goes on
its belly, and whatever goes on all fours, or whatever has
many feet, even all creeping things that creep on the earth,
them you shall not eat; for they are an abomination.
43 You shall not make yourselves abominable with any
creeping thing that creeps. You shall not make yourselves
unclean with them, that you should be defiled by them.
44 For I am God your God. Sanctify yourselves
therefore, and be holy; for I am holy. You shall not defile
yourselves with any kind of creeping thing that moves on
the earth. 45 For I am God who brought you up out of
the land of Egypt, to be your God. You shall therefore be
holy, for I am holy.
46 "'This is the law of the animal, and of the bird, and of
every living creature that moves in the waters, and of
every creature that creeps on the earth, 47 to make a
distinction between the unclean and the clean, and
between the living thing that may be eaten and the living
thing that may not be eaten.'"

Leviticus 12
1 God spoke to Moses, saying, 2 "Speak to the
children of Israel, saying, 'If a woman conceives, and
bears a male child, then she shall be unclean seven days;
as in the days of her monthly period she shall be unclean.
3 In the eighth day the flesh of his foreskin shall be
circumcised. 4 She shall continue in the blood of
purification thirty-three days. She shall not touch any holy
thing, nor come into the sanctuary, until the days of her
purifying are completed. 5 But if she bears a female
child, then she shall be unclean two weeks, as in her
period; and she shall continue in the blood of purification
sixty-six days.
6 "'When the days of her purification are completed for
a son or for a daughter, she shall bring to the priest at the
door of the Tent of Meeting, a year old lamb for a burnt
offering, and a young pigeon or a turtledove, for a sin
offering. 7 He shall offer it before God, and make
atonement for her; then she shall be cleansed from the
fountain of her blood.
"'This is the law for her who bears, whether a male or a
female. 8 If she cannot afford a lamb, then she shall take
two turtledoves or two young pigeons: the one for a burnt
offering, and the other for a sin offering. The priest shall
make atonement for her, and she shall be clean.'"

Leviticus 13
1 God spoke to Moses and to Aaron, saying, 2 "When
a man shall have a swelling in his body's skin, or a scab,
or a bright spot, and it becomes in the skin of his body the
plague of leprosy, then he shall be brought to Aaron the
priest or to one of his sons, the priests. 3 The priest shall
examine the plague in the skin of the body. If the hair in
the plague has turned white, and the appearance of the
plague is deeper than the body's skin, it is the plague of
leprosy; so the priest shall examine him and pronounce
him unclean. 4 If the bright spot is white in the skin of
his body, and its appearance isn't deeper than the skin,
and its hair hasn't turned white, then the priest shall
isolate the infected person for seven days. 5 The priest
shall examine him on the seventh day. Behold, if in his
eyes the plague is arrested and the plague hasn't spread in
the skin, then the priest shall isolate him for seven more
days. 6 The priest shall examine him again on the
seventh day. Behold, if the plague has faded and the
plague hasn't spread in the skin, then the priest shall
pronounce him clean. It is a scab. He shall wash his
clothes, and be clean. 7 But if the scab spreads on the
skin after he has shown himself to the priest for his
cleansing, he shall show himself to the priest again.
8 The priest shall examine him; and behold, if the scab
has spread on the skin, then the priest shall pronounce him
unclean. It is leprosy.
9 "When the plague of leprosy is in a man, then he shall
be brought to the priest; 10 and the priest shall examine
him. Behold, if there is a white swelling in the skin, and it
has turned the hair white, and there is raw flesh in the
swelling, 11 it is a chronic leprosy in the skin of his
body, and the priest shall pronounce him unclean. He
shall not isolate him, for he is already unclean.
12 "If the leprosy breaks out all over the skin, and the
leprosy covers all the skin of the infected person from his
head even to his feet, as far as it appears to the priest,
13 then the priest shall examine him. Behold, if the
leprosy has covered all his flesh, he shall pronounce him
clean of the plague. It has all turned white: he is clean.
14 But whenever raw flesh appears in him, he shall be
unclean. 15 The priest shall examine the raw flesh, and
pronounce him unclean: the raw flesh is unclean. It is
leprosy. 16 Or if the raw flesh turns again, and is
changed to white, then he shall come to the priest.
17 The priest shall examine him. Behold, if the plague
has turned white, then the priest shall pronounce him
clean of the plague. He is clean.
18 "When the body has a boil on its skin, and it has
healed, 19 and in the place of the boil there is a white
swelling, or a bright spot, reddish-white, then it shall be
shown to the priest. 20 The priest shall examine it.
Behold, if its appearance is deeper than the skin, and its
hair has turned white, then the priest shall pronounce him
unclean. It is the plague of leprosy. It has broken out in
the boil. 21 But if the priest examines it, and behold,
there are no white hairs in it, and it isn't deeper than the
skin, but is dim, then the priest shall isolate him seven
days. 22 If it spreads in the skin, then the priest shall
pronounce him unclean. It is a plague. 23 But if the
bright spot stays in its place, and hasn't spread, it is the
scar from the boil; and the priest shall pronounce him
clean.
24 "Or when the body has a burn from fire on its skin,
and the raw flesh of the burn becomes a bright spot,
reddish-white, or white, 25 then the priest shall examine
it; and behold, if the hair in the bright spot has turned
white, and its appearance is deeper than the skin, it is
leprosy. It has broken out in the burning, and the priest
shall pronounce him unclean. It is the plague of leprosy.
26 But if the priest examines it, and behold, there is no
white hair in the bright spot, and it isn't deeper than the
skin, but has faded, then the priest shall isolate him seven
days. 27 The priest shall examine him on the seventh
day. If it has spread in the skin, then the priest shall
pronounce him unclean. It is the plague of leprosy. 28 If
the bright spot stays in its place, and hasn't spread in the
skin, but is faded, it is the swelling from the burn, and the
priest shall pronounce him clean, for it is the scar from the
burn.
29 "When a man or woman has a plague on the head or
on the beard, 30 then the priest shall examine the plague;
and behold, if its appearance is deeper than the skin, and
the hair in it is yellow and thin, then the priest shall
pronounce him unclean. It is an itch. It is leprosy of the
head or of the beard. 31 If the priest examines the plague
of itching, and behold, its appearance isn't deeper than the
skin, and there is no black hair in it, then the priest shall
isolate the person infected with itching seven days.
32 On the seventh day the priest shall examine the
plague; and behold, if the itch hasn't spread, and there is
no yellow hair in it, and the appearance of the itch isn't
deeper than the skin, 33 then he shall be shaved, but he
shall not shave the itch. Then the priest shall isolate the
one who has the itch seven more days. 34 On the
seventh day, the priest shall examine the itch; and behold,
if the itch hasn't spread in the skin, and its appearance
isn't deeper than the skin, then the priest shall pronounce
him clean. He shall wash his clothes and be clean.
35 But if the itch spreads in the skin after his cleansing,
36 then the priest shall examine him; and behold, if the
itch has spread in the skin, the priest shall not look for the
yellow hair; he is unclean. 37 But if in his eyes the itch
is arrested and black hair has grown in it, then the itch is
healed. He is clean. The priest shall pronounce him clean.
38 "When a man or a woman has bright spots in the skin
of the body, even white bright spots, 39 then the priest

---

[106] **11:5** *11:5* or rock badger, or cony

shall examine them. Behold, if the bright spots on the skin
of their body are a dull white, it is a harmless rash. It has
broken out in the skin. He is clean.
40 "If a man's hair has fallen from his head, he is bald.
He is clean. 41 If his hair has fallen off from the front
part of his head, he is forehead bald. He is clean. 42 But
if a reddish-white plague is in the bald head or the bald
forehead, it is leprosy breaking out in his bald head or his
bald forehead. 43 Then the priest shall examine him.
Behold, if the swelling of the plague is reddish-white in
his bald head, or in his bald forehead, like the appearance
of leprosy in the skin of the body, 44 he is a leprous
man. He is unclean. The priest shall surely pronounce him
unclean. His plague is on his head.
45 "The leper in whom the plague is shall wear torn
clothes, and the hair of his head shall hang loose. He shall
cover his upper lip, and shall cry, 'Unclean! Unclean!'
46 All the days in which the plague is in him he shall be
unclean. He is unclean. He shall dwell alone. His dwelling
shall be outside of the camp.
47 "The garment also that the plague of leprosy is in,
whether it is a woolen garment, or a linen garment;
48 whether it is in warp or woof;[107] of linen or of wool;
whether in a leather, or in anything made of leather;
49 if the plague is greenish or reddish in the garment, or
in the leather, or in the warp, or in the woof, or in
anything made of leather; it is the plague of leprosy, and
shall be shown to the priest. 50 The priest shall examine
the plague, and isolate the plague seven days. 51 He
shall examine the plague on the seventh day. If the plague
has spread in the garment, either in the warp, or in the
woof, or in the skin, whatever use the skin is used for, the
plague is a destructive mildew. It is unclean. 52 He shall
burn the garment, whether the warp or the woof, in wool
or in linen, or anything of leather, in which the plague is,
for it is a destructive mildew. It shall be burned in the fire.
53 "If the priest examines it, and behold, the plague
hasn't spread in the garment, either in the warp, or in the
woof, or in anything of skin; 54 then the priest shall
command that they wash the thing that the plague is in,
and he shall isolate it seven more days. 55 Then the
priest shall examine it, after the plague is washed; and
behold, if the plague hasn't changed its color, and the
plague hasn't spread, it is unclean; you shall burn it in the
fire. It is a mildewed spot, whether the bareness is inside
or outside. 56 If the priest looks, and behold, the plague
has faded after it is washed, then he shall tear it out of the
garment, or out of the skin, or out of the warp, or out of
the woof; 57 and if it appears again in the garment,
either in the warp, or in the woof, or in anything of skin, it
is spreading. You shall burn with fire that in which the
plague is. 58 The garment, either the warp, or the woof,
or whatever thing of skin it is, which you shall wash, if
the plague has departed from them, then it shall be
washed the second time, and it will be clean."
59 This is the law of the plague of mildew in a garment
of wool or linen, either in the warp, or the woof, or in
anything of skin, to pronounce it clean, or to pronounce it
unclean.

Leviticus 14

1 God spoke to Moses, saying,
2 "This shall be the law of the leper in the day of his
cleansing: He shall be brought to the priest, 3 and the
priest shall go out of the camp. The priest shall examine
him. Behold, if the plague of leprosy is healed in the
leper, 4 then the priest shall command them to take for
him who is to be cleansed two living clean birds, cedar
wood, scarlet, and hyssop. 5 The priest shall command
them to kill one of the birds in an earthen vessel over
running water. 6 As for the living bird, he shall take it,
the cedar wood, the scarlet, and the hyssop, and shall dip
them and the living bird in the blood of the bird that was
killed over the running water. 7 He shall sprinkle on him
who is to be cleansed from the leprosy seven times, and
shall pronounce him clean, and shall let the living bird go
into the open field.
8 "He who is to be cleansed shall wash his clothes, and
shave off all his hair, and bathe himself in water; and he
shall be clean. After that he shall come into the camp, but
shall dwell outside his tent seven days. 9 It shall be on
the seventh day, that he shall shave all his hair off his
head and his beard and his eyebrows, even all his hair he
shall shave off. He shall wash his clothes, and he shall
bathe his body in water. Then he shall be clean.
10 "On the eighth day he shall take two male lambs
without defect, one ewe lamb a year old without defect,
three tenths of an ephah[108] of fine flour for a meal
offering, mixed with oil, and one log[109] of oil. 11 The
priest who cleanses him shall set the man who is to be
cleansed, and those things, before God, at the door of the
Tent of Meeting.
12 "The priest shall take one of the male lambs, and
offer him for a trespass offering, with the log of oil, and
wave them for a wave offering before God. 13 He shall
kill the male lamb in the place where they kill the sin
offering and the burnt offering, in the place of the
sanctuary; for as the sin offering is the priest's, so is the
trespass offering. It is most holy. 14 The priest shall take
some of the blood of the trespass offering, and the priest
shall put it on the tip of the right ear of him who is to be
cleansed, and on the thumb of his right hand, and on the
big toe of his right foot. 15 The priest shall take some of
the log of oil, and pour it into the palm of his own left
hand. 16 The priest shall dip his right finger in the oil
that is in his left hand, and shall sprinkle some of the oil
with his finger seven times before God. 17 The priest
shall put some of the rest of the oil that is in his hand on
the tip of the right ear of him who is to be cleansed, and
on the thumb of his right hand, and on the big toe of his
right foot, upon the blood of the trespass offering.
18 The rest of the oil that is in the priest's hand he shall
put on the head of him who is to be cleansed, and the
priest shall make atonement for him before God.
19 "The priest shall offer the sin offering, and make
atonement for him who is to be cleansed because of his
uncleanness. Afterward he shall kill the burnt offering;
20 then the priest shall offer the burnt offering and the
meal offering on the altar. The priest shall make
atonement for him, and he shall be clean.
21 "If he is poor, and can't afford so much, then he shall
take one male lamb for a trespass offering to be waved, to
make atonement for him, and one tenth of an ephah[110] of
fine flour mixed with oil for a meal offering, and a log[111]
of oil; 22 and two turtledoves, or two young pigeons,
such as he is able to afford; and the one shall be a sin
offering, and the other a burnt offering.
23 "On the eighth day he shall bring them for his
cleansing to the priest, to the door of the Tent of Meeting,
before God. 24 The priest shall take the lamb of the
trespass offering, and the log of oil, and the priest shall
wave them for a wave offering before God. 25 He shall
kill the lamb of the trespass offering. The priest shall take
some of the blood of the trespass offering and put it on the
tip of the right ear of him who is to be cleansed, and on
the thumb of his right hand, and on the big toe of his right
foot. 26 The priest shall pour some of the oil into the
palm of his own left hand; 27 and the priest shall
sprinkle with his right finger some of the oil that is in his
left hand seven times before God. 28 Then the priest
shall put some of the oil that is in his hand on the tip of
the right ear of him who is to be cleansed, and on the
thumb of his right hand, and on the big toe of his right
foot, on the place of the blood of the trespass offering.
29 The rest of the oil that is in the priest's hand he shall
put on the head of him who is to be cleansed, to make
atonement for him before God. 30 He shall offer one of
the turtledoves, or of the young pigeons, which ever he is
able to afford, 31 of the kind he is able to afford, the one
for a sin offering, and the other for a burnt offering, with
the meal offering. The priest shall make atonement for
him who is to be cleansed before God."
32 This is the law for him in whom is the plague of
leprosy, who is not able to afford the sacrifice for his
cleansing.
33 God spoke to Moses and to Aaron, saying,
34 "When you have come into the land of Canaan,
which I give to you for a possession, and I put a spreading
mildew in a house in the land of your possession,
35 then he who owns the house shall come and tell the
priest, saying, 'There seems to me to be some sort of
plague in the house.' 36 The priest shall command that
they empty the house, before the priest goes in to examine
the plague, that all that is in the house not be made
unclean. Afterward the priest shall go in to inspect the
house. 37 He shall examine the plague; and behold, if
the plague is in the walls of the house with hollow streaks,
greenish or reddish, and it appears to be deeper than the
wall, 38 then the priest shall go out of the house to the
door of the house, and shut up the house seven days.
39 The priest shall come again on the seventh day, and
look. If the plague has spread in the walls of the house,
40 then the priest shall command that they take out the
stones in which is the plague, and cast them into an
unclean place outside of the city. 41 He shall cause the
inside of the house to be scraped all over. They shall pour
out the mortar that they scraped off outside of the city into
an unclean place. 42 They shall take other stones, and
put them in the place of those stones; and he shall take
other mortar, and shall plaster the house.
43 "If the plague comes again, and breaks out in the
house after he has taken out the stones, and after he has
scraped the house, and after it was plastered, 44 then the
priest shall come in and look; and behold, if the plague
has spread in the house, it is a destructive mildew in the
house. It is unclean. 45 He shall break down the house,
its stones, and its timber, and all the house's mortar. He
shall carry them out of the city into an unclean place.
46 "Moreover he who goes into the house while it is
shut up shall be unclean until the evening. 47 He who
lies down in the house shall wash his clothes; and he who
eats in the house shall wash his clothes.
48 "If the priest shall come in, and examine it, and
behold, the plague hasn't spread in the house, after the
house was plastered, then the priest shall pronounce the
house clean, because the plague is healed. 49 To cleanse
the house he shall take two birds, cedar wood, scarlet, and
hyssop. 50 He shall kill one of the birds in an earthen
vessel over running water. 51 He shall take the cedar
wood, the hyssop, the scarlet, and the living bird, and dip
them in the blood of the slain bird, and in the running
water, and sprinkle the house seven times. 52 He shall
cleanse the house with the blood of the bird, and with the
running water, with the living bird, with the cedar wood,
with the hyssop, and with the scarlet; 53 but he shall let
the living bird go out of the city into the open field. So
shall he make atonement for the house; and it shall be
clean."
54 This is the law for any plague of leprosy, and for an
itch, 55 and for the destructive mildew of a garment, and
for a house, 56 and for a swelling, and for a scab, and
for a bright spot; 57 to teach when it is unclean, and
when it is clean.
This is the law of leprosy.

Leviticus 15

1 God spoke to Moses and to Aaron, saying, 2 "Speak
to the children of Israel, and tell them, 'When any man
has a discharge from his body, because of his discharge he
is unclean. 3 This shall be his uncleanness in his
discharge: whether his body runs with his discharge, or
his body has stopped from his discharge, it is his
uncleanness.
4 "'Every bed on which he who has the discharge lies
shall be unclean; and everything he sits on shall be
unclean. 5 Whoever touches his bed shall wash his
clothes, and bathe himself in water, and be unclean until
the evening. 6 He who sits on anything on which the
man who has the discharge sat shall wash his clothes, and
bathe himself in water, and be unclean until the evening.

---

[107] **13:48** *13:48* warp and woof are the vertical and horizontal threads in woven cloth

[108] **14:10** *14:10* 1 ephah is about 22 liters or about 2/3 of a bushel

[109] **14:10** *14:10* a log is a liquid measure of about 300 ml or 10 ounces

[110] **14:21** *14:21* 1 ephah is about 22 liters or about 2/3 of a bushel

[111] **14:21** *14:21* a log is a liquid measure of about 300 ml or 10 ounces

7 “‘He who touches the body of him who has the
discharge shall wash his clothes, and bathe himself in
water, and be unclean until the evening.
8 “‘If he who has the discharge spits on him who is
clean, then he shall wash his clothes, and bathe himself in
water, and be unclean until the evening.
9 “‘Whatever saddle he who has the discharge rides on
shall be unclean. 10 Whoever touches anything that was
under him shall be unclean until the evening. He who
carries those things shall wash his clothes, and bathe
himself in water, and be unclean until the evening.
11 “‘Whomever he who has the discharge touches,
without having rinsed his hands in water, he shall wash
his clothes, and bathe himself in water, and be unclean
until the evening.
12 “‘The earthen vessel, which he who has the discharge
touches, shall be broken; and every vessel of wood shall
be rinsed in water.
13 “‘When he who has a discharge is cleansed of his
discharge, then he shall count to himself seven days for
his cleansing, and wash his clothes; and he shall bathe his
flesh in running water, and shall be clean.
14 “‘On the eighth day he shall take two turtledoves, or
two young pigeons, and come before God to the door of
the Tent of Meeting, and give them to the priest. 15 The
priest shall offer them, the one for a sin offering, and the
other for a burnt offering. The priest shall make
atonement for him before God for his discharge.
16 “‘If any man has an emission of semen, then he shall
bathe all his flesh in water, and be unclean until the
evening. 17 Every garment and every skin which the
semen is on shall be washed with water, and be unclean
until the evening. 18 If a man lies with a woman and
there is an emission of semen, they shall both bathe
themselves in water, and be unclean until the evening.
19 “‘If a woman has a discharge, and her discharge in
her flesh is blood, she shall be in her impurity seven days.
Whoever touches her shall be unclean until the evening.
20 “‘Everything that she lies on in her impurity shall be
unclean. Everything also that she sits on shall be unclean.
21 Whoever touches her bed shall wash his clothes, and
bathe himself in water, and be unclean until the evening.
22 Whoever touches anything that she sits on shall wash
his clothes, and bathe himself in water, and be unclean
until the evening. 23 If it is on the bed, or on anything
she sits on, when he touches it, he shall be unclean until
the evening.
24 “‘If any man lies with her, and her monthly flow is
on him, he shall be unclean seven days; and every bed he
lies on shall be unclean.
25 “‘If a woman has a discharge of her blood many days
not in the time of her period, or if she has a discharge
beyond the time of her period, all the days of the
discharge of her uncleanness shall be as in the days of her
period. She is unclean. 26 Every bed she lies on all the
days of her discharge shall be to her as the bed of her
period. Everything she sits on shall be unclean, as the
uncleanness of her period. 27 Whoever touches these
things shall be unclean, and shall wash his clothes and
bathe himself in water, and be unclean until the evening.
28 “‘But if she is cleansed of her discharge, then she
shall count to herself seven days, and after that she shall
be clean. 29 On the eighth day she shall take two
turtledoves, or two young pigeons, and bring them to the
priest, to the door of the Tent of Meeting. 30 The priest
shall offer the one for a sin offering, and the other for a
burnt offering; and the priest shall make atonement for her
before God for the uncleanness of her discharge.
31 “‘Thus you shall separate the children of Israel from
their uncleanness, so they will not die in their uncleanness
when they defile my tabernacle that is among them.’”
32 This is the law of him who has a discharge, and of
him who has an emission of semen, so that he is unclean
by it; 33 and of her who has her period, and of a man or
woman who has a discharge, and of him who lies with her
who is unclean.

Leviticus 16

1 God spoke to Moses after the death of the two sons of
Aaron, when they came near before God, and died;
2 and God said to Moses, “Tell Aaron your brother not
to come at just any time into the Most Holy Place within
the veil, before the mercy seat which is on the ark; lest he
die; for I will appear in the cloud on the mercy seat.
3 “Aaron shall come into the sanctuary with a young
bull for a sin offering, and a ram for a burnt offering.
4 He shall put on the holy linen tunic. He shall have the
linen trousers on his body, and shall put on the linen sash,
and he shall be clothed with the linen turban. They are the
holy garments. He shall bathe his body in water, and put
them on. 5 He shall take from the congregation of the
children of Israel two male goats for a sin offering, and
one ram for a burnt offering.
6 “Aaron shall offer the bull of the sin offering, which is
for himself, and make atonement for himself and for his
house. 7 He shall take the two goats, and set them before
God at the door of the Tent of Meeting. 8 Aaron shall
cast lots for the two goats: one lot for God, and the other
lot for the scapegoat. 9 Aaron shall present the goat on
which the lot fell for God, and offer him for a sin offering.
10 But the goat on which the lot fell for the scapegoat
shall be presented alive before God, to make atonement
for him, to send him away as the scapegoat into the
wilderness.
11 “Aaron shall present the bull of the sin offering,
which is for himself, and shall make atonement for
himself and for his house, and shall kill the bull of the sin
offering which is for himself. 12 He shall take a censer
full of coals of fire from off the altar before God, and two
handfuls of sweet incense beaten small, and bring it
within the veil. 13 He shall put the incense on the fire
before God, that the cloud of the incense may cover the
mercy seat that is on the covenant, so that he will not die.
14 He shall take some of the blood of the bull, and
sprinkle it with his finger on the mercy seat on the east;
and before the mercy seat he shall sprinkle some of the
blood with his finger seven times.
15 “Then he shall kill the goat of the sin offering that is
for the people, and bring his blood within the veil, and do
with his blood as he did with the blood of the bull, and
sprinkle it on the mercy seat and before the mercy seat.
16 He shall make atonement for the Holy Place, because
of the uncleanness of the children of Israel, and because
of their transgressions, even all their sins; and so he shall
do for the Tent of Meeting that dwells with them in the
middle of their uncleanness. 17 No one shall be in the
Tent of Meeting when he enters to make atonement in the
Holy Place, until he comes out, and has made atonement
for himself and for his household, and for all the assembly
of Israel.
18 “He shall go out to the altar that is before God and
make atonement for it, and shall take some of the bull’s
blood, and some of the goat’s blood, and put it around on
the horns of the altar. 19 He shall sprinkle some of the
blood on it with his finger seven times, and cleanse it, and
make it holy from the uncleanness of the children of
Israel.
20 “When he has finished atoning for the Holy Place,
the Tent of Meeting, and the altar, he shall present the live
goat. 21 Aaron shall lay both his hands on the head of
the live goat, and confess over him all the iniquities of the
children of Israel, and all their transgressions, even all
their sins; and he shall put them on the head of the goat,
and shall send him away into the wilderness by the hand
of a man who is ready. 22 The goat shall carry all their
iniquities on himself to a solitary land, and he shall
release the goat in the wilderness.
23 “Aaron shall come into the Tent of Meeting, and
shall take off the linen garments which he put on when he
went into the Holy Place, and shall leave them there.
24 Then he shall bathe himself in water in a holy place,
put on his garments, and come out and offer his burnt
offering and the burnt offering of the people, and make
atonement for himself and for the people. 25 The fat of
the sin offering he shall burn on the altar.
26 “He who lets the goat go as the scapegoat shall wash
his clothes, and bathe his flesh in water, and afterward he
shall come into the camp. 27 The bull for the sin
offering, and the goat for the sin offering, whose blood
was brought in to make atonement in the Holy Place, shall
be carried outside the camp; and they shall burn their
skins, their flesh, and their dung with fire. 28 He who
burns them shall wash his clothes, and bathe his flesh in
water, and afterward he shall come into the camp.
29 “It shall be a statute to you forever: in the seventh
month, on the tenth day of the month, you shall afflict
your souls, and shall do no kind of work, whether native-
born or a stranger who lives as a foreigner among you;
30 for on this day shall atonement be made for you, to
cleanse you. You shall be clean from all your sins before
God. 31 It is a Sabbath of solemn rest to you, and you
shall afflict your souls. It is a statute forever. 32 The
priest, who is anointed and who is consecrated to be priest
in his father’s place, shall make the atonement, and shall
put on the linen garments, even the holy garments.
33 Then he shall make atonement for the Holy
Sanctuary; and he shall make atonement for the Tent of
Meeting and for the altar; and he shall make atonement
for the priests and for all the people of the assembly.
34 “This shall be an everlasting statute for you, to make
atonement for the children of Israel once in the year
because of all their sins.”
It was done as God commanded Moses.
Leviticus 17
1 God spoke to Moses, saying, 2 “Speak to Aaron, and
to his sons, and to all the children of Israel, and say to
them, ‘This is the thing which God has commanded:
3 Whatever man there is of the house of Israel who kills
a bull, or lamb, or goat in the camp, or who kills it outside
the camp, 4 and hasn’t brought it to the door of the Tent
of Meeting to offer it as an offering to God before God’s
tabernacle: blood shall be imputed to that man. He has
shed blood. That man shall be cut off from among his
people. 5 This is to the end that the children of Israel
may bring their sacrifices, which they sacrifice in the
open field, that they may bring them to God, to the door
of the Tent of Meeting, to the priest, and sacrifice them
for sacrifices of peace offerings to God. 6 The priest
shall sprinkle the blood on God’s altar at the door of the
Tent of Meeting, and burn the fat for a pleasant aroma to
God. 7 They shall no more sacrifice their sacrifices to
the goat idols, after which they play the prostitute. This
shall be a statute forever to them throughout their
generations.’
8 “You shall say to them, ‘Any man there is of the house
of Israel, or of the strangers who live as foreigners among
them, who offers a burnt offering or sacrifice, 9 and
doesn’t bring it to the door of the Tent of Meeting to
sacrifice it to God, that man shall be cut off from his
people.
10 “‘Any man of the house of Israel, or of the strangers
who live as foreigners among them, who eats any kind of
blood, I will set my face against that soul who eats blood,
and will cut him off from among his people. 11 For the
life of the flesh is in the blood. I have given it to you on
the altar to make atonement for your souls; for it is the
blood that makes atonement by reason of the life.
12 Therefore I have said to the children of Israel, “No
person among you may eat blood, nor may any stranger
who lives as a foreigner among you eat blood.”
13 “‘Whatever man there is of the children of Israel, or
of the strangers who live as foreigners among them, who
takes in hunting any animal or bird that may be eaten, he
shall pour out its blood, and cover it with dust. 14 For as
to the life of all flesh, its blood is with its life. Therefore I
said to the children of Israel, “You shall not eat the blood
of any kind of flesh; for the life of all flesh is its blood.
Whoever eats it shall be cut off.”
15 “‘Every person that eats what dies of itself, or that
which is torn by animals, whether he is native-born or a
foreigner, shall wash his clothes, and bathe himself in
water, and be unclean until the evening. Then he shall be
clean. 16 But if he doesn’t wash them, or bathe his flesh,
then he shall bear his iniquity.’”

Leviticus 18

1 God said to Moses, 2 “Speak to the children of Israel,
and say to them, ‘I am God your God. 3 You shall not
do as they do in the land of Egypt, where you lived. You
shall not do as they do in the land of Canaan, where I am
bringing you. You shall not follow their statutes. 4 You
shall do my ordinances. You shall keep my statutes and
walk in them. I am God your God. 5 You shall therefore
keep my statutes and my ordinances, which if a man does,
he shall live in them. I am God.
6 “‘None of you shall approach any close relatives, to
uncover their nakedness: I am God.
7 “‘You shall not uncover the nakedness of your father,
nor the nakedness of your mother: she is your mother.
You shall not uncover her nakedness.
8 “‘You shall not uncover the nakedness of your father’s
wife. It is your father’s nakedness.

9 "'You shall not uncover the nakedness of your sister, the daughter of your father, or the daughter of your mother, whether born at home or born abroad.

10 "'You shall not uncover the nakedness of your son's daughter, or of your daughter's daughter, even their nakedness; for theirs is your own nakedness.

11 "'You shall not uncover the nakedness of your father's wife's daughter, conceived by your father, since she is your sister.

12 "'You shall not uncover the nakedness of your father's sister. She is your father's near kinswoman.

13 "'You shall not uncover the nakedness of your mother's sister, for she is your mother's near kinswoman.

14 "'You shall not uncover the nakedness of your father's brother. You shall not approach his wife. She is your aunt.

15 "'You shall not uncover the nakedness of your daughter-in-law. She is your son's wife. You shall not uncover her nakedness.

16 "'You shall not uncover the nakedness of your brother's wife. It is your brother's nakedness.

17 "'You shall not uncover the nakedness of a woman and her daughter. You shall not take her son's daughter, or her daughter's daughter, to uncover her nakedness. They are near kinswomen. It is wickedness.

18 "'You shall not take a wife in addition to her sister, to be a rival, to uncover her nakedness, while her sister is still alive.

19 "'You shall not approach a woman to uncover her nakedness, as long as she is impure by her uncleanness.

20 "'You shall not lie carnally with your neighbor's wife, and defile yourself with her.

21 "'You shall not give any of your children as a sacrifice to Molech. You shall not profane the name of your God. I am God.

22 "'You shall not lie with a man as with a woman. That is detestable.

23 "'You shall not lie with any animal to defile yourself with it. No woman may give herself to an animal, to lie down with it: it is a perversion.

24 "'Don't defile yourselves in any of these things; for in all these the nations which I am casting out before you were defiled. 25 The land was defiled. Therefore I punished its iniquity, and the land vomited out her inhabitants. 26 You therefore shall keep my statutes and my ordinances, and shall not do any of these abominations; neither the native-born, nor the stranger who lives as a foreigner among you 27 (for the men of the land that were before you had done all these abominations, and the land became defiled), 28 that the land not vomit you out also, when you defile it, as it vomited out the nation that was before you.

29 "'For whoever shall do any of these abominations, even the souls that do them shall be cut off from among their people. 30 Therefore you shall keep my requirements, that you do not practice any of these abominable customs which were practiced before you, and that you do not defile yourselves with them. I am God your God.'"

Leviticus 19

1 God spoke to Moses, saying, 2 "Speak to all the congregation of the children of Israel, and tell them, 'You shall be holy; for I, God your God, am holy.

3 "'Each one of you shall respect his mother and his father. You shall keep my Sabbaths. I am God your God.

4 "'Don't turn to idols, nor make molten gods for yourselves. I am God your God.

5 "'When you offer a sacrifice of peace offerings to God, you shall offer it so that you may be accepted. 6 It shall be eaten the same day you offer it, and on the next day. If anything remains until the third day, it shall be burned with fire. 7 If it is eaten at all on the third day, it is an abomination. It will not be accepted; 8 but everyone who eats it shall bear his iniquity, because he has profaned the holy thing of God, and that soul shall be cut off from his people.

9 "'When you reap the harvest of your land, you shall not wholly reap the corners of your field, neither shall you gather the gleanings of your harvest. 10 You shall not glean your vineyard, neither shall you gather the fallen grapes of your vineyard. You shall leave them for the poor and for the foreigner. I am God your God.

11 "'You shall not steal.
"'You shall not lie.
"'You shall not deceive one another.

12 "'You shall not swear by my name falsely, and profane the name of your God. I am God.

13 "'You shall not oppress your neighbor, nor rob him. "'The wages of a hired servant shall not remain with you all night until the morning.

14 "'You shall not curse the deaf, nor put a stumbling block before the blind; but you shall fear your God. I am God.

15 "'You shall do no injustice in judgment. You shall not be partial to the poor, nor show favoritism to the great; but you shall judge your neighbor in righteousness.

16 "'You shall not go around as a slanderer among your people.
"'You shall not endanger the life[112] of your neighbor. I am God.

17 "'You shall not hate your brother in your heart. You shall surely rebuke your neighbor, and not bear sin because of him.

18 "'You shall not take vengeance, nor bear any grudge against the children of your people; but you shall love your neighbor as yourself. I am God.

19 "'You shall keep my statutes.
"'You shall not cross-breed different kinds of animals.
"'You shall not sow your field with two kinds of seed;
"'Don't wear a garment made of two kinds of material.

20 "'If a man lies carnally with a woman who is a slave girl, pledged to be married to another man, and not ransomed or given her freedom; they shall be punished. They shall not be put to death, because she was not free.

21 He shall bring his trespass offering to God, to the door of the Tent of Meeting, even a ram for a trespass offering. 22 The priest shall make atonement for him with the ram of the trespass offering before God for his sin which he has committed; and the sin which he has committed shall be forgiven him.

23 "'When you come into the land, and have planted all kinds of trees for food, then you shall count their fruit as forbidden.[113] For three years it shall be forbidden to you. It shall not be eaten. 24 But in the fourth year all its fruit shall be holy, for giving praise to God. 25 In the fifth year you shall eat its fruit, that it may yield its increase to you. I am God your God.

26 "'You shall not eat any meat with the blood still in it. You shall not use enchantments, nor practice sorcery.

27 "'You shall not cut the hair on the sides of your head or clip off the edge of your beard.

28 "'You shall not make any cuttings in your flesh for the dead, nor tattoo any marks on you. I am God.

29 "'Don't profane your daughter, to make her a prostitute; lest the land fall to prostitution, and the land become full of wickedness.

30 "'You shall keep my Sabbaths, and reverence my sanctuary; I am God.

31 "'Don't turn to those who are mediums, nor to the wizards. Don't seek them out, to be defiled by them. I am God your God.

32 "'You shall rise up before the gray head and honor the face of the elderly; and you shall fear your God. I am God.

33 "'If a stranger lives as a foreigner with you in your land, you shall not do him wrong. 34 The stranger who lives as a foreigner with you shall be to you as the native-born among you, and you shall love him as yourself; for you lived as foreigners in the land of Egypt. I am God your God.

35 "'You shall do no unrighteousness in judgment, in measures of length, of weight, or of quantity. 36 You shall have just balances, just weights, a just ephah,[114] and a just hin.[115] I am God your God, who brought you out of the land of Egypt.

37 "'You shall observe all my statutes and all my ordinances, and do them. I am God.'"

Leviticus 20

1 God spoke to Moses, saying, 2 "Moreover, you shall tell the children of Israel, 'Anyone of the children of Israel, or of the strangers who live as foreigners in Israel, who gives any of his offspring[116] to Molech shall surely be put to death. The people of the land shall stone that person with stones. 3 I also will set my face against that person, and will cut him off from among his people, because he has given of his offspring to Molech, to defile my sanctuary, and to profane my holy name. 4 If the people of the land all hide their eyes from that person when he gives of his offspring to Molech, and don't put him to death, 5 then I will set my face against that man and against his family, and will cut him off, and all who play the prostitute after him to play the prostitute with Molech, from among their people.

6 "'The person that turns to those who are mediums and wizards, to play the prostitute after them, I will even set my face against that person, and will cut him off from among his people.

7 "'Sanctify yourselves therefore, and be holy; for I am God your God. 8 You shall keep my statutes, and do them. I am God who sanctifies you.

9 "'For everyone who curses his father or his mother shall surely be put to death. He has cursed his father or his mother. His blood shall be upon himself.

10 "'The man who commits adultery with another man's wife, even he who commits adultery with his neighbor's wife, the adulterer and the adulteress shall surely be put to death.

11 "'The man who lies with his father's wife has uncovered his father's nakedness. Both of them shall surely be put to death. Their blood shall be upon themselves.

12 "'If a man lies with his daughter-in-law, both of them shall surely be put to death. They have committed a perversion. Their blood shall be upon themselves.

13 "'If a man lies with a male, as with a woman, both of them have committed an abomination. They shall surely be put to death. Their blood shall be upon themselves.

14 "'If a man takes a wife and her mother, it is wickedness. They shall be burned with fire, both he and they, that there may be no wickedness among you.

15 "'If a man lies with an animal, he shall surely be put to death; and you shall kill the animal.

16 "'If a woman approaches any animal and lies with it, you shall kill the woman and the animal. They shall surely be put to death. Their blood shall be upon them.

17 "'If a man takes his sister—his father's daughter, or his mother's daughter—and sees her nakedness, and she sees his nakedness, it is a shameful thing. They shall be cut off in the sight of the children of their people. He has uncovered his sister's nakedness. He shall bear his iniquity.

18 "'If a man lies with a woman having her monthly period, and uncovers her nakedness, he has made her fountain naked, and she has uncovered the fountain of her blood. Both of them shall be cut off from among their people.

19 "'You shall not uncover the nakedness of your mother's sister, nor of your father's sister, for he has made his close relative naked. They shall bear their iniquity. 20 If a man lies with his uncle's wife, he has uncovered his uncle's nakedness. They shall bear their sin. They shall die childless.

21 "'If a man takes his brother's wife, it is an impurity. He has uncovered his brother's nakedness. They shall be childless.

22 "'You shall therefore keep all my statutes and all my ordinances, and do them, that the land where I am bringing you to dwell may not vomit you out. 23 You shall not walk in the customs of the nation which I am casting out before you; for they did all these things, and therefore I abhorred them. 24 But I have said to you,

---

[112]**19:16** *19:16* literally, "blood"
[113]**19:23** *19:23* literally, "uncircumcised"

[114]**19:36** *19:36* 1 ephah is about 22 liters or about 2/3 of a bushel

[115]**19:36** *19:36* A hin is about 6.5 liters or 1.7 gallons.
[116]**20:2** *20:2* or, seed

"You shall inherit their land, and I will give it to you to
possess it, a land flowing with milk and honey." I am God
your God, who has separated you from the peoples.
25 "'You shall therefore make a distinction between the
clean animal and the unclean, and between the unclean
fowl and the clean. You shall not make yourselves
abominable by animal, or by bird, or by anything with
which the ground teems, which I have separated from you
as unclean for you. 26 You shall be holy to me, for I,
God, am holy, and have set you apart from the peoples,
that you should be mine.
27 "'A man or a woman that is a medium or is a wizard
shall surely be put to death. They shall be stoned with
stones. Their blood shall be upon themselves.'"

Leviticus 21

1 God said to Moses, "Speak to the priests, the sons of
Aaron, and say to them, 'A priest shall not defile himself
for the dead among his people, 2 except for his relatives
that are near to him: for his mother, for his father, for his
son, for his daughter, for his brother, 3 and for his virgin
sister who is near to him, who has had no husband; for her
he may defile himself. 4 He shall not defile himself,
being a chief man among his people, to profane himself.
5 "'They shall not shave their heads or shave off the
corners of their beards or make any cuttings in their flesh.
6 They shall be holy to their God, and not profane the
name of their God, for they offer the offerings of God
made by fire, the bread of their God. Therefore they shall
be holy.
7 "'They shall not marry a woman who is a prostitute, or
profane. A priest shall not marry a woman divorced from
her husband; for he is holy to his God. 8 Therefore you
shall sanctify him, for he offers the bread of your God. He
shall be holy to you, for I God, who sanctify you, am
holy.
9 "'The daughter of any priest, if she profanes herself by
playing the prostitute, she profanes her father. She shall
be burned with fire.
10 "'He who is the high priest among his brothers, upon
whose head the anointing oil is poured, and who is
consecrated to put on the garments, shall not let the hair
of his head hang loose, or tear his clothes. 11 He must
not go in to any dead body, or defile himself for his father
or for his mother. 12 He shall not go out of the
sanctuary, nor profane the sanctuary of his God; for the
crown of the anointing oil of his God is upon him. I am
God.
13 "'He shall take a wife in her virginity. 14 He shall
not marry a widow, or one divorced, or a woman who has
been defiled, or a prostitute. He shall take a virgin of his
own people as a wife. 15 He shall not profane his
offspring among his people, for I am God who sanctifies
him.'"
16 God spoke to Moses, saying, 17 "Say to Aaron,
'None of your offspring throughout their generations who
has a defect may approach to offer the bread of his God.
18 For whatever man he is that has a defect, he shall not
draw near: a blind man, or a lame, or he who has a flat
nose, or any deformity, 19 or a man who has an injured
foot, or an injured hand, 20 or hunchbacked, or a dwarf,
or one who has a defect in his eye, or an itching disease,
or scabs, or who has damaged testicles. 21 No man of
the offspring of Aaron the priest who has a defect shall
come near to offer the offerings of God made by fire.
Since he has a defect, he shall not come near to offer the
bread of his God. 22 He shall eat the bread of his God,
both of the most holy, and of the holy. 23 He shall not
come near to the veil, nor come near to the altar, because
he has a defect; that he may not profane my sanctuaries,
for I am God who sanctifies them.'"
24 So Moses spoke to Aaron, and to his sons, and to all
the children of Israel.

Leviticus 22

1 God spoke to Moses, saying, 2 "Tell Aaron and his
sons to separate themselves from the holy things of the
children of Israel, which they make holy to me, and that
they not profane my holy name. I am God.
3 "Tell them, 'If anyone of all your offspring throughout
your generations approaches the holy things which the
children of Israel make holy to God, having his
uncleanness on him, that soul shall be cut off from before
me. I am God.
4 "'Whoever of the offspring of Aaron is a leper or has a
discharge shall not eat of the holy things until he is clean.
Whoever touches anything that is unclean by the dead, or
a man who has a seminal emission, 5 or whoever
touches any creeping thing whereby he may be made
unclean, or a man from whom he may become unclean,
whatever uncleanness he has— 6 the person that touches
any such shall be unclean until the evening, and shall not
eat of the holy things unless he bathes his body in water.
7 When the sun is down, he shall be clean; and
afterward he shall eat of the holy things, because it is his
bread. 8 He shall not eat that which dies of itself or is
torn by animals, defiling himself by it. I am God.
9 "'They shall therefore follow my commandment, lest
they bear sin for it and die in it, if they profane it. I am
God who sanctifies them.
10 "'No stranger shall eat of the holy thing: a foreigner
living with the priests, or a hired servant, shall not eat of
the holy thing. 11 But if a priest buys a slave, purchased
by his money, he shall eat of it; and those who are born in
his house shall eat of his bread. 12 If a priest's daughter
is married to an outsider, she shall not eat of the heave
offering of the holy things. 13 But if a priest's daughter
is a widow, or divorced, and has no child, and has
returned to her father's house as in her youth, she may eat
of her father's bread; but no stranger shall eat any of it.
14 "'If a man eats something holy unwittingly, then he
shall add the fifth part of its value to it, and shall give the
holy thing to the priest. 15 The priests shall not profane
the holy things of the children of Israel, which they offer
to God, 16 and so cause them to bear the iniquity that
brings guilt when they eat their holy things; for I am God
who sanctifies them.'"
17 God spoke to Moses, saying, 18 "Speak to Aaron,
and to his sons, and to all the children of Israel, and say to
them, 'Whoever is of the house of Israel, or of the
foreigners in Israel, who offers his offering, whether it is
any of their vows or any of their free will offerings, which
they offer to God for a burnt offering; 19 that you may
be accepted, you shall offer a male without defect, of the
bulls, of the sheep, or of the goats. 20 But you shall not
offer whatever has a defect, for it shall not be acceptable
for you. 21 Whoever offers a sacrifice of peace offerings
to God to accomplish a vow, or for a free will offering of
the herd or of the flock, it shall be perfect to be accepted.
It shall have no defect. 22 You shall not offer what is
blind, is injured, is maimed, has a wart, is festering, or has
a running sore to God, nor make an offering by fire of
them on the altar to God. 23 Either a bull or a lamb that
has any deformity or lacking in his parts, that you may
offer for a free will offering; but for a vow it shall not be
accepted. 24 You must not offer to God that which has
its testicles bruised, crushed, broken, or cut. You must not
do this in your land. 25 You must not offer any of these
as the bread of your God from the hand of a foreigner,
because their corruption is in them. There is a defect in
them. They shall not be accepted for you.'"
26 God spoke to Moses, saying, 27 "When a bull, a
sheep, or a goat is born, it shall remain seven days with its
mother. From the eighth day on it shall be accepted for
the offering of an offering made by fire to God.
28 Whether it is a cow or ewe, you shall not kill it and
its young both in one day.
29 "When you sacrifice a sacrifice of thanksgiving to
God, you shall sacrifice it so that you may be accepted.
30 It shall be eaten on the same day; you shall leave
none of it until the morning. I am God.
31 "Therefore you shall keep my commandments, and
do them. I am God. 32 You shall not profane my holy
name, but I will be made holy among the children of
Israel. I am God who makes you holy, 33 who brought
you out of the land of Egypt, to be your God. I am God."

Leviticus 23

1 God spoke to Moses, saying, 2 "Speak to the
children of Israel, and tell them, 'The set feasts of God,
which you shall proclaim to be holy convocations, even
these are my set feasts.
3 "'Six days shall work be done, but on the seventh day
is a Sabbath of solemn rest, a holy convocation; you shall
do no kind of work. It is a Sabbath to God in all your
dwellings.
4 "'These are the set feasts of God, even holy
convocations, which you shall proclaim in their appointed
season. 5 In the first month, on the fourteenth day of the
month in the evening, is God's Passover. 6 On the
fifteenth day of the same month is the feast of unleavened
bread to God. Seven days you shall eat unleavened bread.
7 In the first day you shall have a holy convocation. You
shall do no regular work. 8 But you shall offer an
offering made by fire to God seven days. In the seventh
day is a holy convocation. You shall do no regular
work.'"
9 God spoke to Moses, saying, 10 "Speak to the
children of Israel, and tell them, 'When you have come
into the land which I give to you, and shall reap its
harvest, then you shall bring the sheaf of the first fruits of
your harvest to the priest. 11 He shall wave the sheaf
before God, to be accepted for you. On the next day after
the Sabbath the priest shall wave it. 12 On the day when
you wave the sheaf, you shall offer a male lamb without
defect a year old for a burnt offering to God. 13 The
meal offering with it shall be two tenths of an ephah[117] of
fine flour mixed with oil, an offering made by fire to God
for a pleasant aroma; and the drink offering with it shall
be of wine, the fourth part of a hin.[118] 14 You must not
eat bread, or roasted grain, or fresh grain, until this same
day, until you have brought the offering of your God. This
is a statute forever throughout your generations in all your
dwellings.
15 "'You shall count from the next day after the
Sabbath, from the day that you brought the sheaf of the
wave offering: seven Sabbaths shall be completed.
16 The next day after the seventh Sabbath you shall
count fifty days; and you shall offer a new meal offering
to God. 17 You shall bring out of your habitations two
loaves of bread for a wave offering made of two tenths of
an ephah[119] of fine flour. They shall be baked with yeast,
for first fruits to God. 18 You shall present with the
bread seven lambs without defect a year old, one young
bull, and two rams. They shall be a burnt offering to God,
with their meal offering and their drink offerings, even an
offering made by fire, of a sweet aroma to God. 19 You
shall offer one male goat for a sin offering, and two male
lambs a year old for a sacrifice of peace offerings.
20 The priest shall wave them with the bread of the first
fruits for a wave offering before God, with the two lambs.
They shall be holy to God for the priest. 21 You shall
make proclamation on the same day that there shall be a
holy convocation to you. You shall do no regular work.
This is a statute forever in all your dwellings throughout
your generations.
22 "'When you reap the harvest of your land, you must
not wholly reap into the corners of your field, and you
must not gather the gleanings of your harvest. You must
leave them for the poor, and for the foreigner. I am God
your God.'"
23 God spoke to Moses, saying, 24 "Speak to the
children of Israel, saying, 'In the seventh month, on the
first day of the month, there shall be a solemn rest for
you, a memorial of blowing of trumpets, a holy
convocation. 25 You shall do no regular work. You shall
offer an offering made by fire to God.'"
26 God spoke to Moses, saying, 27 "However on the
tenth day of this seventh month is the day of atonement. It
shall be a holy convocation to you. You shall afflict
yourselves and you shall offer an offering made by fire to
God. 28 You shall do no kind of work in that same day,
for it is a day of atonement, to make atonement for you
before God your God. 29 For whoever it is who shall not
deny himself in that same day shall be cut off from his
people. 30 Whoever does any kind of work in that same
day, I will destroy that person from among his people.

---

[117] **23:13** *23:13* 1 ephah is about 22 liters or about 2/3 of a bushel

[118] **23:13** *23:13* A hin is about 6.5 liters or 1.7 gallons.

[119] **23:17** *23:17* 1 ephah is about 22 liters or about 2/3 of a bushel

31 You shall do no kind of work: it is a statute forever
throughout your generations in all your dwellings. 32 It
shall be a Sabbath of solemn rest for you, and you shall
deny yourselves. In the ninth day of the month at evening,
from evening to evening, you shall keep your Sabbath."
33 God spoke to Moses, saying, 34 "Speak to the
children of Israel, and say, 'On the fifteenth day of this
seventh month is the feast of booths[120] for seven days to
God. 35 On the first day shall be a holy convocation.
You shall do no regular work. 36 Seven days you shall
offer an offering made by fire to God. On the eighth day
shall be a holy convocation to you. You shall offer an
offering made by fire to God. It is a solemn assembly; you
shall do no regular work.
37 "'These are the appointed feasts of God which you
shall proclaim to be holy convocations, to offer an
offering made by fire to God, a burnt offering, a meal
offering, a sacrifice, and drink offerings, each on its own
day— 38 in addition to the Sabbaths of God, and in
addition to your gifts, and in addition to all your vows,
and in addition to all your free will offerings, which you
give to God.
39 "'So on the fifteenth day of the seventh month, when
you have gathered in the fruits of the land, you shall keep
the feast of God seven days. On the first day shall be a
solemn rest, and on the eighth day shall be a solemn rest.
40 You shall take on the first day the fruit of majestic
trees, branches of palm trees, and boughs of thick trees,
and willows of the brook; and you shall rejoice before
God your God seven days. 41 You shall keep it as a
feast to God seven days in the year. It is a statute forever
throughout your generations. You shall keep it in the
seventh month. 42 You shall dwell in temporary
shelters[121] for seven days. All who are native-born in
Israel shall dwell in temporary shelters,[122] 43 that your
generations may know that I made the children of Israel to
dwell in temporary shelters[123] when I brought them out of
the land of Egypt. I am God your God.'"
44 So Moses declared to the children of Israel the
appointed feasts of God.

Leviticus 24

1 God spoke to Moses, saying, 2 "Command the
children of Israel, that they bring to you pure olive oil
beaten for the light, to cause a lamp to burn continually.
3 Outside of the veil of the Testimony, in the Tent of
Meeting, Aaron shall keep it in order from evening to
morning before God continually. It shall be a statute
forever throughout your generations. 4 He shall keep in
order the lamps on the pure gold lamp stand before God
continually.
5 "You shall take fine flour, and bake twelve cakes of it:
two tenths of an ephah[124] shall be in one cake. 6 You
shall set them in two rows, six on a row, on the pure gold
table before God. 7 You shall put pure frankincense on
each row, that it may be to the bread for a memorial, even
an offering made by fire to God. 8 Every Sabbath day he
shall set it in order before God continually. It is an
everlasting covenant on the behalf of the children of
Israel. 9 It shall be for Aaron and his sons. They shall
eat it in a holy place; for it is most holy to him of the
offerings of God made by fire by a perpetual statute."
10 The son of an Israelite woman, whose father was an
Egyptian, went out among the children of Israel; and the
son of the Israelite woman and a man of Israel strove
together in the camp. 11 The son of the Israelite woman
blasphemed the Name, and cursed; and they brought him
to Moses. His mother's name was Shelomith, the daughter
of Dibri, of the tribe of Dan. 12 They put him in custody
until God's will should be declared to them. 13 God
spoke to Moses, saying, 14 "Bring him who cursed out
of the camp; and let all who heard him lay their hands on
his head, and let all the congregation stone him. 15 You
shall speak to the children of Israel, saying, 'Whoever
curses his God shall bear his sin. 16 He who blasphemes
God's name, he shall surely be put to death. All the
congregation shall certainly stone him. The foreigner as
well as the native-born shall be put to death when he
blasphemes the Name.
17 "'He who strikes any man mortally shall surely be
put to death. 18 He who strikes an animal mortally shall
make it good, life for life. 19 If anyone injures his
neighbor, it shall be done to him as he has done:
20 fracture for fracture, eye for eye, tooth for tooth. It
shall be done to him as he has injured someone. 21 He
who kills an animal shall make it good; and he who kills a
man shall be put to death. 22 You shall have one kind of
law for the foreigner as well as the native-born; for I am
God your God.'"
23 Moses spoke to the children of Israel; and they
brought him who had cursed out of the camp, and stoned
him with stones. The children of Israel did as God
commanded Moses.

Leviticus 25

1 God said to Moses in Mount Sinai, 2 "Speak to the
children of Israel, and tell them, 'When you come into the
land which I give you, then the land shall keep a Sabbath
to God. 3 You shall sow your field six years, and you
shall prune your vineyard six years, and gather in its
fruits; 4 but in the seventh year there shall be a Sabbath
of solemn rest for the land, a Sabbath to God. You shall
not sow your field or prune your vineyard. 5 What
grows of itself in your harvest you shall not reap, and you
shall not gather the grapes of your undressed vine. It shall
be a year of solemn rest for the land. 6 The Sabbath of
the land shall be for food for you; for yourself, for your
servant, for your maid, for your hired servant, and for
your stranger, who lives as a foreigner with you. 7 For
your livestock also, and for the animals that are in your
land, shall all its increase be for food.
8 "'You shall count off seven Sabbaths of years, seven
times seven years; and there shall be to you the days of
seven Sabbaths of years, even forty-nine years. 9 Then
you shall sound the loud trumpet on the tenth day of the
seventh month. On the Day of Atonement you shall sound
the trumpet throughout all your land. 10 You shall make
the fiftieth year holy, and proclaim liberty throughout the
land to all its inhabitants. It shall be a jubilee to you; and
each of you shall return to his own property, and each of
you shall return to his family. 11 That fiftieth year shall
be a jubilee to you. In it you shall not sow, neither reap
that which grows of itself, nor gather from the undressed
vines. 12 For it is a jubilee; it shall be holy to you. You
shall eat of its increase out of the field.
13 "'In this Year of Jubilee each of you shall return to
his property.
14 "'If you sell anything to your neighbor, or buy from
your neighbor, you shall not wrong one another.
15 According to the number of years after the Jubilee
you shall buy from your neighbor. According to the
number of years of the crops he shall sell to you.
16 According to the length of the years you shall
increase its price, and according to the shortness of the
years you shall diminish its price; for he is selling the
number of the crops to you. 17 You shall not wrong one
another, but you shall fear your God; for I am God your
God.
18 "'Therefore you shall do my statutes, and keep my
ordinances and do them; and you shall dwell in the land in
safety. 19 The land shall yield its fruit, and you shall eat
your fill, and dwell therein in safety. 20 If you said,
"What shall we eat the seventh year? Behold, we shall not
sow, nor gather in our increase;" 21 then I will
command my blessing on you in the sixth year, and it
shall bear fruit for the three years. 22 You shall sow the
eighth year, and eat of the fruits from the old store until
the ninth year. Until its fruits come in, you shall eat the
old store.
23 "'The land shall not be sold in perpetuity, for the land
is mine; for you are strangers and live as foreigners with
me. 24 In all the land of your possession you shall grant
a redemption for the land.
25 "'If your brother becomes poor, and sells some of his
possessions, then his kinsman who is next to him shall
come, and redeem that which his brother has sold. 26 If
a man has no one to redeem it, and he becomes
prosperous and finds sufficient means to redeem it,
27 then let him reckon the years since its sale, and
restore the surplus to the man to whom he sold it; and he
shall return to his property. 28 But if he isn't able to get
it back for himself, then what he has sold shall remain in
the hand of him who has bought it until the Year of
Jubilee. In the Jubilee it shall be released, and he shall
return to his property.
29 "'If a man sells a dwelling house in a walled city,
then he may redeem it within a whole year after it has
been sold. For a full year he shall have the right of
redemption. 30 If it isn't redeemed within the space of a
full year, then the house that is in the walled city shall be
made sure in perpetuity to him who bought it, throughout
his generations. It shall not be released in the Jubilee.
31 But the houses of the villages which have no wall
around them shall be accounted for with the fields of the
country: they may be redeemed, and they shall be released
in the Jubilee.
32 "'Nevertheless, in the cities of the Levites, the
Levites may redeem the houses in the cities of their
possession at any time. 33 The Levites may redeem the
house that was sold, and the city of his possession, and it
shall be released in the Jubilee; for the houses of the cities
of the Levites are their possession among the children of
Israel. 34 But the field of the pasture lands of their cities
may not be sold, for it is their perpetual possession.
35 "'If your brother has become poor, and his hand can't
support himself among you, then you shall uphold him.
He shall live with you like an alien and a temporary
resident. 36 Take no interest from him or profit; but fear
your God, that your brother may live among you.
37 You shall not lend him your money at interest, nor
give him your food for profit. 38 I am God your God,
who brought you out of the land of Egypt, to give you the
land of Canaan, and to be your God.
39 "'If your brother has grown poor among you, and
sells himself to you, you shall not make him to serve as a
slave. 40 As a hired servant, and as a temporary resident,
he shall be with you; he shall serve with you until the
Year of Jubilee. 41 Then he shall go out from you, he
and his children with him, and shall return to his own
family, and to the possession of his fathers. 42 For they
are my servants, whom I brought out of the land of Egypt.
They shall not be sold as slaves. 43 You shall not rule
over him with harshness, but shall fear your God.
44 "'As for your male and your female slaves, whom
you may have from the nations that are around you, from
them you may buy male and female slaves.
45 Moreover, of the children of the aliens who live
among you, of them you may buy, and of their families
who are with you, which they have conceived in your
land; and they will be your property. 46 You may make
them an inheritance for your children after you, to hold
for a possession. Of them you may take your slaves
forever, but over your brothers the children of Israel you
shall not rule, one over another, with harshness.
47 "'If an alien or temporary resident with you becomes
rich, and your brother beside him has grown poor, and
sells himself to the stranger or foreigner living among
you, or to a member of the stranger's family, 48 after he
is sold he may be redeemed. One of his brothers may
redeem him; 49 or his uncle, or his uncle's son, may
redeem him, or any who is a close relative to him of his
family may redeem him; or if he has grown rich, he may
redeem himself. 50 He shall reckon with him who
bought him from the year that he sold himself to him to
the Year of Jubilee. The price of his sale shall be
according to the number of years; he shall be with him
according to the time of a hired servant. 51 If there are
yet many years, according to them he shall give back the
price of his redemption out of the money that he was
bought for. 52 If there remain but a few years to the year
of jubilee, then he shall reckon with him; according to his

---

[120] **23:34** *23:34* **or, feast of tents, or Succoth**
[121] **23:42** *23:42* **or, booths**
[122] **23:42** *23:42* **or, booths**
[123] **23:43** *23:43* **or, booths**
[124] **24:5** *24:5* **1 ephah is about 22 liters or about 2/3 of a bushel**

years of service he shall give back the price of his redemption. ⁵³ As a servant hired year by year shall he be with him. He shall not rule with harshness over him in your sight. ⁵⁴ If he isn't redeemed by these means, then he shall be released in the Year of Jubilee: he and his children with him. ⁵⁵ For to me the children of Israel are servants; they are my servants whom I brought out of the land of Egypt. I am God your God.

Leviticus 26

¹ "'You shall make for yourselves no idols, and you shall not raise up a carved image or a pillar, and you shall not place any figured stone in your land, to bow down to it; for I am God your God.

² "'You shall keep my Sabbaths, and have reverence for my sanctuary. I am God.

³ "'If you walk in my statutes and keep my commandments, and do them, ⁴ then I will give you your rains in their season, and the land shall yield its increase, and the trees of the field shall yield their fruit.

⁵ Your threshing shall continue until the vintage, and the vintage shall continue until the sowing time. You shall eat your bread to the full, and dwell in your land safely.

⁶ "'I will give peace in the land, and you shall lie down, and no one will make you afraid. I will remove evil animals out of the land, neither shall the sword go through your land. ⁷ You shall chase your enemies, and they shall fall before you by the sword. ⁸ Five of you shall chase a hundred, and a hundred of you shall chase ten thousand; and your enemies shall fall before you by the sword.

⁹ "'I will have respect for you, make you fruitful, multiply you, and will establish my covenant with you.

¹⁰ You shall eat old supplies long kept, and you shall move out the old because of the new. ¹¹ I will set my tent among you, and my soul won't abhor you. ¹² I will walk among you, and will be your God, and you will be my people. ¹³ I am God your God, who brought you out of the land of Egypt, that you should not be their slaves. I have broken the bars of your yoke, and made you walk upright.

¹⁴ "'But if you will not listen to me, and will not do all these commandments, ¹⁵ and if you shall reject my statutes, and if your soul abhors my ordinances, so that you will not do all my commandments, but break my covenant, ¹⁶ I also will do this to you: I will appoint terror over you, even consumption and fever, that shall consume the eyes, and make the soul to pine away. You will sow your seed in vain, for your enemies will eat it.

¹⁷ I will set my face against you, and you will be struck before your enemies. Those who hate you will rule over you; and you will flee when no one pursues.

¹⁸ "'If you in spite of these things will not listen to me, then I will chastise you seven times more for your sins.

¹⁹ I will break the pride of your power, and I will make your sky like iron, and your soil like bronze. ²⁰ Your strength will be spent in vain; for your land won't yield its increase, neither will the trees of the land yield their fruit.

²¹ "'If you walk contrary to me, and won't listen to me, then I will bring seven times more plagues on you according to your sins. ²² I will send the wild animals among you, which will rob you of your children, destroy your livestock, and make you few in number. Your roads will become desolate.

²³ "'If by these things you won't be turned back to me, but will walk contrary to me, ²⁴ then I will also walk contrary to you; and I will strike you, even I, seven times for your sins. ²⁵ I will bring a sword upon you that will execute the vengeance of the covenant. You will be gathered together within your cities, and I will send the pestilence among you. You will be delivered into the hand of the enemy. ²⁶ When I break your staff of bread, ten women shall bake your bread in one oven, and they shall deliver your bread again by weight. You shall eat, and not be satisfied.

²⁷ "'If you in spite of this won't listen to me, but walk contrary to me, ²⁸ then I will walk contrary to you in wrath. I will also chastise you seven times for your sins.

²⁹ You will eat the flesh of your sons, and you will eat the flesh of your daughters. ³⁰ I will destroy your high places, and cut down your incense altars, and cast your dead bodies upon the bodies of your idols; and my soul will abhor you. ³¹ I will lay your cities waste, and will bring your sanctuaries to desolation. I will not take delight in the sweet fragrance of your offerings. ³² I will bring the land into desolation, and your enemies that dwell in it will be astonished at it. ³³ I will scatter you among the nations, and I will draw out the sword after you. Your land will be a desolation, and your cities shall be a waste.

³⁴ Then the land will enjoy its Sabbaths as long as it lies desolate and you are in your enemies' land. Even then the land will rest and enjoy its Sabbaths. ³⁵ As long as it lies desolate it shall have rest, even the rest which it didn't have in your Sabbaths when you lived on it.

³⁶ "'As for those of you who are left, I will send a faintness into their hearts in the lands of their enemies. The sound of a driven leaf will put them to flight; and they shall flee, as one flees from the sword. They will fall when no one pursues. ³⁷ They will stumble over one another, as it were before the sword, when no one pursues. You will have no power to stand before your enemies. ³⁸ You will perish among the nations. The land of your enemies will eat you up. ³⁹ Those of you who are left will pine away in their iniquity in your enemies' lands; and also in the iniquities of their fathers they shall pine away with them.

⁴⁰ "'If they confess their iniquity and the iniquity of their fathers, in their trespass which they trespassed against me; and also that because they walked contrary to me, ⁴¹ I also walked contrary to them, and brought them into the land of their enemies; if then their uncircumcised heart is humbled, and they then accept the punishment of their iniquity, ⁴² then I will remember my covenant with Jacob, my covenant with Isaac, and also my covenant with Abraham; and I will remember the land. ⁴³ The land also will be left by them, and will enjoy its Sabbaths while it lies desolate without them; and they will accept the punishment of their iniquity because they rejected my ordinances, and their soul abhorred my statutes. ⁴⁴ Yet for all that, when they are in the land of their enemies, I will not reject them, neither will I abhor them, to destroy them utterly and to break my covenant with them; for I am God their God. ⁴⁵ But I will for their sake remember the covenant of their ancestors, whom I brought out of the land of Egypt in the sight of the nations, that I might be their God. I am God.'"

⁴⁶ These are the statutes, ordinances, and laws, which God made between him and the children of Israel in Mount Sinai by Moses.

Leviticus 27

¹ God spoke to Moses, saying, ² "Speak to the children of Israel, and say to them, 'When a man consecrates a person to God in a vow, according to your valuation, ³ your valuation of a male from twenty years old to sixty years old shall be fifty shekels of silver, according to the shekel¹²⁵ of the sanctuary. ⁴ If she is a female, then your valuation shall be thirty shekels. ⁵ If the person is from five years old to twenty years old, then your valuation shall be for a male twenty shekels, and for a female ten shekels. ⁶ If the person is from a month old to five years old, then your valuation shall be for a male five shekels of silver, and for a female your valuation shall be three shekels of silver. ⁷ If the person is from sixty years old and upward; if he is a male, then your valuation shall be fifteen shekels, and for a female ten shekels. ⁸ But if he is poorer than your valuation, then he shall be set before the priest, and the priest shall assign a value to him. The priest shall assign a value according to his ability to pay.

⁹ "'If it is an animal of which men offer an offering to God, all that any man gives of such to God becomes holy. ¹⁰ He shall not alter it, nor exchange it, a good for a bad, or a bad for a good. If he shall at all exchange animal for animal, then both it and that for which it is exchanged shall be holy. ¹¹ If it is any unclean animal, of which they do not offer as an offering to God, then he shall set the animal before the priest; ¹² and the priest shall evaluate it, whether it is good or bad. As the priest evaluates it, so it shall be. ¹³ But if he will indeed redeem it, then he shall add the fifth part of it to its valuation.

¹⁴ "'When a man dedicates his house to be holy to God, then the priest shall evaluate it, whether it is good or bad. As the priest evaluates it, so it shall stand. ¹⁵ If he who dedicates it will redeem his house, then he shall add the fifth part of the money of your valuation to it, and it shall be his.

¹⁶ "'If a man dedicates to God part of the field of his possession, then your valuation shall be according to the seed for it. The sowing of a homer ¹²⁶ of barley shall be valued at fifty shekels¹²⁷ of silver. ¹⁷ If he dedicates his field from the Year of Jubilee, according to your valuation it shall stand. ¹⁸ But if he dedicates his field after the Jubilee, then the priest shall reckon to him the money according to the years that remain to the Year of Jubilee; and an abatement shall be made from your valuation.

¹⁹ If he who dedicated the field will indeed redeem it, then he shall add the fifth part of the money of your valuation to it, and it shall remain his. ²⁰ If he will not redeem the field, or if he has sold the field to another man, it shall not be redeemed any more; ²¹ but the field, when it goes out in the Jubilee, shall be holy to God, as a devoted field. It shall be owned by the priests.

²² "'If he dedicates a field to God which he has bought, which is not of the field of his possession, ²³ then the priest shall reckon to him the worth of your valuation up to the Year of Jubilee; and he shall give your valuation on that day, as a holy thing to God. ²⁴ In the Year of Jubilee the field shall return to him from whom it was bought, even to him to whom the possession of the land belongs. ²⁵ All your valuations shall be according to the shekel of the sanctuary: twenty gerahs¹²⁸ to the shekel.¹²⁹

²⁶ "'However the firstborn among animals, which belongs to God as a firstborn, no man may dedicate, whether an ox or a sheep. It is God's. ²⁷ If it is an unclean animal, then he shall buy it back according to your valuation, and shall add to it the fifth part of it; or if it isn't redeemed, then it shall be sold according to your valuation.

²⁸ "'Notwithstanding, no devoted thing that a man devotes to God of all that he has, whether of man or animal, or of the field of his possession, shall be sold or redeemed. Everything that is permanently devoted is most holy to God.

²⁹ "'No one devoted to destruction, who shall be devoted from among men, shall be ransomed. He shall surely be put to death.

³⁰ "'All the tithe of the land, whether of the seed of the land or of the fruit of the trees, is God's. It is holy to God. ³¹ If a man redeems anything of his tithe, he shall add a fifth part to it. ³² All the tithe of the herds or the flocks, whatever passes under the rod, the tenth shall be holy to God. ³³ He shall not examine whether it is good or bad, neither shall he exchange it. If he exchanges it at all, then both it and that for which it is exchanged shall be holy. It shall not be redeemed.'"

³⁴ These are the commandments which God commanded Moses for the children of Israel on Mount Sinai.

---

¹²⁵**27:3** *27:3* A shekel is about 10 grams or about 0.35 ounces.

¹²⁶**27:16** *27:16* 1 homer is about 220 liters or 6 bushels

¹²⁷**27:16** *27:16* A shekel is about 10 grams or about 0.35 ounces.

¹²⁸**27:25** *27:25* A gerah is about 0.5 grams or about 7.7 grains.

¹²⁹**27:25** *27:25* A shekel is about 10 grams or about 0.35 ounces.

The Book of Numbers

Numbers 1

1 God[130] spoke to Moses in the wilderness of Sinai, in the Tent
of Meeting, on the first day of the second month, in the second
year after they had come out of the land of Egypt, saying,
2 "Take a census of all the congregation of the children of Israel,
by their families, by their fathers' houses, according to the
number of the names, every male, one by one, 3 from twenty
years old and upward, all who are able to go out to war in Israel.
You and Aaron shall count them by their divisions. 4 With you
there shall be a man of every tribe, each one head of his fathers'
house. 5 These are the names of the men who shall stand with
you:
Of Reuben: Elizur the son of Shedeur.
6 Of Simeon: Shelumiel the son of Zurishaddai.
7 Of Judah: Nahshon the son of Amminadab.
8 Of Issachar: Nethanel the son of Zuar.
9 Of Zebulun: Eliab the son of Helon.
10 Of the children of Joseph: of Ephraim: Elishama the son of
Ammihud; of Manasseh: Gamaliel the son of Pedahzur.
11 Of Benjamin: Abidan the son of Gideoni.
12 Of Dan: Ahiezer the son of Ammishaddai.
13 Of Asher: Pagiel the son of Ochran.
14 Of Gad: Eliasaph the son of Deuel.
15 Of Naphtali: Ahira the son of Enan."
16 These are those who were called of the congregation, the
princes[131] of the tribes of their fathers; they were the heads of the
thousands of Israel. 17 Moses and Aaron took these men who are
mentioned by name. 18 They assembled all the congregation
together on the first day of the second month; and they declared
their ancestry by their families, by their fathers' houses,
according to the number of the names, from twenty years old and
upward, one by one. 19 As God commanded Moses, so he
counted them in the wilderness of Sinai.
20 The children of Reuben, Israel's firstborn, their generations,
by their families, by their fathers' houses, according to the
number of the names, one by one, every male from twenty years
old and upward, all who were able to go out to war: 21 those
who were counted of them, of the tribe of Reuben, were forty-six
thousand five hundred.
22 Of the children of Simeon, their generations, by their
families, by their fathers' houses, those who were counted of it,
according to the number of the names, one by one, every male
from twenty years old and upward, all who were able to go out to
war: 23 those who were counted of them, of the tribe of Simeon,
were fifty-nine thousand three hundred.
24 Of the children of Gad, their generations, by their families, by
their fathers' houses, according to the number of the names, from
twenty years old and upward, all who were able to go out to war:
25 those who were counted of them, of the tribe of Gad, were
forty-five thousand six hundred fifty.
26 Of the children of Judah, their generations, by their families,
by their fathers' houses, according to the number of the names,
from twenty years old and upward, all who were able to go out to
war: 27 those who were counted of them, of the tribe of Judah,
were seventy-four thousand six hundred.
28 Of the children of Issachar, their generations, by their
families, by their fathers' houses, according to the number of the
names, from twenty years old and upward, all who were able to
go out to war: 29 those who were counted of them, of the tribe of
Issachar, were fifty-four thousand four hundred.
30 Of the children of Zebulun, their generations, by their
families, by their fathers' houses, according to the number of the
names, from twenty years old and upward, all who were able to
go out to war: 31 those who were counted of them, of the tribe of
Zebulun, were fifty-seven thousand four hundred.
32 Of the children of Joseph: of the children of Ephraim, their
generations, by their families, by their fathers' houses, according
to the number of the names, from twenty years old and upward,
all who were able to go out to war: 33 those who were counted
of them, of the tribe of Ephraim, were forty thousand five
hundred.
34 Of the children of Manasseh, their generations, by their
families, by their fathers' houses, according to the number of the
names, from twenty years old and upward, all who were able to
go out to war: 35 those who were counted of them, of the tribe of
Manasseh, were thirty-two thousand two hundred.
36 Of the children of Benjamin, their generations, by their
families, by their fathers' houses, according to the number of the
names, from twenty years old and upward, all who were able to
go out to war: 37 those who were counted of them, of the tribe of
Benjamin, were thirty-five thousand four hundred.
38 Of the children of Dan, their generations, by their families, by
their fathers' houses, according to the number of the names, from
twenty years old and upward, all who were able to go out to war:
39 those who were counted of them, of the tribe of Dan, were
sixty-two thousand seven hundred.
40 Of the children of Asher, their generations, by their families,
by their fathers' houses, according to the number of the names,
from twenty years old and upward, all who were able to go out to
war: 41 those who were counted of them, of the tribe of Asher,
were forty-one thousand five hundred.
42 Of the children of Naphtali, their generations, by their
families, by their fathers' houses, according to the number of the
names, from twenty years old and upward, all who were able to
go out to war: 43 those who were counted of them, of the tribe of
Naphtali, were fifty-three thousand four hundred.
44 These are those who were counted, whom Moses and Aaron
counted, and the twelve men who were princes of Israel, each one
for his fathers' house. 45 So all those who were counted of the
children of Israel by their fathers' houses, from twenty years old
and upward, all who were able to go out to war in Israel— 46 all
those who were counted were six hundred three thousand five
hundred fifty. 47 But the Levites after the tribe of their fathers
were not counted among them. 48 For God spoke to Moses,
saying, 49 "Only the tribe of Levi you shall not count, neither
shall you take a census of them among the children of Israel;
50 but appoint the Levites over the Tabernacle of the Testimony,
and over all its furnishings, and over all that belongs to it. They
shall carry the tabernacle and all its furnishings; and they shall
take care of it, and shall encamp around it. 51 When the
tabernacle is to move, the Levites shall take it down; and when
the tabernacle is to be set up, the Levites shall set it up. The
stranger who comes near shall be put to death. 52 The children
of Israel shall pitch their tents, every man by his own camp, and
every man by his own standard, according to their divisions.
53 But the Levites shall encamp around the Tabernacle of the
Testimony, that there may be no wrath on the congregation of the
children of Israel. The Levites shall be responsible for the
Tabernacle of the Testimony."
54 Thus the children of Israel did. According to all that God
commanded Moses, so they did.

Numbers 2

1 God spoke to Moses and to Aaron, saying, 2 "The children of
Israel shall encamp every man by his own standard, with the
banners of their fathers' houses. They shall encamp around the
Tent of Meeting at a distance from it."
3 Those who encamp on the east side toward the sunrise shall be
of the standard of the camp of Judah, according to their divisions.
The prince of the children of Judah shall be Nahshon the son of
Amminadab. 4 His division, and those who were counted of
them, were seventy-four thousand six hundred.
5 Those who encamp next to him shall be the tribe of Issachar.
The prince of the children of Issachar shall be Nethanel the son of
Zuar. 6 His division, and those who were counted of it, were
fifty-four thousand four hundred.
7 The tribe of Zebulun: the prince of the children of Zebulun
shall be Eliab the son of Helon. 8 His division, and those who
were counted of it, were fifty-seven thousand four hundred.
9 All who were counted of the camp of Judah were one hundred
eighty-six thousand four hundred, according to their divisions.
They shall set out first.
10 "On the south side shall be the standard of the camp of
Reuben according to their divisions. The prince of the children of
Reuben shall be Elizur the son of Shedeur. 11 His division, and
those who were counted of it, were forty-six thousand five
hundred.
12 "Those who encamp next to him shall be the tribe of Simeon.
The prince of the children of Simeon shall be Shelumiel the son
of Zurishaddai. 13 His division, and those who were counted of
them, were fifty-nine thousand three hundred.
14 "The tribe of Gad: the prince of the children of Gad shall be
Eliasaph the son of Reuel. 15 His division, and those who were
counted of them, were forty-five thousand six hundred fifty.
16 "All who were counted of the camp of Reuben were one
hundred fifty-one thousand four hundred fifty, according to their
armies. They shall set out second.
17 "Then the Tent of Meeting shall set out, with the camp of the
Levites in the middle of the camps. As they encamp, so shall they
set out, every man in his place, by their standards.
18 "On the west side shall be the standard of the camp of
Ephraim according to their divisions. The prince of the children
of Ephraim shall be Elishama the son of Ammihud. 19 His
division, and those who were counted of them, were forty
thousand five hundred.
20 "Next to him shall be the tribe of Manasseh. The prince of the
children of Manasseh shall be Gamaliel the son of Pedahzur.
21 His division, and those who were counted of them, were
thirty-two thousand two hundred.
22 "The tribe of Benjamin: the prince of the children of
Benjamin shall be Abidan the son of Gideoni. 23 His army, and
those who were counted of them, were thirty-five thousand four
hundred.
24 "All who were counted of the camp of Ephraim were one
hundred eight thousand one hundred, according to their divisions.
They shall set out third.
25 "On the north side shall be the standard of the camp of Dan
according to their divisions. The prince of the children of Dan
shall be Ahiezer the son of Ammishaddai. 26 His division, and
those who were counted of them, were sixty-two thousand seven
hundred.
27 "Those who encamp next to him shall be the tribe of Asher.
The prince of the children of Asher shall be Pagiel the son of
Ochran. 28 His division, and those who were counted of them,
were forty-one thousand and five hundred.
29 "The tribe of Naphtali: the prince of the children of Naphtali
shall be Ahira the son of Enan. 30 His division, and those who
were counted of them, were fifty-three thousand four hundred.
31 "All who were counted of the camp of Dan were one hundred
fifty-seven thousand six hundred. They shall set out last by their
standards."
32 These are those who were counted of the children of Israel by
their fathers' houses. All who were counted of the camps
according to their armies were six hundred three thousand five
hundred fifty. 33 But the Levites were not counted among the
children of Israel, as God commanded Moses.
34 Thus the children of Israel did. According to all that God
commanded Moses, so they encamped by their standards, and so
they set out, everyone by their families, according to their
fathers' houses.

Numbers 3

1 Now this is the history of the generations of Aaron and Moses
in the day that God spoke with Moses in Mount Sinai. 2 These
are the names of the sons of Aaron: Nadab the firstborn, and
Abihu, Eleazar, and Ithamar.
3 These are the names of the sons of Aaron, the priests who were
anointed, whom he consecrated to minister in the priest's office.
4 Nadab and Abihu died before God when they offered strange
fire before God in the wilderness of Sinai, and they had no
children. Eleazar and Ithamar ministered in the priest's office in
the presence of Aaron their father.
5 God spoke to Moses, saying, 6 "Bring the tribe of Levi near,
and set them before Aaron the priest, that they may minister to
him. 7 They shall keep his requirements, and the requirements of
the whole congregation before the Tent of Meeting, to do the
service of the tabernacle. 8 They shall keep all the furnishings of
the Tent of Meeting, and the obligations of the children of Israel,
to do the service of the tabernacle. 9 You shall give the Levites
to Aaron and to his sons. They are wholly given to him on the
behalf of the children of Israel. 10 You shall appoint Aaron and

[130] **1:1** *1:1* "God" is God's proper Name, sometimes rendered "LORD" (all caps) in other translations.

[131] **1:16** *1:16* or, chiefs, or, leaders

his sons, and they shall keep their priesthood, but the stranger
who comes near shall be put to death."
11 God spoke to Moses, saying, 12 "Behold,[132] I have taken the
Levites from among the children of Israel instead of all the
firstborn who open the womb among the children of Israel; and
the Levites shall be mine, 13 for all the firstborn are mine. On
the day that I struck down all the firstborn in the land of Egypt I
made holy to me all the firstborn in Israel, both man and animal.
They shall be mine. I am God."
14 God spoke to Moses in the wilderness of Sinai, saying,
15 "Count the children of Levi by their fathers' houses, by their
families. You shall count every male from a month old and
upward."
16 Moses counted them according to God's word, as he was
commanded.
17 These were the sons of Levi by their names: Gershon,
Kohath, and Merari.
18 These are the names of the sons of Gershon by their families:
Libni and Shimei.
19 The sons of Kohath by their families: Amram, Izhar, Hebron,
and Uzziel.
20 The sons of Merari by their families: Mahli and Mushi.
These are the families of the Levites according to their fathers'
houses.
21 Of Gershon was the family of the Libnites, and the family of
the Shimeites. These are the families of the Gershonites.
22 Those who were counted of them, according to the number of
all the males from a month old and upward, even those who were
counted of them were seven thousand five hundred.
23 The families of the Gershonites shall encamp behind the
tabernacle westward.
24 Eliasaph the son of Lael shall be the prince of the fathers'
house of the Gershonites. 25 The duty of the sons of Gershon in
the Tent of Meeting shall be the tabernacle, the tent, its covering,
the screen for the door of the Tent of Meeting, 26 the hangings
of the court, the screen for the door of the court which is by the
tabernacle and around the altar, and its cords for all of its service.
27 Of Kohath was the family of the Amramites, the family of the
Izharites, the family of the Hebronites, and the family of the
Uzzielites. These are the families of the Kohathites.
28 According to the number of all the males from a month old
and upward, there were eight thousand six hundred keeping the
requirements of the sanctuary.
29 The families of the sons of Kohath shall encamp on the south
side of the tabernacle. 30 The prince of the fathers' house of the
families of the Kohathites shall be Elizaphan the son of Uzziel.
31 Their duty shall be the ark, the table, the lamp stand, the
altars, the vessels of the sanctuary with which they minister, the
screen, and all its service. 32 Eleazar the son of Aaron the priest
shall be prince of the princes of the Levites, with the oversight of
those who keep the requirements of the sanctuary.
33 Of Merari was the family of the Mahlites and the family of
the Mushites. These are the families of Merari. 34 Those who
were counted of them, according to the number of all the males
from a month old and upward, were six thousand two hundred.[133]
35 The prince of the fathers' house of the families of Merari was
Zuriel the son of Abihail. They shall encamp on the north side of
the tabernacle. 36 The appointed duty of the sons of Merari shall
be the tabernacle's boards, its bars, its pillars, its sockets, all its
instruments, all its service, 37 the pillars of the court around it,
their sockets, their pins, and their cords. 38 Those who encamp
before the tabernacle eastward, in front of the Tent of Meeting
toward the sunrise, shall be Moses, and Aaron and his sons,
keeping the requirements of the sanctuary for the duty of the
children of Israel. The outsider who comes near shall be put to
death. 39 All who were counted of the Levites, whom Moses and
Aaron counted at the commandment of God, by their families, all
the males from a month old and upward, were twenty-two
thousand.
40 God said to Moses, "Count all the firstborn males of the
children of Israel from a month old and upward, and take the
number of their names. 41 You shall take the Levites for me—I
am God—instead of all the firstborn among the children of Israel;
and the livestock of the Levites instead of all the firstborn among
the livestock of the children of Israel."
42 Moses counted, as God commanded him, all the firstborn
among the children of Israel. 43 All the firstborn males
according to the number of names from a month old and upward,
of those who were counted of them, were twenty-two thousand
two hundred seventy-three.
44 God spoke to Moses, saying, 45 "Take the Levites instead of
all the firstborn among the children of Israel, and the livestock of
the Levites instead of their livestock; and the Levites shall be
mine. I am God. 46 For the redemption of the two hundred
seventy-three of the firstborn of the children of Israel who exceed
the number of the Levites, 47 you shall take five shekels apiece
for each one; according to the shekel[134] of the sanctuary you shall
take them (the shekel is twenty gerahs[135]); 48 and you shall give
the money, with which their remainder is redeemed, to Aaron and
to his sons."
49 Moses took the redemption money from those who exceeded
the number of those who were redeemed by the Levites; 50 from
the firstborn of the children of Israel he took the money, one
thousand three hundred sixty-five shekels,[136] according to the
shekel of the sanctuary; 51 and Moses gave the redemption
money to Aaron and to his sons, according to God's word, as
God commanded Moses.

Numbers 4

1 God spoke to Moses and to Aaron, saying, 2 "Take a census
of the sons of Kohath from among the sons of Levi, by their
families, by their fathers' houses, 3 from thirty years old and
upward even until fifty years old, all who enter into the service to
do the work in the Tent of Meeting.
4 "This is the service of the sons of Kohath in the Tent of
Meeting, regarding the most holy things. 5 When the camp
moves forward, Aaron shall go in with his sons; and they shall
take down the veil of the screen, cover the ark of the Testimony
with it, 6 put a covering of sealskin on it, spread a blue cloth
over it, and put in its poles.
7 "On the table of show bread they shall spread a blue cloth, and
put on it the dishes, the spoons, the bowls, and the cups with
which to pour out; and the continual bread shall be on it. 8 They
shall spread on them a scarlet cloth, and cover it with a covering
of sealskin, and shall put in its poles.
9 "They shall take a blue cloth and cover the lamp stand of the
light, its lamps, its snuffers, its snuff dishes, and all its oil vessels,
with which they minister to it. 10 They shall put it and all its
vessels within a covering of sealskin, and shall put it on the
frame.
11 "On the golden altar they shall spread a blue cloth, and cover
it with a covering of sealskin, and shall put in its poles.
12 "They shall take all the vessels of ministry with which they
minister in the sanctuary, and put them in a blue cloth, cover
them with a covering of sealskin, and shall put them on the
frame.
13 "They shall take away the ashes from the altar, and spread a
purple cloth on it. 14 They shall put on it all its vessels with
which they minister about it, the fire pans, the meat hooks, the
shovels, and the basins—all the vessels of the altar; and they shall
spread on it a covering of sealskin, and put in its poles.
15 "When Aaron and his sons have finished covering the
sanctuary and all the furniture of the sanctuary, as the camp
moves forward; after that, the sons of Kohath shall come to carry
it; but they shall not touch the sanctuary, lest they die. The sons
of Kohath shall carry these things belonging to the Tent of
Meeting.
16 "The duty of Eleazar the son of Aaron the priest shall be the
oil for the light, the sweet incense, the continual meal offering,
and the anointing oil, the requirements of all the tabernacle, and
of all that is in it, the sanctuary, and its furnishings."
17 God spoke to Moses and to Aaron, saying, 18 "Don't cut off
the tribe of the families of the Kohathites from among the
Levites; 19 but thus do to them, that they may live, and not die,
when they approach the most holy things: Aaron and his sons
shall go in and appoint everyone to his service and to his burden;
20 but they shall not go in to see the sanctuary even for a
moment, lest they die."
21 God spoke to Moses, saying, 22 "Take a census of the sons
of Gershon also, by their fathers' houses, by their families;
23 you shall count them from thirty years old and upward until
fifty years old: all who enter in to wait on the service, to do the
work in the Tent of Meeting.
24 "This is the service of the families of the Gershonites, in
serving and in bearing burdens: 25 they shall carry the curtains
of the tabernacle and the Tent of Meeting, its covering, the
covering of sealskin that is on it, the screen for the door of the
Tent of Meeting, 26 the hangings of the court, the screen for the
door of the gate of the court which is by the tabernacle and
around the altar, their cords, and all the instruments of their
service, and whatever shall be done with them. They shall serve
in there. 27 At the commandment of Aaron and his sons shall be
all the service of the sons of the Gershonites, in all their burden
and in all their service; and you shall appoint their duty to them
in all their responsibilities. 28 This is the service of the families
of the sons of the Gershonites in the Tent of Meeting. Their duty
shall be under the hand of Ithamar the son of Aaron the priest.
29 "As for the sons of Merari, you shall count them by their
families, by their fathers' houses; 30 you shall count them from
thirty years old and upward even to fifty years old—everyone
who enters on the service, to do the work of the Tent of Meeting.
31 This is the duty of their burden, according to all their service
in the Tent of Meeting: the tabernacle's boards, its bars, its
pillars, its sockets, 32 the pillars of the court around it, their
sockets, their pins, their cords, with all their instruments, and
with all their service. You shall appoint the instruments of the
duty of their burden to them by name. 33 This is the service of
the families of the sons of Merari, according to all their service in
the Tent of Meeting, under the hand of Ithamar the son of Aaron
the priest."
34 Moses and Aaron and the princes of the congregation counted
the sons of the Kohathites by their families, and by their fathers'
houses, 35 from thirty years old and upward even to fifty years
old, everyone who entered into the service for work in the Tent of
Meeting. 36 Those who were counted of them by their families
were two thousand seven hundred fifty. 37 These are those who
were counted of the families of the Kohathites, all who served in
the Tent of Meeting, whom Moses and Aaron counted according
to the commandment of God by Moses.
38 Those who were counted of the sons of Gershon, by their
families, and by their fathers' houses, 39 from thirty years old
and upward even to fifty years old—everyone who entered into
the service for work in the Tent of Meeting, 40 even those who
were counted of them, by their families, by their fathers' houses,
were two thousand six hundred thirty. 41 These are those who
were counted of the families of the sons of Gershon, all who
served in the Tent of Meeting, whom Moses and Aaron counted
according to the commandment of God.
42 Those who were counted of the families of the sons of
Merari, by their families, by their fathers' houses, 43 from thirty
years old and upward even to fifty years old—everyone who
entered into the service for work in the Tent of Meeting, 44 even
those who were counted of them by their families, were three
thousand two hundred. 45 These are those who were counted of
the families of the sons of Merari, whom Moses and Aaron
counted according to the commandment of God by Moses.
46 All those who were counted of the Levites whom Moses and
Aaron and the princes of Israel counted, by their families and by
their fathers' houses, 47 from thirty years old and upward even
to fifty years old, everyone who entered in to do the work of
service and the work of bearing burdens in the Tent of Meeting,
48 even those who were counted of them, were eight thousand
five hundred eighty. 49 According to the commandment of God
they were counted by Moses, everyone according to his service
and according to his burden. Thus they were counted by him, as
God commanded Moses.

Numbers 5

1 God spoke to Moses, saying, 2 "Command the children of
Israel that they put out of the camp every leper, everyone who
has a discharge, and whoever is unclean by a corpse. 3 You shall
put both male and female outside of the camp so that they don't
defile their camp, in the midst of which I dwell."
4 The children of Israel did so, and put them outside of the
camp; as God spoke to Moses, so the children of Israel did.

---

[132]**3:12** *3:12* "Behold", from "הִנֵּה", means look at, take notice, observe, see, or gaze at. It is often used as an interjection.

[133]**3:34** *3:34* + 22,000 is the sum rounded to 2 significant digits. The sum of the Gershonites, Kohathites, and Merarites given above is 22,300, but the traditional Hebrew text has the number rounded to 2 significant digits, not 3 significant digits.

[134]**3:47** *3:47* A shekel is about 10 grams or about 0.35 ounces.

[135]**3:47** *3:47* A gerah is about 0.5 grams or about 7.7 grains.

[136]**3:50** *3:50* A shekel is about 10 grams or about 0.35 ounces, so 1365 shekels is about 13.65 kilograms or about 30 pounds.

5 God spoke to Moses, saying, 6 "Speak to the children of
Israel: 'When a man or woman commits any sin that men
commit, so as to trespass against God, and that soul is guilty,
7 then he shall confess his sin which he has done; and he shall
make restitution for his guilt in full, add to it the fifth part of it,
and give it to him in respect of whom he has been guilty. 8 But if
the man has no kinsman to whom restitution may be made for the
guilt, the restitution for guilt which is made to God shall be the
priest's, in addition to the ram of the atonement, by which
atonement shall be made for him. 9 Every heave offering of all
the holy things of the children of Israel, which they present to the
priest, shall be his. 10 Every man's holy things shall be his;
whatever any man gives the priest, it shall be his.'"
11 God spoke to Moses, saying, 12 "Speak to the children of
Israel, and tell them: 'If any man's wife goes astray and is
unfaithful to him, 13 and a man lies with her carnally, and it is
hidden from the eyes of her husband and this is kept concealed,
and she is defiled, there is no witness against her, and she isn't
taken in the act; 14 and the spirit of jealousy comes on him, and
he is jealous of his wife and she is defiled; or if the spirit of
jealousy comes on him, and he is jealous of his wife and she isn't
defiled; 15 then the man shall bring his wife to the priest, and
shall bring her offering for her: one tenth of an ephah[137] of barley
meal. He shall pour no oil on it, nor put frankincense on it, for it
is a meal offering of jealousy, a meal offering of memorial,
bringing iniquity to memory. 16 The priest shall bring her near,
and set her before God. 17 The priest shall take holy water in an
earthen vessel; and the priest shall take some of the dust that is on
the floor of the tabernacle and put it into the water. 18 The priest
shall set the woman before God, and let the hair of the woman's
head go loose, and put the meal offering of memorial in her
hands, which is the meal offering of jealousy. The priest shall
have in his hand the water of bitterness that brings a curse.
19 The priest shall cause her to take an oath and shall tell the
woman, "If no man has lain with you, and if you haven't gone
aside to uncleanness, being under your husband's authority, be
free from this water of bitterness that brings a curse. 20 But if
you have gone astray, being under your husband's authority, and
if you are defiled, and some man has lain with you besides your
husband—" 21 then the priest shall cause the woman to swear
with the oath of cursing, and the priest shall tell the woman,
"May God make you a curse and an oath among your people,
when God allows your thigh to fall away, and your body to swell;
22 and this water that brings a curse will go into your bowels,
and make your body swell, and your thigh fall away." The
woman shall say, "Amen, Amen."
23 "'The priest shall write these curses in a book, and he shall
wipe them into the water of bitterness. 24 He shall make the
woman drink the water of bitterness that causes the curse; and the
water that causes the curse shall enter into her and become bitter.
25 The priest shall take the meal offering of jealousy out of the
woman's hand, and shall wave the meal offering before God, and
bring it to the altar. 26 The priest shall take a handful of the meal
offering, as its memorial portion, and burn it on the altar, and
afterward shall make the woman drink the water. 27 When he
has made her drink the water, then it shall happen, if she is
defiled and has committed a trespass against her husband, that the
water that causes the curse will enter into her and become bitter,
and her body will swell, and her thigh will fall away; and the
woman will be a curse among her people. 28 If the woman isn't
defiled, but is clean; then she shall be free, and shall conceive
offspring.[138]
29 "'This is the law of jealousy, when a wife, being under her
husband, goes astray, and is defiled, 30 or when the spirit of
jealousy comes on a man, and he is jealous of his wife; then he
shall set the woman before God, and the priest shall execute on
her all this law. 31 The man shall be free from iniquity, and that
woman shall bear her iniquity.'"

Numbers 6

1 God spoke to Moses, saying, 2 "Speak to the children of
Israel, and tell them: 'When either man or woman shall make a
special vow, the vow of a Nazirite, to separate himself to God,
3 he shall separate himself from wine and strong drink. He shall
drink no vinegar of wine, or vinegar of fermented drink, neither
shall he drink any juice of grapes, nor eat fresh grapes or dried.
4 All the days of his separation he shall eat nothing that is made
of the grapevine, from the seeds even to the skins.
5 "'All the days of his vow of separation no razor shall come on
his head, until the days are fulfilled in which he separates himself
to God. He shall be holy. He shall let the locks of the hair of his
head grow long.
6 "'All the days that he separates himself to God he shall not go
near a dead body. 7 He shall not make himself unclean for his
father, or for his mother, for his brother, or for his sister, when
they die, because his separation to God[139] is on his head. 8 All
the days of his separation he is holy to God.
9 "'If any man dies very suddenly beside him, and he defiles the
head of his separation, then he shall shave his head in the day of
his cleansing. On the seventh day he shall shave it. 10 On the
eighth day he shall bring two turtledoves or two young pigeons to
the priest, to the door of the Tent of Meeting. 11 The priest shall
offer one for a sin offering, and the other for a burnt offering, and
make atonement for him, because he sinned by reason of the
dead, and shall make his head holy that same day. 12 He shall
separate to God the days of his separation, and shall bring a male
lamb a year old for a trespass offering; but the former days shall
be void, because his separation was defiled.
13 "'This is the law of the Nazirite: when the days of his
separation are fulfilled, he shall be brought to the door of the
Tent of Meeting, 14 and he shall offer his offering to God: one
male lamb a year old without defect for a burnt offering, one ewe
lamb a year old without defect for a sin offering, one ram without
defect for peace offerings, 15 a basket of unleavened bread,
cakes of fine flour mixed with oil, and unleavened wafers
anointed with oil with their meal offering and their drink
offerings. 16 The priest shall present them before God, and shall
offer his sin offering and his burnt offering. 17 He shall offer the
ram for a sacrifice of peace offerings to God, with the basket of
unleavened bread. The priest shall offer also its meal offering and
its drink offering. 18 The Nazirite shall shave the head of his
separation at the door of the Tent of Meeting, take the hair of the
head of his separation, and put it on the fire which is under the
sacrifice of peace offerings. 19 The priest shall take the boiled
shoulder of the ram, one unleavened cake out of the basket, and
one unleavened wafer, and shall put them on the hands of the
Nazirite after he has shaved the head of his separation; 20 and
the priest shall wave them for a wave offering before God. They
are holy for the priest, together with the breast that is waved and
the thigh that is offered. After that the Nazirite may drink wine.
21 "'This is the law of the Nazirite who vows and of his offering
to God for his separation, in addition to that which he is able to
afford. According to his vow which he vows, so he must do after
the law of his separation.'"
22 God spoke to Moses, saying, 23 "Speak to Aaron and to his
sons, saying, 'This is how you shall bless the children of Israel.'
You shall tell them,
24 'God bless you, and keep you.
25 God make his face to shine on you,
and be gracious to you.
26 God lift up his face toward you,
and give you peace.'
27 "So they shall put my name on the children of Israel; and I
will bless them."

Numbers 7

1 On the day that Moses had finished setting up the tabernacle,
and had anointed it and sanctified it with all its furniture, and the
altar with all its vessels, and had anointed and sanctified them;
2 the princes of Israel, the heads of their fathers' houses, offered.
These were the princes of the tribes. These are they who were
over those who were counted; 3 and they brought their offering
before God, six covered wagons and twelve oxen; a wagon for
every two of the princes, and for each one an ox. They presented
them before the tabernacle. 4 God spoke to Moses, saying,
5 "Accept these from them, that they may be used in doing the
service of the Tent of Meeting; and you shall give them to the
Levites, to every man according to his service."
6 Moses took the wagons and the oxen, and gave them to the
Levites. 7 He gave two wagons and four oxen to the sons of
Gershon, according to their service. 8 He gave four wagons and
eight oxen to the sons of Merari, according to their service, under
the direction of Ithamar the son of Aaron the priest. 9 But to the
sons of Kohath he gave none, because the service of the
sanctuary belonged to them; they carried it on their shoulders.
10 The princes gave offerings for the dedication of the altar in
the day that it was anointed. The princes gave their offerings
before the altar.
11 God said to Moses, "They shall offer their offering, each
prince on his day, for the dedication of the altar."
12 He who offered his offering the first day was Nahshon the
son of Amminadab, of the tribe of Judah, 13 and his offering
was:
one silver platter, the weight of which was one hundred thirty
shekels,[140]
one silver bowl of seventy shekels, according to the shekel of the
sanctuary; both of them full of fine flour mixed with oil for a
meal offering;
14 one golden ladle of ten shekels, full of incense;
15 one young bull,
one ram,
one male lamb a year old, for a burnt offering;
16 one male goat for a sin offering;
17 and for the sacrifice of peace offerings, two head of cattle,
five rams, five male goats, and five male lambs a year old. This
was the offering of Nahshon the son of Amminadab.
18 On the second day Nethanel the son of Zuar, prince of
Issachar, gave his offering. 19 He offered for his offering:
one silver platter, the weight of which was one hundred thirty
shekels,
one silver bowl of seventy shekels, according to the shekel of the
sanctuary; both of them full of fine flour mixed with oil for a
meal offering;
20 one golden ladle of ten shekels, full of incense;
21 one young bull,
one ram,
one male lamb a year old, for a burnt offering;
22 one male goat for a sin offering;
23 and for the sacrifice of peace offerings, two head of cattle,
five rams, five male goats, five male lambs a year old. This was
the offering of Nethanel the son of Zuar.
24 On the third day Eliab the son of Helon, prince of the children
of Zebulun, 25 gave his offering:
one silver platter, the weight of which was a hundred and thirty
shekels,
one silver bowl of seventy shekels, according to the shekel of the
sanctuary; both of them full of fine flour mixed with oil for a
meal offering;
26 one golden ladle of ten shekels, full of incense;
27 one young bull,
one ram,
one male lamb a year old, for a burnt offering;
28 one male goat for a sin offering;
29 and for the sacrifice of peace offerings, two head of cattle,
five rams, five male goats, and five male lambs a year old. This
was the offering of Eliab the son of Helon.
30 On the fourth day Elizur the son of Shedeur, prince of the
children of Reuben, 31 gave his offering:
one silver platter, the weight of which was one hundred thirty
shekels,
one silver bowl of seventy shekels, according to the shekel of the
sanctuary; both of them full of fine flour mixed with oil for a
meal offering;
32 one golden ladle of ten shekels, full of incense;
33 one young bull,
one ram,
one male lamb a year old, for a burnt offering;
34 one male goat for a sin offering;
35 and for the sacrifice of peace offerings, two head of cattle,
five rams, five male goats, and five male lambs a year old. This
was the offering of Elizur the son of Shedeur.
36 On the fifth day Shelumiel the son of Zurishaddai, prince of
the children of Simeon, 37 gave his offering:
one silver platter, the weight of which was one hundred thirty
shekels,
one silver bowl of seventy shekels, according to the shekel of the
sanctuary; both of them full of fine flour mixed with oil for a
meal offering;
38 one golden ladle of ten shekels, full of incense;
39 one young bull,
one ram,
one male lamb a year old, for a burnt offering;
40 one male goat for a sin offering;

---

[137] **5:15** *5:15* 1 ephah is about 22 liters or about 2/3 of a bushel

[138] **5:28** *5:28* or, seed

[139] **6:7** *6:7* The Hebrew word rendered "God" is "אֱלֹהִים" (Elohim).

[140] **7:13** *7:13* A shekel is about 10 grams or about 0.35 ounces.

41 and for the sacrifice of peace offerings, two head of cattle,
five rams, five male goats, and five male lambs a year old: this
was the offering of Shelumiel the son of Zurishaddai.
42 On the sixth day, Eliasaph the son of Deuel, prince of the
children of Gad, **43** gave his offering:
one silver platter, the weight of which was one hundred thirty
shekels,
one silver bowl of seventy shekels, according to the shekel of the
sanctuary; both of them full of fine flour mixed with oil for a
meal offering;
44 one golden ladle of ten shekels, full of incense;
45 one young bull,
one ram,
one male lamb a year old, for a burnt offering;
46 one male goat for a sin offering;
47 and for the sacrifice of peace offerings, two head of cattle,
five rams, five male goats, and five male lambs a year old. This
was the offering of Eliasaph the son of Deuel.
48 On the seventh day Elishama the son of Ammihud, prince of
the children of Ephraim, **49** gave his offering:
one silver platter, the weight of which was one hundred thirty
shekels,
one silver bowl of seventy shekels, according to the shekel of the
sanctuary; both of them full of fine flour mixed with oil for a
meal offering;
50 one golden ladle of ten shekels, full of incense;
51 one young bull,
one ram,
one male lamb a year old, for a burnt offering;
52 one male goat for a sin offering;
53 and for the sacrifice of peace offerings, two head of cattle,
five rams, five male goats, and five male lambs a year old. This
was the offering of Elishama the son of Ammihud.
54 On the eighth day Gamaliel the son of Pedahzur, prince of the
children of Manasseh, **55** gave his offering:
one silver platter, the weight of which was one hundred thirty
shekels,
one silver bowl of seventy shekels, according to the shekel of the
sanctuary; both of them full of fine flour mixed with oil for a
meal offering;
56 one golden ladle of ten shekels, full of incense;
57 one young bull,
one ram,
one male lamb a year old, for a burnt offering;
58 one male goat for a sin offering;
59 and for the sacrifice of peace offerings, two head of cattle,
five rams, five male goats, and five male lambs a year old. This
was the offering of Gamaliel the son of Pedahzur.
60 On the ninth day Abidan the son of Gideoni, prince of the
children of Benjamin, **61** gave his offering:
one silver platter, the weight of which was one hundred thirty
shekels,
one silver bowl of seventy shekels, according to the shekel of the
sanctuary; both of them full of fine flour mixed with oil for a
meal offering;
62 one golden ladle of ten shekels, full of incense;
63 one young bull,
one ram,
one male lamb a year old, for a burnt offering;
64 one male goat for a sin offering;
65 and for the sacrifice of peace offerings, two head of cattle,
five rams, five male goats, and five male lambs a year old. This
was the offering of Abidan the son of Gideoni.
66 On the tenth day Ahiezer the son of Ammishaddai, prince of
the children of Dan, **67** gave his offering:
one silver platter, the weight of which was one hundred thirty
shekels,
one silver bowl of seventy shekels, according to the shekel of the
sanctuary; both of them full of fine flour mixed with oil for a
meal offering;
68 one golden ladle of ten shekels, full of incense;
69 one young bull,
one ram,
one male lamb a year old, for a burnt offering;
70 one male goat for a sin offering;
71 and for the sacrifice of peace offerings, two head of cattle,
five rams, five male goats, and five male lambs a year old. This
was the offering of Ahiezer the son of Ammishaddai.
72 On the eleventh day Pagiel the son of Ochran, prince of the
children of Asher, **73** gave his offering:
one silver platter, the weight of which was one hundred thirty
shekels,
one silver bowl of seventy shekels, according to the shekel of the
sanctuary; both of them full of fine flour mixed with oil for a
meal offering;
74 one golden ladle of ten shekels, full of incense;
75 one young bull,
one ram,
one male lamb a year old, for a burnt offering;
76 one male goat for a sin offering;
77 and for the sacrifice of peace offerings, two head of cattle,
five rams, five male goats, and five male lambs a year old. This
was the offering of Pagiel the son of Ochran.
78 On the twelfth day Ahira the son of Enan, prince of the
children of Naphtali, **79** gave his offering:
one silver platter, the weight of which was one hundred thirty
shekels,
one silver bowl of seventy shekels, according to the shekel of the
sanctuary; both of them full of fine flour mixed with oil for a
meal offering;
80 one golden spoon of ten shekels, full of incense;
81 one young bull,
one ram,
one male lamb a year old, for a burnt offering;
82 one male goat for a sin offering;
83 and for the sacrifice of peace offerings, two head of cattle,
five rams, five male goats, and five male lambs a year old. This
was the offering of Ahira the son of Enan.
84 This was the dedication offering of the altar, on the day when
it was anointed, by the princes of Israel: twelve silver platters,
twelve silver bowls, twelve golden ladles; **85** each silver platter
weighing one hundred thirty shekels, and each bowl seventy; all
the silver of the vessels two thousand four hundred shekels,
according to the shekel of the sanctuary; **86** the twelve golden
ladles, full of incense, weighing ten shekels apiece, according to
the shekel of the sanctuary; all the gold of the ladles weighed one
hundred twenty shekels; **87** all the cattle for the burnt offering
twelve bulls, the rams twelve, the male lambs a year old twelve,
and their meal offering; and twelve male goats for a sin offering;
88 and all the cattle for the sacrifice of peace offerings: twenty-
four bulls, sixty rams, sixty male goats, and sixty male lambs a
year old. This was the dedication offering of the altar, after it was
anointed.
89 When Moses went into the Tent of Meeting to speak with
God, he heard his voice speaking to him from above the mercy
seat that was on the ark of the Testimony, from between the two
cherubim; and he spoke to him.

Numbers 8

1 God spoke to Moses, saying, **2** "Speak to Aaron, and tell him,
'When you light the lamps, the seven lamps shall give light in
front of the lamp stand.'"
3 Aaron did so. He lit its lamps to light the area in front of the
lamp stand, as God commanded Moses. **4** This was the
workmanship of the lamp stand, beaten work of gold. From its
base to its flowers, it was beaten work. He made the lamp stand
according to the pattern which God had shown Moses.
5 God spoke to Moses, saying, **6** "Take the Levites from among
the children of Israel, and cleanse them. **7** You shall do this to
them, to cleanse them: sprinkle the water of cleansing on them,
let them shave their whole bodies with a razor, let them wash
their clothes, and cleanse themselves. **8** Then let them take a
young bull and its meal offering, fine flour mixed with oil; and
another young bull you shall take for a sin offering. **9** You shall
present the Levites before the Tent of Meeting. You shall
assemble the whole congregation of the children of Israel.
10 You shall present the Levites before God. The children of
Israel shall lay their hands on the Levites, **11** and Aaron shall
offer the Levites before God for a wave offering on the behalf of
the children of Israel, that it may be theirs to do the service of
God.
12 "The Levites shall lay their hands on the heads of the bulls,
and you shall offer the one for a sin offering and the other for a
burnt offering to God, to make atonement for the Levites.
13 You shall set the Levites before Aaron and before his sons,
and offer them as a wave offering to God. **14** Thus you shall
separate the Levites from among the children of Israel, and the
Levites shall be mine.
15 "After that, the Levites shall go in to do the service of the
Tent of Meeting. You shall cleanse them, and offer them as a
wave offering. **16** For they are wholly given to me from among
the children of Israel; instead of all who open the womb, even the
firstborn of all the children of Israel, I have taken them to me.
17 For all the firstborn among the children of Israel are mine,
both man and animal. On the day that I struck all the firstborn in
the land of Egypt, I sanctified them for myself. **18** I have taken
the Levites instead of all the firstborn among the children of
Israel. **19** I have given the Levites as a gift to Aaron and to his
sons from among the children of Israel, to do the service of the
children of Israel in the Tent of Meeting, and to make atonement
for the children of Israel, so that there will be no plague among
the children of Israel when the children of Israel come near to the
sanctuary."
20 Moses, and Aaron, and all the congregation of the children of
Israel did so to the Levites. According to all that God
commanded Moses concerning the Levites, so the children of
Israel did to them. **21** The Levites purified themselves from sin,
and they washed their clothes; and Aaron offered them for a
wave offering before God and Aaron made atonement for them to
cleanse them. **22** After that, the Levites went in to do their
service in the Tent of Meeting before Aaron and before his sons:
as God had commanded Moses concerning the Levites, so they
did to them.
23 God spoke to Moses, saying, **24** "This is what is assigned to
the Levites: from twenty-five years old and upward they shall go
in to wait on the service in the work of the Tent of Meeting;
25 and from the age of fifty years they shall retire from doing the
work, and shall serve no more, **26** but shall assist their brothers
in the Tent of Meeting, to perform the duty, and shall perform no
service. This is how you shall have the Levites do their duties."

Numbers 9

1 God spoke to Moses in the wilderness of Sinai, in the first
month of the second year after they had come out of the land of
Egypt, saying, **2** "Let the children of Israel keep the Passover in
its appointed season. **3** On the fourteenth day of this month, at
evening, you shall keep it in its appointed season. You shall keep
it according to all its statutes and according to all its ordinances."
4 Moses told the children of Israel that they should keep the
Passover. **5** They kept the Passover in the first month, on the
fourteenth day of the month at evening, in the wilderness of
Sinai. According to all that God commanded Moses, so the
children of Israel did. **6** There were certain men, who were
unclean because of the dead body of a man, so that they could not
keep the Passover on that day, and they came before Moses and
Aaron on that day. **7** Those men said to him, "We are unclean
because of the dead body of a man. Why are we kept back, that
we may not offer the offering of God in its appointed season
among the children of Israel?"
8 Moses answered them, "Wait, that I may hear what God will
command concerning you."
9 God spoke to Moses, saying, **10** "Say to the children of Israel,
'If any man of you or of your generations is unclean by reason of
a dead body, or is on a journey far away, he shall still keep the
Passover to God. **11** In the second month, on the fourteenth day
at evening they shall keep it; they shall eat it with unleavened
bread and bitter herbs. **12** They shall leave none of it until the
morning, nor break a bone of it. According to all the statute of the
Passover they shall keep it. **13** But the man who is clean, and is
not on a journey, and fails to keep the Passover, that soul shall be
cut off from his people. Because he didn't offer the offering of
God in its appointed season, that man shall bear his sin.
14 "'If a foreigner lives among you, and desires to keep the
Passover to God, then he shall do so according to the statute of
the Passover, and according to its ordinance. You shall have one
statute, both for the foreigner, and for him who is born in the
land.'"
15 On the day that the tabernacle was raised up, the cloud
covered the tabernacle, even the Tent of the Testimony. At
evening it was over the tabernacle, as it were the appearance of
fire, until morning. **16** So it was continually. The cloud covered
it, and the appearance of fire by night. **17** Whenever the cloud
was taken up from over the Tent, then after that the children of
Israel traveled; and in the place where the cloud remained, there
the children of Israel encamped. **18** At the commandment of
God, the children of Israel traveled, and at the commandment of
God they encamped. As long as the cloud remained on the
tabernacle they remained encamped. **19** When the cloud stayed
on the tabernacle many days, then the children of Israel kept
God's command, and didn't travel. **20** Sometimes the cloud was
a few days on the tabernacle; then according to the
commandment of God they remained encamped, and according
to the commandment of God they traveled. **21** Sometimes the
cloud was from evening until morning; and when the cloud was
taken up in the morning, they traveled; or by day and by night,
when the cloud was taken up, they traveled. **22** Whether it was
two days, or a month, or a year that the cloud stayed on the
tabernacle, remaining on it, the children of Israel remained
encamped, and didn't travel; but when it was taken up, they
traveled. **23** At the commandment of God they encamped, and at

the commandment of God they traveled. They kept God's command, at the commandment of God by Moses.

Numbers 10

¹ God spoke to Moses, saying, ² "Make two trumpets of silver. You shall make them of beaten work. You shall use them for the calling of the congregation, and for the journeying of the camps. ³ When they blow them, all the congregation shall gather themselves to you at the door of the Tent of Meeting. ⁴ If they blow just one, then the princes, the heads of the thousands of Israel, shall gather themselves to you. ⁵ When you blow an alarm, the camps that lie on the east side shall go forward. ⁶ When you blow an alarm the second time, the camps that lie on the south side shall go forward. They shall blow an alarm for their journeys. ⁷ But when the assembly is to be gathered together, you shall blow, but you shall not sound an alarm. ⁸ "The sons of Aaron, the priests, shall blow the trumpets. This shall be to you for a statute forever throughout your generations. ⁹ When you go to war in your land against the adversary who oppresses you, then you shall sound an alarm with the trumpets. Then you will be remembered before God your God, and you will be saved from your enemies. ¹⁰ "Also in the day of your gladness, and in your set feasts, and in the beginnings of your months, you shall blow the trumpets over your burnt offerings, and over the sacrifices of your peace offerings; and they shall be to you for a memorial before your God. I am God your God."

¹¹ In the second year, in the second month, on the twentieth day of the month, the cloud was taken up from over the tabernacle of the covenant. ¹² The children of Israel went forward on their journeys out of the wilderness of Sinai; and the cloud stayed in the wilderness of Paran. ¹³ They first went forward according to the commandment of God by Moses.

¹⁴ First, the standard of the camp of the children of Judah went forward according to their armies. Nahshon the son of Amminadab was over his army. ¹⁵ Nethanel the son of Zuar was over the army of the tribe of the children of Issachar. ¹⁶ Eliab the son of Helon was over the army of the tribe of the children of Zebulun. ¹⁷ The tabernacle was taken down; and the sons of Gershon and the sons of Merari, who bore the tabernacle, went forward. ¹⁸ The standard of the camp of Reuben went forward according to their armies. Elizur the son of Shedeur was over his army. ¹⁹ Shelumiel the son of Zurishaddai was over the army of the tribe of the children of Simeon. ²⁰ Eliasaph the son of Deuel was over the army of the tribe of the children of Gad.

²¹ The Kohathites set forward, bearing the sanctuary. The others set up the tabernacle before they arrived.

²² The standard of the camp of the children of Ephraim set forward according to their armies. Elishama the son of Ammihud was over his army. ²³ Gamaliel the son of Pedahzur was over the army of the tribe of the children of Manasseh. ²⁴ Abidan the son of Gideoni was over the army of the tribe of the children of Benjamin.

²⁵ The standard of the camp of the children of Dan, which was the rear guard of all the camps, set forward according to their armies. Ahiezer the son of Ammishaddai was over his army.

²⁶ Pagiel the son of Ochran was over the army of the tribe of the children of Asher. ²⁷ Ahira the son of Enan was over the army of the tribe of the children of Naphtali. ²⁸ Thus were the travels of the children of Israel according to their armies; and they went forward.

²⁹ Moses said to Hobab, the son of Reuel the Midianite, Moses' father-in-law, "We are journeying to the place of which God said, 'I will give it to you.' Come with us, and we will treat you well; for God has spoken good concerning Israel."

³⁰ He said to him, "I will not go; but I will depart to my own land, and to my relatives."

³¹ Moses said, "Don't leave us, please; because you know how we are to encamp in the wilderness, and you can be our eyes. ³² It shall be, if you go with us—yes, it shall be—that whatever good God does to us, we will do the same to you."

³³ They set forward from the Mount of God three days' journey. The ark of God's covenant went before them three days' journey, to seek out a resting place for them. ³⁴ The cloud of God was over them by day, when they set forward from the

camp. ³⁵ When the ark went forward, Moses said, "Rise up, God, and let your enemies be scattered! Let those who hate you flee before you!" ³⁶ When it rested, he said, "Return, God, to the ten thousands of the thousands of Israel."

Numbers 11

¹ The people were complaining in the ears of God. When God heard it, his anger burned; and God's fire burned among them, and consumed some of the outskirts of the camp. ² The people cried to Moses; and Moses prayed to God, and the fire abated. ³ The name of that place was called Taberah,¹⁴¹ because God's fire burned among them.

⁴ The mixed multitude that was among them lusted exceedingly; and the children of Israel also wept again, and said, "Who will give us meat to eat? ⁵ We remember the fish, which we ate in Egypt for nothing; the cucumbers, and the melons, and the leeks, and the onions, and the garlic; ⁶ but now we have lost our appetite. There is nothing at all except this manna to look at."

⁷ The manna was like coriander seed, and it looked like bdellium.¹⁴² ⁸ The people went around, gathered it, and ground it in mills, or beat it in mortars, and boiled it in pots, and made cakes of it. Its taste was like the taste of fresh oil. ⁹ When the dew fell on the camp in the night, the manna fell on it.

¹⁰ Moses heard the people weeping throughout their families, every man at the door of his tent; and God's anger burned greatly; and Moses was displeased. ¹¹ Moses said to God, "Why have you treated your servant so badly? Why haven't I found favor in your sight, that you lay the burden of all this people on me? ¹² Have I conceived all this people? Have I brought them out, that you should tell me, 'Carry them in your bosom, as a nurse carries a nursing infant, to the land which you swore to their fathers?' ¹³ Where could I get meat to give all these people? For they weep before me, saying, 'Give us meat, that we may eat.' ¹⁴ I am not able to bear all this people alone, because it is too heavy for me. ¹⁵ If you treat me this way, please kill me right now, if I have found favor in your sight; and don't let me see my wretchedness."

¹⁶ God said to Moses, "Gather to me seventy men of the elders of Israel, whom you know to be the elders of the people and officers over them; and bring them to the Tent of Meeting, that they may stand there with you. ¹⁷ I will come down and talk with you there. I will take of the Spirit which is on you, and will put it on them; and they shall bear the burden of the people with you, that you don't bear it yourself alone.

¹⁸ "Say to the people, 'Sanctify yourselves in preparation for tomorrow, and you will eat meat; for you have wept in the ears of God, saying, "Who will give us meat to eat? For it was well with us in Egypt." Therefore God will give you meat, and you will eat. ¹⁹ You will not eat just one day, or two days, or five days, or ten days, or twenty days, ²⁰ but a whole month, until it comes out at your nostrils, and it is loathsome to you; because you have rejected God who is among you, and have wept before him, saying, "Why did we come out of Egypt?"'"

²¹ Moses said, "The people, among whom I am, are six hundred thousand men on foot; and you have said, 'I will give them meat, that they may eat a whole month.' ²² Shall flocks and herds be slaughtered for them, to be sufficient for them? Shall all the fish of the sea be gathered together for them, to be sufficient for them?"

²³ God said to Moses, "Has God's hand grown short? Now you will see whether my word will happen to you or not."

²⁴ Moses went out, and told the people God's words; and he gathered seventy men of the elders of the people, and set them around the Tent. ²⁵ God came down in the cloud, and spoke to him, and took of the Spirit that was on him, and put it on the seventy elders. When the Spirit rested on them, they prophesied, but they did so no more. ²⁶ But two men remained in the camp. The name of one was Eldad, and the name of the other Medad; and the Spirit rested on them. They were of those who were written, but had not gone out to the Tent; and they prophesied in the camp. ²⁷ A young man ran, and told Moses, and said, "Eldad and Medad are prophesying in the camp!"

²⁸ Joshua the son of Nun, the servant of Moses, one of his chosen men, answered, "My lord Moses, forbid them!"

²⁹ Moses said to him, "Are you jealous for my sake? I wish that all God's people were prophets, that God would put his Spirit on them!"

³⁰ Moses went into the camp, he and the elders of Israel. ³¹ A wind from God went out and brought quails from the sea, and let them fall by the camp, about a day's journey on this side, and a day's journey on the other side, around the camp, and about two cubits¹⁴³ above the surface of the earth. ³² The people rose up all that day, and all of that night, and all the next day, and gathered the quails. He who gathered least gathered ten homers;¹⁴⁴ and they spread them all out for themselves around the camp.

³³ While the meat was still between their teeth, before it was chewed, God's anger burned against the people, and God struck the people with a very great plague. ³⁴ The name of that place was called Kibroth Hattaavah,¹⁴⁵ because there they buried the people who lusted.

³⁵ From Kibroth Hattaavah the people traveled to Hazeroth; and they stayed at Hazeroth.

Numbers 12

¹ Miriam and Aaron spoke against Moses because of the Cushite woman whom he had married; for he had married a Cushite woman. ² They said, "Has God indeed spoken only with Moses? Hasn't he spoken also with us?" And God heard it.

³ Now the man Moses was very humble, more than all the men who were on the surface of the earth. ⁴ God spoke suddenly to Moses, to Aaron, and to Miriam, "You three come out to the Tent of Meeting!"

The three of them came out. ⁵ God came down in a pillar of cloud, and stood at the door of the Tent, and called Aaron and Miriam; and they both came forward. ⁶ He said, "Now hear my words. If there is a prophet among you, I, God, will make myself known to him in a vision. I will speak with him in a dream. ⁷ My servant Moses is not so. He is faithful in all my house. ⁸ With him, I will speak mouth to mouth, even plainly, and not in riddles; and he shall see God's form. Why then were you not afraid to speak against my servant, against Moses?" ⁹ God's anger burned against them; and he departed.

¹⁰ The cloud departed from over the Tent; and behold, Miriam was leprous, as white as snow. Aaron looked at Miriam, and behold, she was leprous.

¹¹ Aaron said to Moses, "Oh, my lord, please don't count this sin against us, in which we have done foolishly, and in which we have sinned. ¹² Let her not, I pray, be as one dead, of whom the flesh is half consumed when he comes out of his mother's womb."

¹³ Moses cried to God, saying, "Heal her, God, I beg you!"

¹⁴ God said to Moses, "If her father had but spit in her face, shouldn't she be ashamed seven days? Let her be shut up outside of the camp seven days, and after that she shall be brought in again."

¹⁵ Miriam was shut up outside of the camp seven days, and the people didn't travel until Miriam was brought in again.

¹⁶ Afterward the people traveled from Hazeroth, and encamped in the wilderness of Paran.

Numbers 13

¹ God spoke to Moses, saying, ² "Send men, that they may spy out the land of Canaan, which I give to the children of Israel. Of every tribe of their fathers, you shall send a man, every one a prince among them."

³ Moses sent them from the wilderness of Paran according to the commandment of God. All of them were men who were heads of the children of Israel. ⁴ These were their names:
Of the tribe of Reuben, Shammua the son of Zaccur.

⁵ Of the tribe of Simeon, Shaphat the son of Hori.

⁶ Of the tribe of Judah, Caleb the son of Jephunneh.

⁷ Of the tribe of Issachar, Igal the son of Joseph.

⁸ Of the tribe of Ephraim, Hoshea the son of Nun.

⁹ Of the tribe of Benjamin, Palti the son of Raphu.

¹⁰ Of the tribe of Zebulun, Gaddiel the son of Sodi.

¹¹ Of the tribe of Joseph, of the tribe of Manasseh, Gaddi the son of Susi.

¹² Of the tribe of Dan, Ammiel the son of Gemalli.

¹³ Of the tribe of Asher, Sethur the son of Michael.

¹⁴ Of the tribe of Naphtali, Nahbi the son of Vophsi.

¹⁵ Of the tribe of Gad, Geuel the son of Machi.

---

¹⁴¹**11:3** *11:3* Taberah means "burning"

¹⁴²**11:7** *11:7* Bdellium is a resin extracted from certain African trees.

¹⁴³**11:31** *11:31* A cubit is the length from the tip of the middle finger to the elbow on a man's arm, or about 18 inches or 46 centimeters.

¹⁴⁴**11:32** *11:32* 1 homer is about 220 liters or 6 bushels

¹⁴⁵**11:34** *11:34* Kibroth Hattaavah means "graves of lust"

16 These are the names of the men who Moses sent to spy out
the land. Moses called Hoshea the son of Nun Joshua. 17 Moses
sent them to spy out the land of Canaan, and said to them, “Go up
this way by the South, and go up into the hill country. 18 See
the land, what it is; and the people who dwell therein, whether
they are strong or weak, whether they are few or many; 19 and
what the land is that they dwell in, whether it is good or bad; and
what cities they are that they dwell in, whether in camps, or in
strongholds; 20 and what the land is, whether it is fertile or
poor, whether there is wood therein, or not. Be courageous, and
bring some of the fruit of the land.” Now the time was the time of
the first-ripe grapes.
21 So they went up, and spied out the land from the wilderness
of Zin to Rehob, to the entrance of Hamath. 22 They went up by
the South, and came to Hebron; and Ahiman, Sheshai, and
Talmai, the children of Anak, were there. (Now Hebron was built
seven years before Zoan in Egypt.) 23 They came to the valley
of Eshcol, and cut down from there a branch with one cluster of
grapes, and they bore it on a staff between two. They also
brought some of the pomegranates and figs. 24 That place was
called the valley of Eshcol, because of the cluster which the
children of Israel cut down from there. 25 They returned from
spying out the land at the end of forty days. 26 They went and
came to Moses, to Aaron, and to all the congregation of the
children of Israel, to the wilderness of Paran, to Kadesh; and
brought back word to them and to all the congregation. They
showed them the fruit of the land. 27 They told him, and said,
“We came to the land where you sent us. Surely it flows with
milk and honey, and this is its fruit. 28 However, the people
who dwell in the land are strong, and the cities are fortified and
very large. Moreover, we saw the children of Anak there.
29 Amalek dwells in the land of the South. The Hittite, the
Jebusite, and the Amorite dwell in the hill country. The Canaanite
dwells by the sea, and along the side of the Jordan.”
30 Caleb stilled the people before Moses, and said, “Let’s go up
at once, and possess it; for we are well able to overcome it!”
31 But the men who went up with him said, “We aren’t able to
go up against the people; for they are stronger than we.”
32 They brought up an evil report of the land which they had
spied out to the children of Israel, saying, “The land, through
which we have gone to spy it out, is a land that eats up its
inhabitants; and all the people who we saw in it are men of great
stature. 33 There we saw the Nephilim, [146] the sons of Anak,
who come from the Nephilim.[147] We were in our own sight as
grasshoppers, and so we were in their sight.”

Numbers 14

1 All the congregation lifted up their voice, and cried; and the
people wept that night. 2 All the children of Israel murmured
against Moses and against Aaron. The whole congregation said to
them, “We wish that we had died in the land of Egypt, or that we
had died in this wilderness! 3 Why does God bring us to this
land, to fall by the sword? Our wives and our little ones will be
captured or killed! Wouldn’t it be better for us to return into
Egypt?” 4 They said to one another, “Let’s choose a leader, and
let’s return into Egypt.”
5 Then Moses and Aaron fell on their faces before all the
assembly of the congregation of the children of Israel.
6 Joshua the son of Nun and Caleb the son of Jephunneh, who
were of those who spied out the land, tore their clothes. 7 They
spoke to all the congregation of the children of Israel, saying,
“The land, which we passed through to spy it out, is an
exceedingly good land. 8 If God delights in us, then he will
bring us into this land, and give it to us: a land which flows with
milk and honey. 9 Only don’t rebel against God, neither fear the
people of the land; for they are bread for us. Their defense is
removed from over them, and God is with us. Don’t fear them.”
10 But all the congregation threatened to stone them with
stones.
God’s glory appeared in the Tent of Meeting to all the children of
Israel. 11 God said to Moses, “How long will this people
despise me? and how long will they not believe in me, for all the
signs which I have worked among them? 12 I will strike them
with the pestilence, and disinherit them, and will make of you a
nation greater and mightier than they.”
13 Moses said to God, “Then the Egyptians will hear it; for you
brought up this people in your might from among them.
14 They will tell it to the inhabitants of this land. They have
heard that you God are among this people; for you God are seen
face to face, and your cloud stands over them, and you go before
them, in a pillar of cloud by day, and in a pillar of fire by night.
15 Now if you killed this people as one man, then the nations
which have heard the fame of you will speak, saying,
16 ‘Because God was not able to bring this people into the land
which he swore to them, therefore he has slain them in the
wilderness.’ 17 Now please let the power of the Lord[148] be
great, according as you have spoken, saying, 18 ‘God is slow to
anger, and abundant in loving kindness, forgiving iniquity and
disobedience; and he will by no means clear the guilty, visiting
the iniquity of the fathers on the children, on the third and on the
fourth generation.’ 19 Please pardon the iniquity of this people
according to the greatness of your loving kindness, and just as
you have forgiven this people, from Egypt even until now.”
20 God said, “I have pardoned according to your word; 21 but
in very deed—as I live, and as all the earth shall be filled with
God’s glory— 22 because all those men who have seen my
glory, and my signs, which I worked in Egypt and in the
wilderness, yet have tempted me these ten times, and have not
listened to my voice; 23 surely they shall not see the land which
I swore to their fathers, neither shall any of those who despised
me see it. 24 But my servant Caleb, because he had another
spirit with him, and has followed me fully, him I will bring into
the land into which he went. His offspring shall possess it.
25 Since the Amalekite and the Canaanite dwell in the valley,
tomorrow turn and go into the wilderness by the way to the Red
Sea.” 26 God spoke to Moses and to Aaron, saying, 27 “How
long shall I bear with this evil congregation that complain against
me? I have heard the complaints of the children of Israel, which
they complain against me. 28 Tell them, ‘As I live, says God,
surely as you have spoken in my ears, so I will do to you.
29 Your dead bodies shall fall in this wilderness; and all who
were counted of you, according to your whole number, from
twenty years old and upward, who have complained against me,
30 surely you shall not come into the land concerning which I
swore that I would make you dwell therein, except Caleb the son
of Jephunneh, and Joshua the son of Nun. 31 But I will bring
your little ones that you said should be captured or killed in, and
they shall know the land which you have rejected. 32 But as for
you, your dead bodies shall fall in this wilderness. 33 Your
children shall be wanderers in the wilderness forty years, and
shall bear your prostitution, until your dead bodies are consumed
in the wilderness. 34 After the number of the days in which you
spied out the land, even forty days, for every day a year, you will
bear your iniquities, even forty years, and you will know my
alienation.’ 35 I, God, have spoken. I will surely do this to all
this evil congregation who are gathered together against me. In
this wilderness they shall be consumed, and there they shall die.”
36 The men whom Moses sent to spy out the land, who returned
and made all the congregation to murmur against him by bringing
up an evil report against the land, 37 even those men who
brought up an evil report of the land, died by the plague before
God. 38 But Joshua the son of Nun and Caleb the son of
Jephunneh remained alive of those men who went to spy out the
land.
39 Moses told these words to all the children of Israel, and the
people mourned greatly. 40 They rose up early in the morning
and went up to the top of the mountain, saying, “Behold, we are
here, and will go up to the place which God has promised; for we
have sinned.”
41 Moses said, “Why now do you disobey the commandment of
God, since it shall not prosper? 42 Don’t go up, for God isn’t
among you; that way you won’t be struck down before your
enemies. 43 For there the Amalekite and the Canaanite are
before you, and you will fall by the sword because you turned
back from following God; therefore God will not be with you.”
44 But they presumed to go up to the top of the mountain.
Nevertheless, the ark of God’s covenant and Moses didn’t depart
out of the camp. 45 Then the Amalekites came down, and the
Canaanites who lived in that mountain, and struck them and beat
them down, even to Hormah.

Numbers 15

1 God spoke to Moses, saying, 2 “Speak to the children of
Israel, and tell them, ‘When you have come into the land of your
habitations, which I give to you, 3 and will make an offering by
fire to God—a burnt offering, or a sacrifice, to accomplish a vow,
or as a free will offering, or in your set feasts, to make a pleasant
aroma to God, of the herd, or of the flock— 4 then he who
offers his offering shall offer to God a meal offering of one tenth
of an ephah[149] of fine flour mixed with one fourth of a hin[150] of
oil. 5 You shall prepare wine for the drink offering, one fourth
of a hin, with the burnt offering or for the sacrifice, for each
lamb.
6 “‘For a ram, you shall prepare for a meal offering two tenths
of an ephah[151] of fine flour mixed with the third part of a hin of
oil; 7 and for the drink offering you shall offer the third part of a
hin of wine, of a pleasant aroma to God. 8 When you prepare a
bull for a burnt offering or for a sacrifice, to accomplish a vow,
or for peace offerings to God, 9 then he shall offer with the bull
a meal offering of three tenths of an ephah[152] of fine flour mixed
with half a hin of oil; 10 and you shall offer for the drink
offering half a hin of wine, for an offering made by fire, of a
pleasant aroma to God. 11 Thus it shall be done for each bull,
for each ram, for each of the male lambs, or of the young goats.
12 According to the number that you shall prepare, so you shall
do to everyone according to their number.
13 “‘All who are native-born shall do these things in this way,
in offering an offering made by fire, of a pleasant aroma to God.
14 If a stranger lives as a foreigner with you, or whoever may
be among you throughout your generations, and will offer an
offering made by fire, of a pleasant aroma to God, as you do, so
he shall do. 15 For the assembly, there shall be one statute for
you and for the stranger who lives as a foreigner, a statute forever
throughout your generations. As you are, so the foreigner shall be
before God. 16 One law and one ordinance shall be for you and
for the stranger who lives as a foreigner with you.’”
17 God spoke to Moses, saying, 18 “Speak to the children of
Israel, and tell them, ‘When you come into the land where I bring
you, 19 then it shall be that when you eat of the bread of the
land, you shall offer up a wave offering to God. 20 Of the first
of your dough you shall offer up a cake for a wave offering. As
the wave offering of the threshing floor, so you shall heave it.
21 Of the first of your dough, you shall give to God a wave
offering throughout your generations.
22 “‘When you err, and don’t observe all these commandments
which God has spoken to Moses— 23 even all that God has
commanded you by Moses, from the day that God gave
commandment and onward throughout your generations—
24 then it shall be, if it was done unwittingly, without the
knowledge of the congregation, that all the congregation shall
offer one young bull for a burnt offering, for a pleasant aroma to
God, with its meal offering and its drink offering, according to
the ordinance, and one male goat for a sin offering. 25 The
priest shall make atonement for all the congregation of the
children of Israel, and they shall be forgiven; for it was an error,
and they have brought their offering, an offering made by fire to
God, and their sin offering before God, for their error. 26 All
the congregation of the children of Israel shall be forgiven, as
well as the stranger who lives as a foreigner among them; for
with regard to all the people, it was done unwittingly.
27 “‘If a person sins unwittingly, then he shall offer a female
goat a year old for a sin offering. 28 The priest shall make
atonement for the soul who errs when he sins unwittingly before
God. He shall make atonement for him; and he shall be forgiven.
29 You shall have one law for him who does anything
unwittingly, for him who is native-born among the children of
Israel, and for the stranger who lives as a foreigner among them.
30 “‘But the soul who does anything with a high hand, whether
he is native-born or a foreigner, blasphemes God. That soul shall
be cut off from among his people. 31 Because he has despised
God’s word, and has broken his commandment, that soul shall be
utterly cut off. His iniquity shall be on him.’”
32 While the children of Israel were in the wilderness, they
found a man gathering sticks on the Sabbath day. 33 Those who
found him gathering sticks brought him to Moses and Aaron, and
to all the congregation. 34 They put him in custody, because it
had not been declared what should be done to him.

---

[146] **13:33** *13:33* or, giants

[147] **13:33** *13:33* or, giants

[148] **14:17** *14:17* The word translated “Lord” is “Adonai.”

[149] **15:4** *15:4* 1 ephah is about 22 liters or about 2/3 of a bushel

[150] **15:4** *15:4* A hin is about 6.5 liters or 1.7 gallons.

[151] **15:6** *15:6* 1 ephah is about 22 liters or about 2/3 of a bushel

[152] **15:9** *15:9* 1 ephah is about 22 liters or about 2/3 of a bushel

35 God said to Moses, "The man shall surely be put to death.
All the congregation shall stone him with stones outside of the
camp." 36 All the congregation brought him outside of the
camp, and stoned him to death with stones, as God commanded
Moses.
37 God spoke to Moses, saying, 38 "Speak to the children of
Israel, and tell them that they should make themselves fringes[153]
on the borders of their garments throughout their generations, and
that they put on the fringe [154] of each border a cord of blue. 39 It
shall be to you for a fringe,[155] that you may see it, and remember
all God's commandments, and do them; and that you don't
follow your own heart and your own eyes, after which you used
to play the prostitute; 40 so that you may remember and do all
my commandments, and be holy to your God. 41 I am God your
God, who brought you out of the land of Egypt, to be your God: I
am God your God."

Numbers 16

1 Now Korah, the son of Izhar, the son of Kohath, the son of
Levi, with Dathan and Abiram, the sons of Eliab, and On, the son
of Peleth, sons of Reuben, took some men. 2 They rose up
before Moses, with some of the children of Israel, two hundred
fifty princes of the congregation, called to the assembly, men of
renown. 3 They assembled themselves together against Moses
and against Aaron, and said to them, "You take too much on
yourself, since all the congregation are holy, everyone of them,
and God is among them! Why do you lift yourselves up above
God's assembly?"
4 When Moses heard it, he fell on his face. 5 He said to Korah
and to all his company, "In the morning, God will show who are
his, and who is holy, and will cause him to come near to him.
Even him whom he shall choose, he will cause to come near to
him. 6 Do this: have Korah and all his company take censers,
7 put fire in them, and put incense on them before God
tomorrow. It shall be that the man whom God chooses, he shall
be holy. You have gone too far, you sons of Levi!"
8 Moses said to Korah, "Hear now, you sons of Levi! 9 Is it a
small thing to you that the God of Israel has separated you from
the congregation of Israel, to bring you near to himself, to do the
service of God's tabernacle, and to stand before the congregation
to minister to them; 10 and that he has brought you near, and all
your brothers the sons of Levi with you? Do you seek the
priesthood also? 11 Therefore you and all your company have
gathered together against God! What is Aaron that you complain
against him?"
12 Moses sent to call Dathan and Abiram, the sons of Eliab; and
they said, "We won't come up! 13 Is it a small thing that you
have brought us up out of a land flowing with milk and honey, to
kill us in the wilderness, but you must also make yourself a
prince over us? 14 Moreover you haven't brought us into a land
flowing with milk and honey, nor given us inheritance of fields
and vineyards. Will you put out the eyes of these men? We won't
come up."
15 Moses was very angry, and said to God, "Don't respect their
offering. I have not taken one donkey from them, neither have I
hurt one of them."
16 Moses said to Korah, "You and all your company go before
God, you, and they, and Aaron, tomorrow. 17 Each man take
his censer and put incense on it, and each man bring before God
his censer, two hundred fifty censers; you also, and Aaron, each
with his censer."
18 They each took his censer, and put fire in it, and laid incense
on it, and stood at the door of the Tent of Meeting with Moses
and Aaron. 19 Korah assembled all the congregation opposite
them to the door of the Tent of Meeting.
God's glory appeared to all the congregation. 20 God spoke to
Moses and to Aaron, saying, 21 "Separate yourselves from
among this congregation, that I may consume them in a
moment!"
22 They fell on their faces, and said, "God, the God of the
spirits of all flesh, shall one man sin, and will you be angry with
all the congregation?"
23 God spoke to Moses, saying, 24 "Speak to the
congregation, saying, 'Get away from around the tent of Korah,
Dathan, and Abiram!'"
25 Moses rose up and went to Dathan and Abiram; and the
elders of Israel followed him. 26 He spoke to the congregation,
saying, "Depart, please, from the tents of these wicked men, and
touch nothing of theirs, lest you be consumed in all their sins!"
27 So they went away from the tent of Korah, Dathan, and
Abiram, on every side. Dathan and Abiram came out, and stood
at the door of their tents with their wives, their sons, and their
little ones.
28 Moses said, "Hereby you shall know that God has sent me to
do all these works; for they are not from my own mind. 29 If
these men die the common death of all men, or if they experience
what all men experience, then God hasn't sent me. 30 But if
God makes a new thing, and the ground opens its mouth, and
swallows them up with all that belong to them, and they go down
alive into Sheol,[156] then you shall understand that these men have
despised God."
31 As he finished speaking all these words, the ground that was
under them split apart. 32 The earth opened its mouth and
swallowed them up with their households, all of Korah's men,
and all their goods. 33 So they, and all that belonged to them
went down alive into Sheol. [157] The earth closed on them, and
they perished from among the assembly. 34 All Israel that were
around them fled at their cry; for they said, "Lest the earth
swallow us up!" 35 Fire came out from God, and devoured the
two hundred fifty men who offered the incense.
36 God spoke to Moses, saying, 37 "Speak to Eleazar the son
of Aaron the priest, that he take up the censers out of the burning,
and scatter the fire away from the camp; for they are holy,
38 even the censers of those who sinned against their own lives.
Let them be beaten into plates for a covering of the altar, for they
offered them before God. Therefore they are holy. They shall be
a sign to the children of Israel."
39 Eleazar the priest took the bronze censers which those who
were burned had offered; and they beat them out for a covering of
the altar, 40 to be a memorial to the children of Israel, to the end
that no stranger who isn't of the offspring of Aaron, would come
near to burn incense before God, that he not be as Korah, and as
his company; as God spoke to him by Moses.
41 But on the next day all the congregation of the children of
Israel complained against Moses and against Aaron, saying, "You
have killed God's people!"
42 When the congregation was assembled against Moses and
against Aaron, they looked toward the Tent of Meeting. Behold,
the cloud covered it, and God's glory appeared. 43 Moses and
Aaron came to the front of the Tent of Meeting. 44 God spoke
to Moses, saying, 45 "Get away from among this congregation,
that I may consume them in a moment!" They fell on their faces.
46 Moses said to Aaron, "Take your censer, put fire from the
altar in it, lay incense on it, carry it quickly to the congregation,
and make atonement for them; for wrath has gone out from God!
The plague has begun."
47 Aaron did as Moses said, and ran into the middle of the
assembly. The plague had already begun among the people. He
put on the incense, and made atonement for the people. 48 He
stood between the dead and the living; and the plague was stayed.
49 Now those who died by the plague were fourteen thousand
and seven hundred, in addition to those who died about the matter
of Korah. 50 Aaron returned to Moses to the door of the Tent of
Meeting, and the plague was stopped.

Numbers 17

1 God spoke to Moses, saying, 2 "Speak to the children of
Israel, and take rods from them, one for each fathers' house, of
all their princes according to their fathers' houses, twelve rods.
Write each man's name on his rod. 3 You shall write Aaron's
name on Levi's rod. There shall be one rod for each head of their
fathers' houses. 4 You shall lay them up in the Tent of Meeting
before the covenant, where I meet with you. 5 It shall happen
that the rod of the man whom I shall choose shall bud. I will
make the murmurings of the children of Israel, which they
murmur against you, cease from me."
6 Moses spoke to the children of Israel; and all their princes
gave him rods, for each prince one, according to their fathers'
houses, a total of twelve rods. Aaron's rod was among their rods.
7 Moses laid up the rods before God in the Tent of the
Testimony.
8 On the next day, Moses went into the Tent of the Testimony;
and behold, Aaron's rod for the house of Levi had sprouted,
budded, produced blossoms, and bore ripe almonds. 9 Moses
brought out all the rods from before God to all the children of
Israel. They looked, and each man took his rod.
10 God said to Moses, "Put back the rod of Aaron before the
covenant, to be kept for a token against the children of rebellion;
that you may make an end of their complaining against me, that
they not die." 11 Moses did so. As God commanded him, so he
did.
12 The children of Israel spoke to Moses, saying, "Behold, we
perish! We are undone! We are all undone! 13 Everyone who
keeps approaching God's tabernacle, dies! Will we all perish?"

Numbers 18

1 God said to Aaron, "You and your sons and your fathers'
house with you shall bear the iniquity of the sanctuary; and you
and your sons with you shall bear the iniquity of your priesthood.
2 Bring your brothers also, the tribe of Levi, the tribe of your
father, near with you, that they may be joined to you, and
minister to you; but you and your sons with you shall be before
the Tent of the Testimony. 3 They shall keep your commands
and the duty of the whole Tent; only they shall not come near to
the vessels of the sanctuary and to the altar, that they not die,
neither they nor you. 4 They shall be joined to you and keep the
responsibility of the Tent of Meeting, for all the service of the
Tent. A stranger shall not come near to you.
5 "You shall perform the duty of the sanctuary and the duty of
the altar, that there be no more wrath on the children of Israel.
6 Behold, I myself have taken your brothers the Levites from
among the children of Israel. They are a gift to you, dedicated to
God, to do the service of the Tent of Meeting. 7 You and your
sons with you shall keep your priesthood for everything of the
altar, and for that within the veil. You shall serve. I give you the
service of the priesthood as a gift. The stranger who comes near
shall be put to death."
8 God spoke to Aaron, "Behold, I myself have given you the
command of my wave offerings, even all the holy things of the
children of Israel. I have given them to you by reason of the
anointing, and to your sons, as a portion forever. 9 This shall be
yours of the most holy things from the fire: every offering of
theirs, even every meal offering of theirs, and every sin offering
of theirs, and every trespass offering of theirs, which they shall
render to me, shall be most holy for you and for your sons.
10 You shall eat of it like the most holy things. Every male shall
eat of it. It shall be holy to you.
11 "This is yours, too: the wave offering of their gift, even all
the wave offerings of the children of Israel. I have given them to
you, and to your sons and to your daughters with you, as a
portion forever. Everyone who is clean in your house shall eat of
it.
12 "I have given to you all the best of the oil, all the best of the
vintage, and of the grain, the first fruits of them which they give
to God. 13 The first-ripe fruits of all that is in their land, which
they bring to God, shall be yours. Everyone who is clean in your
house shall eat of it.
14 "Everything devoted in Israel shall be yours. 15 Everything
that opens the womb, of all flesh which they offer to God, both of
man and animal, shall be yours. Nevertheless, you shall surely
redeem the firstborn of man, and you shall redeem the firstborn
of unclean animals. 16 You shall redeem those who are to be
redeemed of them from a month old, according to your
estimation, for five shekels of money, according to the shekel[158]
of the sanctuary, which weighs twenty gerahs.[159]
17 "But you shall not redeem the firstborn of a cow, or the
firstborn of a sheep, or the firstborn of a goat. They are holy. You
shall sprinkle their blood on the altar, and shall burn their fat for
an offering made by fire, for a pleasant aroma to God. 18 Their
meat shall be yours, as the wave offering breast and as the right
thigh, it shall be yours. 19 All the wave offerings of the holy
things which the children of Israel offer to God, I have given you
and your sons and your daughters with you, as a portion forever.
It is a covenant of salt forever before God to you and to your
offspring with you."
20 God said to Aaron, "You shall have no inheritance in their
land, neither shall you have any portion among them. I am your
portion and your inheritance among the children of Israel.
21 "To the children of Levi, behold, I have given all the tithe in
Israel for an inheritance, in return for their service which they

---

[153] **15:38** *15:38* or, tassels (Hebrew ציצת)

[154] **15:38** *15:38* or, tassel

[155] **15:39** *15:39* or, tassel

[156] **16:30** *16:30* Sheol is the place of the dead.

[157] **16:33** *16:33* Sheol is the place of the dead.

[158] **18:16** *18:16* A shekel is about 10 grams or about 0.35 ounces.

[159] **18:16** *18:16* A gerah is about 0.5 grams or about 7.7 grains.

serve, even the service of the Tent of Meeting. 22 Henceforth
the children of Israel shall not come near the Tent of Meeting,
lest they bear sin, and die. 23 But the Levites shall do the
service of the Tent of Meeting, and they shall bear their iniquity.
It shall be a statute forever throughout your generations. Among
the children of Israel, they shall have no inheritance. 24 For the
tithe of the children of Israel, which they offer as a wave offering
to God, I have given to the Levites for an inheritance. Therefore I
have said to them, 'Among the children of Israel they shall have
no inheritance.'"

25 God spoke to Moses, saying, 26 "Moreover you shall speak
to the Levites, and tell them, 'When you take of the children of
Israel the tithe which I have given you from them for your
inheritance, then you shall offer up a wave offering of it for God,
a tithe of the tithe. 27 Your wave offering shall be credited to
you, as though it were the grain of the threshing floor, and as the
fullness of the wine press. 28 Thus you also shall offer a wave
offering to God of all your tithes, which you receive of the
children of Israel; and of it you shall give God's wave offering to
Aaron the priest. 29 Out of all your gifts, you shall offer every
wave offering to God, of all its best parts, even the holy part of
it.'

30 "Therefore you shall tell them, 'When you heave its best
from it, then it shall be credited to the Levites as the increase of
the threshing floor, and as the increase of the wine press.

31 You may eat it anywhere, you and your households, for it is
your reward in return for your service in the Tent of Meeting.

32 You shall bear no sin by reason of it, when you have heaved
from it its best. You shall not profane the holy things of the
children of Israel, that you not die.'"

Numbers 19

1 God spoke to Moses and to Aaron, saying, 2 "This is the
statute of the law which God has commanded. Tell the children
of Israel to bring you a red heifer without spot, in which is no
defect, and which was never yoked. 3 You shall give her to
Eleazar the priest, and he shall bring her outside of the camp, and
one shall kill her before his face. 4 Eleazar the priest shall take
some of her blood with his finger, and sprinkle her blood toward
the front of the Tent of Meeting seven times. 5 One shall burn
the heifer in his sight; her skin, and her meat, and her blood, with
her dung, shall he burn. 6 The priest shall take cedar wood,
hyssop, and scarlet, and cast it into the middle of the burning of
the heifer. 7 Then the priest shall wash his clothes, and he shall
bathe his flesh in water, and afterward he shall come into the
camp, and the priest shall be unclean until the evening. 8 He
who burns her shall wash his clothes in water, and bathe his flesh
in water, and shall be unclean until the evening.

9 "A man who is clean shall gather up the ashes of the heifer,
and lay them up outside of the camp in a clean place; and it shall
be kept for the congregation of the children of Israel for use in
water for cleansing impurity. It is a sin offering. 10 He who
gathers the ashes of the heifer shall wash his clothes, and be
unclean until the evening. It shall be to the children of Israel, and
to the stranger who lives as a foreigner among them, for a statute
forever.

11 "He who touches the dead body of any man shall be unclean
seven days. 12 He shall purify himself with water on the third
day, and on the seventh day he shall be clean; but if he doesn't
purify himself the third day, then the seventh day he shall not be
clean. 13 Whoever touches a dead person, the body of a man
who has died, and doesn't purify himself, defiles God's
tabernacle; and that soul shall be cut off from Israel; because the
water for impurity was not sprinkled on him, he shall be unclean.
His uncleanness is yet on him.

14 "This is the law when a man dies in a tent: everyone who
comes into the tent, and everyone who is in the tent, shall be
unclean seven days. 15 Every open vessel, which has no
covering bound on it, is unclean.

16 "Whoever in the open field touches one who is slain with a
sword, or a dead body, or a bone of a man, or a grave, shall be
unclean seven days.

17 "For the unclean, they shall take of the ashes of the burning
of the sin offering; and running water shall be poured on them in
a vessel. 18 A clean person shall take hyssop, dip it in the water,
and sprinkle it on the tent, on all the vessels, on the persons who
were there, and on him who touched the bone, or the slain, or the
dead, or the grave. 19 The clean person shall sprinkle on the
unclean on the third day, and on the seventh day. On the seventh
day, he shall purify him. He shall wash his clothes and bathe
himself in water, and shall be clean at evening. 20 But the man
who shall be unclean, and shall not purify himself, that soul shall
be cut off from among the assembly, because he has defiled the
sanctuary of God. The water for impurity has not been sprinkled
on him. He is unclean. 21 It shall be a perpetual statute to them.
He who sprinkles the water for impurity shall wash his clothes,
and he who touches the water for impurity shall be unclean until
evening.

22 "Whatever the unclean person touches shall be unclean; and
the soul that touches it shall be unclean until evening."

Numbers 20

1 The children of Israel, even the whole congregation, came
into the wilderness of Zin in the first month. The people stayed in
Kadesh. Miriam died there, and was buried there. 2 There was
no water for the congregation; and they assembled themselves
together against Moses and against Aaron. 3 The people
quarreled with Moses, and spoke, saying, "We wish that we had
died when our brothers died before God! 4 Why have you
brought God's assembly into this wilderness, that we should die
there, we and our animals? 5 Why have you made us to come
up out of Egypt, to bring us in to this evil place? It is no place of
seed, or of figs, or of vines, or of pomegranates; neither is there
any water to drink."

6 Moses and Aaron went from the presence of the assembly to
the door of the Tent of Meeting, and fell on their faces. God's
glory appeared to them. 7 God spoke to Moses, saying,

8 "Take the rod, and assemble the congregation, you, and Aaron
your brother, and speak to the rock before their eyes, that it pour
out its water. You shall bring water to them out of the rock; so
you shall give the congregation and their livestock drink."

9 Moses took the rod from before God, as he commanded him.

10 Moses and Aaron gathered the assembly together before the
rock, and he said to them, "Hear now, you rebels! Shall we bring
water out of this rock for you?" 11 Moses lifted up his hand,
and struck the rock with his rod twice, and water came out
abundantly. The congregation and their livestock drank.

12 God said to Moses and Aaron, "Because you didn't believe
in me, to sanctify me in the eyes of the children of Israel,
therefore you shall not bring this assembly into the land which I
have given them."

13 These are the waters of Meribah;[160] because the children of
Israel strove with God, and he was sanctified in them.

14 Moses sent messengers from Kadesh to the king of Edom,
saying:
"Your brother Israel says: You know all the travail that has
happened to us; 15 how our fathers went down into Egypt, and
we lived in Egypt a long time. The Egyptians mistreated us and
our fathers. 16 When we cried to God, he heard our voice, sent
an angel, and brought us out of Egypt. Behold, we are in Kadesh,
a city in the edge of your border.

17 "Please let us pass through your land. We will not pass
through field or through vineyard, neither will we drink from the
water of the wells. We will go along the king's highway. We will
not turn away to the right hand nor to the left, until we have
passed your border."

18 Edom said to him, "You shall not pass through me, lest I
come out with the sword against you."

19 The children of Israel said to him, "We will go up by the
highway; and if we drink your water, I and my livestock, then I
will give its price. Only let me, without doing anything else, pass
through on my feet."

20 He said, "You shall not pass through." Edom came out
against him with many people, and with a strong hand. 21 Thus
Edom refused to give Israel passage through his border, so Israel
turned away from him.

22 They traveled from Kadesh, and the children of Israel, even
the whole congregation, came to Mount Hor. 23 God spoke to
Moses and Aaron in Mount Hor, by the border of the land of
Edom, saying, 24 "Aaron shall be gathered to his people; for he
shall not enter into the land which I have given to the children of
Israel, because you rebelled against my word at the waters of
Meribah. 25 Take Aaron and Eleazar his son, and bring them up
to Mount Hor; 26 and strip Aaron of his garments, and put them
on Eleazar his son. Aaron shall be gathered, and shall die there."

27 Moses did as God commanded. They went up onto Mount
Hor in the sight of all the congregation. 28 Moses stripped
Aaron of his garments, and put them on Eleazar his son. Aaron
died there on the top of the mountain, and Moses and Eleazar
came down from the mountain. 29 When all the congregation
saw that Aaron was dead, they wept for Aaron thirty days, even
all the house of Israel.

Numbers 21

1 The Canaanite, the king of Arad, who lived in the South,
heard that Israel came by the way of Atharim. He fought against
Israel, and took some of them captive. 2 Israel vowed a vow to
God, and said, "If you will indeed deliver this people into my
hand, then I will utterly destroy their cities." 3 God listened to
the voice of Israel, and delivered up the Canaanites; and they
utterly destroyed them and their cities. The name of the place was
called Hormah.[161]

4 They traveled from Mount Hor by the way to the Red Sea, to
go around the land of Edom. The soul of the people was very
discouraged because of the journey. 5 The people spoke against
God and against Moses: "Why have you brought us up out of
Egypt to die in the wilderness? For there is no bread, there is no
water, and our soul loathes this disgusting food!"

6 God sent venomous snakes among the people, and they bit the
people. Many people of Israel died. 7 The people came to
Moses, and said, "We have sinned, because we have spoken
against God and against you. Pray to God, that he take away the
serpents from us." Moses prayed for the people.

8 God said to Moses, "Make a venomous snake, and set it on a
pole. It shall happen that everyone who is bitten, when he sees it,
shall live." 9 Moses made a serpent of bronze, and set it on the
pole. If a serpent had bitten any man, when he looked at the
serpent of bronze, he lived.

10 The children of Israel traveled, and encamped in Oboth.

11 They traveled from Oboth, and encamped at Iyeabarim, in
the wilderness which is before Moab, toward the sunrise.

12 From there they traveled, and encamped in the valley of
Zered. 13 From there they traveled, and encamped on the other
side of the Arnon, which is in the wilderness that comes out of
the border of the Amorites; for the Arnon is the border of Moab,
between Moab and the Amorites. 14 Therefore it is said in the
book of the Wars of God, "Vaheb in Suphah, the valleys of the
Arnon, 15 the slope of the valleys that incline toward the
dwelling of Ar, leans on the border of Moab."

16 From there they traveled to Beer; that is the well of which
God said to Moses, "Gather the people together, and I will give
them water."

17 Then Israel sang this song:
"Spring up, well! Sing to it,

18 the well, which the princes dug,
which the nobles of the people dug,
with the scepter, and with their poles."
From the wilderness they traveled to Mattanah; 19 and from
Mattanah to Nahaliel; and from Nahaliel to Bamoth; 20 and
from Bamoth to the valley that is in the field of Moab, to the top
of Pisgah, which looks down on the desert. 21 Israel sent
messengers to Sihon king of the Amorites, saying, 22 "Let me
pass through your land. We will not turn away into field or
vineyard. We will not drink of the water of the wells. We will go
by the king's highway, until we have passed your border."

23 Sihon would not allow Israel to pass through his border, but
Sihon gathered all his people together, and went out against Israel
into the wilderness, and came to Jahaz. He fought against Israel.

24 Israel struck him with the edge of the sword, and possessed
his land from the Arnon to the Jabbok, even to the children of
Ammon; for the border of the children of Ammon was fortified.

25 Israel took all these cities. Israel lived in all the cities of the
Amorites, in Heshbon, and in all its villages. 26 For Heshbon
was the city of Sihon the king of the Amorites, who had fought
against the former king of Moab, and taken all his land out of his
hand, even to the Arnon. 27 Therefore those who speak in
proverbs say,
"Come to Heshbon.
Let the city of Sihon be built and established;

28 for a fire has gone out of Heshbon,
a flame from the city of Sihon.
It has devoured Ar of Moab,
The lords of the high places of the Arnon.

29 Woe to you, Moab!
You are undone, people of Chemosh!
He has given his sons as fugitives,
and his daughters into captivity,
to Sihon king of the Amorites.

30 We have shot at them.

[160] **20:13** *20:13* **"Meribah" means "quarreling".**

[161] **21:3** *21:3* **"Hormah" means "destruction".**

Heshbon has perished even to Dibon.
We have laid waste even to Nophah,
Which reaches to Medeba."
31 Thus Israel lived in the land of the Amorites. 32 Moses
sent to spy out Jazer. They took its villages, and drove out the
Amorites who were there. 33 They turned and went up by the
way of Bashan. Og the king of Bashan went out against them, he
and all his people, to battle at Edrei.
34 God said to Moses, "Don't fear him, for I have delivered him
into your hand, with all his people, and his land. You shall do to
him as you did to Sihon king of the Amorites, who lived at
Heshbon."
35 So they struck him, with his sons and all his people, until
there were no survivors; and they possessed his land.

Numbers 22

1 The children of Israel traveled, and encamped in the plains of
Moab beyond the Jordan at Jericho. 2 Balak the son of Zippor
saw all that Israel had done to the Amorites. 3 Moab was very
afraid of the people, because they were many. Moab was
distressed because of the children of Israel. 4 Moab said to the
elders of Midian, "Now this multitude will lick up all that is
around us, as the ox licks up the grass of the field."
Balak the son of Zippor was king of Moab at that time. 5 He
sent messengers to Balaam the son of Beor, to Pethor, which is
by the River, to the land of the children of his people, to call him,
saying, "Behold, there is a people who came out of Egypt.
Behold, they cover the surface of the earth, and they are staying
opposite me. 6 Please come now therefore, and curse this
people for me; for they are too mighty for me. Perhaps I shall
prevail, that we may strike them, and that I may drive them out of
the land; for I know that he whom you bless is blessed, and he
whom you curse is cursed."
7 The elders of Moab and the elders of Midian departed with
the rewards of divination in their hand. They came to Balaam,
and spoke to him the words of Balak.
8 He said to them, "Lodge here this night, and I will bring you
word again, as God shall speak to me." The princes of Moab
stayed with Balaam.
9 God came to Balaam, and said, "Who are these men with
you?"
10 Balaam said to God, "Balak the son of Zippor, king of
Moab, has said to me, 11 'Behold, the people that has come out
of Egypt covers the surface of the earth. Now, come curse me
them. Perhaps I shall be able to fight against them, and shall drive
them out.'"
12 God said to Balaam, "You shall not go with them. You shall
not curse the people, for they are blessed."
13 Balaam rose up in the morning, and said to the princes of
Balak, "Go to your land; for God refuses to permit me to go with
you."
14 The princes of Moab rose up, and they went to Balak, and
said, "Balaam refuses to come with us."
15 Balak again sent princes, more, and more honorable than
they. 16 They came to Balaam, and said to him, "Balak the son
of Zippor says, 'Please let nothing hinder you from coming to
me, 17 for I will promote you to very great honor, and whatever
you say to me I will do. Please come therefore, and curse this
people for me.'"
18 Balaam answered the servants of Balak, "If Balak would
give me his house full of silver and gold, I can't go beyond the
word of God my God, to do less or more. 19 Now therefore
please stay here tonight as well, that I may know what else God
will speak to me."
20 God came to Balaam at night, and said to him, "If the men
have come to call you, rise up, go with them; but only the word
which I speak to you, that you shall do."
21 Balaam rose up in the morning, and saddled his donkey, and
went with the princes of Moab. 22 God's anger burned because
he went; and God's angel placed himself in the way as an
adversary against him. Now he was riding on his donkey, and his
two servants were with him. 23 The donkey saw God's angel
standing in the way, with his sword drawn in his hand; and the
donkey turned out of the path, and went into the field. Balaam
struck the donkey, to turn her into the path. 24 Then God's
angel stood in a narrow path between the vineyards, a wall being
on this side, and a wall on that side. 25 The donkey saw God's
angel, and she thrust herself to the wall, and crushed Balaam's
foot against the wall. He struck her again.
26 God's angel went further, and stood in a narrow place, where
there was no way to turn either to the right hand or to the left.
27 The donkey saw God's angel, and she lay down under
Balaam. Balaam's anger burned, and he struck the donkey with
his staff.
28 God opened the mouth of the donkey, and she said to
Balaam, "What have I done to you, that you have struck me these
three times?"
29 Balaam said to the donkey, "Because you have mocked me, I
wish there were a sword in my hand, for now I would have killed
you."
30 The donkey said to Balaam, "Am I not your donkey, on
which you have ridden all your life long until today? Was I ever
in the habit of doing so to you?"
He said, "No."
31 Then God opened the eyes of Balaam, and he saw God's
angel standing in the way, with his sword drawn in his hand; and
he bowed his head, and fell on his face. 32 God's angel said to
him, "Why have you struck your donkey these three times?
Behold, I have come out as an adversary, because your way is
perverse before me. 33 The donkey saw me, and turned away
before me these three times. Unless she had turned away from
me, surely now I would have killed you, and saved her alive."
34 Balaam said to God's angel, "I have sinned; for I didn't
know that you stood in the way against me. Now therefore, if it
displeases you, I will go back again."
35 God's angel said to Balaam, "Go with the men; but only the
word that I shall speak to you, that you shall speak."
So Balaam went with the princes of Balak. 36 When Balak
heard that Balaam had come, he went out to meet him to the City
of Moab, which is on the border of the Arnon, which is in the
utmost part of the border. 37 Balak said to Balaam, "Didn't I
earnestly send for you to summon you? Why didn't you come to
me? Am I not able indeed to promote you to honor?"
38 Balaam said to Balak, "Behold, I have come to you. Have I
now any power at all to speak anything? The word that God puts
in my mouth, that shall I speak."
39 Balaam went with Balak, and they came to Kiriath Huzoth.
40 Balak sacrificed cattle and sheep, and sent to Balaam, and to
the princes who were with him. 41 In the morning, Balak took
Balaam, and brought him up into the high places of Baal; and he
saw from there part of the people.

Numbers 23

1 Balaam said to Balak, "Build here seven altars for me, and
prepare here seven bulls and seven rams for me."
2 Balak did as Balaam had spoken; and Balak and Balaam
offered on every altar a bull and a ram. 3 Balaam said to Balak,
"Stand by your burnt offering, and I will go. Perhaps God will
come to meet me. Whatever he shows me I will tell you."
He went to a bare height. 4 God met Balaam, and he said to
him, "I have prepared the seven altars, and I have offered up a
bull and a ram on every altar."
5 God put a word in Balaam's mouth, and said, "Return to
Balak, and thus you shall speak."
6 He returned to him, and behold, he was standing by his burnt
offering, he, and all the princes of Moab. 7 He took up his
parable, and said,
"From Aram has Balak brought me,
the king of Moab from the mountains of the East.
Come, curse Jacob for me.
Come, defy Israel.
8 How shall I curse whom God has not cursed?
How shall I defy whom God has not defied?
9 For from the top of the rocks I see him.
From the hills I see him.
Behold, it is a people that dwells alone,
and shall not be listed among the nations.
10 Who can count the dust of Jacob,
or count the fourth part of Israel?
Let me die the death of the righteous!
Let my last end be like his!"
11 Balak said to Balaam, "What have you done to me? I took
you to curse my enemies, and behold, you have blessed them
altogether."
12 He answered and said, "Must I not take heed to speak that
which God puts in my mouth?"
13 Balak said to him, "Please come with me to another place,
where you may see them. You shall see just part of them, and
shall not see them all. Curse them from there for me."
14 He took him into the field of Zophim, to the top of Pisgah,
and built seven altars, and offered up a bull and a ram on every
altar. 15 He said to Balak, "Stand here by your burnt offering,
while I meet God over there."
16 God met Balaam, and put a word in his mouth, and said,
"Return to Balak, and say this."
17 He came to him, and behold, he was standing by his burnt
offering, and the princes of Moab with him. Balak said to him,
"What has God spoken?"
18 He took up his parable, and said,
"Rise up, Balak, and hear!
Listen to me, you son of Zippor.
19 God is not a man, that he should lie,
nor a son of man, that he should repent.
Has he said, and will he not do it?
Or has he spoken, and will he not make it good?
20 Behold, I have received a command to bless.
He has blessed, and I can't reverse it.
21 He has not seen iniquity in Jacob.
Neither has he seen perverseness in Israel.
God his God is with him.
The shout of a king is among them.
22 God brings them out of Egypt.
He has as it were the strength of the wild ox.
23 Surely there is no enchantment with Jacob;
Neither is there any divination with Israel.
Now it shall be said of Jacob and of Israel,
'What has God done!'
24 Behold, a people rises up as a lioness.
As a lion he lifts himself up.
He shall not lie down until he eats of the prey,
and drinks the blood of the slain."
25 Balak said to Balaam, "Neither curse them at all, nor bless
them at all."
26 But Balaam answered Balak, "Didn't I tell you, saying, 'All
that God speaks, that I must do?'"
27 Balak said to Balaam, "Come now, I will take you to another
place; perhaps it will please God that you may curse them for me
from there."
28 Balak took Balaam to the top of Peor, that looks down on the
desert. 29 Balaam said to Balak, "Build seven altars for me
here, and prepare seven bulls and seven rams for me here."
30 Balak did as Balaam had said, and offered up a bull and a
ram on every altar.

Numbers 24

1 When Balaam saw that it pleased God to bless Israel, he
didn't go, as at the other times, to use divination, but he set his
face toward the wilderness. 2 Balaam lifted up his eyes, and he
saw Israel dwelling according to their tribes; and the Spirit of
God came on him. 3 He took up his parable, and said,
"Balaam the son of Beor says,
the man whose eyes are open says;
4 he says, who hears the words of God,
who sees the vision of the Almighty,
falling down, and having his eyes open:
5 How goodly are your tents, Jacob,
and your dwellings, Israel!
6 As valleys they are spread out,
as gardens by the riverside,
as aloes which God has planted,
as cedar trees beside the waters.
7 Water shall flow from his buckets.
His seed shall be in many waters.
His king shall be higher than Agag.
His kingdom shall be exalted.
8 God brings him out of Egypt.
He has as it were the strength of the wild ox.
He shall consume the nations his adversaries,
shall break their bones in pieces,
and pierce them with his arrows.
9 He couched, he lay down as a lion,
as a lioness;
who shall rouse him up?
Everyone who blesses you is blessed.
Everyone who curses you is cursed."
10 Balak's anger burned against Balaam, and he struck his
hands together. Balak said to Balaam, "I called you to curse my
enemies, and, behold, you have altogether blessed them these
three times. 11 Therefore, flee to your place, now! I thought to
promote you to great honor; but, behold, God has kept you back
from honor."
12 Balaam said to Balak, "Didn't I also tell your messengers
whom you sent to me, saying, 13 'If Balak would give me his
house full of silver and gold, I can't go beyond God's word, to do
either good or bad from my own mind. I will say what God
says'? 14 Now, behold, I go to my people. Come, I will inform
you what this people shall do to your people in the latter days."
15 He took up his parable, and said,
"Balaam the son of Beor says,
the man whose eyes are open says;
16 he says, who hears the words of God,
knows the knowledge of the Most High,
and who sees the vision of the Almighty,

Falling down, and having his eyes open:
17 I see him, but not now.
I see him, but not near.
A star will come out of Jacob.
A scepter will rise out of Israel,
and shall strike through the corners of Moab,
and crush all the sons of Sheth.
18 Edom shall be a possession.
Seir, his enemies, also shall be a possession,
while Israel does valiantly.
19 Out of Jacob shall one have dominion,
and shall destroy the remnant from the city."
20 He looked at Amalek, and took up his parable, and said,
"Amalek was the first of the nations,
But his latter end shall come to destruction."
21 He looked at the Kenite, and took up his parable, and said,
"Your dwelling place is strong.
Your nest is set in the rock.
22 Nevertheless Kain shall be wasted,
until Asshur carries you away captive."
23 He took up his parable, and said,
"Alas, who shall live when God does this?
24 But ships shall come from the coast of Kittim.
They shall afflict Asshur, and shall afflict Eber.
He also shall come to destruction."
25 Balaam rose up, and went and returned to his place; and
Balak also went his way.

Numbers 25

1 Israel stayed in Shittim; and the people began to play the
prostitute with the daughters of Moab; 2 for they called the
people to the sacrifices of their gods. The people ate and bowed
down to their gods. 3 Israel joined himself to Baal Peor, and
God's anger burned against Israel. 4 God said to Moses, "Take
all the chiefs of the people, and hang them up to God before the
sun, that the fierce anger of God may turn away from Israel."
5 Moses said to the judges of Israel, "Everyone kill his men
who have joined themselves to Baal Peor."
6 Behold, one of the children of Israel came and brought to his
brothers a Midianite woman in the sight of Moses, and in the
sight of all the congregation of the children of Israel, while they
were weeping at the door of the Tent of Meeting. 7 When
Phinehas, the son of Eleazar, the son of Aaron the priest, saw it,
he rose up from the middle of the congregation, and took a spear
in his hand. 8 He went after the man of Israel into the pavilion,
and thrust both of them through, the man of Israel, and the
woman through her body. So the plague was stopped among the
children of Israel. 9 Those who died by the plague were twenty-
four thousand.
10 God spoke to Moses, saying, 11 "Phinehas, the son of
Eleazar, the son of Aaron the priest, has turned my wrath away
from the children of Israel, in that he was jealous with my
jealousy among them, so that I didn't consume the children of
Israel in my jealousy. 12 Therefore say, 'Behold, I give to him
my covenant of peace. 13 It shall be to him, and to his offspring
after him, the covenant of an everlasting priesthood, because he
was jealous for his God, and made atonement for the children of
Israel.'"
14 Now the name of the man of Israel that was slain, who was
slain with the Midianite woman, was Zimri, the son of Salu, a
prince of a fathers' house among the Simeonites. 15 The name
of the Midianite woman who was slain was Cozbi, the daughter
of Zur. He was head of the people of a fathers' house in Midian.
16 God spoke to Moses, saying, 17 "Harass the Midianites,
and strike them; 18 for they harassed you with their wiles,
wherein they have deceived you in the matter of Peor, and in the
incident regarding Cozbi, the daughter of the prince of Midian,
their sister, who was slain on the day of the plague in the matter
of Peor."

Numbers 26

1 After the plague, God spoke to Moses and to Eleazar the son
of Aaron the priest, saying, 2 "Take a census of all the
congregation of the children of Israel, from twenty years old and
upward, by their fathers' houses, all who are able to go out to war
in Israel." 3 Moses and Eleazar the priest spoke with them in
the plains of Moab by the Jordan at Jericho, saying, 4 "Take a
census, from twenty years old and upward, as God commanded
Moses and the children of Israel."
These are those that came out of the land of Egypt. 5 Reuben,
the firstborn of Israel; the sons of Reuben: of Hanoch, the family
of the Hanochites; of Pallu, the family of the Palluites; 6 of
Hezron, the family of the Hezronites; of Carmi, the family of the
Carmites. 7 These are the families of the Reubenites; and those
who were counted of them were forty-three thousand seven
hundred thirty. 8 The son of Pallu: Eliab. 9 The sons of Eliab:
Nemuel, Dathan, and Abiram. These are that Dathan and Abiram
who were called by the congregation, who rebelled against Moses
and against Aaron in the company of Korah when they rebelled
against God; 10 and the earth opened its mouth, and swallowed
them up together with Korah when that company died; at the time
the fire devoured two hundred fifty men, and they became a sign.
11 Notwithstanding, the sons of Korah didn't die. 12 The sons
of Simeon after their families: of Nemuel, the family of the
Nemuelites; of Jamin, the family of the Jaminites; of Jachin, the
family of the Jachinites; 13 of Zerah, the family of the
Zerahites; of Shaul, the family of the Shaulites. 14 These are the
families of the Simeonites, twenty-two thousand two hundred.
15 The sons of Gad after their families: of Zephon, the family
of the Zephonites; of Haggi, the family of the Haggites; of Shuni,
the family of the Shunites; 16 of Ozni, the family of the
Oznites; of Eri, the family of the Erites; 17 of Arod, the family
of the Arodites; of Areli, the family of the Arelites. 18 These
are the families of the sons of Gad according to those who were
counted of them, forty thousand and five hundred. 19 The sons
of Judah: Er and Onan. Er and Onan died in the land of Canaan.
20 The sons of Judah after their families were: of Shelah, the
family of the Shelanites; of Perez, the family of the Perezites; of
Zerah, the family of the Zerahites. 21 The sons of Perez were:
of Hezron, the family of the Hezronites; of Hamul, the family of
the Hamulites. 22 These are the families of Judah according to
those who were counted of them, seventy-six thousand five
hundred. 23 The sons of Issachar after their families: of Tola,
the family of the Tolaites; of Puvah, the family of the Punites;
24 of Jashub, the family of the Jashubites; of Shimron, the
family of the Shimronites. 25 These are the families of Issachar
according to those who were counted of them, sixty-four
thousand three hundred. 26 The sons of Zebulun after their
families: of Sered, the family of the Seredites; of Elon, the family
of the Elonites; of Jahleel, the family of the Jahleelites.
27 These are the families of the Zebulunites according to those
who were counted of them, sixty thousand five hundred. 28 The
sons of Joseph after their families: Manasseh and Ephraim.
29 The sons of Manasseh: of Machir, the family of the
Machirites; and Machir became the father of Gilead; of Gilead,
the family of the Gileadites. 30 These are the sons of Gilead: of
Iezer, the family of the Iezerites; of Helek, the family of the
Helekites; 31 and Asriel, the family of the Asrielites; and
Shechem, the family of the Shechemites; 32 and Shemida, the
family of the Shemidaites; and Hepher, the family of the
Hepherites. 33 Zelophehad the son of Hepher had no sons, but
daughters: and the names of the daughters of Zelophehad were
Mahlah, Noah, Hoglah, Milcah, and Tirzah. 34 These are the
families of Manasseh. Those who were counted of them were
fifty-two thousand seven hundred. 35 These are the sons of
Ephraim after their families: of Shuthelah, the family of the
Shuthelahites; of Becher, the family of the Becherites; of Tahan,
the family of the Tahanites. 36 These are the sons of Shuthelah:
of Eran, the family of the Eranites. 37 These are the families of
the sons of Ephraim according to those who were counted of
them, thirty-two thousand five hundred. These are the sons of
Joseph after their families. 38 The sons of Benjamin after their
families: of Bela, the family of the Belaites; of Ashbel, the family
of the Ashbelites; of Ahiram, the family of the Ahiramites;
39 of Shephupham, the family of the Shuphamites; of Hupham,
the family of the Huphamites. 40 The sons of Bela were Ard
and Naaman: the family of the Ardites; and of Naaman, the
family of the Naamites. 41 These are the sons of Benjamin after
their families; and those who were counted of them were forty-
five thousand six hundred. 42 These are the sons of Dan after
their families: of Shuham, the family of the Shuhamites. These
are the families of Dan after their families. 43 All the families
of the Shuhamites, according to those who were counted of them,
were sixty-four thousand four hundred. 44 The sons of Asher
after their families: of Imnah, the family of the Imnites; of Ishvi,
the family of the Ishvites; of Beriah, the family of the Berites.
45 Of the sons of Beriah: of Heber, the family of the Heberites;
of Malchiel, the family of the Malchielites. 46 The name of the
daughter of Asher was Serah. 47 These are the families of the
sons of Asher according to those who were counted of them,
fifty-three thousand and four hundred. 48 The sons of Naphtali
after their families: of Jahzeel, the family of the Jahzeelites; of
Guni, the family of the Gunites; 49 of Jezer, the family of the
Jezerites; of Shillem, the family of the Shillemites. 50 These are
the families of Naphtali according to their families; and those
who were counted of them were forty-five thousand four
hundred. 51 These are those who were counted of the children
of Israel, six hundred one thousand seven hundred thirty.
52 God spoke to Moses, saying, 53 "To these the land shall be
divided for an inheritance according to the number of names.
54 To the more you shall give the more inheritance, and to the
fewer you shall give the less inheritance. To everyone according
to those who were counted of him shall his inheritance be given.
55 Notwithstanding, the land shall be divided by lot. According
to the names of the tribes of their fathers they shall inherit.
56 According to the lot shall their inheritance be divided
between the more and the fewer."
57 These are those who were counted of the Levites after their
families: of Gershon, the family of the Gershonites; of Kohath,
the family of the Kohathites; of Merari, the family of the
Merarites. 58 These are the families of Levi: the family of the
Libnites, the family of the Hebronites, the family of the Mahlites,
the family of the Mushites, and the family of the Korahites.
Kohath became the father of Amram. 59 The name of Amram's
wife was Jochebed, the daughter of Levi, who was born to Levi
in Egypt. She bore to Amram Aaron and Moses, and Miriam their
sister. 60 To Aaron were born Nadab and Abihu, Eleazar and
Ithamar. 61 Nadab and Abihu died when they offered strange
fire before God. 62 Those who were counted of them were
twenty-three thousand, every male from a month old and upward;
for they were not counted among the children of Israel, because
there was no inheritance given them among the children of Israel.
63 These are those who were counted by Moses and Eleazar the
priest, who counted the children of Israel in the plains of Moab
by the Jordan at Jericho. 64 But among these there was not a
man of them who were counted by Moses and Aaron the priest,
who counted the children of Israel in the wilderness of Sinai.
65 For God had said of them, "They shall surely die in the
wilderness." There was not a man left of them, except Caleb the
son of Jephunneh, and Joshua the son of Nun.

Numbers 27

1 Then the daughters of Zelophehad, the son of Hepher, the son
of Gilead, the son of Machir, the son of Manasseh, of the families
of Manasseh the son of Joseph came near. These are the names of
his daughters: Mahlah, Noah, Hoglah, Milcah, and Tirzah.
2 They stood before Moses, before Eleazar the priest, and
before the princes and all the congregation, at the door of the
Tent of Meeting, saying, 3 "Our father died in the wilderness.
He was not among the company of those who gathered
themselves together against God in the company of Korah, but he
died in his own sin. He had no sons. 4 Why should the name of
our father be taken away from among his family, because he had
no son? Give to us a possession among the brothers of our
father."
5 Moses brought their cause before God. 6 God spoke to
Moses, saying, 7 "The daughters of Zelophehad speak right.
You shall surely give them a possession of an inheritance among
their father's brothers. You shall cause the inheritance of their
father to pass to them. 8 You shall speak to the children of
Israel, saying, 'If a man dies, and has no son, then you shall cause
his inheritance to pass to his daughter. 9 If he has no daughter,
then you shall give his inheritance to his brothers. 10 If he has
no brothers, then you shall give his inheritance to his father's
brothers. 11 If his father has no brothers, then you shall give his
inheritance to his kinsman who is next to him of his family, and
he shall possess it. This shall be a statute and ordinance for the
children of Israel, as God commanded Moses.'"
12 God said to Moses, "Go up into this mountain of Abarim,
and see the land which I have given to the children of Israel.
13 When you have seen it, you also shall be gathered to your
people, as Aaron your brother was gathered; 14 because in the
strife of the congregation, you rebelled against my word in the
wilderness of Zin, to honor me as holy at the waters before their
eyes." (These are the waters of Meribah of Kadesh in the
wilderness of Zin.)
15 Moses spoke to God, saying, 16 "Let God, the God of the
spirits of all flesh, appoint a man over the congregation, 17 who
may go out before them, and who may come in before them, and
who may lead them out, and who may bring them in, that the
congregation of God may not be as sheep which have no
shepherd."
18 God said to Moses, "Take Joshua the son of Nun, a man in
whom is the Spirit, and lay your hand on him. 19 Set him before
Eleazar the priest, and before all the congregation; and
commission him in their sight. 20 You shall give authority to
him, that all the congregation of the children of Israel may obey.
21 He shall stand before Eleazar the priest, who shall inquire for
him by the judgment of the Urim before God. At his word they
shall go out, and at his word they shall come in, both he and all
the children of Israel with him, even all the congregation."

22 Moses did as God commanded him. He took Joshua, and set
him before Eleazar the priest and before all the congregation.
23 He laid his hands on him and commissioned him, as God
spoke by Moses.

Numbers 28

1 God spoke to Moses, saying, 2 "Command the children of
Israel, and tell them, 'See that you present my offering, my food
for my offerings made by fire, as a pleasant aroma to me, in their
due season.' 3 You shall tell them, 'This is the offering made by
fire which you shall offer to God: male lambs a year old without
defect, two day by day, for a continual burnt offering. 4 You
shall offer the one lamb in the morning, and you shall offer the
other lamb at evening, 5 with one tenth of an ephah[162] of fine
flour for a meal offering, mixed with the fourth part of a hin[163] of
beaten oil. 6 It is a continual burnt offering which was ordained
in Mount Sinai for a pleasant aroma, an offering made by fire to
God. 7 Its drink offering shall be the fourth part of a hin[164] for
each lamb. You shall pour out a drink offering of strong drink to
God in the holy place. 8 The other lamb you shall offer at
evening. As the meal offering of the morning, and as its drink
offering, you shall offer it, an offering made by fire, for a
pleasant aroma to God.
9 "'On the Sabbath day, you shall offer two male lambs a year
old without defect, and two tenths of an ephah[165] of fine flour for
a meal offering mixed with oil, and its drink offering: 10 this is
the burnt offering of every Sabbath, in addition to the continual
burnt offering and its drink offering.
11 "'In the beginnings of your months, you shall offer a burnt
offering to God: two young bulls, one ram, seven male lambs a
year old without defect, 12 and three tenths of an ephah[166] of
fine flour for a meal offering mixed with oil, for each bull; and
two tenth parts of fine flour for a meal offering mixed with oil,
for the one ram; 13 and one tenth part of fine flour mixed with
oil for a meal offering to every lamb, as a burnt offering of a
pleasant aroma, an offering made by fire to God. 14 Their drink
offerings shall be half a hin of wine for a bull, the third part of a
hin for the ram, and the fourth part of a hin for a lamb. This is the
burnt offering of every month throughout the months of the year.
15 Also, one male goat for a sin offering to God shall be offered
in addition to the continual burnt offering and its drink offering.
16 "'In the first month, on the fourteenth day of the month, is
God's Passover. 17 On the fifteenth day of this month shall be a
feast. Unleavened bread shall be eaten for seven days. 18 In the
first day shall be a holy convocation. You shall do no regular
work, 19 but you shall offer an offering made by fire, a burnt
offering to God: two young bulls, one ram, and seven male lambs
a year old. They shall be without defect, 20 with their meal
offering, fine flour mixed with oil. You shall offer three tenths
for a bull, and two tenths for the ram. 21 You shall offer one
tenth for every lamb of the seven lambs; 22 and one male goat
for a sin offering, to make atonement for you. 23 You shall
offer these in addition to the burnt offering of the morning, which
is for a continual burnt offering. 24 In this way you shall offer
daily, for seven days, the food of the offering made by fire, of a
pleasant aroma to God. It shall be offered in addition to the
continual burnt offering and its drink offering. 25 On the
seventh day you shall have a holy convocation. You shall do no
regular work.
26 "'Also in the day of the first fruits, when you offer a new
meal offering to God in your feast of weeks, you shall have a
holy convocation. You shall do no regular work; 27 but you
shall offer a burnt offering for a pleasant aroma to God: two
young bulls, one ram, seven male lambs a year old; 28 and their
meal offering, fine flour mixed with oil, three tenths for each
bull, two tenths for the one ram, 29 one tenth for every lamb of
the seven lambs; 30 and one male goat, to make atonement for
you. 31 Besides the continual burnt offering and its meal
offering, you shall offer them and their drink offerings. See that
they are without defect.

Numbers 29

1 "'In the seventh month, on the first day of the month, you
shall have a holy convocation; you shall do no regular work. It is
a day of blowing of trumpets to you. 2 You shall offer a burnt
offering for a pleasant aroma to God: one young bull, one ram,
seven male lambs a year old without defect; 3 and their meal
offering, fine flour mixed with oil: three tenths for the bull, two
tenths for the ram, 4 and one tenth for every lamb of the seven
lambs; 5 and one male goat for a sin offering, to make
atonement for you; 6 in addition to the burnt offering of the new
moon with its meal offering, and the continual burnt offering
with its meal offering, and their drink offerings, according to
their ordinance, for a pleasant aroma, an offering made by fire to
God.
7 "'On the tenth day of this seventh month you shall have a
holy convocation. You shall afflict your souls. You shall do no
kind of work; 8 but you shall offer a burnt offering to God for a
pleasant aroma: one young bull, one ram, seven male lambs a
year old, all without defect; 9 and their meal offering, fine flour
mixed with oil: three tenths for the bull, two tenths for the one
ram, 10 one tenth for every lamb of the seven lambs; 11 one
male goat for a sin offering, in addition to the sin offering of
atonement, and the continual burnt offering, and its meal
offering, and their drink offerings.
12 "'On the fifteenth day of the seventh month you shall have a
holy convocation. You shall do no regular work. You shall keep a
feast to God seven days. 13 You shall offer a burnt offering, an
offering made by fire, of a pleasant aroma to God: thirteen young
bulls, two rams, fourteen male lambs a year old, all without
defect; 14 and their meal offering, fine flour mixed with oil:
three tenths for every bull of the thirteen bulls, two tenths for
each ram of the two rams, 15 and one tenth for every lamb of
the fourteen lambs; 16 and one male goat for a sin offering, in
addition to the continual burnt offering, its meal offering, and its
drink offering.
17 "'On the second day you shall offer twelve young bulls, two
rams, and fourteen male lambs a year old without defect; 18 and
their meal offering and their drink offerings for the bulls, for the
rams, and for the lambs, according to their number, after the
ordinance; 19 and one male goat for a sin offering, in addition
to the continual burnt offering, with its meal offering and their
drink offerings.
20 "'On the third day: eleven bulls, two rams, fourteen male
lambs a year old without defect; 21 and their meal offering and
their drink offerings for the bulls, for the rams, and for the lambs,
according to their number, after the ordinance; 22 and one male
goat for a sin offering, in addition to the continual burnt offering,
and its meal offering, and its drink offering.
23 "'On the fourth day ten bulls, two rams, fourteen male lambs
a year old without defect; 24 their meal offering and their drink
offerings for the bulls, for the rams, and for the lambs, according
to their number, after the ordinance; 25 and one male goat for a
sin offering; in addition to the continual burnt offering, its meal
offering, and its drink offering.
26 "'On the fifth day: nine bulls, two rams, fourteen male lambs
a year old without defect; 27 and their meal offering and their
drink offerings for the bulls, for the rams, and for the lambs,
according to their number, after the ordinance, 28 and one male
goat for a sin offering, in addition to the continual burnt offering,
and its meal offering, and its drink offering.
29 "'On the sixth day: eight bulls, two rams, fourteen male
lambs a year old without defect; 30 and their meal offering and
their drink offerings for the bulls, for the rams, and for the lambs,
according to their number, after the ordinance, 31 and one male
goat for a sin offering; in addition to the continual burnt offering,
its meal offering, and the drink offerings of it.
32 "'On the seventh day: seven bulls, two rams, fourteen male
lambs a year old without defect; 33 and their meal offering and
their drink offerings for the bulls, for the rams, and for the lambs,
according to their number, after the ordinance, 34 and one male
goat for a sin offering; in addition to the continual burnt offering,
its meal offering, and its drink offering.
35 "'On the eighth day you shall have a solemn assembly. You
shall do no regular work; 36 but you shall offer a burnt offering,
an offering made by fire, a pleasant aroma to God: one bull, one
ram, seven male lambs a year old without defect; 37 their meal
offering and their drink offerings for the bull, for the ram, and for
the lambs, shall be according to their number, after the ordinance,
38 and one male goat for a sin offering, in addition to the
continual burnt offering, with its meal offering, and its drink
offering.
39 "'You shall offer these to God in your set feasts—in addition
to your vows and your free will offerings—for your burnt
offerings, your meal offerings, your drink offerings, and your
peace offerings.'"
40 Moses told the children of Israel according to all that God
commanded Moses.

Numbers 30

1 Moses spoke to the heads of the tribes of the children of
Israel, saying, "This is the thing which God has commanded.
2 When a man vows a vow to God, or swears an oath to bind his
soul with a bond, he shall not break his word. He shall do
according to all that proceeds out of his mouth.
3 "Also, when a woman vows a vow to God and binds herself
by a pledge, being in her father's house, in her youth, 4 and her
father hears her vow and her pledge with which she has bound
her soul, and her father says nothing to her, then all her vows
shall stand, and every pledge with which she has bound her soul
shall stand. 5 But if her father forbids her in the day that he
hears, none of her vows or of her pledges with which she has
bound her soul, shall stand. God will forgive her, because her
father has forbidden her.
6 "If she has a husband, while her vows are on her, or the rash
utterance of her lips with which she has bound her soul, 7 and
her husband hears it, and says nothing to her in the day that he
hears it; then her vows shall stand, and her pledges with which
she has bound her soul shall stand. 8 But if her husband forbids
her in the day that he hears it, then he makes void her vow which
is on her and the rash utterance of her lips, with which she has
bound her soul. God will forgive her.
9 "But the vow of a widow, or of her who is divorced,
everything with which she has bound her soul shall stand against
her.
10 "If she vowed in her husband's house or bound her soul by a
bond with an oath, 11 and her husband heard it, and held his
peace at her and didn't disallow her, then all her vows shall stand,
and every pledge with which she bound her soul shall stand.
12 But if her husband made them null and void in the day that
he heard them, then whatever proceeded out of her lips
concerning her vows, or concerning the bond of her soul, shall
not stand. Her husband has made them void. God will forgive
her. 13 Every vow, and every binding oath to afflict the soul,
her husband may establish it, or her husband may make it void.
14 But if her husband says nothing to her from day to day, then
he establishes all her vows or all her pledges which are on her.
He has established them, because he said nothing to her in the
day that he heard them. 15 But if he makes them null and void
after he has heard them, then he shall bear her iniquity."
16 These are the statutes which God commanded Moses,
between a man and his wife, between a father and his daughter,
being in her youth, in her father's house.

Numbers 31

1 God spoke to Moses, saying, 2 "Avenge the children of
Israel on the Midianites. Afterward you shall be gathered to your
people."
3 Moses spoke to the people, saying, "Arm men from among
you for war, that they may go against Midian, to execute God's
vengeance on Midian. 4 You shall send one thousand out of
every tribe, throughout all the tribes of Israel, to the war." 5 So
there were delivered, out of the thousands of Israel, a thousand
from every tribe, twelve thousand armed for war. 6 Moses sent
them, one thousand of every tribe, to the war with Phinehas the
son of Eleazar the priest, to the war, with the vessels of the
sanctuary and the trumpets for the alarm in his hand. 7 They
fought against Midian, as God commanded Moses. They killed
every male. 8 They killed the kings of Midian with the rest of
their slain: Evi, Rekem, Zur, Hur, and Reba, the five kings of
Midian. They also killed Balaam the son of Beor with the sword.
9 The children of Israel took the women of Midian captive with
their little ones; and all their livestock, all their flocks, and all
their goods, they took as plunder. 10 All their cities in the
places in which they lived, and all their encampments, they
burned with fire. 11 They took all the captives, and all the

---

[162] **28:5** *28:5* 1 ephah is about 22 liters or about 2/3 of a bushel

[163] **28:5** *28:5* A hin is about 6.5 liters or 1.7 gallons.

[164] **28:7** *28:7* One hin is about 6.5 liters, so 1/4 hin is about 1.6 liters or 1.7 quarts.

[165] **28:9** *28:9* 1 ephah is about 22 liters or about 2/3 of a bushel

[166] **28:12** *28:12* 1 ephah is about 22 liters or about 2/3 of a bushel

plunder, both of man and of animal. 12 They brought the
captives with the prey and the plunder, to Moses, and to Eleazar
the priest, and to the congregation of the children of Israel, to the
camp at the plains of Moab, which are by the Jordan at Jericho.
13 Moses and Eleazar the priest, with all the princes of the
congregation, went out to meet them outside of the camp.
14 Moses was angry with the officers of the army, the captains
of thousands and the captains of hundreds, who came from the
service of the war. 15 Moses said to them, "Have you saved all
the women alive? 16 Behold, these caused the children of Israel,
through the counsel of Balaam, to commit trespass against God in
the matter of Peor, and so the plague was among the congregation
of God. 17 Now therefore kill every male among the little ones,
and kill every woman who has known man by lying with him.
18 But all the girls, who have not known man by lying with
him, keep alive for yourselves.
19 "Encamp outside of the camp for seven days. Whoever has
killed any person, and whoever has touched any slain, purify
yourselves on the third day and on the seventh day, you and your
captives. 20 You shall purify every garment, and all that is
made of skin, and all work of goats' hair, and all things made of
wood."
21 Eleazar the priest said to the men of war who went to the
battle, "This is the statute of the law which God has commanded
Moses: 22 however the gold, and the silver, the bronze, the iron,
the tin, and the lead, 23 everything that may withstand the fire,
you shall make to go through the fire, and it shall be clean;
nevertheless it shall be purified with the water for impurity. All
that doesn't withstand the fire you shall make to go through the
water. 24 You shall wash your clothes on the seventh day, and
you shall be clean. Afterward you shall come into the camp."
25 God spoke to Moses, saying, 26 "Count the plunder that
was taken, both of man and of animal, you, and Eleazar the
priest, and the heads of the fathers' households of the
congregation; 27 and divide the plunder into two parts: between
the men skilled in war, who went out to battle, and all the
congregation. 28 Levy a tribute to God of the men of war who
went out to battle: one soul of five hundred; of the persons, of the
cattle, of the donkeys, and of the flocks. 29 Take it from their
half, and give it to Eleazar the priest, for God's wave offering.
30 Of the children of Israel's half, you shall take one drawn out
of every fifty, of the persons, of the cattle, of the donkeys, and of
the flocks, of all the livestock, and give them to the Levites, who
perform the duty of God's tabernacle."
31 Moses and Eleazar the priest did as God commanded Moses.
32 Now the plunder, over and above the booty which the men
of war took, was six hundred seventy-five thousand sheep,
33 seventy-two thousand head of cattle, 34 sixty-one thousand
donkeys, 35 and thirty-two thousand persons in all, of the
women who had not known man by lying with him. 36 The
half, which was the portion of those who went out to war, was in
number three hundred thirty-seven thousand five hundred sheep;
37 and God's tribute of the sheep was six hundred seventy-five.
38 The cattle were thirty-six thousand, of which God's tribute
was seventy-two. 39 The donkeys were thirty thousand five
hundred, of which God's tribute was sixty-one. 40 The persons
were sixteen thousand, of whom God's tribute was thirty-two
persons. 41 Moses gave the tribute, which was God's wave
offering, to Eleazar the priest, as God commanded Moses.
42 Of the children of Israel's half, which Moses divided off
from the men who fought 43 (now the congregation's half was
three hundred thirty-seven thousand five hundred sheep,
44 thirty-six thousand head of cattle, 45 thirty thousand five
hundred donkeys, 46 and sixteen thousand persons), 47 even
of the children of Israel's half, Moses took one drawn out of
every fifty, both of man and of animal, and gave them to the
Levites, who performed the duty of God's tabernacle, as God
commanded Moses.
48 The officers who were over the thousands of the army, the
captains of thousands, and the captains of hundreds, came near to
Moses. 49 They said to Moses, "Your servants have taken the
sum of the men of war who are under our command, and there
lacks not one man of us. 50 We have brought God's offering,
what every man found: gold ornaments, armlets, bracelets, signet
rings, earrings, and necklaces, to make atonement for our souls
before God."
51 Moses and Eleazar the priest took their gold, even all worked
jewels. 52 All the gold of the wave offering that they offered up
to God, of the captains of thousands, and of the captains of
hundreds, was sixteen thousand seven hundred fifty shekels.[167]
53 The men of war had taken booty, every man for himself.
54 Moses and Eleazar the priest took the gold of the captains of
thousands and of hundreds, and brought it into the Tent of
Meeting for a memorial for the children of Israel before God.

Numbers 32

1 Now the children of Reuben and the children of Gad had a
very great multitude of livestock. They saw the land of Jazer, and
the land of Gilead. Behold, the place was a place for livestock.
2 Then the children of Gad and the children of Reuben came
and spoke to Moses, and to Eleazar the priest, and to the princes
of the congregation, saying, 3 "Ataroth, Dibon, Jazer, Nimrah,
Heshbon, Elealeh, Sebam, Nebo, and Beon, 4 the land which
God struck before the congregation of Israel, is a land for
livestock; and your servants have livestock." 5 They said, "If
we have found favor in your sight, let this land be given to your
servants for a possession. Don't bring us over the Jordan."
6 Moses said to the children of Gad, and to the children of
Reuben, "Shall your brothers go to war while you sit here?
7 Why do you discourage the heart of the children of Israel
from going over into the land which God has given them?
8 Your fathers did so when I sent them from Kadesh Barnea to
see the land. 9 For when they went up to the valley of Eshcol,
and saw the land, they discouraged the heart of the children of
Israel, that they should not go into the land which God had given
them. 10 God's anger burned in that day, and he swore, saying,
11 'Surely none of the men who came up out of Egypt, from
twenty years old and upward, shall see the land which I swore to
Abraham, to Isaac, and to Jacob; because they have not wholly
followed me, 12 except Caleb the son of Jephunneh the
Kenizzite, and Joshua the son of Nun, because they have
followed God completely.' 13 God's anger burned against
Israel, and he made them wander back and forth in the wilderness
forty years, until all the generation who had done evil in God's
sight was consumed.
14 "Behold, you have risen up in your fathers' place, an
increase of sinful men, to increase the fierce anger of God toward
Israel. 15 For if you turn away from after him, he will yet again
leave them in the wilderness; and you will destroy all these
people."
16 They came near to him, and said, "We will build sheepfolds
here for our livestock, and cities for our little ones; 17 but we
ourselves will be ready armed to go before the children of Israel,
until we have brought them to their place. Our little ones shall
dwell in the fortified cities because of the inhabitants of the land.
18 We will not return to our houses until the children of Israel
have all received their inheritance. 19 For we will not inherit
with them on the other side of the Jordan and beyond, because
our inheritance has come to us on this side of the Jordan
eastward."
20 Moses said to them: "If you will do this thing, if you will
arm yourselves to go before God to the war, 21 and every one
of your armed men will pass over the Jordan before God until he
has driven out his enemies from before him, 22 and the land is
subdued before God; then afterward you shall return, and be clear
of obligation to God and to Israel. Then this land shall be your
possession before God.
23 "But if you will not do so, behold, you have sinned against
God; and be sure your sin will find you out. 24 Build cities for
your little ones, and folds for your sheep; and do that which has
proceeded out of your mouth."
25 The children of Gad and the children of Reuben spoke to
Moses, saying, "Your servants will do as my lord commands.
26 Our little ones, our wives, our flocks, and all our livestock
shall be there in the cities of Gilead; 27 but your servants will
pass over, every man who is armed for war, before God to battle,
as my lord says."
28 So Moses commanded concerning them to Eleazar the priest,
and to Joshua the son of Nun, and to the heads of the fathers'
households of the tribes of the children of Israel. 29 Moses said
to them, "If the children of Gad and the children of Reuben will
pass with you over the Jordan, every man who is armed to battle
before God, and the land is subdued before you, then you shall
give them the land of Gilead for a possession; 30 but if they will
not pass over with you armed, they shall have possessions among
you in the land of Canaan."
31 The children of Gad and the children of Reuben answered,
saying, "As God has said to your servants, so will we do. 32 We
will pass over armed before God into the land of Canaan, and the
possession of our inheritance shall remain with us beyond the
Jordan."
33 Moses gave to them, even to the children of Gad, and to the
children of Reuben, and to the half-tribe of Manasseh the son of
Joseph, the kingdom of Sihon king of the Amorites, and the
kingdom of Og king of Bashan; the land, according to its cities
and borders, even the cities of the surrounding land. 34 The
children of Gad built Dibon, Ataroth, Aroer, 35 Atroth-shophan,
Jazer, Jogbehah, 36 Beth Nimrah, and Beth Haran: fortified
cities and folds for sheep. 37 The children of Reuben built
Heshbon, Elealeh, Kiriathaim, 38 Nebo, and Baal Meon, (their
names being changed), and Sibmah. They gave other names to
the cities which they built. 39 The children of Machir the son of
Manasseh went to Gilead, took it, and dispossessed the Amorites
who were therein. 40 Moses gave Gilead to Machir the son of
Manasseh; and he lived therein. 41 Jair the son of Manasseh
went and took its villages, and called them Havvoth Jair.
42 Nobah went and took Kenath and its villages, and called it
Nobah, after his own name.

Numbers 33

1 These are the journeys of the children of Israel, when they
went out of the land of Egypt by their armies under the hand of
Moses and Aaron. 2 Moses wrote the starting points of their
journeys by the commandment of God. These are their journeys
according to their starting points. 3 They traveled from Rameses
in the first month, on the fifteenth day of the first month; on the
next day after the Passover, the children of Israel went out with a
high hand in the sight of all the Egyptians, 4 while the
Egyptians were burying all their firstborn, whom God had struck
among them. God also executed judgments on their gods. 5 The
children of Israel traveled from Rameses, and encamped in
Succoth. 6 They traveled from Succoth, and encamped in
Etham, which is in the edge of the wilderness. 7 They traveled
from Etham, and turned back to Pihahiroth, which is before Baal
Zephon, and they encamped before Migdol. 8 They traveled
from before Hahiroth, and crossed through the middle of the sea
into the wilderness. They went three days' journey in the
wilderness of Etham, and encamped in Marah. 9 They traveled
from Marah, and came to Elim. In Elim, there were twelve
springs of water and seventy palm trees, and they encamped
there. 10 They traveled from Elim, and encamped by the Red
Sea. 11 They traveled from the Red Sea, and encamped in the
wilderness of Sin. 12 They traveled from the wilderness of Sin,
and encamped in Dophkah. 13 They traveled from Dophkah,
and encamped in Alush. 14 They traveled from Alush, and
encamped in Rephidim, where there was no water for the people
to drink. 15 They traveled from Rephidim, and encamped in the
wilderness of Sinai. 16 They traveled from the wilderness of
Sinai, and encamped in Kibroth Hattaavah. 17 They traveled
from Kibroth Hattaavah, and encamped in Hazeroth. 18 They
traveled from Hazeroth, and encamped in Rithmah. 19 They
traveled from Rithmah, and encamped in Rimmon Perez.
20 They traveled from Rimmon Perez, and encamped in
Libnah. 21 They traveled from Libnah, and encamped in
Rissah. 22 They traveled from Rissah, and encamped in
Kehelathah. 23 They traveled from Kehelathah, and encamped
in Mount Shepher. 24 They traveled from Mount Shepher, and
encamped in Haradah. 25 They traveled from Haradah, and
encamped in Makheloth. 26 They traveled from Makheloth, and
encamped in Tahath. 27 They traveled from Tahath, and
encamped in Terah. 28 They traveled from Terah, and
encamped in Mithkah. 29 They traveled from Mithkah, and
encamped in Hashmonah. 30 They traveled from Hashmonah,
and encamped in Moseroth. 31 They traveled from Moseroth,
and encamped in Bene Jaakan. 32 They traveled from Bene
Jaakan, and encamped in Hor Haggidgad. 33 They traveled

[167] **31:52** *31:52* **A shekel is about 10 grams or about 0.35 ounces, so 16,750 shekels is about 167.5 kilograms or about 368.5 pounds.**

from Hor Haggidgad, and encamped in Jotbathah. **34** They traveled from Jotbathah, and encamped in Abronah. **35** They traveled from Abronah, and encamped in Ezion Geber. **36** They traveled from Ezion Geber, and encamped at Kadesh in the wilderness of Zin. **37** They traveled from Kadesh, and encamped in Mount Hor, in the edge of the land of Edom.

38 Aaron the priest went up into Mount Hor at the commandment of God and died there, in the fortieth year after the children of Israel had come out of the land of Egypt, in the fifth month, on the first day of the month. **39** Aaron was one hundred twenty-three years old when he died in Mount Hor. **40** The Canaanite king of Arad, who lived in the South in the land of Canaan, heard of the coming of the children of Israel. **41** They traveled from Mount Hor, and encamped in Zalmonah. **42** They traveled from Zalmonah, and encamped in Punon. **43** They traveled from Punon, and encamped in Oboth. **44** They traveled from Oboth, and encamped in Iye Abarim, in the border of Moab.

45 They traveled from Iyim, and encamped in Dibon Gad.

46 They traveled from Dibon Gad, and encamped in Almon Diblathaim. **47** They traveled from Almon Diblathaim, and encamped in the mountains of Abarim, before Nebo. **48** They traveled from the mountains of Abarim, and encamped in the plains of Moab by the Jordan at Jericho. **49** They encamped by the Jordan, from Beth Jeshimoth even to Abel Shittim in the plains of Moab. **50** God spoke to Moses in the plains of Moab by the Jordan at Jericho, saying, **51** Speak to the children of Israel, and tell them, "When you pass over the Jordan into the land of Canaan, **52** then you shall drive out all the inhabitants of the land from before you, destroy all their stone idols, destroy all their molten images, and demolish all their high places. **53** You shall take possession of the land, and dwell therein; for I have given the land to you to possess it. **54** You shall inherit the land by lot according to your families; to the more you shall give the more inheritance, and to the fewer you shall give the less inheritance. Wherever the lot falls to any man, that shall be his. You shall inherit according to the tribes of your fathers.

55 "But if you do not drive out the inhabitants of the land from before you, then those you let remain of them will be like pricks in your eyes and thorns in your sides. They will harass you in the land in which you dwell. **56** It shall happen that as I thought to do to them, so I will do to you."

Numbers 34

1 God spoke to Moses, saying, **2** "Command the children of Israel, and tell them, 'When you come into the land of Canaan (this is the land that shall fall to you for an inheritance, even the land of Canaan according to its borders), **3** then your south quarter shall be from the wilderness of Zin along by the side of Edom, and your south border shall be from the end of the Salt Sea eastward. **4** Your border shall turn about southward of the ascent of Akrabbim, and pass along to Zin; and it shall pass southward of Kadesh Barnea; and it shall go from there to Hazar Addar, and pass along to Azmon. **5** The border shall turn about from Azmon to the brook of Egypt, and it shall end at the sea.

6 "'For the western border, you shall have the great sea and its border. This shall be your west border.

7 "'This shall be your north border: from the great sea you shall mark out for yourselves Mount Hor. **8** From Mount Hor you shall mark out to the entrance of Hamath; and the border shall pass by Zedad. **9** Then the border shall go to Ziphron, and it shall end at Hazar Enan. This shall be your north border.

10 "'You shall mark out your east border from Hazar Enan to Shepham. **11** The border shall go down from Shepham to Riblah, on the east side of Ain. The border shall go down, and shall reach to the side of the sea of Chinnereth eastward. **12** The border shall go down to the Jordan, and end at the Salt Sea. This shall be your land according to its borders around it."

13 Moses commanded the children of Israel, saying, "This is the land which you shall inherit by lot, which God has commanded to give to the nine tribes, and to the half-tribe; **14** for the tribe of the children of Reuben according to their fathers' houses, the tribe of the children of Gad according to their fathers' houses, and the half-tribe of Manasseh have received their inheritance.

15 The two tribes and the half-tribe have received their inheritance beyond the Jordan at Jericho eastward, toward the sunrise."

16 God spoke to Moses, saying, **17** "These are the names of the men who shall divide the land to you for inheritance: Eleazar the priest, and Joshua the son of Nun. **18** You shall take one prince of every tribe, to divide the land for inheritance.

19 These are the names of the men: Of the tribe of Judah, Caleb the son of Jephunneh. **20** Of the tribe of the children of Simeon, Shemuel the son of Ammihud. **21** Of the tribe of Benjamin, Elidad the son of Chislon. **22** Of the tribe of the children of Dan a prince, Bukki the son of Jogli. **23** Of the children of Joseph: of the tribe of the children of Manasseh a prince, Hanniel the son of Ephod. **24** Of the tribe of the children of Ephraim a prince, Kemuel the son of Shiphtan. **25** Of the tribe of the children of Zebulun a prince, Elizaphan the son of Parnach. **26** Of the tribe of the children of Issachar a prince, Paltiel the son of Azzan.

27 Of the tribe of the children of Asher a prince, Ahihud the son of Shelomi. **28** Of the tribe of the children of Naphtali a prince, Pedahel the son of Ammihud." **29** These are they whom God commanded to divide the inheritance to the children of Israel in the land of Canaan.

Numbers 35

1 God spoke to Moses in the plains of Moab by the Jordan at Jericho, saying, **2** "Command the children of Israel to give to the Levites cities to dwell in out of their inheritance. You shall give pasture lands for the cities around them to the Levites.

3 They shall have the cities to dwell in. Their pasture lands shall be for their livestock, and for their possessions, and for all their animals.

4 "The pasture lands of the cities, which you shall give to the Levites, shall be from the wall of the city and outward one thousand cubits[168] around it. **5** You shall measure outside of the city for the east side two thousand cubits, and for the south side two thousand cubits, and for the west side two thousand cubits, and for the north side two thousand cubits, the city being in the middle. This shall be the pasture lands of their cities.

6 "The cities which you shall give to the Levites, they shall be the six cities of refuge, which you shall give for the man slayer to flee to. Besides them you shall give forty-two cities. **7** All the cities which you shall give to the Levites shall be forty-eight cities together with their pasture lands. **8** Concerning the cities which you shall give of the possession of the children of Israel, from the many you shall take many, and from the few you shall take few. Everyone according to his inheritance which he inherits shall give some of his cities to the Levites." **9** God spoke to Moses, saying, **10** "Speak to the children of Israel, and tell them, 'When you pass over the Jordan into the land of Canaan, **11** then you shall appoint for yourselves cities to be cities of refuge for you, that the man slayer who kills any person unwittingly may flee there. **12** The cities shall be for your refuge from the avenger, that the man slayer not die until he stands before the congregation for judgment. **13** The cities which you shall give shall be for you six cities of refuge.

14 You shall give three cities beyond the Jordan, and you shall give three cities in the land of Canaan. They shall be cities of refuge. **15** For the children of Israel, and for the stranger and for the foreigner living among them, shall these six cities be for refuge, that everyone who kills any person unwittingly may flee there.

16 "'But if he struck him with an instrument of iron, so that he died, he is a murderer. The murderer shall surely be put to death.

17 If he struck him with a stone in the hand, by which a man may die, and he died, he is a murderer. The murderer shall surely be put to death.

---

[168]**35:4** *35:4* A cubit is the length from the tip of the middle finger to the elbow on a man's arm, or about 18 inches or 46 centimeters.

The Book of Deuteronomy

Deuteronomy 1

1 These are the words which Moses spoke to all Israel beyond
the Jordan in the wilderness, in the Arabah opposite Suf, between
Paran, Tophel, Laban, Hazeroth, and Dizahab. 2 It is eleven
days' journey from Horeb by the way of Mount Seir to Kadesh
Barnea. 3 In the fortieth year, in the eleventh month, on the first
day of the month, Moses spoke to the children of Israel according
to all that God[169] had given him in commandment to them,
4 after he had struck Sihon the king of the Amorites who lived in
Heshbon, and Og the king of Bashan who lived in Ashtaroth, at
Edrei. 5 Beyond the Jordan, in the land of Moab, Moses began to
declare this law, saying, 6 "God our God[170] spoke to us in
Horeb, saying, 'You have lived long enough at this mountain.
7 Turn, and take your journey, and go to the hill country of the
Amorites and to all the places near there: in the Arabah, in the
hill country, in the lowland, in the South, by the seashore, in the
land of the Canaanites, and in Lebanon as far as the great river,
the river Euphrates. 8 Behold,[171] I have set the land before you.
Go in and possess the land which God swore to your fathers—to
Abraham, to Isaac, and to Jacob—to give to them and to their
offspring[172] after them.'"
9 I spoke to you at that time, saying, "I am not able to bear you
myself alone. 10 God your God has multiplied you, and behold,
you are today as the stars of the sky for multitude. 11 God, the
God of your fathers, make you a thousand times as many as you
are and bless you, as he has promised you! 12 How can I myself
alone bear your problems, your burdens, and your strife?
13 Take wise men of understanding who are respected among
your tribes, and I will make them heads over you."
14 You answered me, and said, "The thing which you have
spoken is good to do." 15 So I took the heads of your tribes, wise
and respected men, and made them heads over you, captains of
thousands, captains of hundreds, captains of fifties, captains of
tens, and officers, according to your tribes. 16 I commanded
your judges at that time, saying, "Hear cases between your
brothers and judge righteously between a man and his brother,
and the foreigner who is living with him. 17 You shall not show
partiality in judgment; you shall hear the small and the great
alike. You shall not be afraid of the face of man, for the judgment
is God's. The case that is too hard for you, you shall bring to me,
and I will hear it." 18 I commanded you at that time all the
things which you should do. 19 We traveled from Horeb and
went through all that great and terrible wilderness which you
saw, by the way to the hill country of the Amorites, as God our
God commanded us; and we came to Kadesh Barnea. 20 I said to
you, "You have come to the hill country of the Amorites, which
God our God gives to us. 21 Behold, God your God has set the
land before you. Go up, take possession, as God the God of your
fathers has spoken to you. Don't be afraid, neither be dismayed."
22 You came near to me, everyone of you, and said, "Let's send
men before us, that they may search the land for us, and bring
back to us word of the way by which we must go up, and the
cities to which we shall come."
23 The thing pleased me well. I took twelve of your men, one
man for every tribe. 24 They turned and went up into the hill
country, and came to the valley of Eshcol, and spied it out.
25 They took some of the fruit of the land in their hands and
brought it down to us, and brought us word again, and said, "It is
a good land which God our God gives to us."
26 Yet you wouldn't go up, but rebelled against the
commandment of God your God. 27 You murmured in your
tents, and said, "Because God hated us, he has brought us out of
the land of Egypt, to deliver us into the hand of the Amorites to
destroy us. 28 Where are we going up? Our brothers have made
our heart melt, saying, 'The people are greater and taller than we.
The cities are great and fortified up to the sky. Moreover we have
seen the sons of the Anakim there!'"
29 Then I said to you, "Don't be terrified. Don't be afraid of
them. 30 God your God, who goes before you, he will fight for
you, according to all that he did for you in Egypt before your
eyes, 31 and in the wilderness where you have seen how that
God your God carried you, as a man carries his son, in all the
way that you went, until you came to this place."
32 Yet in this thing you didn't believe God your God, 33 who
went before you on the way, to seek out a place for you to pitch
your tents in: in fire by night, to show you by what way you
should go, and in the cloud by day. 34 God heard the voice of
your words and was angry, and swore, saying, 35 "Surely not
one of these men of this evil generation shall see the good land
which I swore to give to your fathers, 36 except Caleb the son of
Jephunneh. He shall see it. I will give the land that he has trodden
on to him and to his children, because he has wholly followed
God."
37 Also God was angry with me for your sakes, saying, "You
also shall not go in there. 38 Joshua the son of Nun, who stands
before you, shall go in there. Encourage him, for he shall cause
Israel to inherit it. 39 Moreover your little ones, whom you said
would be captured or killed, your children, who today have no
knowledge of good or evil, shall go in there. I will give it to
them, and they shall possess it. 40 But as for you, turn, and take
your journey into the wilderness by the way to the Red Sea."
41 Then you answered and said to me, "We have sinned against
God. We will go up and fight, according to all that God our God
commanded us." Every man of you put on his weapons of war,
and presumed to go up into the hill country.
42 God said to me, "Tell them, 'Don't go up and don't fight; for
I am not among you, lest you be struck before your enemies.'"
43 So I spoke to you, and you didn't listen; but you rebelled
against the commandment of God, and were presumptuous, and
went up into the hill country. 44 The Amorites, who lived in that
hill country, came out against you and chased you as bees do, and
beat you down in Seir, even to Hormah. 45 You returned and
wept before God; but God didn't listen to your voice, nor turn his
ear to you. 46 So you stayed in Kadesh many days, according to
the days that you remained.

Deuteronomy 2

1 Then we turned, and took our journey into the wilderness by
the way to the Red Sea, as God spoke to me; and we encircled
Mount Seir many days.
2 God spoke to me, saying, 3 "You have encircled this
mountain long enough. Turn northward. 4 Command the people,
saying, 'You are to pass through the border of your brothers, the
children of Esau, who dwell in Seir; and they will be afraid of
you. Therefore be careful. 5 Don't contend with them; for I will
not give you any of their land, no, not so much as for the sole of
the foot to tread on, because I have given Mount Seir to Esau for
a possession. 6 You shall purchase food from them for money,
that you may eat. You shall also buy water from them for money,
that you may drink.'"
7 For God your God has blessed you in all the work of your
hands. He has known your walking through this great wilderness.
These forty years, God your God has been with you. You have
lacked nothing.
8 So we passed by from our brothers, the children of Esau, who
dwell in Seir, from the way of the Arabah from Elath and from
Ezion Geber. We turned and passed by the way of the wilderness
of Moab.
9 God said to me, "Don't bother Moab, neither contend with
them in battle; for I will not give you any of his land for a
possession, because I have given Ar to the children of Lot for a
possession."
10 (The Emim lived there before, a great and numerous people,
and tall as the Anakim. 11 These also are considered to be
Rephaim, as the Anakim; but the Moabites call them Emim.
12 The Horites also lived in Seir in the past, but the children of
Esau succeeded them. They destroyed them from before them,
and lived in their place, as Israel did to the land of his possession,
which God gave to them.)
13 "Now rise up, and cross over the brook Zered." We went over
the brook Zered.
14 The days in which we came from Kadesh Barnea until we had
come over the brook Zered were thirty-eight years: until all the
generation of the men of war were consumed from the middle of
the camp, as God swore to them. 15 Moreover God's hand was
against them, to destroy them from the middle of the camp, until
they were consumed. 16 So, when all the men of war were
consumed and dead from among the people, 17 God spoke to
me, saying, 18 "You are to pass over Ar, the border of Moab,
today. 19 When you come near the border of the children of
Ammon, don't bother them, nor contend with them; for I will not
give you any of the land of the children of Ammon for a
possession, because I have given it to the children of Lot for a
possession."
20 (That also is considered a land of Rephaim. Rephaim lived
there in the past, but the Ammonites call them Zamzummim,
21 a great people, many, and tall, as the Anakim; but God
destroyed them from before Israel, and they succeeded them, and
lived in their place; 22 as he did for the children of Esau who
dwell in Seir, when he destroyed the Horites from before them;
and they succeeded them, and lived in their place even to this
day. 23 Then the Avvim, who lived in villages as far as Gaza:
the Caphtorim, who came out of Caphtor, destroyed them and
lived in their place.)
24 "Rise up, take your journey, and pass over the valley of the
Arnon. Behold, I have given into your hand Sihon the Amorite,
king of Heshbon, and his land; begin to possess it, and contend
with him in battle. 25 Today I will begin to put the dread of you
and the fear of you on the peoples who are under the whole sky,
who shall hear the report of you, and shall tremble and be in
anguish because of you."
26 I sent messengers out of the wilderness of Kedemoth to Sihon
king of Heshbon with words of peace, saying, 27 "Let me pass
through your land. I will go along by the highway. I will turn
neither to the right hand nor to the left. 28 You shall sell me food
for money, that I may eat; and give me water for money, that I
may drink. Just let me pass through on my feet, 29 as the
children of Esau who dwell in Seir, and the Moabites who dwell
in Ar, did to me; until I pass over the Jordan into the land which
God our God gives us." 30 But Sihon king of Heshbon would
not let us pass by him; for God your God hardened his spirit and
made his heart obstinate, that he might deliver him into your
hand, as it is today.
31 God said to me, "Behold, I have begun to deliver up Sihon
and his land before you. Begin to possess, that you may inherit
his land." 32 Then Sihon came out against us, he and all his
people, to battle at Jahaz. 33 God our God delivered him up
before us; and we struck him, his sons, and all his people. 34 We
took all his cities at that time, and utterly destroyed every
inhabited city, with the women and the little ones. We left no one
remaining. 35 Only the livestock we took for plunder for
ourselves, with the plunder of the cities which we had taken.
36 From Aroer, which is on the edge of the valley of the Arnon,
and the city that is in the valley, even to Gilead, there was not a
city too high for us. God our God delivered up all before us.
37 Only to the land of the children of Ammon you didn't come
near: all the banks of the river Jabbok, and the cities of the hill
country, and wherever God our God forbade us.

Deuteronomy 3

1 Then we turned, and went up the way to Bashan. Og the king
of Bashan came out against us, he and all his people, to battle at
Edrei. 2 God said to me, "Don't fear him; for I have delivered
him, with all his people, and his land, into your hand. You shall
do to him as you did to Sihon king of the Amorites, who lived at
Heshbon."
3 So God our God delivered into our hand Og also, the king of
Bashan, and all his people. We struck him until no one was left to
him remaining. 4 We took all his cities at that time. There was
not a city which we didn't take from them: sixty cities, all the
region of Argob, the kingdom of Og in Bashan. 5 All these were
cities fortified with high walls, gates, and bars, in addition to a
great many villages without walls. 6 We utterly destroyed them,
as we did to Sihon king of Heshbon, utterly destroying every
inhabited city, with the women and the little ones. 7 But all the
livestock, and the plunder of the cities, we took for plunder for
ourselves. 8 We took the land at that time out of the hand of the
two kings of the Amorites who were beyond the Jordan, from the
valley of the Arnon to Mount Hermon. 9 (The Sidonians call
Hermon Sirion, and the Amorites call it Senir.) 10 We took all
the cities of the plain, and all Gilead, and all Bashan, to Salecah

---

[169] **1:3** *1:3* "God" is God's proper Name, sometimes rendered "LORD" (all caps) in other translations.

[170] **1:6** *1:6* The Hebrew word rendered "God" is "אֱלֹהִים" (Elohim).

[171] **1:8** *1:8* "Behold", from "הִנֵּה", means look at, take notice, observe, see, or gaze at. It is often used as an interjection.

[172] **1:8** *1:8* or, seed

and Edrei, cities of the kingdom of Og in Bashan. **11** (For only Og king of Bashan remained of the remnant of the Rephaim. Behold, his bedstead was a bedstead of iron. Isn't it in Rabbah of the children of Ammon? Nine cubits[173] was its length, and four cubits its width, after the cubit of a man.) **12** This land we took in possession at that time: from Aroer, which is by the valley of the Arnon, and half the hill country of Gilead with its cities, I gave to the Reubenites and to the Gadites; **13** and the rest of Gilead, and all Bashan, the kingdom of Og, I gave to the half-tribe of Manasseh—all the region of Argob, even all Bashan. (The same is called the land of Rephaim. **14** Jair the son of Manasseh took all the region of Argob, to the border of the Geshurites and the Maacathites, and called them, even Bashan, after his own name, Havvoth Jair, to this day.) **15** I gave Gilead to Machir. **16** To the Reubenites and to the Gadites I gave from Gilead even to the valley of the Arnon, the middle of the valley, and its border, even to the river Jabbok, which is the border of the children of Ammon; **17** the Arabah also, and the Jordan and its border, from Chinnereth even to the sea of the Arabah, the Salt Sea, under the slopes of Pisgah eastward.

18 I commanded you at that time, saying, "God your God has given you this land to possess it. All of you men of valor shall pass over armed before your brothers, the children of Israel.

19 But your wives, and your little ones, and your livestock, (I know that you have much livestock), shall live in your cities which I have given you, **20** until God gives rest to your brothers, as to you, and they also possess the land which God your God gives them beyond the Jordan. Then you shall each return to his own possession, which I have given you."

21 I commanded Joshua at that time, saying, "Your eyes have seen all that God your God has done to these two kings. So shall God do to all the kingdoms where you go over. **22** You shall not fear them; for God your God himself fights for you."

23 I begged God at that time, saying, **24** "Lord[174] God, you have begun to show your servant your greatness, and your strong hand. For what god is there in heaven or in earth that can do works like yours, and mighty acts like yours? **25** Please let me go over and see the good land that is beyond the Jordan, that fine mountain, and Lebanon."

26 But God was angry with me because of you, and didn't listen to me. God said to me, "That is enough! Speak no more to me of this matter. **27** Go up to the top of Pisgah, and lift up your eyes westward, and northward, and southward, and eastward, and see with your eyes; for you shall not go over this Jordan. **28** But commission Joshua, and encourage him, and strengthen him; for he shall go over before this people, and he shall cause them to inherit the land which you shall see." **29** So we stayed in the valley near Beth Peor.

Deuteronomy 4

1 Now, Israel, listen to the statutes and to the ordinances which I teach you, to do them; that you may live, and go in and possess the land which God, the God of your fathers, gives you. **2** You shall not add to the word which I command you, neither shall you take away from it, that you may keep the commandments of God your God which I command you. **3** Your eyes have seen what God did because of Baal Peor; for God your God has destroyed all the men who followed Baal Peor from among you. **4** But you who were faithful to God your God are all alive today. **5** Behold, I have taught you statutes and ordinances, even as God my God commanded me, that you should do so in the middle of the land where you go in to possess it. **6** Keep therefore and do them; for this is your wisdom and your understanding in the sight of the peoples who shall hear all these statutes and say, "Surely this great nation is a wise and understanding people." **7** For what great nation is there that has a god so near to them as God our God is whenever we call on him? **8** What great nation is there that has statutes and ordinances so righteous as all this law which I set before you today?

9 Only be careful, and keep your soul diligently, lest you forget the things which your eyes saw, and lest they depart from your heart all the days of your life; but make them known to your children and your children's children— **10** the day that you stood before God your God in Horeb, when God said to me, "Assemble the people to me, and I will make them hear my words, that they may learn to fear me all the days that they live on the earth, and that they may teach their children." **11** You came near and stood under the mountain. The mountain burned with fire to the heart of the sky, with darkness, cloud, and thick darkness. **12** God spoke to you out of the middle of the fire: you heard the voice of words, but you saw no form; you only heard a voice. **13** He declared to you his covenant, which he commanded you to perform, even the ten commandments. He wrote them on two stone tablets. **14** God commanded me at that time to teach you statutes and ordinances, that you might do them in the land where you go over to possess it. **15** Be very careful, for you saw no kind of form on the day that God spoke to you in Horeb out of the middle of the fire, **16** lest you corrupt yourselves, and make yourself a carved image in the form of any figure, the likeness of male or female, **17** the likeness of any animal that is on the earth, the likeness of any winged bird that flies in the sky, **18** the likeness of anything that creeps on the ground, the likeness of any fish that is in the water under the earth; **19** and lest you lift up your eyes to the sky, and when you see the sun and the moon and the stars, even all the army of the sky, you are drawn away and worship them, and serve them, which God your God has allotted to all the peoples under the whole sky. **20** But God has taken you, and brought you out of the iron furnace, out of Egypt, to be to him a people of inheritance, as it is today. **21** Furthermore God was angry with me for your sakes, and swore that I should not go over the Jordan, and that I should not go in to that good land which God your God gives you for an inheritance; **22** but I must die in this land. I must not go over the Jordan, but you shall go over and possess that good land. **23** Be careful, lest you forget the covenant of God your God, which he made with you, and make yourselves a carved image in the form of anything which God your God has forbidden you. **24** For God your God is a devouring fire, a jealous God. **25** When you shall father children and children's children, and you shall have been long in the land, and shall corrupt yourselves, and make a carved image in the form of anything, and shall do that which is evil in God your God's sight to provoke him to anger, **26** I call heaven and earth to witness against you today, that you will soon utterly perish from off the land which you go over the Jordan to possess it. You will not prolong your days on it, but will utterly be destroyed.

27 God will scatter you among the peoples, and you will be left few in number among the nations where God will lead you away.

28 There you shall serve gods, the work of men's hands, wood and stone, which neither see, nor hear, nor eat, nor smell. **29** But from there you shall seek God your God, and you shall find him when you search after him with all your heart and with all your soul. **30** When you are in oppression, and all these things have come on you, in the latter days you shall return to God your God and listen to his voice. **31** For God your God is a merciful God. He will not fail you nor destroy you, nor forget the covenant of your fathers which he swore to them. **32** For ask now of the days that are past, which were before you, since the day that God created man on the earth, and from the one end of the sky to the other, whether there has been anything as great as this thing is, or has been heard like it? **33** Did a people ever hear the voice of God speaking out of the middle of the fire, as you have heard, and live? **34** Or has God tried to go and take a nation for himself from among another nation, by trials, by signs, by wonders, by war, by a mighty hand, by an outstretched arm, and by great terrors, according to all that God your God did for you in Egypt before your eyes? **35** It was shown to you so that you might know that God is God. There is no one else besides him. **36** Out of heaven he made you to hear his voice, that he might instruct you. On earth he made you to see his great fire; and you heard his words out of the middle of the fire. **37** Because he loved your fathers, therefore he chose their offspring after them, and brought you out with his presence, with his great power, out of Egypt;

38 to drive out nations from before you greater and mightier than you, to bring you in, to give you their land for an inheritance, as it is today. **39** Know therefore today, and take it to heart, that God himself is God in heaven above and on the earth beneath. There is no one else. **40** You shall keep his statutes and his commandments which I command you today, that it may go well with you and with your children after you, and that you may prolong your days in the land which God your God gives you for all time.

41 Then Moses set apart three cities beyond the Jordan toward the sunrise, **42** that the man slayer might flee there, who kills his neighbor unintentionally and didn't hate him in time past, and that fleeing to one of these cities he might live: **43** Bezer in the wilderness, in the plain country, for the Reubenites; and Ramoth in Gilead for the Gadites; and Golan in Bashan for the Manassites.

44 This is the law which Moses set before the children of Israel.

45 These are the testimonies, and the statutes, and the ordinances which Moses spoke to the children of Israel when they came out of Egypt, **46** beyond the Jordan, in the valley opposite Beth Peor, in the land of Sihon king of the Amorites, who lived at Heshbon, whom Moses and the children of Israel struck when they came out of Egypt. **47** They took possession of his land and the land of Og king of Bashan, the two kings of the Amorites, who were beyond the Jordan toward the sunrise; **48** from Aroer, which is on the edge of the valley of the Arnon, even to Mount Sion (also called Hermon), **49** and all the Arabah beyond the Jordan eastward, even to the sea of the Arabah, under the slopes of Pisgah.

Deuteronomy 5

1 Moses called to all Israel, and said to them, "Hear, Israel, the statutes and the ordinances which I speak in your ears today, that you may learn them, and observe to do them." **2** God our God made a covenant with us in Horeb. **3** God didn't make this covenant with our fathers, but with us, even us, who are all of us here alive today. **4** God spoke with you face to face on the mountain out of the middle of the fire, **5** (I stood between God and you at that time, to show you God's word; for you were afraid because of the fire, and didn't go up onto the mountain) saying,

6 "I am God your God, who brought you out of the land of Egypt, out of the house of bondage.

7 "You shall have no other gods before me.

8 "You shall not make a carved image for yourself—any likeness of what is in heaven above, or what is in the earth beneath, or that is in the water under the earth. **9** You shall not bow yourself down to them, nor serve them; for I, God your God, am a jealous God, visiting the iniquity of the fathers on the children and on the third and on the fourth generation of those who hate me; **10** and showing loving kindness to thousands of those who love me and keep my commandments.

11 "You shall not misuse the name of God your God;[175] for God will not hold him guiltless who misuses his name.

12 "Observe the Sabbath day, to keep it holy, as God your God commanded you. **13** You shall labor six days, and do all your work; **14** but the seventh day is a Sabbath to God your God, in which you shall not do any work— neither you, nor your son, nor your daughter, nor your male servant, nor your female servant, nor your ox, nor your donkey, nor any of your livestock, nor your stranger who is within your gates; that your male servant and your female servant may rest as well as you. **15** You shall remember that you were a servant in the land of Egypt, and God your God brought you out of there by a mighty hand and by an outstretched arm. Therefore God your God commanded you to keep the Sabbath day.

16 "Honor your father and your mother, as God your God commanded you; that your days may be long, and that it may go well with you in the land which God your God gives you.

17 "You shall not murder.

18 "You shall not commit adultery.

19 "You shall not steal.

20 "You shall not give false testimony against your neighbor.

21 "You shall not covet your neighbor's wife. Neither shall you desire your neighbor's house, his field, or his male servant, or his female servant, his ox, or his donkey, or anything that is your neighbor's."

22 God spoke these words to all your assembly on the mountain out of the middle of the fire, of the cloud, and of the thick darkness, with a great voice. He added no more. He wrote them on two stone tablets, and gave them to me. **23** When you heard the voice out of the middle of the darkness, while the mountain was burning with fire, you came near to me, even all the heads of your tribes, and your elders; **24** and you said, "Behold, God our God has shown us his glory and his greatness, and we have heard his voice out of the middle of the fire. We have seen today that God does speak with man, and he lives. **25** Now therefore, why should we die? For this great fire will consume us. If we hear God our God's voice any more, then we shall die. **26** For who is there of all flesh, that has heard the voice of the living God

[173] **3:11** *3:11* A cubit is the length from the tip of the middle finger to the elbow on a man's arm, or about 18 inches or 46 centimeters.

[174] **3:24** *3:24* The word translated "Lord" is "Adonai."

[175] **5:11** *5:11* or, You shall not take the name of God your God in vain;

speaking out of the middle of the fire, as we have, and lived?
27 Go near, and hear all that God our God shall say, and tell us
all that God our God tells you; and we will hear it, and do it."
28 God heard the voice of your words when you spoke to me;
and God said to me, "I have heard the voice of the words of this
people which they have spoken to you. They have well said all
that they have spoken. 29 Oh that there were such a heart in
them that they would fear me and keep all my commandments
always, that it might be well with them and with their children
forever!
30 "Go tell them, 'Return to your tents.' 31 But as for you,
stand here by me, and I will tell you all the commandments, and
the statutes, and the ordinances, which you shall teach them, that
they may do them in the land which I give them to possess."
32 You shall observe to do therefore as God your God has
commanded you. You shall not turn away to the right hand or to
the left. 33 You shall walk in all the way which God your God
has commanded you, that you may live and that it may be well
with you, and that you may prolong your days in the land which
you shall possess.

Deuteronomy 6

1 Now these are the commandments, the statutes, and the
ordinances, which God your God commanded to teach you, that
you might do them in the land that you go over to possess; 2 that
you might fear God your God, to keep all his statutes and his
commandments, which I command you—you, your son, and your
son's son, all the days of your life; and that your days may be
prolonged. 3 Hear therefore, Israel, and observe to do it, that it
may be well with you, and that you may increase mightily, as
God, the God of your fathers, has promised to you, in a land
flowing with milk and honey.
4 Hear, Israel: God is our God. God is one. 5 You shall love
God your God with all your heart, with all your soul, and with all
your might. 6 These words, which I command you today, shall
be on your heart; 7 and you shall teach them diligently to your
children, and shall talk of them when you sit in your house, and
when you walk by the way, and when you lie down, and when
you rise up. 8 You shall bind them for a sign on your hand, and
they shall be for frontlets between your eyes. 9 You shall write
them on the door posts of your house and on your gates.
10 It shall be, when God your God brings you into the land
which he swore to your fathers, to Abraham, to Isaac, and to
Jacob, to give you, great and goodly cities which you didn't
build, 11 and houses full of all good things which you didn't fill,
and cisterns dug out which you didn't dig, vineyards and olive
trees which you didn't plant, and you shall eat and be full;
12 then beware lest you forget God, who brought you out of the
land of Egypt, out of the house of bondage. 13 You shall fear
God your God; and you shall serve him, and shall swear by his
name. 14 You shall not go after other gods, of the gods of the
peoples who are around you, 15 for God your God among you is
a jealous God, lest the anger of God your God be kindled against
you, and he destroy you from off the face of the earth. 16 You
shall not tempt God your God, as you tempted him in Massah.
17 You shall diligently keep the commandments of God your
God, and his testimonies, and his statutes, which he has
commanded you. 18 You shall do that which is right and good in
God's sight, that it may be well with you and that you may go in
and possess the good land which God swore to your fathers,
19 to thrust out all your enemies from before you, as God has
spoken.
20 When your son asks you in time to come, saying, "What do
the testimonies, the statutes, and the ordinances, which God our
God has commanded you mean?" 21 then you shall tell your son,
"We were Pharaoh's slaves in Egypt. God brought us out of
Egypt with a mighty hand; 22 and God showed great and
awesome signs and wonders on Egypt, on Pharaoh, and on all his
house, before our eyes; 23 and he brought us out from there, that
he might bring us in, to give us the land which he swore to our
fathers. 24 God commanded us to do all these statutes, to fear
God our God, for our good always, that he might preserve us
alive, as we are today. 25 It shall be righteousness to us, if we
observe to do all these commandments before God our God, as he
has commanded us."

Deuteronomy 7

1 When God your God brings you into the land where you go to
possess it, and casts out many nations before you—the Hittite, the
Girgashite, the Amorite, the Canaanite, the Perizzite, the Hivite,
and the Jebusite—seven nations greater and mightier than you;
2 and when God your God delivers them up before you, and you
strike them, then you shall utterly destroy them. You shall make
no covenant with them, nor show mercy to them. 3 You shall not
make marriages with them. You shall not give your daughter to
his son, nor shall you take his daughter for your son. 4 For that
would turn away your sons from following me, that they may
serve other gods. So God's anger would be kindled against you,
and he would destroy you quickly. 5 But you shall deal with
them like this: you shall break down their altars, dash their pillars
in pieces, cut down their Asherah poles, and burn their engraved
images with fire. 6 For you are a holy people to God your God.
God your God has chosen you to be a people for his own
possession, above all peoples who are on the face of the earth.
7 God didn't set his love on you nor choose you, because you
were more in number than any people; for you were the fewest of
all peoples; 8 but because God loves you, and because he desires
to keep the oath which he swore to your fathers, God has brought
you out with a mighty hand and redeemed you out of the house of
bondage, from the hand of Pharaoh king of Egypt. 9 Know
therefore that God your God himself is God, the faithful God,
who keeps covenant and loving kindness with them who love him
and keep his commandments to a thousand generations, 10 and
repays those who hate him to their face, to destroy them. He will
not be slack to him who hates him. He will repay him to his face.
11 You shall therefore keep the commandments, the statutes, and
the ordinances which I command you today, to do them. 12 It
shall happen, because you listen to these ordinances and keep and
do them, that God your God will keep with you the covenant and
the loving kindness which he swore to your fathers. 13 He will
love you, bless you, and multiply you. He will also bless the fruit
of your body and the fruit of your ground, your grain and your
new wine and your oil, the increase of your livestock and the
young of your flock, in the land which he swore to your fathers to
give you. 14 You will be blessed above all peoples. There won't
be male or female barren among you, or among your livestock.
15 God will take away from you all sickness; and he will put
none of the evil diseases of Egypt, which you know, on you, but
will lay them on all those who hate you. 16 You shall consume
all the peoples whom God your God shall deliver to you. Your
eye shall not pity them. You shall not serve their gods; for that
would be a snare to you. 17 If you shall say in your heart, "These
nations are more than I; how can I dispossess them?" 18 you
shall not be afraid of them. You shall remember well what God
your God did to Pharaoh and to all Egypt: 19 the great trials
which your eyes saw, the signs, the wonders, the mighty hand,
and the outstretched arm, by which God your God brought you
out. So shall God your God do to all the peoples of whom you are
afraid. 20 Moreover God your God will send the hornet among
them, until those who are left, and hide themselves, perish from
before you. 21 You shall not be scared of them; for God your
God is among you, a great and awesome God. 22 God your God
will cast out those nations before you little by little. You may not
consume them at once, lest the animals of the field increase on
you. 23 But God your God will deliver them up before you, and
will confuse them with a great confusion, until they are
destroyed. 24 He will deliver their kings into your hand, and you
shall make their name perish from under the sky. No one will be
able to stand before you until you have destroyed them. 25 You
shall burn the engraved images of their gods with fire. You shall
not covet the silver or the gold that is on them, nor take it for
yourself, lest you be snared in it; for it is an abomination to God
your God. 26 You shall not bring an abomination into your
house and become a devoted thing like it. You shall utterly detest
it. You shall utterly abhor it; for it is a devoted thing.

Deuteronomy 8

1 You shall observe to do all the commandments which I
command you today, that you may live, and multiply, and go in
and possess the land which God swore to your fathers. 2 You
shall remember all the way which God your God has led you
these forty years in the wilderness, that he might humble you, to
test you, to know what was in your heart, whether you would
keep his commandments or not. 3 He humbled you, allowed you
to be hungry, and fed you with manna, which you didn't know,
neither did your fathers know, that he might teach you that man
does not live by bread only, but man lives by every word that
proceeds out of God's mouth. 4 Your clothing didn't grow old
on you, neither did your foot swell, these forty years. 5 You shall
consider in your heart that as a man disciplines his son, so God
your God disciplines you. 6 You shall keep the commandments
of God your God, to walk in his ways, and to fear him. 7 For
God your God brings you into a good land, a land of brooks of
water, of springs, and underground water flowing into valleys
and hills; 8 a land of wheat, barley, vines, fig trees, and
pomegranates; a land of olive trees and honey; 9 a land in which
you shall eat bread without scarcity, you shall not lack anything
in it; a land whose stones are iron, and out of whose hills you
may dig copper. 10 You shall eat and be full, and you shall bless
God your God for the good land which he has given you.
11 Beware lest you forget God your God, in not keeping his
commandments, his ordinances, and his statutes, which I
command you today; 12 lest, when you have eaten and are full,
and have built fine houses and lived in them; 13 and when your
herds and your flocks multiply, and your silver and your gold is
multiplied, and all that you have is multiplied; 14 then your heart
might be lifted up, and you forget God your God, who brought
you out of the land of Egypt, out of the house of bondage;
15 who led you through the great and terrible wilderness, with
venomous snakes and scorpions, and thirsty ground where there
was no water; who poured water for you out of the rock of flint;
16 who fed you in the wilderness with manna, which your
fathers didn't know, that he might humble you, and that he might
prove you, to do you good at your latter end; 17 and lest you say
in your heart, "My power and the might of my hand has gotten
me this wealth." 18 But you shall remember God your God, for
it is he who gives you power to get wealth, that he may establish
his covenant which he swore to your fathers, as it is today.
19 It shall be, if you shall forget God your God, and walk after
other gods, and serve them and worship them, I testify against
you today that you shall surely perish. 20 As the nations that
God makes to perish before you, so you shall perish, because you
wouldn't listen to God your God's voice.

Deuteronomy 9

1 Hear, Israel! You are to pass over the Jordan today, to go in to
dispossess nations greater and mightier than yourself, cities great
and fortified up to the sky, 2 a people great and tall, the sons of
the Anakim, whom you know, and of whom you have heard say,
"Who can stand before the sons of Anak?" 3 Know therefore
today that God your God is he who goes over before you as a
devouring fire. He will destroy them and he will bring them down
before you. So you shall drive them out and make them perish
quickly, as God has spoken to you.
4 Don't say in your heart, after God your God has thrust them
out from before you, "For my righteousness God has brought me
in to possess this land;" because God drives them out before you
because of the wickedness of these nations. 5 Not for your
righteousness or for the uprightness of your heart do you go in to
possess their land; but for the wickedness of these nations God
your God does drive them out from before you, and that he may
establish the word which God swore to your fathers, to Abraham,
to Isaac, and to Jacob. 6 Know therefore that God your God
doesn't give you this good land to possess for your righteousness,
for you are a stiff-necked people. 7 Remember, and don't forget,
how you provoked God your God to wrath in the wilderness.
From the day that you left the land of Egypt until you came to
this place, you have been rebellious against God. 8 Also in
Horeb you provoked God to wrath, and God was angry with you
to destroy you. 9 When I had gone up onto the mountain to
receive the stone tablets, even the tablets of the covenant which
God made with you, then I stayed on the mountain forty days and
forty nights. I neither ate bread nor drank water. 10 God
delivered to me the two stone tablets written with God's finger.
On them were all the words which God spoke with you on the
mountain out of the middle of the fire in the day of the assembly.
11 It came to pass at the end of forty days and forty nights that
God gave me the two stone tablets, even the tablets of the
covenant. 12 God said to me, "Arise, get down quickly from
here; for your people whom you have brought out of Egypt have
corrupted themselves. They have quickly turned away from the
way which I commanded them. They have made a molten image
for themselves!"
13 Furthermore God spoke to me, saying, "I have seen this
people, and behold, it is a stiff-necked people. 14 Leave me
alone, that I may destroy them, and blot out their name from
under the sky; and I will make of you a nation mightier and
greater than they."
15 So I turned and came down from the mountain, and the
mountain was burning with fire. The two tablets of the covenant
were in my two hands. 16 I looked, and behold, you had sinned
against God your God. You had made yourselves a molded calf.
You had quickly turned away from the way which God had
commanded you. 17 I took hold of the two tablets, and threw
them out of my two hands, and broke them before your eyes.
18 I fell down before God, as at the first, forty days and forty
nights. I neither ate bread nor drank water, because of all your sin
which you sinned, in doing that which was evil in God's sight, to
provoke him to anger. 19 For I was afraid of the anger and hot
displeasure with which God was angry against you to destroy
you. But God listened to me that time also. 20 God was angry

enough with Aaron to destroy him. I prayed for Aaron also at the
same time. 21 I took your sin, the calf which you had made, and
burned it with fire, and crushed it, grinding it very small, until it
was as fine as dust. I threw its dust into the brook that descended
out of the mountain. 22 At Taberah, at Massah, and at Kibroth
Hattaavah you provoked God to wrath. 23 When God sent you
from Kadesh Barnea, saying, "Go up and possess the land which
I have given you," you rebelled against the commandment of
God your God, and you didn't believe him or listen to his voice.
24 You have been rebellious against God from the day that I
knew you. 25 So I fell down before God the forty days and forty
nights that I fell down, because God had said he would destroy
you. 26 I prayed to God, and said, "Lord God, don't destroy your
people and your inheritance that you have redeemed through your
greatness, that you have brought out of Egypt with a mighty
hand. 27 Remember your servants, Abraham, Isaac, and Jacob.
Don't look at the stubbornness of this people, nor at their
wickedness, nor at their sin, 28 lest the land you brought us out
from say, 'Because God was not able to bring them into the land
which he promised to them, and because he hated them, he has
brought them out to kill them in the wilderness.' 29 Yet they are
your people and your inheritance, which you brought out by your
great power and by your outstretched arm."

Deuteronomy 10

1 At that time God said to me, "Cut two stone tablets like the
first, and come up to me onto the mountain, and make an ark of
wood. 2 I will write on the tablets the words that were on the
first tablets which you broke, and you shall put them in the ark."
3 So I made an ark of acacia wood, and cut two stone tablets
like the first, and went up onto the mountain, having the two
tablets in my hand. 4 He wrote on the tablets, according to the
first writing, the ten commandments, which God spoke to you on
the mountain out of the middle of the fire in the day of the
assembly; and God gave them to me. 5 I turned and came down
from the mountain, and put the tablets in the ark which I had
made; and there they are as God commanded me.
6 (The children of Israel traveled from Beeroth Bene Jaakan to
Moserah. There Aaron died, and there he was buried; and Eleazar
his son ministered in the priest's office in his place. 7 From
there they traveled to Gudgodah; and from Gudgodah to
Jotbathah, a land of brooks of water. 8 At that time God set
apart the tribe of Levi to bear the ark of God's covenant, to stand
before God to minister to him, and to bless in his name, to this
day. 9 Therefore Levi has no portion nor inheritance with his
brothers; God is his inheritance, according as God your God
spoke to him.)
10 I stayed on the mountain, as at the first time, forty days and
forty nights; and God listened to me that time also. God would
not destroy you. 11 God said to me, "Arise, take your journey
before the people; and they shall go in and possess the land which
I swore to their fathers to give to them."
12 Now, Israel, what does God your God require of you, but to
fear God your God, to walk in all his ways, to love him, and to
serve God your God with all your heart and with all your soul,
13 to keep God's commandments and statutes, which I
command you today for your good? 14 Behold, to God your
God belongs heaven, the heaven of heavens, and the earth, with
all that is therein. 15 Only God had a delight in your fathers to
love them, and he chose their offspring after them, even you
above all peoples, as it is today. 16 Circumcise therefore the
foreskin of your heart, and be no more stiff-necked. 17 For God
your God, he is God of gods and Lord of lords, the great God, the
mighty, and the awesome, who doesn't respect persons or take
bribes. 18 He executes justice for the fatherless and widow and
loves the foreigner in giving him food and clothing.
19 Therefore love the foreigner, for you were foreigners in the
land of Egypt. 20 You shall fear God your God. You shall serve
him. You shall cling to him, and you shall swear by his name.
21 He is your praise, and he is your God, who has done for you
these great and awesome things which your eyes have seen.
22 Your fathers went down into Egypt with seventy persons;
and now God your God has made you as the stars of the sky for
multitude.

Deuteronomy 11

1 Therefore you shall love God your God, and keep his
instructions, his statutes, his ordinances, and his commandments,
always. 2 Know this day—for I don't speak with your children
who have not known, and who have not seen the chastisement of
God your God, his greatness, his mighty hand, his outstretched
arm, 3 his signs, and his works, which he did in the middle of
Egypt to Pharaoh the king of Egypt, and to all his land; 4 and
what he did to the army of Egypt, to their horses, and to their
chariots; how he made the water of the Red Sea to overflow them
as they pursued you, and how God has destroyed them to this
day; 5 and what he did to you in the wilderness until you came
to this place; 6 and what he did to Dathan and Abiram, the sons
of Eliab, the son of Reuben—how the earth opened its mouth and
swallowed them up, with their households, their tents, and every
living thing that followed them, in the middle of all Israel; 7 but
your eyes have seen all of God's great work which he did.
8 Therefore you shall keep the entire commandment which I
command you today, that you may be strong, and go in and
possess the land that you go over to possess; 9 and that you may
prolong your days in the land which God swore to your fathers to
give to them and to their offspring, a land flowing with milk and
honey. 10 For the land, where you go in to possess isn't like the
land of Egypt that you came out of, where you sowed your seed
and watered it with your foot, as a garden of herbs; 11 but the
land that you go over to possess is a land of hills and valleys
which drinks water from the rain of the sky, 12 a land which
God your God cares for. God your God's eyes are always on it,
from the beginning of the year even to the end of the year. 13 It
shall happen, if you shall listen diligently to my commandments
which I command you today, to love God your God, and to serve
him with all your heart and with all your soul, 14 that I will give
the rain for your land in its season, the early rain and the latter
rain, that you may gather in your grain, your new wine, and your
oil. 15 I will give grass in your fields for your livestock, and
you shall eat and be full. 16 Be careful, lest your heart be
deceived, and you turn away to serve other gods and worship
them; 17 and God's anger be kindled against you, and he shut
up the sky so that there is no rain, and the land doesn't yield its
fruit; and you perish quickly from off the good land which God
gives you. 18 Therefore you shall lay up these words of mine in
your heart and in your soul. You shall bind them for a sign on
your hand, and they shall be for frontlets between your eyes.
19 You shall teach them to your children, talking of them when
you sit in your house, when you walk by the way, when you lie
down, and when you rise up. 20 You shall write them on the
door posts of your house and on your gates; 21 that your days
and your children's days may be multiplied in the land which
God swore to your fathers to give them, as the days of the
heavens above the earth. 22 For if you shall diligently keep all
these commandments which I command you—to do them, to love
God your God, to walk in all his ways, and to cling to him—
23 then God will drive out all these nations from before you,
and you shall dispossess nations greater and mightier than
yourselves. 24 Every place on which the sole of your foot treads
shall be yours: from the wilderness and Lebanon, from the river,
the river Euphrates, even to the western sea shall be your border.
25 No man will be able to stand before you. God your God will
lay the fear of you and the dread of you on all the land that you
tread on, as he has spoken to you. 26 Behold, I set before you
today a blessing and a curse: 27 the blessing, if you listen to the
commandments of God your God, which I command you today;
28 and the curse, if you do not listen to the commandments of
God your God, but turn away out of the way which I command
you today, to go after other gods which you have not known.
29 It shall happen, when God your God brings you into the land
that you go to possess, that you shall set the blessing on Mount
Gerizim, and the curse on Mount Ebal. 30 Aren't they beyond
the Jordan, behind the way of the going down of the sun, in the
land of the Canaanites who dwell in the Arabah near Gilgal,
beside the oaks of Moreh? 31 For you are to pass over the
Jordan to go in to possess the land which God your God gives
you, and you shall possess it and dwell in it. 32 You shall
observe to do all the statutes and the ordinances which I set
before you today.

Deuteronomy 12

1 These are the statutes and the ordinances which you shall
observe to do in the land which God, the God of your fathers, has
given you to possess all the days that you live on the earth.
2 You shall surely destroy all the places in which the nations
that you shall dispossess served their gods: on the high
mountains, and on the hills, and under every green tree. 3 You
shall break down their altars, dash their pillars in pieces, and burn
their Asherah poles with fire. You shall cut down the engraved
images of their gods. You shall destroy their name out of that
place. 4 You shall not do so to God your God. 5 But to the
place which God your God shall choose out of all your tribes, to
put his name there, you shall seek his habitation, and you shall
come there. 6 You shall bring your burnt offerings, your
sacrifices, your tithes, the wave offering of your hand, your vows,
your free will offerings, and the firstborn of your herd and of
your flock there. 7 There you shall eat before God your God,
and you shall rejoice in all that you put your hand to, you and
your households, in which God your God has blessed you.
8 You shall not do all the things that we do here today, every
man whatever is right in his own eyes; 9 for you haven't yet
come to the rest and to the inheritance which God your God gives
you. 10 But when you go over the Jordan and dwell in the land
which God your God causes you to inherit, and he gives you rest
from all your enemies around you, so that you dwell in safety,
11 then it shall happen that to the place which God your God
shall choose, to cause his name to dwell there, there you shall
bring all that I command you: your burnt offerings, your
sacrifices, your tithes, the wave offering of your hand, and all
your choice vows which you vow to God. 12 You shall rejoice
before God your God—you, and your sons, your daughters, your
male servants, your female servants, and the Levite who is within
your gates, because he has no portion nor inheritance with you.
13 Be careful that you don't offer your burnt offerings in every
place that you see; 14 but in the place which God chooses in
one of your tribes, there you shall offer your burnt offerings, and
there you shall do all that I command you.
15 Yet you may kill and eat meat within all your gates, after all
the desire of your soul, according to God your God's blessing
which he has given you. The unclean and the clean may eat of it,
as of the gazelle and the deer. 16 Only you shall not eat the
blood. You shall pour it out on the earth like water. 17 You may
not eat within your gates the tithe of your grain, or of your new
wine, or of your oil, or the firstborn of your herd or of your flock,
nor any of your vows which you vow, nor your free will
offerings, nor the wave offering of your hand; 18 but you shall
eat them before God your God in the place which God your God
shall choose: you, your son, your daughter, your male servant,
your female servant, and the Levite who is within your gates.
You shall rejoice before God your God in all that you put your
hand to. 19 Be careful that you don't forsake the Levite as long
as you live in your land.
20 When God your God enlarges your border, as he has
promised you, and you say, "I want to eat meat," because your
soul desires to eat meat, you may eat meat, after all the desire of
your soul. 21 If the place which God your God shall choose to
put his name is too far from you, then you shall kill of your herd
and of your flock, which God has given you, as I have
commanded you; and you may eat within your gates, after all the
desire of your soul. 22 Even as the gazelle and as the deer is
eaten, so you shall eat of it. The unclean and the clean may eat of
it alike. 23 Only be sure that you don't eat the blood; for the
blood is the life. You shall not eat the life with the meat. 24 You
shall not eat it. You shall pour it out on the earth like water.
25 You shall not eat it, that it may go well with you and with
your children after you, when you do that which is right in God's
eyes. 26 Only your holy things which you have, and your vows,
you shall take and go to the place which God shall choose.
27 You shall offer your burnt offerings, the meat and the blood,
on God your God's altar. The blood of your sacrifices shall be
poured out on God your God's altar, and you shall eat the meat.
28 Observe and hear all these words which I command you, that
it may go well with you and with your children after you forever,
when you do that which is good and right in God your God's
eyes.
29 When God your God cuts off the nations from before you
where you go in to dispossess them, and you dispossess them and
dwell in their land, 30 be careful that you are not ensnared to
follow them after they are destroyed from before you, and that
you not inquire after their gods, saying, "How do these nations
serve their gods? I will do likewise." 31 You shall not do so to
God your God; for every abomination to God, which he hates,
they have done to their gods; for they even burn their sons and
their daughters in the fire to their gods. 32 Whatever thing I
command you, that you shall observe to do. You shall not add to
it, nor take away from it.

Deuteronomy 13

1 If a prophet or a dreamer of dreams arises among you, and he
gives you a sign or a wonder, 2 and the sign or the wonder
comes to pass, of which he spoke to you, saying, "Let's go after
other gods" (which you have not known) "and let's serve them,"
3 you shall not listen to the words of that prophet, or to that
dreamer of dreams; for God your God is testing you, to know
whether you love God your God with all your heart and with all
your soul. 4 You shall walk after God your God, fear him, keep
his commandments, and obey his voice. You shall serve him, and
cling to him. 5 That prophet, or that dreamer of dreams, shall be
put to death, because he has spoken rebellion against God your
God, who brought you out of the land of Egypt and redeemed

you out of the house of bondage, to draw you aside out of the
way which God your God commanded you to walk in. So you
shall remove the evil from among you.

6 If your brother, the son of your mother, or your son, or your
daughter, or the wife of your bosom, or your friend who is as
your own soul, entices you secretly, saying, "Let's go and serve
other gods"—which you have not known, you, nor your fathers;

7 of the gods of the peoples who are around you, near to you, or
far off from you, from the one end of the earth even to the other
end of the earth— 8 you shall not consent to him nor listen to
him; neither shall your eye pity him, neither shall you spare,
neither shall you conceal him; 9 but you shall surely kill him.
Your hand shall be first on him to put him to death, and
afterwards the hands of all the people. 10 You shall stone him
to death with stones, because he has sought to draw you away
from God your God, who brought you out of the land of Egypt,
out of the house of bondage. 11 All Israel shall hear, and fear,
and shall not do any more wickedness like this among you.

12 If you hear about one of your cities, which God your God
gives you to dwell there, that 13 certain wicked fellows have
gone out from among you and have drawn away the inhabitants
of their city, saying, "Let's go and serve other gods," which you
have not known, 14 then you shall inquire, investigate, and ask
diligently. Behold, if it is true, and the thing certain, that such
abomination was done among you, 15 you shall surely strike the
inhabitants of that city with the edge of the sword, destroying it
utterly, with all that is therein and its livestock, with the edge of
the sword. 16 You shall gather all its plunder into the middle of
its street, and shall burn with fire the city, with all of its plunder,
to God your God. It shall be a heap forever. It shall not be built
again. 17 Nothing of the devoted thing shall cling to your hand,
that God may turn from the fierceness of his anger and show you
mercy, and have compassion on you and multiply you, as he has
sworn to your fathers, 18 when you listen to God your God's
voice, to keep all his commandments which I command you
today, to do that which is right in God your God's eyes.

Deuteronomy 14

1 You are the children of God your God. You shall not cut
yourselves, nor make any baldness between your eyes for the
dead. 2 For you are a holy people to God your God, and God
has chosen you to be a people for his own possession, above all
peoples who are on the face of the earth.

3 You shall not eat any abominable thing. 4 These are the
animals which you may eat: the ox, the sheep, the goat, 5 the
deer, the gazelle, the roebuck, the wild goat, the ibex, the
antelope, and the chamois. 6 Every animal that parts the hoof,
and has the hoof split in two and chews the cud, among the
animals, you may eat. 7 Nevertheless these you shall not eat of
them that chew the cud, or of those who have the hoof split: the
camel, the hare, and the rabbit. Because they chew the cud but
don't part the hoof, they are unclean to you. 8 The pig, because
it has a split hoof but doesn't chew the cud, is unclean to you.
You shall not eat their meat. You shall not touch their carcasses.

9 These you may eat of all that are in the waters: you may eat
whatever has fins and scales. 10 You shall not eat whatever
doesn't have fins and scales. It is unclean to you. 11 Of all clean
birds you may eat. 12 But these are they of which you shall not
eat: the eagle, the vulture, the osprey, 13 the red kite, the falcon,
the kite after its kind, 14 every raven after its kind, 15 the
ostrich, the owl, the seagull, the hawk after its kind, 16 the little
owl, the great owl, the horned owl, 17 the pelican, the vulture,
the cormorant, 18 the stork, the heron after its kind, the hoopoe,
and the bat. 19 All winged creeping things are unclean to you.
They shall not be eaten. 20 Of all clean birds you may eat.

21 You shall not eat of anything that dies of itself. You may
give it to the foreigner living among you who is within your
gates, that he may eat it; or you may sell it to a foreigner; for you
are a holy people to God your God.
You shall not boil a young goat in its mother's milk.

22 You shall surely tithe all the increase of your seed, that
which comes out of the field year by year. 23 You shall eat
before God your God, in the place which he chooses to cause his
name to dwell, the tithe of your grain, of your new wine, and of
your oil, and the firstborn of your herd and of your flock; that you
may learn to fear God your God always. 24 If the way is too
long for you, so that you are not able to carry it because the place
which God your God shall choose to set his name there is too far
from you, when God your God blesses you, 25 then you shall
turn it into money, bind up the money in your hand, and shall go
to the place which God your God shall choose. 26 You shall
trade the money for whatever your soul desires: for cattle, or for
sheep, or for wine, or for strong drink, or for whatever your soul
asks of you. You shall eat there before God your God, and you
shall rejoice, you and your household. 27 You shall not forsake
the Levite who is within your gates, for he has no portion nor
inheritance with you. 28 At the end of every three years you
shall bring all the tithe of your increase in the same year, and
shall store it within your gates. 29 The Levite, because he has
no portion nor inheritance with you, as well as the foreigner
living among you, the fatherless, and the widow who are within
your gates shall come, and shall eat and be satisfied; that God
your God may bless you in all the work of your hand which you
do.

Deuteronomy 15

1 At the end of every seven years, you shall cancel debts.

2 This is the way it shall be done: every creditor shall release
that which he has lent to his neighbor. He shall not require
payment from his neighbor and his brother, because God's
release has been proclaimed. 3 Of a foreigner you may require
it; but whatever of yours is with your brother, your hand shall
release. 4 However there will be no poor with you (for God will
surely bless you in the land which God your God gives you for an
inheritance to possess) 5 if only you diligently listen to God
your God's voice, to observe to do all this commandment which I
command you today. 6 For God your God will bless you, as he
promised you. You will lend to many nations, but you will not
borrow. You will rule over many nations, but they will not rule
over you. 7 If a poor man, one of your brothers, is with you
within any of your gates in your land which God your God gives
you, you shall not harden your heart, nor shut your hand from
your poor brother; 8 but you shall surely open your hand to him,
and shall surely lend him sufficient for his need, which he lacks.

9 Beware that there not be a wicked thought in your heart,
saying, "The seventh year, the year of release, is at hand," and
your eye be evil against your poor brother and you give him
nothing; and he cry to God against you, and it be sin to you.

10 You shall surely give, and your heart shall not be grieved
when you give to him, because it is for this thing God your God
will bless you in all your work and in all that you put your hand
to. 11 For the poor will never cease out of the land. Therefore I
command you to surely open your hand to your brother, to your
needy, and to your poor, in your land. 12 If your brother, a
Hebrew man, or a Hebrew woman, is sold to you and serves you
six years, then in the seventh year you shall let him go free from
you. 13 When you let him go free from you, you shall not let
him go empty. 14 You shall furnish him liberally out of your
flock, out of your threshing floor, and out of your wine press. As
God your God has blessed you, you shall give to him. 15 You
shall remember that you were a slave in the land of Egypt, and
God your God redeemed you. Therefore I command you this
thing today. 16 It shall be, if he tells you, "I will not go out from
you," because he loves you and your house, because he is well
with you, 17 then you shall take an awl, and thrust it through his
ear to the door, and he shall be your servant forever. Also to your
female servant you shall do likewise. 18 It shall not seem hard
to you when you let him go free from you; for he has been double
the value of a hired hand as he served you six years. God your
God will bless you in all that you do. 19 You shall dedicate all
the firstborn males that are born of your herd and of your flock to
God your God. You shall do no work with the firstborn of your
herd, nor shear the firstborn of your flock. 20 You shall eat it
before God your God year by year in the place which God shall
choose, you and your household. 21 If it has any defect—is
lame or blind, or has any defect whatever, you shall not sacrifice
it to God your God. 22 You shall eat it within your gates. The`
unclean and the clean shall eat it alike, as the gazelle and as the
deer. 23 Only you shall not eat its blood. You shall pour it out
on the ground like water.

Deuteronomy 16

1 Observe the month of Abib, and keep the Passover to God
your God; for in the month of Abib God your God brought you
out of Egypt by night. 2 You shall sacrifice the Passover to God
your God, of the flock and the herd, in the place which God shall
choose to cause his name to dwell there. 3 You shall eat no
leavened bread with it. You shall eat unleavened bread with it
seven days, even the bread of affliction (for you came out of the
land of Egypt in haste) that you may remember the day when you
came out of the land of Egypt all the days of your life. 4 No
yeast shall be seen with you in all your borders seven days;
neither shall any of the meat, which you sacrifice the first day at
evening, remain all night until the morning. 5 You may not
sacrifice the Passover within any of your gates which God your
God gives you; 6 but at the place which God your God shall
choose to cause his name to dwell in, there you shall sacrifice the
Passover at evening, at the going down of the sun, at the season
that you came out of Egypt. 7 You shall roast and eat it in the
place which God your God chooses. In the morning you shall
return to your tents. 8 Six days you shall eat unleavened bread.
On the seventh day shall be a solemn assembly to God your God.
You shall do no work. 9 You shall count for yourselves seven
weeks. From the time you begin to put the sickle to the standing
grain you shall begin to count seven weeks. 10 You shall keep
the feast of weeks to God your God with a tribute of a free will
offering of your hand, which you shall give according to how
God your God blesses you. 11 You shall rejoice before God
your God: you, your son, your daughter, your male servant, your
female servant, the Levite who is within your gates, the foreigner,
the fatherless, and the widow who are among you, in the place
which God your God shall choose to cause his name to dwell
there. 12 You shall remember that you were a slave in Egypt.
You shall observe and do these statutes. 13 You shall keep the
feast of booths seven days, after you have gathered in from your
threshing floor and from your wine press. 14 You shall rejoice
in your feast, you, your son, your daughter, your male servant,
your female servant, the Levite, the foreigner, the fatherless, and
the widow who are within your gates. 15 You shall keep a feast
to God your God seven days in the place which God chooses,
because God your God will bless you in all your increase and in
all the work of your hands, and you shall be altogether joyful.

16 Three times in a year all of your males shall appear before
God your God in the place which he chooses: in the feast of
unleavened bread, in the feast of weeks, and in the feast of
booths. They shall not appear before God empty. 17 Every man
shall give as he is able, according to God your God's blessing
which he has given you. 18 You shall make judges and officers
in all your gates, which God your God gives you, according to
your tribes; and they shall judge the people with righteous
judgment. 19 You shall not pervert justice. You shall not show
partiality. You shall not take a bribe, for a bribe blinds the eyes of
the wise and perverts the words of the righteous. 20 You shall
follow that which is altogether just, that you may live and inherit
the land which God your God gives you. 21 You shall not plant
for yourselves an Asherah of any kind of tree beside God your
God's altar, which you shall make for yourselves. 22 Neither
shall you set yourself up a sacred stone which God your God
hates.

Deuteronomy 17

1 You shall not sacrifice to God your God an ox or a sheep in
which is a defect or anything evil; for that is an abomination to
God your God.

2 If there is found among you, within any of your gates which
God your God gives you, a man or woman who does that which
is evil in God your God's sight in transgressing his covenant,

3 and has gone and served other gods and worshiped them, or
the sun, or the moon, or any of the stars of the sky, which I have
not commanded, 4 and you are told, and you have heard of it,
then you shall inquire diligently. Behold, if it is true, and the
thing certain, that such abomination is done in Israel, 5 then you
shall bring out that man or that woman who has done this evil
thing to your gates, even that same man or woman; and you shall
stone them to death with stones. 6 At the mouth of two
witnesses, or three witnesses, he who is to die shall be put to
death. At the mouth of one witness he shall not be put to death.

7 The hands of the witnesses shall be first on him to put him to
death, and afterward the hands of all the people. So you shall
remove the evil from among you.

8 If there arises a matter too hard for you in judgment, between
blood and blood, between plea and plea, and between stroke and
stroke, being matters of controversy within your gates, then you
shall arise, and go up to the place which God your God chooses.

9 You shall come to the priests who are Levites and to the judge
who shall be in those days. You shall inquire, and they shall give
you the verdict. 10 You shall do according to the decisions of
the verdict which they shall give you from that place which God
chooses. You shall observe to do according to all that they shall
teach you. 11 According to the decisions of the law which they
shall teach you, and according to the judgment which they shall
tell you, you shall do. You shall not turn away from the sentence
which they announce to you, to the right hand, nor to the left.

12 The man who does presumptuously in not listening to the
priest who stands to minister there before God your God, or to
the judge, even that man shall die. You shall put away the evil
from Israel. 13 All the people shall hear and fear, and do no
more presumptuously.

14 When you have come to the land which God your God gives
you, and possess it and dwell in it, and say, "I will set a king over

me, like all the nations that are around me," 15 you shall surely
set him whom God your God chooses as king over yourselves.
You shall set as king over you one from among your brothers.
You may not put a foreigner over you, who is not your brother.
16 Only he shall not multiply horses to himself, nor cause the
people to return to Egypt, to the end that he may multiply horses;
because God has said to you, "You shall not go back that way
again." 17 He shall not multiply wives to himself, that his heart
not turn away. He shall not greatly multiply to himself silver and
gold.
18 It shall be, when he sits on the throne of his kingdom, that he
shall write himself a copy of this law in a book, out of that which
is before the Levitical priests. 19 It shall be with him, and he
shall read from it all the days of his life, that he may learn to fear
God his God, to keep all the words of this law and these statutes,
to do them; 20 that his heart not be lifted up above his brothers,
and that he not turn away from the commandment to the right
hand, or to the left, to the end that he may prolong his days in his
kingdom, he and his children, in the middle of Israel.

Deuteronomy 18

1 The priests and the Levites—all the tribe of Levi—shall have
no portion nor inheritance with Israel. They shall eat the offerings
of God made by fire and his portion. 2 They shall have no
inheritance among their brothers. God is their inheritance, as he
has spoken to them. 3 This shall be the priests' due from the
people, from those who offer a sacrifice, whether it be ox or
sheep, that they shall give to the priest: the shoulder, the two
cheeks, and the inner parts. 4 You shall give him the first fruits
of your grain, of your new wine, and of your oil, and the first of
the fleece of your sheep. 5 For God your God has chosen him
out of all your tribes to stand to minister in God's name, him and
his sons forever.
6 If a Levite comes from any of your gates out of all Israel
where he lives, and comes with all the desire of his soul to the
place which God shall choose, 7 then he shall minister in the
name of God his God, as all his brothers the Levites do, who
stand there before God. 8 They shall have like portions to eat, in
addition to that which comes from the sale of his family
possessions.
9 When you have come into the land which God your God gives
you, you shall not learn to imitate the abominations of those
nations. 10 There shall not be found with you anyone who
makes his son or his daughter to pass through the fire, one who
uses divination, one who tells fortunes, or an enchanter, or a
sorcerer, 11 or a charmer, or someone who consults with a
familiar spirit, or a wizard, or a necromancer. 12 For whoever
does these things is an abomination to God. Because of these
abominations, God your God drives them out from before you.
13 You shall be blameless with God your God. 14 For these
nations that you shall dispossess listen to those who practice
sorcery and to diviners; but as for you, God your God has not
allowed you so to do. 15 God your God will raise up to you a
prophet from among you, of your brothers, like me. You shall
listen to him. 16 This is according to all that you desired of God
your God in Horeb in the day of the assembly, saying, "Let me
not hear again God my God's voice, neither let me see this great
fire any more, that I not die."
17 God said to me, "They have well said that which they have
spoken. 18 I will raise them up a prophet from among their
brothers, like you. I will put my words in his mouth, and he shall
speak to them all that I shall command him. 19 It shall happen,
that whoever will not listen to my words which he shall speak in
my name, I will require it of him. 20 But the prophet who
speaks a word presumptuously in my name, which I have not
commanded him to speak, or who speaks in the name of other
gods, that same prophet shall die."
21 You may say in your heart, "How shall we know the word
which God has not spoken?" 22 When a prophet speaks in
God's name, if the thing doesn't follow, nor happen, that is the
thing which God has not spoken. The prophet has spoken it
presumptuously. You shall not be afraid of him.

Deuteronomy 19

1 When God your God cuts off the nations whose land God
your God gives you, and you succeed them and dwell in their
cities and in their houses, 2 you shall set apart three cities for
yourselves in the middle of your land, which God your God gives
you to possess. 3 You shall prepare the way, and divide the
borders of your land which God your God causes you to inherit
into three parts, that every man slayer may flee there. 4 This is
the case of the man slayer who shall flee there and live: Whoever
kills his neighbor unintentionally, and didn't hate him in time
past— 5 as when a man goes into the forest with his neighbor to
chop wood and his hand swings the ax to cut down the tree, and
the head slips from the handle and hits his neighbor so that he
dies—he shall flee to one of these cities and live. 6 Otherwise,
the avenger of blood might pursue the man slayer while hot anger
is in his heart and overtake him, because the way is long, and
strike him mortally, even though he was not worthy of death,
because he didn't hate him in time past. 7 Therefore I command
you to set apart three cities for yourselves. 8 If God your God
enlarges your border, as he has sworn to your fathers, and gives
you all the land which he promised to give to your fathers;
9 and if you keep all this commandment to do it, which I
command you today, to love God your God, and to walk ever in
his ways, then you shall add three cities more for yourselves, in
addition to these three. 10 This is so that innocent blood will not
be shed in the middle of your land which God your God gives
you for an inheritance, leaving blood guilt on you. 11 But if any
man hates his neighbor, lies in wait for him, rises up against him,
strikes him mortally so that he dies, and he flees into one of these
cities; 12 then the elders of his city shall send and bring him
there, and deliver him into the hand of the avenger of blood, that
he may die. 13 Your eye shall not pity him, but you shall purge
the innocent blood from Israel that it may go well with you.
14 You shall not remove your neighbor's landmark, which they
of old time have set, in your inheritance which you shall inherit,
in the land that God your God gives you to possess.
15 One witness shall not rise up against a man for any iniquity,
or for any sin that he sins. At the mouth of two witnesses, or at
the mouth of three witnesses, shall a matter be established. 16 If
an unrighteous witness rises up against any man to testify against
him of wrongdoing, 17 then both the men, between whom the
controversy is, shall stand before God, before the priests and the
judges who shall be in those days; 18 and the judges shall make
diligent inquisition; and behold, if the witness is a false witness,
and has testified falsely against his brother, 19 then you shall do
to him as he had thought to do to his brother. So you shall
remove the evil from among you. 20 Those who remain shall
hear, and fear, and will never again commit any such evil among
you. 21 Your eyes shall not pity: life for life, eye for eye, tooth
for tooth, hand for hand, foot for foot.

Deuteronomy 20

1 When you go out to battle against your enemies, and see
horses, chariots, and a people more numerous than you, you shall
not be afraid of them; for God your God is with you, who brought
you up out of the land of Egypt. 2 It shall be, when you draw
near to the battle, that the priest shall approach and speak to the
people, 3 and shall tell them, "Hear, Israel, you draw near today
to battle against your enemies. Don't let your heart faint! Don't
be afraid, nor tremble, neither be scared of them; 4 for God your
God is he who goes with you, to fight for you against your
enemies, to save you."
5 The officers shall speak to the people, saying, "What man is
there who has built a new house, and has not dedicated it? Let
him go and return to his house, lest he die in the battle, and
another man dedicate it. 6 What man is there who has planted a
vineyard, and has not used its fruit? Let him go and return to his
house, lest he die in the battle, and another man use its fruit.
7 What man is there who has pledged to be married to a wife,
and has not taken her? Let him go and return to his house, lest he
die in the battle, and another man take her." 8 The officers shall
speak further to the people, and they shall say, "What man is
there who is fearful and faint-hearted? Let him go and return to
his house, lest his brother's heart melt as his heart." 9 It shall
be, when the officers have finished speaking to the people, that
they shall appoint captains of armies at the head of the people.
10 When you draw near to a city to fight against it, then
proclaim peace to it. 11 It shall be, if it gives you answer of
peace and opens to you, then it shall be that all the people who
are found therein shall become forced laborers to you, and shall
serve you. 12 If it will make no peace with you, but will make
war against you, then you shall besiege it. 13 When God your
God delivers it into your hand, you shall strike every male of it
with the edge of the sword; 14 but the women, the little ones,
the livestock, and all that is in the city, even all its plunder, you
shall take for plunder for yourself. You may use the plunder of
your enemies, which God your God has given you. 15 Thus you
shall do to all the cities which are very far off from you, which
are not of the cities of these nations. 16 But of the cities of these
peoples that God your God gives you for an inheritance, you shall
save alive nothing that breathes; 17 but you shall utterly destroy
them: the Hittite, the Amorite, the Canaanite, the Perizzite, the
Hivite, and the Jebusite, as God your God has commanded you;
18 that they not teach you to follow all their abominations,
which they have done for their gods; so would you sin against
God your God. 19 When you shall besiege a city a long time, in
making war against it to take it, you shall not destroy its trees by
wielding an ax against them; for you may eat of them. You shall
not cut them down, for is the tree of the field man, that it should
be besieged by you? 20 Only the trees that you know are not
trees for food, you shall destroy and cut them down. You shall
build bulwarks against the city that makes war with you, until it
falls.

Deuteronomy 21

1 If someone is found slain in the land which God your God
gives you to possess, lying in the field, and it isn't known who
has struck him, 2 then your elders and your judges shall come
out, and they shall measure to the cities which are around him
who is slain. 3 It shall be that the elders of the city which is
nearest to the slain man shall take a heifer of the herd, which
hasn't been worked with and which has not drawn in the yoke.
4 The elders of that city shall bring the heifer down to a valley
with running water, which is neither plowed nor sown, and shall
break the heifer's neck there in the valley. 5 The priests the sons
of Levi shall come near, for them God your God has chosen to
minister to him, and to bless in God's name; and according to
their word shall every controversy and every assault be decided.
6 All the elders of that city which is nearest to the slain man
shall wash their hands over the heifer whose neck was broken in
the valley. 7 They shall answer and say, "Our hands have not
shed this blood, neither have our eyes seen it. 8 Forgive, God,
your people Israel, whom you have redeemed, and don't allow
innocent blood among your people Israel." The blood shall be
forgiven them. 9 So you shall put away the innocent blood from
among you, when you shall do that which is right in God's eyes.
10 When you go out to battle against your enemies, and God
your God delivers them into your hands and you carry them away
captive, 11 and see among the captives a beautiful woman, and
you are attracted to her, and desire to take her as your wife,
12 then you shall bring her home to your house. She shall shave
her head and trim her nails. 13 She shall take off the clothing of
her captivity, and shall remain in your house, and bewail her
father and her mother a full month. After that you shall go in to
her and be her husband, and she shall be your wife. 14 It shall
be, if you have no delight in her, then you shall let her go where
she desires; but you shall not sell her at all for money. You shall
not deal with her as a slave, because you have humbled her.
15 If a man has two wives, the one beloved and the other hated,
and they have borne him children, both the beloved and the
hated, and if the firstborn son is hers who was hated, 16 then it
shall be, in the day that he causes his sons to inherit that which he
has, that he may not give the son of the beloved the rights of the
firstborn before the son of the hated, who is the firstborn; 17 but
he shall acknowledge the firstborn, the son of the hated, by
giving him a double portion of all that he has; for he is the
beginning of his strength. The right of the firstborn is his.
18 If a man has a stubborn and rebellious son who will not obey
the voice of his father or the voice of his mother, and though they
chasten him, will not listen to them, 19 then his father and his
mother shall take hold of him and bring him out to the elders of
his city and to the gate of his place. 20 They shall tell the elders
of his city, "This our son is stubborn and rebellious. He will not
obey our voice. He is a glutton and a drunkard." 21 All the men
of his city shall stone him to death with stones. So you shall
remove the evil from among you. All Israel shall hear, and fear.
22 If a man has committed a sin worthy of death, and he is put
to death, and you hang him on a tree, 23 his body shall not
remain all night on the tree, but you shall surely bury him the
same day; for he who is hanged is accursed of God. Don't defile
your land which God your God gives you for an inheritance.

Deuteronomy 22

1 You shall not see your brother's ox or his sheep go astray and
hide yourself from them. You shall surely bring them again to
your brother. 2 If your brother isn't near to you, or if you don't
know him, then you shall bring it home to your house, and it shall
be with you until your brother comes looking for it, and you shall
restore it to him. 3 So you shall do with his donkey. So you
shall do with his garment. So you shall do with every lost thing of
your brother's, which he has lost and you have found. You may
not hide yourself. 4 You shall not see your brother's donkey or
his ox fallen down by the way, and hide yourself from them. You
shall surely help him to lift them up again.
5 A woman shall not wear men's clothing, neither shall a man
put on women's clothing; for whoever does these things is an
abomination to God your God.

6 If you come across a bird's nest on the way, in any tree or on
the ground, with young ones or eggs, and the hen sitting on the
young, or on the eggs, you shall not take the hen with the young.
7 You shall surely let the hen go, but the young you may take
for yourself, that it may be well with you, and that you may
prolong your days.
8 When you build a new house, then you shall make a railing
around your roof, so that you don't bring blood on your house if
anyone falls from there.
9 You shall not sow your vineyard with two kinds of seed, lest
all the fruit be defiled, the seed which you have sown, and the
increase of the vineyard. 10 You shall not plow with an ox and
a donkey together. 11 You shall not wear clothes of wool and
linen woven together.
12 You shall make yourselves fringes[176] on the four corners of
your cloak with which you cover yourself.
13 If any man takes a wife, and goes in to her, hates her,
14 accuses her of shameful things, gives her a bad name, and
says, "I took this woman, and when I came near to her, I didn't
find in her the tokens of virginity;" 15 then the young lady's
father and mother shall take and bring the tokens of the young
lady's virginity to the elders of the city in the gate. 16 The
young lady's father shall tell the elders, "I gave my daughter to
this man as his wife, and he hates her. 17 Behold, he has
accused her of shameful things, saying, 'I didn't find in your
daughter the tokens of virginity;' and yet these are the tokens of
my daughter's virginity." They shall spread the cloth before the
elders of the city. 18 The elders of that city shall take the man
and chastise him. 19 They shall fine him one hundred shekels of
silver,[177] and give them to the father of the young lady, because
he has given a bad name to a virgin of Israel. She shall be his
wife. He may not put her away all his days.
20 But if this thing is true, that the tokens of virginity were not
found in the young lady, 21 then they shall bring out the young
lady to the door of her father's house, and the men of her city
shall stone her to death with stones, because she has done folly in
Israel, to play the prostitute in her father's house. So you shall
remove the evil from among you.
22 If a man is found lying with a woman married to a husband,
then they shall both die, the man who lay with the woman and the
woman. So you shall remove the evil from Israel. 23 If there is
a young lady who is a virgin pledged to be married to a husband,
and a man finds her in the city, and lies with her, 24 then you
shall bring them both out to the gate of that city, and you shall
stone them to death with stones; the lady, because she didn't cry,
being in the city; and the man, because he has humbled his
neighbor's wife. So you shall remove the evil from among you.
25 But if the man finds the lady who is pledged to be married in
the field, and the man forces her and lies with her, then only the
man who lay with her shall die; 26 but to the lady you shall do
nothing. There is in the lady no sin worthy of death; for as when
a man rises against his neighbor and kills him, even so is this
matter; 27 for he found her in the field, the pledged to be
married lady cried, and there was no one to save her. 28 If a
man finds a lady who is a virgin, who is not pledged to be
married, grabs her and lies with her, and they are found, 29 then
the man who lay with her shall give to the lady's father fifty
shekels[178] of silver. She shall be his wife, because he has
humbled her. He may not put her away all his days. 30 A man
shall not take his father's wife, and shall not uncover his father's
skirt.

Deuteronomy 23

1 He who is emasculated by crushing or cutting shall not enter
into God's assembly. 2 A person born of a forbidden union shall
not enter into God's assembly; even to the tenth generation shall
no one of his enter into God's assembly. 3 An Ammonite or a
Moabite shall not enter into God's assembly; even to the tenth
generation shall no one belonging to them enter into God's
assembly forever, 4 because they didn't meet you with bread
and with water on the way when you came out of Egypt, and
because they hired against you Balaam the son of Beor from
Pethor of Mesopotamia, to curse you. 5 Nevertheless God your
God wouldn't listen to Balaam, but God your God turned the
curse into a blessing to you, because God your God loved you.
6 You shall not seek their peace nor their prosperity all your
days forever. 7 You shall not abhor an Edomite, for he is your
brother. You shall not abhor an Egyptian, because you lived as a
foreigner in his land. 8 The children of the third generation who
are born to them may enter into God's assembly.
9 When you go out and camp against your enemies, then you
shall keep yourselves from every evil thing. 10 If there is
among you any man who is not clean by reason of that which
happens to him by night, then shall he go outside of the camp. He
shall not come within the camp; 11 but it shall be, when
evening comes, he shall bathe himself in water. When the sun is
down, he shall come within the camp. 12 You shall have a place
also outside of the camp where you go relieve yourself. 13 You
shall have a trowel among your weapons. It shall be, when you
relieve yourself, you shall dig with it, and shall turn back and
cover your excrement; 14 for God your God walks in the
middle of your camp, to deliver you, and to give up your enemies
before you. Therefore your camp shall be holy, that he may not
see an unclean thing in you, and turn away from you.
15 You shall not deliver to his master a servant who has
escaped from his master to you. 16 He shall dwell with you,
among you, in the place which he shall choose within one of your
gates, where it pleases him best. You shall not oppress him.
17 There shall be no prostitute of the daughters of Israel, neither
shall there be a sodomite of the sons of Israel. 18 You shall not
bring the hire of a prostitute, or the wages of a male prostitute,[179]
into the house of God your God for any vow; for both of these are
an abomination to God your God.
19 You shall not lend on interest to your brother: interest of
money, interest of food, interest of anything that is lent on
interest. 20 You may charge a foreigner interest; but you shall
not your brother interest, that God your God may bless you in all
that you put your hand to, in the land where you go in to possess
it.
21 When you vow a vow to God your God, you shall not be
slack to pay it, for God your God will surely require it of you;
and it would be sin in you. 22 But if you refrain from making a
vow, it shall be no sin in you. 23 You shall observe and do that
which has gone out of your lips. Whatever you have vowed to
God your God as a free will offering, which you have promised
with your mouth, you must do. 24 When you come into your
neighbor's vineyard, then you may eat your fill of grapes at your
own pleasure; but you shall not put any in your container.
25 When you come into your neighbor's standing grain, then
you may pluck the ears with your hand; but you shall not use a
sickle on your neighbor's standing grain.

Deuteronomy 24

1 When a man takes a wife and marries her, then it shall be, if
she finds no favor in his eyes because he has found some
unseemly thing in her, that he shall write her a certificate of
divorce, put it in her hand, and send her out of his house.
2 When she has departed out of his house, she may go and be
another man's wife. 3 If the latter husband hates her, and write
her a certificate of divorce, puts it in her hand, and sends her out
of his house; or if the latter husband dies, who took her to be his
wife; 4 her former husband, who sent her away, may not take
her again to be his wife after she is defiled; for that would be an
abomination to God. You shall not cause the land to sin, which
God your God gives you for an inheritance. 5 When a man
takes a new wife, he shall not go out in the army, neither shall he
be assigned any business. He shall be free at home one year, and
shall cheer his wife whom he has taken.
6 No man shall take the mill or the upper millstone as a pledge,
for he takes a life in pledge. 7 If a man is found stealing any of
his brothers of the children of Israel, and he deals with him as a
slave, or sells him, then that thief shall die. So you shall remove
the evil from among you. 8 Be careful in the plague of leprosy,
that you observe diligently and do according to all that the
Levitical priests teach you. As I commanded them, so you shall
observe to do. 9 Remember what God your God did to Miriam,
by the way as you came out of Egypt.
10 When you lend your neighbor any kind of loan, you shall not
go into his house to get his pledge. 11 You shall stand outside,
and the man to whom you lend shall bring the pledge outside to
you. 12 If he is a poor man, you shall not sleep with his pledge.
13 You shall surely restore to him the pledge when the sun goes
down, that he may sleep in his garment and bless you. It shall be
righteousness to you before God your God.
14 You shall not oppress a hired servant who is poor and needy,
whether he is one of your brothers or one of the foreigners who
are in your land within your gates. 15 In his day you shall give
him his wages, neither shall the sun go down on it; for he is poor
and sets his heart on it; lest he cry against you to God, and it be
sin to you.
16 The fathers shall not be put to death for the children, neither
shall the children be put to death for the fathers. Every man shall
be put to death for his own sin.
17 You shall not deprive the foreigner or the fatherless of
justice, nor take a widow's clothing in pledge; 18 but you shall
remember that you were a slave in Egypt, and God your God
redeemed you there. Therefore I command you to do this thing.
19 When you reap your harvest in your field, and have forgotten
a sheaf in the field, you shall not go again to get it. It shall be for
the foreigner, for the fatherless, and for the widow, that God your
God may bless you in all the work of your hands. 20 When you
beat your olive tree, you shall not go over the boughs again. It
shall be for the foreigner, for the fatherless, and for the widow.
21 When you harvest your vineyard, you shall not glean it after
yourselves. It shall be for the foreigner, for the fatherless, and for
the widow. 22 You shall remember that you were a slave in the
land of Egypt. Therefore I command you to do this thing.

Deuteronomy 25

1 If there is a controversy between men, and they come to
judgment and the judges judge them, then they shall justify the
righteous and condemn the wicked. 2 It shall be, if the wicked
man is worthy to be beaten, that the judge shall cause him to lie
down and to be beaten before his face, according to his
wickedness, by number. 3 He may sentence him to no more
than forty stripes. He shall not give more, lest if he should give
more and beat him more than that many stripes, then your brother
will be degraded in your sight.
4 You shall not muzzle the ox when he treads out the grain.
5 If brothers dwell together, and one of them dies and has no
son, the wife of the dead shall not be married outside to a
stranger. Her husband's brother shall go in to her, and take her as
his wife, and perform the duty of a husband's brother to her. 6 It
shall be that the firstborn whom she bears shall succeed in the
name of his brother who is dead, that his name not be blotted out
of Israel.
7 If the man doesn't want to take his brother's wife, then his
brother's wife shall go up to the gate to the elders, and say, "My
husband's brother refuses to raise up to his brother a name in
Israel. He will not perform the duty of a husband's brother to
me." 8 Then the elders of his city shall call him, and speak to
him. If he stands and says, "I don't want to take her," 9 then his
brother's wife shall come to him in the presence of the elders,
and loose his sandal from off his foot, and spit in his face. She
shall answer and say, "So shall it be done to the man who does
not build up his brother's house." 10 His name shall be called in
Israel, "The house of him who had his sandal removed."
11 When men strive against each other, and the wife of one
draws near to deliver her husband out of the hand of him who
strikes him, and puts out her hand, and grabs him by his private
parts, 12 then you shall cut off her hand. Your eye shall have no
pity.
13 You shall not have in your bag diverse weights, one heavy
and one light. 14 You shall not have in your house diverse
measures, one large and one small. 15 You shall have a perfect
and just weight. You shall have a perfect and just measure, that
your days may be long in the land which God your God gives
you. 16 For all who do such things, all who do unrighteously,
are an abomination to God your God.
17 Remember what Amalek did to you by the way as you came
out of Egypt; 18 how he met you by the way, and struck the
rearmost of you, all who were feeble behind you, when you were
faint and weary; and he didn't fear God. 19 Therefore it shall
be, when God your God has given you rest from all your enemies
all around, in the land which God your God gives you for an
inheritance to possess it, that you shall blot out the memory of
Amalek from under the sky. You shall not forget.

Deuteronomy 26

1 It shall be, when you have come in to the land which God
your God gives you for an inheritance, possess it, and dwell in it,

[176] **22:12** *22:12* or, tassels

[177] **22:19** *22:19* A shekel is about 10 grams or about 0.35 ounces, so 100 shekels is about a kilogram or 2.2 pounds.

[178] **22:29** *22:29* A shekel is about 10 grams or about 0.35 ounces.

[179] **23:18** *23:18* literally, dog

2 that you shall take some of the first of all the fruit of the
ground, which you shall bring in from your land that God your
God gives you. You shall put it in a basket, and shall go to the
place which God your God shall choose to cause his name to
dwell there. 3 You shall come to the priest who shall be in those
days, and tell him, "I profess today to God your God, that I have
come to the land which God swore to our fathers to give us."
4 The priest shall take the basket out of your hand, and set it
down before God your God's altar. 5 You shall answer and say
before God your God, "My father[180] was a Syrian ready to perish.
He went down into Egypt, and lived there, few in number. There
he became a great, mighty, and populous nation. 6 The
Egyptians mistreated us, afflicted us, and imposed hard labor on
us. 7 Then we cried to God, the God of our fathers. God heard
our voice, and saw our affliction, our toil, and our oppression.
8 God brought us out of Egypt with a mighty hand, with an
outstretched arm, with great terror, with signs, and with wonders;
9 and he has brought us into this place, and has given us this
land, a land flowing with milk and honey. 10 Now, behold, I
have brought the first of the fruit of the ground, which you, God,
have given me." You shall set it down before God your God, and
worship before God your God. 11 You shall rejoice in all the
good which God your God has given to you, and to your house,
you, and the Levite, and the foreigner who is among you.
12 When you have finished tithing all the tithe of your increase
in the third year, which is the year of tithing, then you shall give
it to the Levite, to the foreigner, to the fatherless, and to the
widow, that they may eat within your gates and be filled.
13 You shall say before God your God, "I have put away the
holy things out of my house, and also have given them to the
Levite, to the foreigner, to the fatherless, and to the widow,
according to all your commandment which you have commanded
me. I have not transgressed any of your commandments, neither
have I forgotten them. 14 I have not eaten of it in my mourning,
neither have I removed any of it while I was unclean, nor given
of it for the dead. I have listened to God my God's voice. I have
done according to all that you have commanded me. 15 Look
down from your holy habitation, from heaven, and bless your
people Israel, and the ground which you have given us, as you
swore to our fathers, a land flowing with milk and honey."
16 Today God your God commands you to do these statutes and
ordinances. You shall therefore keep and do them with all your
heart and with all your soul. 17 You have declared today that
God is your God, and that you would walk in his ways, keep his
statutes, his commandments, and his ordinances, and listen to his
voice. 18 God has declared today that you are a people for his
own possession, as he has promised you, and that you should
keep all his commandments. 19 He will make you high above
all nations that he has made, in praise, in name, and in honor; and
that you may be a holy people to God your God, as he has
spoken.

Deuteronomy 27

1 Moses and the elders of Israel commanded the people, saying,
"Keep all the commandment which I command you today. 2 It
shall be on the day when you shall pass over the Jordan to the
land which God your God gives you, that you shall set yourself
up great stones, and coat them with plaster. 3 You shall write on
them all the words of this law, when you have passed over, that
you may go in to the land which God your God gives you, a land
flowing with milk and honey, as God, the God of your fathers,
has promised you. 4 It shall be, when you have crossed over the
Jordan, that you shall set up these stones, which I command you
today, on Mount Ebal, and you shall coat them with plaster.
5 There you shall build an altar to God your God, an altar of
stones. You shall not use any iron tool on them. 6 You shall
build God your God's altar of uncut stones. You shall offer burnt
offerings on it to God your God. 7 You shall sacrifice peace
offerings, and shall eat there. You shall rejoice before God your
God. 8 You shall write on the stones all the words of this law
very plainly."
9 Moses and the Levitical priests spoke to all Israel, saying, "Be
silent and listen, Israel! Today you have become the people of
God your God. 10 You shall therefore obey God your God's
voice, and do his commandments and his statutes, which I
command you today."
11 Moses commanded the people the same day, saying,
12 "These shall stand on Mount Gerizim to bless the people,
when you have crossed over the Jordan: Simeon, Levi, Judah,
Issachar, Joseph, and Benjamin. 13 These shall stand on Mount
Ebal for the curse: Reuben, Gad, Asher, Zebulun, Dan, and
Naphtali. 14 With a loud voice, the Levites shall say to all the
men of Israel, 15 'Cursed is the man who makes an engraved or
molten image, an abomination to God, the work of the hands of
the craftsman, and sets it up in secret.'
All the people shall answer and say, 'Amen.'
16 'Cursed is he who dishonors his father or his mother.'
All the people shall say, 'Amen.'
17 'Cursed is he who removes his neighbor's landmark.'
All the people shall say, 'Amen.'
18 'Cursed is he who leads the blind astray on the road.'
All the people shall say, 'Amen.'
19 'Cursed is he who withholds justice from the foreigner,
fatherless, and widow.'
All the people shall say, 'Amen.'
20 'Cursed is he who lies with[181] his father's wife, because he
dishonors his father's bed.'
All the people shall say, 'Amen.'
21 'Cursed is he who lies with any kind of animal.'
All the people shall say, 'Amen.'
22 'Cursed is he who lies with his sister, his father's daughter or
his mother's daughter.'
All the people shall say, 'Amen.'
23 'Cursed is he who lies with his mother-in-law.'
All the people shall say, 'Amen.'
24 'Cursed is he who secretly kills his neighbor.'
All the people shall say, 'Amen.'
25 'Cursed is he who takes a bribe to kill an innocent person.'
All the people shall say, 'Amen.'
26 'Cursed is he who doesn't uphold the words of this law by
doing them.'
All the people shall say, 'Amen.'"

Deuteronomy 28

1 It shall happen, if you shall listen diligently to God your
God's voice, to observe to do all his commandments which I
command you today, that God your God will set you high above
all the nations of the earth. 2 All these blessings will come upon
you, and overtake you, if you listen to God your God's voice.
3 You shall be blessed in the city, and you shall be blessed in
the field. 4 You shall be blessed in the fruit of your body, the
fruit of your ground, the fruit of your animals, the increase of
your livestock, and the young of your flock. 5 Your basket and
your kneading trough shall be blessed. 6 You shall be blessed
when you come in, and you shall be blessed when you go out.
7 God will cause your enemies who rise up against you to be
struck before you. They will come out against you one way, and
will flee before you seven ways. 8 God will command the
blessing on you in your barns, and in all that you put your hand
to. He will bless you in the land which God your God gives you.
9 God will establish you for a holy people to himself, as he has
sworn to you, if you shall keep the commandments of God your
God, and walk in his ways. 10 All the peoples of the earth shall
see that you are called by God's name, and they will be afraid of
you. 11 God will grant you abundant prosperity in the fruit of
your body, in the fruit of your livestock, and in the fruit of your
ground, in the land which God swore to your fathers to give you.
12 God will open to you his good treasure in the sky, to give the
rain of your land in its season, and to bless all the work of your
hand. You will lend to many nations, and you will not borrow.
13 God will make you the head, and not the tail. You will be
above only, and you will not be beneath, if you listen to the
commandments of God your God which I command you today,
to observe and to do, 14 and shall not turn away from any of the
words which I command you today, to the right hand or to the
left, to go after other gods to serve them.
15 But it shall come to pass, if you will not listen to God your
God's voice, to observe to do all his commandments and his
statutes which I command you today, that all these curses will
come on you and overtake you. 16 You will be cursed in the
city, and you will be cursed in the field. 17 Your basket and
your kneading trough will be cursed. 18 The fruit of your body,
the fruit of your ground, the increase of your livestock, and the
young of your flock will be cursed. 19 You will be cursed when
you come in, and you will be cursed when you go out. 20 God
will send on you cursing, confusion, and rebuke in all that you
put your hand to do, until you are destroyed and until you perish
quickly, because of the evil of your doings, by which you have
forsaken me. 21 God will make the pestilence cling to you, until
he has consumed you from off the land where you go in to
possess it. 22 God will strike you with consumption, with fever,
with inflammation, with fiery heat, with the sword, with blight,
and with mildew. They will pursue you until you perish.
23 Your sky that is over your head will be bronze, and the earth
that is under you will be iron. 24 God will make the rain of your
land powder and dust. It will come down on you from the sky,
until you are destroyed. 25 God will cause you to be struck
before your enemies. You will go out one way against them, and
will flee seven ways before them. You will be tossed back and
forth among all the kingdoms of the earth. 26 Your dead bodies
will be food to all birds of the sky, and to the animals of the
earth; and there will be no one to frighten them away. 27 God
will strike you with the boils of Egypt, with the tumors, with the
scurvy, and with the itch, of which you can not be healed.
28 God will strike you with madness, with blindness, and with
astonishment of heart. 29 You will grope at noonday, as the
blind gropes in darkness, and you shall not prosper in your ways.
You will only be oppressed and robbed always, and there will be
no one to save you. 30 You will betroth a wife, and another man
shall lie with her. You will build a house, and you won't dwell in
it. You will plant a vineyard, and not use its fruit. 31 Your ox
will be slain before your eyes, and you will not eat any of it. Your
donkey will be violently taken away from before your face, and
will not be restored to you. Your sheep will be given to your
enemies, and you will have no one to save you. 32 Your sons
and your daughters will be given to another people. Your eyes
will look, and fail with longing for them all day long. There will
be no power in your hand. 33 A nation which you don't know
will eat the fruit of your ground and all of your work. You will
only be oppressed and crushed always, 34 so that the sights that
you see with your eyes will drive you mad. 35 God will strike
you in the knees and in the legs with a sore boil, of which you
cannot be healed, from the sole of your foot to the crown of your
head. 36 God will bring you, and your king whom you will set
over yourselves, to a nation that you have not known, you nor
your fathers. There you will serve other gods of wood and stone.
37 You will become an astonishment, a proverb, and a byword
among all the peoples where God will lead you away. 38 You
will carry much seed out into the field, and will gather little in,
for the locust will consume it. 39 You will plant vineyards and
dress them, but you will neither drink of the wine, nor harvest,
because worms will eat them. 40 You will have olive trees
throughout all your borders, but you won't anoint yourself with
the oil, for your olives will drop off. 41 You will father sons
and daughters, but they will not be yours, for they will go into
captivity. 42 Locusts will consume all of your trees and the fruit
of your ground. 43 The foreigner who is among you will mount
up above you higher and higher, and you will come down lower
and lower. 44 He will lend to you, and you won't lend to him.
He will be the head, and you will be the tail.
45 All these curses will come on you, and will pursue you and
overtake you, until you are destroyed, because you didn't listen to
God your God's voice, to keep his commandments and his
statutes which he commanded you. 46 They will be for a sign
and for a wonder to you and to your offspring forever.
47 Because you didn't serve God your God with joyfulness and
with gladness of heart, by reason of the abundance of all things;
48 therefore you will serve your enemies whom God sends
against you, in hunger, in thirst, in nakedness, and in lack of all
things. He will put an iron yoke on your neck until he has
destroyed you. 49 God will bring a nation against you from far,
from the end of the earth, as the eagle flies: a nation whose
language you will not understand, 50 a nation of fierce facial
expressions, that doesn't respect the elderly, nor show favor to
the young. 51 They will eat the fruit of your livestock and the
fruit of your ground, until you are destroyed. They also won't
leave you grain, new wine, oil, the increase of your livestock, or
the young of your flock, until they have caused you to perish.
52 They will besiege you in all your gates until your high and
fortified walls in which you trusted come down throughout all
your land. They will besiege you in all your gates throughout all
your land which God your God has given you. 53 You will eat
the fruit of your own body, the flesh of your sons and of your
daughters, whom God your God has given you, in the siege and
in the distress with which your enemies will distress you.
54 The man who is tender among you, and very delicate, his eye
will be evil toward his brother, toward the wife whom he loves,
and toward the remnant of his children whom he has remaining,

---

[180] **26:5** *26:5* or, forefather

[181] **27:20** *27:20* i.e., has sexual relations with

55 so that he will not give to any of them of the flesh of his
children whom he will eat, because he has nothing left to him, in
the siege and in the distress with which your enemy will distress
you in all your gates. 56 The tender and delicate woman among
you, who would not venture to set the sole of her foot on the
ground for delicateness and tenderness, her eye will be evil
toward the husband that she loves, toward her son, toward her
daughter, 57 toward her young one who comes out from
between her feet, and toward her children whom she bears; for
she will eat them secretly for lack of all things in the siege and in
the distress with which your enemy will distress you in your
gates. 58 If you will not observe to do all the words of this law
that are written in this book, that you may fear this glorious and
fearful name, YAHWEH your God, 59 then God will make
your plagues and the plagues of your offspring fearful, even great
plagues, and of long duration, and severe sicknesses, and of long
duration. 60 He will bring on you again all the diseases of
Egypt, which you were afraid of; and they will cling to you.
61 Also every sickness and every plague which is not written in
the book of this law, God will bring them on you until you are
destroyed. 62 You will be left few in number, even though you
were as the stars of the sky for multitude, because you didn't
listen to God your God's voice. 63 It will happen that as God
rejoiced over you to do you good, and to multiply you, so God
will rejoice over you to cause you to perish and to destroy you.
You will be plucked from the land that you are going in to
possess. 64 God will scatter you among all peoples, from one
end of the earth to the other end of the earth. There you will serve
other gods which you have not known, you nor your fathers, even
wood and stone. 65 Among these nations you will find no ease,
and there will be no rest for the sole of your foot; but God will
give you there a trembling heart, failing of eyes, and pining of
soul. 66 Your life will hang in doubt before you. You will be
afraid night and day, and will have no assurance of your life.
67 In the morning you will say, "I wish it were evening!" and at
evening you will say, "I wish it were morning!" for the fear of
your heart which you will fear, and for the sights which your eyes
will see. 68 God will bring you into Egypt again with ships, by
the way of which I told to you that you would never see it again.
There you will offer yourselves to your enemies for male and
female slaves, and nobody will buy you.

Deuteronomy 29

1 These are the words of the covenant which God commanded
Moses to make with the children of Israel in the land of Moab, in
addition to the covenant which he made with them in Horeb.
2 Moses called to all Israel, and said to them:
Your eyes have seen all that God did in the land of Egypt to
Pharaoh, and to all his servants, and to all his land; 3 the great
trials which your eyes saw, the signs, and those great wonders.
4 But God has not given you a heart to know, eyes to see, and
ears to hear, to this day. 5 I have led you forty years in the
wilderness. Your clothes have not grown old on you, and your
sandals have not grown old on your feet. 6 You have not eaten
bread, neither have you drunk wine or strong drink, that you may
know that I am God your God. 7 When you came to this place,
Sihon the king of Heshbon and Og the king of Bashan came out
against us to battle, and we struck them. 8 We took their land,
and gave it for an inheritance to the Reubenites, and to the
Gadites, and to the half-tribe of the Manassites. 9 Therefore
keep the words of this covenant and do them, that you may
prosper in all that you do. 10 All of you stand today in the
presence of God your God: your heads, your tribes, your elders,
and your officers, even all the men of Israel, 11 your little ones,
your wives, and the foreigners who are in the middle of your
camps, from the one who cuts your wood to the one who draws
your water, 12 that you may enter into the covenant of God
your God, and into his oath, which God your God makes with
you today, 13 that he may establish you today as his people, and
that he may be your God, as he spoke to you and as he swore to
your fathers, to Abraham, to Isaac, and to Jacob. 14 Neither do I
make this covenant and this oath with you only, 15 but with
those who stand here with us today before God our God, and also
with those who are not here with us today 16 (for you know
how we lived in the land of Egypt, and how we came through the
middle of the nations through which you passed; 17 and you
have seen their abominations and their idols of wood, stone,
silver, and gold, which were among them); 18 lest there should
be among you man, woman, family, or tribe whose heart turns
away today from God our God, to go to serve the gods of those
nations; lest there should be among you a root that produces
bitter poison; 19 and it happen, when he hears the words of this
curse, that he bless himself in his heart, saying, "I shall have
peace, though I walk in the stubbornness of my heart," to destroy
the moist with the dry. 20 God will not pardon him, but then
God's anger and his jealousy will smoke against that man, and all
the curse that is written in this book will fall on him, and God
will blot out his name from under the sky. 21 God will set him
apart for evil out of all the tribes of Israel, according to all the
curses of the covenant written in this book of the law.
22 The generation to come—your children who will rise up
after you, and the foreigner who will come from a far land—will
say, when they see the plagues of that land, and the sicknesses
with which God has made it sick, 23 that all of its land is
sulfur, salt, and burning, that it is not sown, doesn't produce, nor
does any grass grow in it, like the overthrow of Sodom,
Gomorrah, Admah, and Zeboiim, which God overthrew in his
anger, and in his wrath. 24 Even all the nations will say, "Why
has God done this to this land? What does the heat of this great
anger mean?"
25 Then men will say, "Because they abandoned the covenant
of God, the God of their fathers, which he made with them when
he brought them out of the land of Egypt, 26 and went and
served other gods and worshiped them, gods that they didn't
know and that he had not given to them. 27 Therefore God's
anger burned against this land, to bring on it all the curses that are
written in this book. 28 God rooted them out of their land in
anger, in wrath, and in great indignation, and thrust them into
another land, as it is today."
29 The secret things belong to God our God; but the things that
are revealed belong to us and to our children forever, that we may
do all the words of this law.

Deuteronomy 30

1 It shall happen, when all these things have come on you, the
blessing and the curse, which I have set before you, and you shall
call them to mind among all the nations where God your God has
driven you, 2 and return to God your God and obey his voice
according to all that I command you today, you and your
children, with all your heart and with all your soul, 3 that then
God your God will release you from captivity, have compassion
on you, and will return and gather you from all the peoples where
God your God has scattered you. 4 If your outcasts are in the
uttermost parts of the heavens, from there God your God will
gather you, and from there he will bring you back. 5 God your
God will bring you into the land which your fathers possessed,
and you will possess it. He will do you good, and increase your
numbers more than your fathers. 6 God your God will
circumcise your heart, and the heart of your offspring, to love
God your God with all your heart and with all your soul, that you
may live. 7 God your God will put all these curses on your
enemies and on those who hate you, who persecuted you. 8 You
shall return and obey God's voice, and do all his commandments
which I command you today. 9 God your God will make you
prosperous in all the work of your hand, in the fruit of your body,
in the fruit of your livestock, and in the fruit of your ground, for
good; for God will again rejoice over you for good, as he rejoiced
over your fathers, 10 if you will obey God your God's voice, to
keep his commandments and his statutes which are written in this
book of the law; if you turn to God your God with all your heart
and with all your soul.
11 For this commandment which I command you today is not
too hard for you or too distant. 12 It is not in heaven, that you
should say, "Who will go up for us to heaven, bring it to us, and
proclaim it to us, that we may do it?" 13 Neither is it beyond the
sea, that you should say, "Who will go over the sea for us, bring
it to us, and proclaim it to us, that we may do it?" 14 But the
word is very near to you, in your mouth and in your heart, that
you may do it. 15 Behold, I have set before you today life and
prosperity, and death and evil. 16 For I command you today to
love God your God, to walk in his ways and to keep his
commandments, his statutes, and his ordinances, that you may
live and multiply, and that God your God may bless you in the
land where you go in to possess it. 17 But if your heart turns
away, and you will not hear, but are drawn away and worship
other gods, and serve them, 18 I declare to you today that you
will surely perish. You will not prolong your days in the land
where you pass over the Jordan to go in to possess it. 19 I call
heaven and earth to witness against you today that I have set
before you life and death, the blessing and the curse. Therefore
choose life, that you may live, you and your descendants, 20 to
love God your God, to obey his voice, and to cling to him; for he
is your life, and the length of your days, that you may dwell in
the land which God swore to your fathers, to Abraham, to Isaac,
and to Jacob, to give them.

Deuteronomy 31

1 Moses went and spoke these words to all Israel. 2 He said to
them, "I am one hundred twenty years old today. I can no more
go out and come in. God has said to me, 'You shall not go over
this Jordan.' 3 God your God himself will go over before you.
He will destroy these nations from before you, and you shall
dispossess them. Joshua will go over before you, as God has
spoken. 4 God will do to them as he did to Sihon and to Og, the
kings of the Amorites, and to their land, when he destroyed them.
5 God will deliver them up before you, and you shall do to them
according to all the commandment which I have commanded
you. 6 Be strong and courageous. Don't be afraid or scared of
them; for God your God himself is who goes with you. He will
not fail you nor forsake you."
7 Moses called to Joshua, and said to him in the sight of all
Israel, "Be strong and courageous, for you shall go with this
people into the land which God has sworn to their fathers to give
them; and you shall cause them to inherit it. 8 God himself is
who goes before you. He will be with you. He will not fail you
nor forsake you. Don't be afraid. Don't be discouraged."
9 Moses wrote this law and delivered it to the priests the sons of
Levi, who bore the ark of God's covenant, and to all the elders of
Israel. 10 Moses commanded them, saying, "At the end of every
seven years, in the set time of the year of release, in the feast of
booths, 11 when all Israel has come to appear before God your
God in the place which he will choose, you shall read this law
before all Israel in their hearing. 12 Assemble the people, the
men and the women and the little ones, and the foreigners who
are within your gates, that they may hear, learn, fear God your
God, and observe to do all the words of this law, 13 and that
their children, who have not known, may hear and learn to fear
God your God, as long as you live in the land where you go over
the Jordan to possess it."
14 God said to Moses, "Behold, your days approach that you
must die. Call Joshua, and present yourselves in the Tent of
Meeting, that I may commission him."
Moses and Joshua went, and presented themselves in the Tent of
Meeting.
15 God appeared in the Tent in a pillar of cloud, and the pillar
of cloud stood over the Tent's door. 16 God said to Moses,
"Behold, you shall sleep with your fathers. This people will rise
up and play the prostitute after the strange gods of the land where
they go to be among them, and will forsake me and break my
covenant which I have made with them. 17 Then my anger shall
be kindled against them in that day, and I will forsake them, and I
will hide my face from them, and they shall be devoured, and
many evils and troubles shall come on them; so that they will say
in that day, 'Haven't these evils come on us because our God is
not among us?' 18 I will surely hide my face in that day for all
the evil which they have done, in that they have turned to other
gods.
19 "Now therefore write this song for yourselves, and teach it to
the children of Israel. Put it in their mouths, that this song may be
a witness for me against the children of Israel. 20 For when I
have brought them into the land which I swore to their fathers,
flowing with milk and honey, and they have eaten and filled
themselves, and grown fat, then they will turn to other gods, and
serve them, and despise me, and break my covenant. 21 It will
happen, when many evils and troubles have come on them, that
this song will testify before them as a witness; for it will not be
forgotten out of the mouths of their descendants; for I know their
ways and what they are doing today, before I have brought them
into the land which I promised them."
22 So Moses wrote this song the same day, and taught it to the
children of Israel.
23 He commissioned Joshua the son of Nun, and said, "Be
strong and courageous; for you shall bring the children of Israel
into the land which I swore to them. I will be with you."
24 When Moses had finished writing the words of this law in a
book, until they were finished, 25 Moses commanded the
Levites, who bore the ark of God's covenant, saying, 26 "Take
this book of the law, and put it by the side of the ark of God your
God's covenant, that it may be there for a witness against you.
27 For I know your rebellion and your stiff neck. Behold, while
I am yet alive with you today, you have been rebellious against
God. How much more after my death? 28 Assemble to me all
the elders of your tribes and your officers, that I may speak these
words in their ears, and call heaven and earth to witness against
them. 29 For I know that after my death you will utterly corrupt
yourselves, and turn away from the way which I have
commanded you; and evil will happen to you in the latter days,
because you will do that which is evil in God's sight, to provoke
him to anger through the work of your hands."
30 Moses spoke in the ears of all the assembly of Israel the
words of this song, until they were finished.

Deuteronomy 32

1 Give ear, you heavens, and I will speak.
Let the earth hear the words of my mouth.

2 My doctrine will drop as the rain.
My speech will condense as the dew,
as the misty rain on the tender grass,
as the showers on the herb.

3 For I will proclaim God's name.
Ascribe greatness to our God!

4 The Rock: his work is perfect,
for all his ways are just.
A God of faithfulness who does no wrong,
just and right is he.

5 They have dealt corruptly with him.
They are not his children, because of their defect.
They are a perverse and crooked generation.

6 Is this the way you repay God,
foolish and unwise people?
Isn't he your father who has bought you?
He has made you and established you.

7 Remember the days of old.
Consider the years of many generations.
Ask your father, and he will show you;
your elders, and they will tell you.

8 When the Most High gave to the nations their inheritance,
when he separated the children of men,
he set the bounds of the peoples
according to the number of the children of Israel.

9 For God's portion is his people.
Jacob is the lot of his inheritance.

10 He found him in a desert land,
in the waste howling wilderness.
He surrounded him.
He cared for him.
He kept him as the apple of his eye.

11 As an eagle that stirs up her nest,
that flutters over her young,
he spread abroad his wings,
he took them,
he bore them on his feathers.

12 God alone led him.
There was no foreign god with him.

13 He made him ride on the high places of the earth.
He ate the increase of the field.
He caused him to suck honey out of the rock,
oil out of the flinty rock;

14 butter from the herd, and milk from the flock,
with fat of lambs,
rams of the breed of Bashan, and goats,
with the finest of the wheat.
From the blood of the grape, you drank wine.

15 But Jeshurun grew fat, and kicked.
You have grown fat.
You have grown thick.
You have become sleek.
Then he abandoned God who made him,
and rejected the Rock of his salvation.

16 They moved him to jealousy with strange gods.
They provoked him to anger with abominations.

17 They sacrificed to demons, not God,
to gods that they didn't know,
to new gods that came up recently,
which your fathers didn't dread.

18 Of the Rock who became your father, you are unmindful,
and have forgotten God who gave you birth.

19 God saw and abhorred,
because of the provocation of his sons and his daughters.

20 He said, "I will hide my face from them.
I will see what their end will be;
for they are a very perverse generation,
children in whom is no faithfulness.

21 They have moved me to jealousy with that which is not God.
They have provoked me to anger with their vanities.
I will move them to jealousy with those who are not a people.
I will provoke them to anger with a foolish nation.

22 For a fire is kindled in my anger,
that burns to the lowest Sheol,[182]
devours the earth with its increase,
and sets the foundations of the mountains on fire.

23 "I will heap evils on them.
I will spend my arrows on them.

24 They shall be wasted with hunger,
and devoured with burning heat
and bitter destruction.
I will send the teeth of animals on them,
with the venom of vipers that glide in the dust.

25 Outside the sword will bereave,
and in the rooms,
terror on both young man and virgin,
the nursing infant with the gray-haired man.

26 I said that I would scatter them afar.
I would make their memory to cease from among men;

27 were it not that I feared the provocation of the enemy,
lest their adversaries should judge wrongly,
lest they should say, 'Our hand is exalted,
God has not done all this.'"

28 For they are a nation void of counsel.
There is no understanding in them.

29 Oh that they were wise, that they understood this,
that they would consider their latter end!

30 How could one chase a thousand,
and two put ten thousand to flight,
unless their Rock had sold them,
and God had delivered them up?

31 For their rock is not as our Rock,
even our enemies themselves concede.

32 For their vine is of the vine of Sodom,
of the fields of Gomorrah.
Their grapes are poison grapes.
Their clusters are bitter.

33 Their wine is the poison of serpents,
the cruel venom of asps.

34 "Isn't this laid up in store with me,
sealed up among my treasures?

35 Vengeance is mine, and recompense,
at the time when their foot slides;
for the day of their calamity is at hand.
Their doom rushes at them."

36 For God will judge his people,
and have compassion on his servants,
when he sees that their power is gone;
that there is no one remaining, shut up or left at large.

37 He will say, "Where are their gods,
the rock in which they took refuge;

38 which ate the fat of their sacrifices,
and drank the wine of their drink offering?
Let them rise up and help you!
Let them be your protection.

39 "See now that I myself am he.
There is no god with me.
I kill and I make alive.
I wound and I heal.
There is no one who can deliver out of my hand.

40 For I lift up my hand to heaven and declare,
as I live forever,

41 if I sharpen my glittering sword,
my hand grasps it in judgment;
I will take vengeance on my adversaries,
and will repay those who hate me.

42 I will make my arrows drunk with blood.
My sword shall devour flesh with the blood of the slain and the captives,
from the head of the leaders of the enemy."

43 Rejoice, you nations, with his people,
for he will avenge the blood of his servants.
He will take vengeance on his adversaries,
and will make atonement for his land and for his people.[183]

44 Moses came and spoke all the words of this song in the ears of the people, he and Joshua the son of Nun. **45** Moses finished reciting all these words to all Israel. **46** He said to them, "Set your heart to all the words which I testify to you today, which you shall command your children to observe to do, all the words of this law. **47** For it is no vain thing for you, because it is your life, and through this thing you shall prolong your days in the land, where you go over the Jordan to possess it."

48 God spoke to Moses that same day, saying, **49** "Go up into this mountain of Abarim, to Mount Nebo, which is in the land of Moab, that is across from Jericho; and see the land of Canaan, which I give to the children of Israel for a possession. **50** Die on the mountain where you go up, and be gathered to your people, as Aaron your brother died on Mount Hor, and was gathered to his people; **51** because you trespassed against me among the children of Israel at the waters of Meribah of Kadesh, in the wilderness of Zin; because you didn't uphold my holiness among the children of Israel. **52** For you shall see the land from a distance; but you shall not go there into the land which I give the children of Israel."

Deuteronomy 33

1 This is the blessing with which Moses the man of God blessed the children of Israel before his death. **2** He said,

"God came from Sinai,
and rose from Seir to them.
He shone from Mount Paran.
He came from the ten thousands of holy ones.
At his right hand was a fiery law for them.[184]

3 Yes, he loves the people.
All his saints are in your hand.
They sat down at your feet.
Each receives your words.

4 Moses commanded us a law,
an inheritance for the assembly of Jacob.

5 He was king in Jeshurun,
when the heads of the people were gathered,
all the tribes of Israel together.

6 "Let Reuben live, and not die;
Nor let his men be few."

7 This is for Judah. He said,
"Hear, God, the voice of Judah.
Bring him in to his people.
With his hands he contended for himself.
You shall be a help against his adversaries."

8 About Levi he said,
"Your Thummim and your Urim are with your godly one,
whom you proved at Massah,
with whom you contended at the waters of Meribah.

9 He said of his father, and of his mother, 'I have not seen him.'
He didn't acknowledge his brothers,
nor did he know his own children;
for they have observed your word,
and keep your covenant.

10 They shall teach Jacob your ordinances,
and Israel your law.
They shall put incense before you,
and whole burnt offering on your altar.

11 God, bless his skills.
Accept the work of his hands.
Strike through the hips of those who rise up against him,
of those who hate him, that they not rise again."

12 About Benjamin he said,
"The beloved of God will dwell in safety by him.
He covers him all day long.
He dwells between his shoulders."

13 About Joseph he said,
"His land is blessed by God,
for the precious things of the heavens, for the dew,
for the deep that couches beneath,

14 for the precious things of the fruits of the sun,
for the precious things that the moon can yield,

15 for the best things of the ancient mountains,
for the precious things of the everlasting hills,

16 for the precious things of the earth and its fullness,
the good will of him who lived in the bush.[185]
Let this come on the head of Joseph,
on the crown of the head of him who was separated from his brothers.

17 Majesty belongs to the firstborn of his herd.
His horns are the horns of the wild ox.
With them he will push all the peoples to the ends of the earth.

---

[182] **32:22** *32:22* Sheol is the place of the dead.

[183] **32:43** *32:43* For this verse, LXX reads: Rejoice, you heavens, with him, and let all the angels of God worship him; rejoice you Gentiles, with his people, and let all the sons of God strengthen themselves in him; for he will avenge the blood of his sons, and he will render vengeance, and recompense justice to his enemies, and will reward them that hate him; and the Lord shall purge the land of his people.

[184] 33:2 33:2 another manuscript reads "He came with myriads of holy ones from the south, from his mountain slopes."

[185] **33:16** *33:16* i.e., the burning bush of Exodus 3:3-4.

They are the ten thousands of Ephraim.
They are the thousands of Manasseh."

18 About Zebulun he said,
"Rejoice, Zebulun, in your going out;
and Issachar, in your tents.

19 They will call the peoples to the mountain.
There they will offer sacrifices of righteousness,
for they will draw out the abundance of the seas,
the hidden treasures of the sand."

20 About Gad he said,
"He who enlarges Gad is blessed.
He dwells as a lioness,
and tears the arm and the crown of the head.

21 He provided the first part for himself,
for the lawgiver's portion reserved was reserved for him.
He came with the heads of the people.
He executed the righteousness of God,
His ordinances with Israel."

22 About Dan he said,
"Dan is a lion's cub
that leaps out of Bashan."

23 About Naphtali he said,
"Naphtali, satisfied with favor,
full of God's'blessing,
Possess the west and the south."

24 About Asher he said,
"Asher is blessed with children.
Let him be acceptable to his brothers.

Let him dip his foot in oil.

25 Your bars will be iron and bronze.
As your days, so your strength will be.

26 "There is no one like God, Jeshurun,
who rides on the heavens for your help,
in his excellency on the skies.

27 The eternal God is your dwelling place.
Underneath are the everlasting arms.
He thrust out the enemy from before you,
and said, 'Destroy!'

28 Israel dwells in safety,
the fountain of Jacob alone,
In a land of grain and new wine.
Yes, his heavens drop down dew.

29 You are happy, Israel!
Who is like you, a people saved by God,
the shield of your help,
the sword of your excellency?
Your enemies will submit themselves to you.
You will tread on their high places."

Deuteronomy 34

1 Moses went up from the plains of Moab to Mount Nebo, to the top of Pisgah, that is opposite Jericho. God showed him all the land of Gilead to Dan, **2** and all Naphtali, and the land of Ephraim and Manasseh, and all the land of Judah, to the Western Sea, **3** and the south,[186] and the Plain of the valley of Jericho the city of palm trees, to Zoar. **4** God said to him, "This is the land which I swore to Abraham, to Isaac, and to Jacob, saying, 'I will give it to your offspring.' I have caused you to see it with your eyes, but you shall not go over there."

5 So Moses the servant of God died there in the land of Moab, according to God's word. **6** He buried him in the valley in the land of Moab opposite Beth Peor, but no man knows where his tomb is to this day. **7** Moses was one hundred twenty years old when he died. His eye was not dim, nor his strength gone. **8** The children of Israel wept for Moses in the plains of Moab thirty days, until the days of weeping in the mourning for Moses were ended. **9** Joshua the son of Nun was full of the spirit of wisdom, for Moses had laid his hands on him. The children of Israel listened to him, and did as God commanded Moses. **10** Since then, there has not arisen a prophet in Israel like Moses, whom God knew face to face, **11** in all the signs and the wonders which God sent him to do in the land of Egypt, to Pharaoh, and to all his servants, and to all his land, **12** and in all the mighty hand, and in all the awesome deeds, which Moses did in the sight of all Israel.

---

[186]**34:3** *34:3* or, Negev

Journaling Notebook

Made in the USA
Coppell, TX
14 December 2023

26061112R00155